Empires Without Imperialism

Empires Without Imperialism

Anglo-American Decline and the Politics of Deflection

JEANNE MOREFIELD

OXFORD
UNIVERSITY PRESS

OXFORD

UNIVERSITY PRESS

Oxford University Press is a department of the University of Oxford.
It furthers the University's objective of excellence in research, scholarship,
and education by publishing worldwide.

Oxford   New York

Auckland   Cape Town   Dar es Salaam   Hong Kong   Karachi
Kuala Lumpur   Madrid   Melbourne   Mexico City   Nairobi
New Delhi   Shanghai   Taipei   Toronto

With offices in

Argentina   Austria   Brazil   Chile   Czech Republic   France   Greece
Guatemala   Hungary   Italy   Japan   Poland   Portugal   Singapore
South Korea   Switzerland   Thailand   Turkey   Ukraine   Vietnam

Oxford is a registered trademark of Oxford University Press
in the UK and certain other countries.

Published in the United States of America by
Oxford University Press
198 Madison Avenue, New York, NY 10016

CIP data is on file at the Library of Congress

ISBN 978–0–19–938732–8 (hbk)
ISBN 978–0–19–938725–0 (pbk)

1 3 5 7 9 8 6 4 2
Printed in the United States of America
on acid-free paper

For Paul. Of course.

CONTENTS

ACKNOWLEDGEMENTS

This book reflects the voices, critiques, work, and inspiration of so many people that it is difficult to properly honor them all here. I am immensely grateful to those friends, colleagues, and reviewers who took the time to read this manuscript in its various iterations and offer invaluable insight. Special thanks to Sam Moyn, Duncan Bell, Karuna Mantena, Elizabeth Vandiver, and Onur Ulas Ince for their thoughtful and incredibly helpful comments. David Lupher deserves special mention for his unbelievably careful reading of those portions of the manuscript dealing with classical texts. Because of David, I feel slightly less like the interloper that I am in the world of antiquity. Others who have commented on portions or fragments of what would become the book include George Ciccariello-Maher, Mark Mazower, Duncan Kelly, Hagar Kotef, Romand Coles, Elizabeth Wingrove, Jennifer Pitts, James Tully, Ian Hall, Mark Bevir, Gaurav Majumdar, Peter Steinberger, Sam Chambers, Keally McBride, Megan Thomas, Tamara Metz, Burke Hendrix, Andrew Valls, and the students of "Politics 308: Liberalism and Its Discontents." As always, I could not have done any of the archival work for this project without the generous help of talented librarians, particularly Colin Harris at the Bodleian Library Modern Papers Collection, and Lisette Matano at the Georgetown University Library Special Collections Research Center, Washington, D.C. I would also like to thank Whitman College, especially President George Bridges and the Trustees of the College, for so wisely continuing to fund the sabbatical policy that made this book possible and makes this institution one of the jewels in the crown of liberal arts colleges in the United States. Finally, thanks to my editor, David McBride, for his patience and excellent advice as well as Alexandra Dauler at OUP for all things production.

I am immensely grateful for the support, camaraderie, political acumen, snarkiness, intellectual brilliance, and all-around goodness of the Politics Department at Whitman College. Your courage in the face of the neoliberal assault on liberal arts gives me hope for the future of higher education in America. I have also leaned heavily on the support of my *fierce* women colleagues and friends, the Women of Maxey Building: Shampa Biswas, Elyse Semerdjian, Brooke Vick, Susanne Beechey, Susanne Morrissey, Melisa Casumbal, Lynn Sharp, and Kristy King. Without you all taking up space, none of this would have been possible. Anna and Niko Apostolidis also deserve special mention for all the love and patience they displayed while their mother was grumpy and distracted by writing. And finally, Paul Apostolidis has spent more time with this text than everyone else combined. In so, so, so, many ways: without him, not.

Introduction

Who We Are

Being an American is not easy. It is hard. We are required to keep some
serious promises. We are judged by a high standard, one we crafted for
ourselves in the founding documents of the republic, the ones that talk
about the equality of all people, the ones that tell us that government is
of the people, by the people and for the people. We need to live by this,
at home and abroad, and it is just about the only thing we can do to face
the hatred of those who want to destroy us. Our best defense is to stay
true to who we are. Our best defense is to refuse to live in fear, of them,
of ourselves, of anyone.
                    —Michael Ignatieff, "Living Fearlessly in a Fearful World"

On March 11, 2012, Staff Sergeant Robert Bales walked out of the American
Army outpost where he was stationed in the Panjwai District of Kandahar,
Afghanistan, made his way to a local village, and began a shooting rampage that
resulted in the deaths of sixteen Afghan civilians, including nine children. The
incident occurred two weeks after the burning of *Qur'ans* at a military base,
which had sparked massive protests in Afghanistan, and two months after the
release of a video, shot by American troops, that showed four Marines urinating
on the corpses of dead Afghans. President Obama responded to these events in
his first public comments after the massacre in Kandahar by claiming, "It's not
who we are as a country."[1] His words prefigured and echoed almost exactly those
of Hillary Clinton, Leon Panetta, and General John Allen, all of whom rendered
some version of the same sentiment: this is just not who we are.[2]

This book is a sustained engagement with the prolix rhetorical phenomenon
that makes this kind of response to political violence possible. At its core, however, the book is less concerned with the denial of political responsibility on the
part of liberal imperial powers like the United States and Great Britain as it is with
the sustained historical and contemporary narratives that enable these powers to
deflect responsibility for imperial violence away from themselves in an ongoing,
systematic way. In this sense, the book focuses on imperial narratives that tell the

kinds of stories best captured by Michael Ignatieff's response to the revelations regarding the extensive use of torture and humiliation by American soldiers at Abu Ghraib prison in Iraq. Rather than wring his hands and declare that this is "not who we are," Ignatieff exhorted his audience of graduating college seniors to look imperial violence in the eye and "stay true to who we are."[3]

This deflective impulse—aimed at drawing critical attention away from the liberal empire's illiberalism by insisting upon its fundamental character—has deep roots in the tradition of liberal imperial apologetics.[4] We see this phenomenon in starkest relief, however, during those moments when critical numbers of politicians and public intellectuals begin to feel terrorized by the possibility of their empire's imminent decline and the rise of societies and civilizations they deem illiberal, barbarian, or simply, in Niall Ferguson's words, "the Rest." As this book explains in greater detail, British liberal imperialists just before and during World War I suffered from what Lord Milner, a prominent colonial administrator, described as "chronic" anxiety about the demise of the British Empire—what many of them referred to simply as the "imperial problem"—and it is hardly surprising that we see an upsurge of "who we are" narratives in the speeches and writings of the Empire's most ardent liberal defenders of the time.[5]

A similarly palpable anxiety has run through American foreign policy discourse since the end of the Cold War, but particularly since September 11, 2001. During this time we have witnessed a remarkable consensus developing among neoconservatives and liberal internationalists on the benefits of intervention and the need to assert more explicitly America's leadership role in the world.[6] Then Governor George W. Bush set the tone for this approach in a 1999 speech entitled "A Distinctly American Internationalism" when he argued,

> Some have tried to pose a choice between American ideals and American interests—between who we are and how we act. But the choice is false. America, by decision and destiny, promotes political freedom—and gains the most when democracy advances. America believes in free markets and free trade—and benefits most when markets are opened. America is a peaceful power—and gains the greatest dividend from democratic stability.[7]

In one fell swoop, Bush brushes aside the troubling discrepancy between what American foreign policy leaders tell the world their state represents and the American state's acts of military, economic, and political aggression by simply returning to the issue of identity. America "by decision and destiny" promotes freedom; therefore, everything it ever does serves that end. Importantly, this emphasis on "who we are" rather than "how we act" is hardly unique to the Bush administration, with its epic reliance on the bellicose foreign policy objectives of influential neoconservatives in the Administration or associated with the powerful think tank, the Project for a New American Century. For example, even as Obama advisor and International Relations (IR) scholar Anne-Marie Slaughter disparages Bush's "for us or against us" rhetoric in her 2007 book, *The Idea that is America: Keeping Faith with our Values in a Dangerous World,* she simultaneously grounds her post-Bush-era approach to American foreign policy in the same, deflective logic. For Slaughter, "engagement with the world" not only ought to define American leadership, it is "built into the very core of who we are as a nation."[8] In other words, the idea that the best way to respond to questions about American power in the world is to return, almost instinctively, to a narrative about "who we are" has become one of the most sustaining elements in the rhetorical air we breathe, from the pages of the *National Review,* to the Princeton Project on National Security, to virtually all of Obama's comments on terrorism, drone strikes, and the prisoners at Guantanamo Bay.[9]

To explore this historical and contemporary phenomenon from the inside out, this book burrows deeply into three imperial stories told by British public intellectuals just before and during World War I and three imperial stories told by American public intellectuals today. During both eras, I argue, liberals have felt compelled to narrate the history of "who we are" in response to their empire's perceived decline in a manner that consistently forgets the imperial state's forays into illiberality in the past and present. While the scope and shape of this forgetting differs from author to author, the narratives are similar in the extent to which they rely not merely upon historical omission but, rather, upon prolonged and creative forms of deflection that consistently ask the reader to avert her eyes, away from colonial violence and economic exploitation, and back toward the liberal nature of the imperial society. Each of these narratives thus engages in the complicated temporal dance of creating contemporary truth by intervening in the past in ways that intentionally misrecognize the imperial state and, in the process, make it, in Slavoj Žižek words, "become what it always was."[10] Each of these narratives also engenders an interventionist political vision grounded in an understanding of the colonizer as the unwitting victim of what John Robert Seeley once referred to as its "absence of mind."[11] Additionally, the cynical form of imperial politics in the passive that emerges from these narratives allows liberal imperialists to have their cake and eat it too: in their world visions, the imperial state is compelled to act imperially to save the world from illiberalism, and yet is never responsible for having created the conditions that require it to save the world in the first place because it was always, even when it was not, just being who it was. Finally, the public intellectuals at the heart of this book are able to inspire liberal imperialist political visions that straddle the past, present, and future by drawing upon a variety of deflective strategies that fall roughly into the three categories reflected in the three sections of this book: strategies that situate the liberal empire in antiquity; strategies that bind the liberal empire to global and epoch-spanning metanarratives; and strategies that insist upon the consistency of the imperial state's liberal character over time. Together these strategies forge the links in a rhetorical armor that enables Anglo-American public intellectuals—then and now—to deflect attention away from the violence and illiberalism of the imperial state. In other words, strategies of deflection embolden these thinkers to imagine a world of empires without imperialism.

Empire: Britain Then, America Now

Scholars and political actors have defined empire and imperialism in a variety of ways over the past two hundred years.[12] For the purposes of this book, an empire is a state that engages in the direct or indirect rule over dependent or colonial territories.[13] "Imperialism," in this sense, refers simply to, in Michael Doyle's words, the "process or policy of establishing or maintaining an empire."[14] However, beneath this deceptively simple exterior, the approach I take in this book also understands the "process or policy of establishing or maintaining an empire" as always a dimension of power, one that is inherently asymmetrical and scalar, and which orders political, social, and economic relations through discursive, rhetorical, economic, military, and political processes that differentiate between types of peoples and regimes. The ultimate product of imperial power is a political terrain characterized by overlapping relations of, as Paul Kramer puts it, "hierarchy, discipline, dispossession, extraction, and exploitation."[15]

Thus, as a state practice and a political ideology, imperialism presents perhaps the ultimate challenge to the founding narratives of liberal equality, individual freedom, and sovereign autonomy; over the last fifteen years in particular, much work has been done to explore this challenge in the context of the British Empire.[16] In some fashion, political theorists and historians writing in this vein are all interested in the way liberal writers have responded to circumstances that challenge the tradition's universalism. Thinkers like Uday Mehta thus push against standard readings of the history of liberal thought in Europe that characterize the exclusion of women, non-freemen, and colonized peoples from the nascent theory's understandings of universal humanity as simply accidental byproducts of the time and argue, instead, that the theoretical vision of liberalism from the seventeenth century to the present "is unmistakably marked by the systematic and sustained political exclusion of various groups and 'types' of people."[17] For Mehta, the "strategies of exclusion" developed by thinkers like Locke and Mill to fend off the incursion of undesirables into their imagined liberal universals were not ancillary, but rather absolutely essential to, the development of liberal thought. In other words, for a considerable time, liberals have been adjusting the contours of their theories to rationalize violating the tradition's founding narratives in the name of those same narratives. Imperialism intensifies the contradiction considerably, forcing liberal supporters of empire to work even harder to stretch the skin of universal rhetoric over the corpus of a fundamentally exclusionary worldview.

The imperial visions that I critically examine in this book can be considered liberal insofar as all of the public intellectuals associated with these visions understand their imperial state and imperial society in distinctly liberal terms. In other words, from Alfred Zimmern to Donald Kagan, from Lionel Curtis to Niall Ferguson, from Jan Smuts to Michael Ignatieff, every single thinker under consideration here believes that the British and American Empires are ultimately, at their core, based on the liberal principles of freedom, individualism, and universal equality. These thinkers differ, of course, in the extent to which they emphasize various ancillary liberal values. Smuts and Ignatieff, for example, both consistently underscore the link between their empires and universal human rights, while Ferguson and Curtis (and the other thinkers associated with his pro-imperial organization, the Round Table) identify the imperial state's commitment to the "rule of law" as one of its most singular and noble qualities. These thinkers differ, as do liberals more generally, in the extent to which freedom of trade and property rights take center stage in their imperial visions, but all of them reject both economic collectivism and state-run economies as inherently anathema to liberal principles, and they all make frequent negative comparisons between the freedom-loving qualities of their empires and the state-oriented polities of their day—namely, Germany, the Soviet Union, and China. These thinkers are also influenced by different liberal traditions. Zimmern and the Round Table thinkers, for instance, were molded by the New Liberalism that dominated Oxford in the late nineteenth and early twentieth centuries, which made them more sympathetic to the kinds of welfare state politics that Ferguson, a confirmed Thatcherite, instinctively reviles. Kagan's vision was forged in the midst of the neoconservative rejection of identity politics in the 1960s, while Smuts's self-serving liberalism emerged out of his long-term struggle to identify white South Africa with progressive politics. However, despite these and other differences, every one of these authors would insist, without a moment of hesitation or a second thought, that their Empires (as opposed to the Soviet Union, or Germany, or China) are always conditioned by a core respect for freedom, individualism, and equality for all people.

Ultimately, what makes the pro-imperial liberalism of early-twentieth-century Britain and contemporary America so fascinating is just how taut the liberal skin has to be drawn in both periods to make these thinkers' political visions—and the bodies of theory and historical narratives that accompany them—appear whole, coherent, and natural. Evaluating this tautness, I argue, has much to tell us about the relationship between liberalism, empire, and the politics of deflection more generally, as well as offering us invaluable insight into the genealogical assumptions of twentieth- and twenty-first-century internationalism, informal imperialism, and the resurgence of explicit imperial rhetoric since September 11, 2001.

The book is thus also premised on the assumption that there is a compelling comparison to be made between the liberal imperialist rhetoric and political theorizing of the early twentieth-century and today. Indeed, with regard to empire, a number of contemporary pro-imperialists (Ferguson) and skeptics (Fareed Zakaria) make this comparison themselves, suggesting that the historical circumstances surrounding the decline of the British Empire and the perceived crisis of American geopolitical dominance today might be usefully contrasted so as to extract "lessons" (Ferguson's term) for global power.[18] In this book, however, I am drawn to the comparison between the imperialist arguments of these two periods not because I believe the circumstances can be mined for lessons but, rather, because of an intriguing similarity in the rhetorical responses to those circumstances. Zimmern's insistence, for example, that the kernel of Britain's liberal empire can be found in a completely literal interpretation of Pericles's funeral oration in *The History of the Peloponnesian War* is strikingly similar to the way Kagan—again, with no ironic sense of anachronism whatsoever—reads an embattled American hegemon into his loving description of Athens as a "school for Hellas." Likewise, the Round Table's metahistorical narrative of a British Empire moved through time by its Anglo-Saxon longing for freedom limns very close to Ferguson's narrative of the long-term benefits of "Anglobalization." Smuts's organicist conviction that the British Empire was "actuated" by the principles of freedom, equality, and equity, sounds similar to Michael Ignatieff's proclamation that the response of liberal states to global terrorism lies in a retrenched commitment to inhabiting the basic truths of "who we are."

The similarities between liberal imperial rhetorics during these periods are hardly coincidental. Rather, such similarities reflect the fraught, transitional qualities of both political moments and locations—qualities that themselves push against the grain of dominant reflections on the high imperialism of both eras. Thus, for most imperial critics, comparing the American and British Empires requires a basic recognition of the extent to which the word "empire" itself has always resonated differently for the two societies. As Edward Said rightly observes, despite the fact that the American state was founded on a presumption of imperium over the continent, the dominant discourse of exceptionalism, altruism, and greatness bound up with most Americans' sense of their country as anti-imperial in nature and origin have resulted in a long-standing denial of the US's actual imperial power in the world. America, in Said's sense, is an Empire that cannot say its name. By contrast, he argues, for citizens of nineteenth-century Britain and France, "empire was a major topic of unembarrassed cultural attention. British India and French North Africa alone played inestimable roles in the imagination, economy, political life, and social fabric of British and French society."[19] Britain, in this interpretation, was an empire that proudly declared itself to be so.

However, by the first two decades of the twentieth-century, British imperialists themselves were no longer "unembarrassed" about their Empire, despite the fact that groups like the Round Table worked assiduously to save it and everything it stood for. Rather, as the Round Table's purposeful decision in 1914 to refer to the Empire in all their official publications as the "Commonwealth" suggests, many liberal imperialists were increasingly uncomfortable with the connotations of the word itself and the possible comparisons it might evoke between British imperial power and the kinds of power associated with states they believed to be antiliberal in nature, primarily Germany. By contrast, from the opposite rhetorical direction at the opposite end of the century, contemporary America is currently witnessing a renaissance of interest in the word "empire" and in resuscitating its reputation as a benign form of global governance. Particularly since September 11, 2001, scholars and foreign policy pundits like Ferguson, Ignatieff, Max Boot, and others have called upon Americans to shake off their shame and denial about being an imperial power and to embrace the concept fully, to rise to the occasion and proudly bear the burden they already shoulder.

And yet, while thinkers during these moments may appear to be making inverse political moves—away from and toward the idea of empire—the status of imperial rhetoric is similar in both cases in that, in both Britain and America, liberals have engaged, or are engaging, the concept of empire in order to save their imperial state from perceived decline. Calling the empire something else, or encouraging an empire that has refused to say its name to do so, are both salvage efforts, attempts at repair and recuperation, despite the fact that the thinkers who theorize these transitions often do so in the name of innovation and a canny break with the past. In these two historical moments, when the linguistic status of the word empire itself was and is in flux and decline seems to loom ominously on the horizon, imperialists turn to narratives that both consolidate and legitimate the empire's power and naturalize its liberal character, at the same time they deflect attention away from its violence and illiberalism.

Fear of decline is, of course, a regular feature of imperial power and, during the historical course of the British Empire, Edwardians were hardly alone in expressing it. Indeed, anxiety about imperial decline was palpable among British political leaders and intellectuals during the period of the Empire's most rapid expansion in the last three decades of the nineteenth-century, an anxiety reflected in the thought of both what Peter Cain terms "ultra-imperialists" like Lord Curzon and in the work of the imperial Federationists such as Seeley and J. A. Froude.[20] As Duncan Bell argues, the various responses of the Federationists to the emergence of Germany, Russia, and the United States as competing economic and political powers demonstrate the "disquieting effect that the impending loss of great power status had on a generation of thinkers."[21] What differentiated the responses of liberal imperialists writing shortly before and during the First World War from the generation of worried imperialists that preceded them was both the intensity with which they expressed their fears, and the particular political context that conditioned that expression.

In 1909, at the moment when Lord Milner claimed to be experiencing "chronic, but as I think, reasonable anxiety" about the Empire's future, the British Empire was actually more powerful than it ever had been and ever would be again.[22] At the pinnacle of its success, anxiety over the Empire's future was reflected in lengthy debates over tariff reform and in the emergence during this same period of a record number of voluntary organizations and think tanks, like the Round Table, formed to address the "imperial problem."[23] The same period saw an overall spike in cynical attitudes toward the Empire in popular culture and, in particular, toward the boundless and enthusiastic future articulated by the likes of Rhodes and Kipling.[24] In Ronald Hyam's words, "Pessimism was in fact an all pervasive and quintessential characteristic of Edwardian thinking about Empire."[25] This pessimism was also fed by the rise of anti-imperial sentiment during the same period (particularly among liberals and radicals) that developed in response to the highly visible economic exploitation of the late nineteenth-century, the publication in 1902 of J. A. Hobson's *Imperialism: A Study* (which would have an abiding effect on early-twentieth-century thinkers, most notably Lenin), and the violence of the Boer War.[26] At the same time, as Gregory Claeys explains, the Boer War also "assisted a shift for many on the left towards tion with empire," a phenomenon mirrored in the formation, during various cross-party conversation groups such as the Rainbow Circle fficients, which were designed to explore the political connections ral social policy and imperialism.[27]

During this period of heightened pessimism, scrutiny, and conversation about the future of the Empire, liberal imperialists found that the justificatory logic of nineteenth-century liberals like John Stuart Mill was being pulled up hard against the shore of its own contradictions. Mill's exclusionary rhetoric relied on a theoretical vision that combined his commitment to understand "man as a progressive being" with a detailed hermeneutic of civilization in which the colonized, like children, lagged behind on the path to progress, always not quite mature enough for political subjecthood. The central legerdemain at work in this exclusionary strategy, argues Mehta, involved an interpretation of "backwardness" as "a temporal deficit or stasis" that required the colonized to remain hitched to the imperial engine of history, thus linking the "caboose of politics to the time of the future."[28] In an alternative metaphor, Dipesh Chakrabarty describes this temporal deficit as the "waiting room of history," the space of the perennial "not yet."[29] But by the turn of the last century, several different historical circumstances were combining to make this waiting room seem not only a less powerful, but also a less palatable and benevolent, place to while away the time before civilizational maturity.

First, the rising global power of Russia, the United States, and Germany, coupled with these states' increasing reach into the remaining "waste space" of the earth, haunted the imaginations of imperialists during this period, who feared the decline of British economic and military hegemony. But it was Germany's empire that posed the thorniest rhetorical problems for liberal imperialists. Rapid German imperial expansion (and the increasingly nationalist language that motivated it) led to an anti-German backlash in Britain in the decade before the First World War, when the press routinely portrayed Germany as fundamentally aggressive and antithetical to liberal notions of freedom through images of, in Paul Kennedy's words, "Hohensollern autocracy, of jackboots and mailed fists and preventative wars."[30] The Germans, in this popular imaginary, were racist, nationalist thugs hell-bent on dominating the world through the expansion of their superior *Kultur*. In addition, during this time, the rise of racial segregation in the American South and then in the newly unified South Africa resulted in a backlash against crude, racialized forms of jingoism in England and intensified liberal and radical critiques of racial politics.[31] The trick for imperialists during this time (and particularly for liberal imperialists) was thus to adequately explain for themselves, and for the public, the difference between racist and expansionist German imperialism and a British imperialism grounded in "racial individuality" and the growth of freedom.[32]

Second, during the late nineteenth-century, imperial Federationists had excluded India from their political visions of the future Empire because of what Seeley identified in 1883's *The Expansion of England* as the "great burden which is imposed by India on foreign policy."[33] Instead, Seeley suggested that British rule in India ought to continue only as long as there was no major threat of a widespread, Indian nationalist movement. Twenty years later, however, what Seeley imagined as a future possibility had become a reality. By the turn of century, nationalists in India, Ireland, and Egypt had begun to challenge imperial authority, often by forgoing conciliatory appeals to the British liberal conscience and demanding the kind of autonomy and self-governance that the "civilizing mission" held out as only a remote possibility.[34] At the same time, liberal supporters of the Empire were becoming increasingly clear eyed (in a way that Seeley had not been) about the centrality of India to the Empire's financial stability and hegemony. Without India, Philip Kerr of the Round Table noted in 1910, "we sink to the level of a trade competitor with Germany and the United States" rather than the world's foremost military and economic power.[35] And yet, Edwardian liberals remained as committed as their nineteenth-century predecessors to the idea that Indians were a "subject race," not yet ready for, or incapable of, self-government. This meant that whatever solution these liberals proposed to the "imperial problem" had to stress India's necessary role in the future Empire and avoid alienating sympathetic elites in India, while simultaneously couching this argument in a manner that would effectively exclude most Indians from practices of democratic citizenship without using the German-sounding language of racial superiority to justify that exclusion.

Third, equally distressing to many Edwardian supporters of empire was the increase in nonwhite immigration within the Empire during this period, creating "diasporas of people of color" who were, as Ira Christopher Fletcher argues, "changing the nature of colonial encounters" in Australia, Canada, and South Africa.[36] In response to the rising numbers of Indian workers throughout the Empire, imperialists like Milner fretted about the effects of "alien colored races, even if they be British subjects" on the already precarious status of white minorities, even as he acknowledged that such migrations (and the racial encounters they engendered) were inevitable.[37] At the same time, the turn of the twentieth-century also witnessed the transformation of the British settler colonies of Australia, New Zealand, Canada, and South Africa into self-governing dominions. While imperial administrators treated the "distinctive national aspirations of the new white peoples of the Empire" differently from the national aspirations of nonwhite peoples, the rise of nation-oriented politics in the new dominions was still a cause for concern both for the government and for supporters of empire.[38] For these observers, the natural relationship between mother country and colonial children had been reversed, and policy was now being dictated to the center from the periphery—a sentiment perhaps best captured in the words of two pro-imperial, Liberal prime ministers, uttered twenty-five years apart. Thus, in 1894, Rosebery complained that, "Our foreign policy has become a colonial policy" that was "in reality dictated much more from the extremities of the Empire than from London itself."[39] Lloyd George clearly felt the same way shortly after World War I when he quipped petulantly, "There was a time when Downing Street ruled the Empire. Now the Empire rules Downing Street."[40]

In sum, liberal imperialists during this era looked around at what they saw as an increasingly frayed Empire in danger of decline and knew they had to develop a vision for its future that stressed its holism in a manner that avoided sounding totalizing and German. In other words, this British imperial vision could not be grounded in an explicit sense of cultural or racial superiority and coherence. Simultaneously, these thinkers believed that there *was* something uniquely blessed about the British. Thus, the Anglo-Saxon values of freedom and equality upon which the Empire was built, they argued, were both universally true and distinctly British. In addition, these thinkers had no intention of expanding political participation for nonwhite citizens of the Empire but, again, could not use the language of race to justify this omission and thus were forced to articulate exclusive ends through what looked like a universal logic. At the same time, they could not ignore the rise of anticolonial nationalism and therefore had to come up with some way of acknowledging its existence without legitimizing its demands.

And yet, while this bundle of contextual limits was unique to the Edwardian period, I argue that it was also similar in key ways to the circumstances that shape American pro-imperial rhetoric today. To clarify, in making this connection between rhetorical epochs, I in no way claim that the two moments are mere reflections of each other, or that the world has not undergone huge and systemic changes in the interim—changes which give shape to the current historical landscape and affect the way early-twenty-first-century imperialists both conceptualize and peddle their political visions. Obviously, between the end of the Great War and today the world witnessed the rise and fall of fascism in Europe, the Second World War, the expansion of anticolonial movements and their violent repression, the creation of the League of Nations and the United Nations, decolonization, the rise of America as a global world power, the beginning and end of the Cold War, the expansion of neoliberal economic policies throughout both the Global South and developed world, and the rise of China and India as economic powers. Many scholars describe the major form of imperialism since decolonization as "informal" and they argue that the Great Powers or G8 nations are able to rule informally through international banking institutions, nongovernmental organizations, and covert military intervention.[41] James Tully takes this point even further, arguing that liberals have been empowered during the so-called "postcolonial" period to drop the word "empire" from their vocabulary altogether, because they simply do not need it to rule. The very language of civil liberties, he argues, and the historical process of nation state formation in the West have been so deeply entwined with the imperial project that they render the imperial impulses of liberal ideas like "global citizenship" all but invisible to the postcolonial eye.[42]

The work of these scholars also reflects a major shift in academic culture regarding the study of British and American imperialism: a move away from a celebration of imperial benefits, and toward a critique of its negative effects. From Gallagher and Robinson's 1953 critique of Britain's "free trade imperialism," to Theodore Mommsen's analyses of informal empire, to Harry Magdoff's take on America's "imperialism without colonies," two generations of historians have argued that the British and American imposition of free trade by gunboat has had long-term, devastating effects on the economic and political well-being of formerly colonized states.[43] At the same time, a generation of scholars from the former colonies has taken on the ideological and cultural underpinnings of the British Empire and its effects on postcolonial societies in ways that often turn the colonial gaze back on the assumptions of the imperialists themselves, while filling in the silences and omissions of imperial history. For Chakrabarty this has meant looking at the way Western forms of historical analysis have been normalized in India and "been made to look 'obvious' far beyond the ground where they originated."[44] For Said, studying the role of Orientalist discourse in European imperialism in the context of what was happening throughout the British and French Empires demonstrates that it was never the case that the imperial encounter "pitted an active Western intruder against a supine or inert non-Western native; there was always some form of active resistance."[45] Finally, recent scholarship by Mike Davis, Kenneth Morgan, David Anderson, and others has suggested that the British Empire was far more violent and had a far deeper environmental, political, and economic impact on the former colonies than had previously been calculated.[46] In other words, mainstream academic thought in Britain and America has complicated the history of empire, reversed the colonial gaze, and turned decidedly against its economic and political agenda.

Perhaps the most important difference between Edwardian and contemporary American imperialism, however, is the fact that the current discussion of the United States as an empire takes shape within the shadow of American exceptionalism and the widespread perception that America was founded on anti-imperial principles and went on to create a democracy like no other. As Richard Immerman describes it, to "classify the United States with its imperial ancestor, let alone more recent exemplars and wannabes—the Germans and Soviets for example—seems perverse, an affront to America's self identity as well as history."[47] This insistence on American exceptionalism has existed alongside and in tension with America's history of expansion (on the North American continent), its formal occupation of states like Cuba, the Philippines, and Haiti, its usurpation of formerly independent regimes like Hawaii, its covert interference in democratic states throughout the twentieth-century, and its current status as a global power with an astonishing 725 military bases scattered throughout the world, organized into four regional commands that resemble, in Tully's words, the "proconsuls of the Roman empire and the governors-general of the British."[48] In the face of this reality, critics of American imperialism consistently confront the longstanding myth continually propagated by pundits, politicians, and scholars alike that the United States acquired its power over the continent and the world through "invitation" or historical accident.[49] These same supporters of American power in the world have for years struggled to find words other than "empire" to describe America's global power, often falling back on such anodyne alternatives as "super power" or the recent favorite of IR scholars, "hegemon."

Something began to shift, however, among political pundits and IR scholars in the early 1990s, following the end of the Cold War. During this period, in the sudden absence of all the certainties associated with living in a bipolar world, key observers of world politics began to argue more forcefully for the benefits of a liberal interventionism that often looked, for all intents and purposes, like imperialism.[50] In 1995, in response to the chaos engendered in the former Yugoslavia by the collapse of the Soviet Union, Ignatieff argued that citizens of liberal, democratic states must move beyond their instinctive "moral disgust" with imperialism and embrace a new kind of interventionist foreign policy, one that was "ill-suited to the post-Cold War style of instant intervention and quick exit" and which would require "long-term, unspectacular, patient commitment to a molecular rebuilding of society itself." "In the nineteenth-century," he continued, "such work was the white man's burden" and, by Ignatieff's lights, this burden was something once again worth taking up.[51]

But, as Michael Cox has argued, while public intellectuals like Ignatieff might have been working up to a theory of contemporary empire throughout the 1990s, it took the events of September 11, 2001, a "crisis of almost biblical proportions," to launch the word "empire" itself into the mainstream of public discourse.[52] For many thinkers, September 11, 2001 was the wake-up call that Americans needed, living proof that while their polity was supremely powerful, it was also vulnerable to the "barbarians at the gate," teetering on the precipice of decline.[53] Since the terrorist attacks of that day, an increasing number of self–styled liberal imperialists have fallen into line with the opinion that the language of hegemony and the policies and practices of informal imperialism are no longer enough to preserve American power. In response to the existential threat of a chaotic, barbarian world crystallized in the worldview of Islamic extremism, these thinkers have championed a vision of liberal imperialism that evokes the kinds of explicitly nostalgic, justificatory celebration of empire rarely seen in either public or academic culture in Britain and America since formal decolonization. Like the Edwardians, contemporary America imperialists are concerned with imagining and inventing an approach to empire that is deeply committed to the racial hierarchy of the international status quo, but claims to be both novel and universally valid—an approach which celebrates the uniqueness of American culture while insisting upon its global relevance. In the words of George W. Bush, America's power is grounded in "our heritage and our principles" but also "right and true for every person, in every society."[54] But, while Bush consistently refused to call American hegemony "imperial" (declaring in 2004 that "We are not an imperial power…we are a liberating power"), other thinkers have been much less reticent in this regard.[55] Their rhetorically complex goal, since September 11,

2001 has been to articulate a vision of American Empire that can resist all of the rhetorical pressures stacked against it by appearing both universal and particular, traditional and novel, and, most importantly, the solution in perpetuity to the problem of American decline.

In sum, both Edwardian and contemporary liberal imperialists have sought to negotiate the tension between liberal universalism and the exclusive politics of empire in contexts where that tension is particularly fraught, and where the very idea of empire is being challenged at the same time it is being justified. In Wendy Brown's terms, both of these historical eras represent moments of discursive disruption, when the political and epistemological certainties of dominant liberal narratives begin to splinter and fragment, producing new and troubling political formations.[56] Like their Edwardian predecessors, the American thinkers examined in this book have negotiated the heightened tensions of this disruption by employing a number of different narrative strategies that enable them to tell stories about the Empire—its present, its past, and its future—that seem to resolve the tension between universalism and exclusion by conveniently forgetting the Empire's own illiberalism. And, like the Edwardians, contemporary champions of American empire have done this by telling stories that simultaneously deflect attention away from the liberal empire's illiberalism and draw that attention back to itself.

Deflection, Forgetting, and Nostalgia

Scholars interested in the theory and politics of historical interpretation have long argued that forgetting plays an essential role in the way historians construct narratives of the past, even as they imagine what they are doing in terms of recovery or remembering. In *Memory, History, Forgetting* (2004), Paul Ricoeur explains that historians typically read history "as a struggle against forgetting. Herodotus strives to preserve the glory of the Greeks and the Barbarians from oblivion. And our celebrated duty of memory is proclaimed in the form of an exhortation not to forget."[57] But the practice of historical recovery is just as much about forgetting, according to Ricoeur, as it is about remembering. As Hayden White argues in his lucid review of *Memory, History, Forgetting*, the writing of history itself is always concerned, in some way, with identifying a "collective" past in the present and with establishing some foundation upon which a "collective identity" can be built. "History seeks to discipline memory," he suggests, "by setting up standards regarding what should be remembered and in what manner," standards which then stage the problem that preoccupies Ricoeur: "the problem of unbinding an individual or a group from its past, of being able to forget events of the past 'that won't go away.' "[58]

Both Edwardian and contemporary liberal advocates of American empire must, by necessity, engage in a similar process of unbinding the liberal imperial state (and its people) from its illiberal past and present. The set of rhetorical hurdles that condition this unbinding, however, is especially high given the sheer breadth and complexity of their projects. Liberal imperialists insist that we understand Britain and America as essentially liberal societies, but, at the same time, commit themselves to a politics that supports the global status quo—in particular, that insists upon the continuing economic, military, and political domination of much of the world's population. Liberal imperialists argue that their brand of liberalism is absolutely unique, that it was formed within the crucible of Anglo-Saxon culture—as Round Table scholar Lionel Curtis put it, "a sort of spontaneous growth so closely bound up with the life of a people that we can hardly treat it as a product of human will and energy"— and, at the same time, insist that it is universally true for the whole world.[59] They express revulsion at violations of liberal human rights throughout the world, and yet insist that the ongoing abrogation of these rights for those who fall within the liberal imperial state's sphere of influence remains a regrettable but necessary path to liberal ends. They claim that their empires have become great through sheer liberal moxie, and yet take no responsibility for either the contemporary ire of the colonized or the current state of their own decline. In essence, liberal imperialists then and now consistently desire to have their cake and eat it too, to square the circle between liberal freedom and colonial order, to unbind the liberal empire from its illiberal actions so that no one can ever call its intentions into question.

In his work on the architectural, economic, and cultural transformation of Los Angeles in the twentieth-century, Norman Klein explores one approach to this process of memorial unbinding, an approach that resembles what psychologists call "distraction," where "one false memory allows another memory to be removed in plain view without complaint—forgotten."[60] Liberal imperialists depend upon ways of telling stories about the state's historical development and its relationship to the current political configuration of the world that resemble a form of distraction but, at the same time, can never allow painful memories to be entirely "removed in plain view." In other words, the very complexities of their political project prevents them from telling stories (intentionally or unintentionally) in a way that encourages the reader to look away, while they blithely reach under the table and replace one set of memories with another, or simply allow some memories to disappear from the flow of time. Rather, liberal imperialists must confront the continuing presence of Britain or America as occupiers in India or Afghanistan and their continuing use of illiberal means in these occupied spaces. In this sense, liberal imperialist narratives cannot merely tap us on the shoulder, tell us to look away, and make memories disappear. Rather, they must develop means to acknowledge illiberalism without allowing it to become the center of attention.

The nature of this forgetting both resembles and departs from the way that critical and sympathetic observers of nationalism and national identity have understood the relationship between narratives of nation-making and forgetting. As Ernst Renan famously argued in his 1882 essay, *What is a Nation?*, forgetfulness and historical error are essential to the creation of a nation. "Every French citizen must have forgotten the night of St. Bartholomew and the massacres in the thirteenth century in the South."[61] But as Benedict Anderson rightly points out, even the act of remembering the massacre of St. Bartholomew in order to then forget it calls upon "French" people to understand themselves as one people who engaged in a violent, self-immolating act. Anderson labels this the "assurance of fratricide," the well-heeled historical conviction that one side of the family killed another, thus reconfirming that they were a family in the first place while neatly burying the memory in the safety of the past.[62] As with liberal imperialist narratives, nationalist forgetting doesn't just replace one memory with another. In ritualistically calling upon the remembering community to forget, it gestures toward the violence of the past and then purges that violence by asking members of the community to dwell deeper in the familial whole that emerged from such fratricidal rage. This form of forgetting is, in a deeply Foucaultian sense, never simply about the repression of uncomfortable memories but always, rather, about the production of national identity through remembering to forget fratricide.[63]

But liberal imperialists who similarly ask us to look and then look away from imperial violence and illiberalism cannot assume that this cozy-but-deadly set of ritualized family connections will salve the indignity of one side of the family's rage against another, precisely because that rage, and that violence, is still ongoing. Thus, Edwardian imperialists who traced the movement of the Anglo-Saxon Empire through time did so in the context of understanding, rationalizing, and explaining its current expansionist policies in Asia and Africa. Contemporary supporters of American Empire must similarly explain America's military history in light of its continuing occupation of Afghanistan or the ongoing drone war in Pakistan and Yemen. There is, then, never any resolution to this kind of historical narrative, never a moment when liberal imperialists can breathe a sigh of relief and say, like nationalists, "well, that was then, but now it's over, and we're all family." Liberal imperialists, writing in moments of decline, have even given up the comfort of thinking that some day, down the line, when the children are grown, we can actually all be one liberal family of mankind. Committed to the continued domination of their state, unwilling to imagine a future without it, and always fearful of the decline just around the bend, liberal imperialists develop hyperbolic strategies of forgetting that are constantly engaged in acts of deflection. They steer us toward the brink of illiberalism, always hinting at the presence of violence, military aggression, and occupation through the passive voice (e.g. acts of violence "were committed" and mistakes "were made"), but then instructing us to look away from such acts toward the rich, unfolding narrative of Britain and America's liberal identity in history—or their liberal identity in the present. This sleight of hand nods stoically at illiberalism and violence while simultaneously constructing all-consuming, empathetic accounts of Britain and America's liberal character. In this worldview, the illiberal practices of the liberal imperial state fall just outside of our peripheral vision, so that we are aware of their presence but unable to draw them into focus for too long because we are so distracted by liberal imperialists insistently demanding: "don't look over there! Look at me!" In essence, the nature of liberal imperialist justification in times of pressure and decline requires its devotees to develop historical and contemporary narratives of their empire's liberal identity sufficiently heavy enough to serve as a constant, reiterated counterweight to the necessary pull of the empire's ongoing illiberalism.

Because this exercise in self-promotion usually entails prolonged dwelling on myths about the liberal empire's origins and glory days, it is almost always profoundly backward looking and nostalgic in a way that seems to strain against the definitional sensibilities of political theorists, who are used to imagining liberal theory as primarily oriented toward progress. For Judith Shklar, both utopianism and nostalgia are inherently conservative responses to the end of "great ideological systems," the warning signs that the liberal imagination has been stymied "by our inability to think as creatively as the ancients apparently did."[64] In a similar vein, Wendy Brown argues, prior to the end of the Cold War, "only modernity's critics (who were also critics of liberalism)" had questioned the forward and improving nature of history by constructing "mytho-historical accounts" of the "corruption and decline of a once great polity."[65] Themes of nostalgia and decline, according to Brown, "framed Thucydides' telling of the Peloponnesian War and Machiavelli's account of the demise of ancient Rome," but, she suggests, such accounts are almost unheard of in modernity and, indeed, only since the end of the Cold War have liberals given up on the promise of modern progress in the wake of new forms of global capitalism, ensuing challenges to liberal understandings of sovereignty, and the rise of identity politics.[66] What startles Brown so much about the present day is the nostalgic longing of someone like Gore Vidal for a mythical golden moment in the America liberal past. This suggests, she argues, that some liberals thinkers have simply given up on the progressive movement of history (so central to liberal thought and modernity itself) altogether. What happens, Brown wonders, to the liberal project when it ceases to imagine time in these forward terms, when it moves "out of history"?

Contrary to Shklar's observation that nostalgia signifies a break with liberal values, I argue that liberal theorists have, in the past, turned to nostalgic musings about their polity's liberal history in order to chart a way out of its current predicaments, particularly when confronted with the contradiction between liberal principles and illiberal politics. And, contrary to Brown's assertions that this turn is somehow shockingly new and distinctly American, it is clear that liberals were developing such "mytho-historical accounts" of the past in Britain long before Gore Vidal ever cast a nostalgic glance back at the 1950s. In other words, in order to pull against the spectacle of the empire's constant violation of its own liberal principles, liberal imperialists are forced to turn, again and again, to a fixed understanding of what the empire is in its essence, in a space that was both forged in the fires of a golden past and locked still within its imperial husk. Both Zimmern and Kagan, for instance, weave their narratives of British and American power into a mournful story of Athenian democracy, preserved in some form, within the British and American present. Curtis (with the Round Table) and Ferguson construct elaborate metanarrative histories of the British Empire that consistently look backward, toward a moment that was both more decidedly Anglo-Saxon than the present and more innocently liberal. Ignatieff's vision of the democratic "we" at the heart of his imperial vision feels always tragically poised at the brink of letting go of better times. Hence, in order to give the empire sufficient liberal heft to deflect attention away from its antiliberal policies, supporters of liberal empire, like the thinkers examined in this book, fashion their narratives around densely nostalgic musing about the empire's liberal origins that consistently suggest, even as they point toward the future, that its best days—the days that made it who it is now—are gone.

In this sense, these thinkers are often nostalgic in ways that are both redemptive and, in Ian Baucum's words, "proleptic." Thus, in his work on historical debates and discourses about Englishness in the context of Empire, Baucum argues that there is nothing "new and unusual" about a nostalgia that both mourns the loss of an English past and is "at once an embrace and a repudiation of the imperial beyond."[67] For Baucum, debates and discourses about English character have historically used nostalgic visions of a golden English past as a way of both reconciling and forgetting the violence of Britain's Empire and its contemporary legacy. Moreover, Baucum argues that at times these nostalgic narratives have taken on a "proleptic" quality, reveling in the pleasure associated with remembering England in a lost, blessed time, but doing so by imagining this moment in the future. "This proleptic nostalgia," he argues in his chapter on Ruskin's historical vision, " . . . anticipates the bitter pleasure of occupying the present only in memory" and thus begins "the work of forgetting or evacuating the present in order that it might be later remembered or infinitely reoccupied." Such an impulse is particularly evident in what he calls "the practices of tourism, in the buying of the souvenir or the taking of the photograph, moments in which the present begins to annul itself by anticipating its representation as an artifact of memory."[68] Imagining a time in the future that looks back on the time that is now allowed thinkers like Ruskin to "evacuate the present," to empty the now of the kinds of discomforting contradictions that clustered around the intersection of liberalism and empire, of Englishness and Britishness. The nostalgia of all the thinkers under consideration in this book, to a greater or lesser extent, similarly evacuates the present of uncomfortable contradictions by dwelling on the now from the position of the past and/or the future while mourning the loss of the liberal imperial polity's greatness. Contra Shklar and Brown, nostalgia in this imperial context is not merely conservative or "out of history": it is productive, it gives rise to redemptive narratives of the Empire's liberal past and evacuated present that legitimate not only contemporary imperial practices but future forms of imperial governance.

Ideology, Intention, and Political Theory

Several years ago, while writing my first book, I presented a chapter to a group of colleagues from the Politics, History, and Philosophy Departments who gathered once a month to read each other's works in progress. The chapter dealt with the intersection between an emerging body of internationalist thought in Britain after the First World War and the legacy of German idealism on a generation of Oxford thinkers. After the meeting, one of my colleagues in Philosophy came up to me and asked, quite earnestly, why it was that I wanted to study "bad Hegelians." This colleague's comments reflect a broader phenomenon identified by Michael Freeden in his 1996 book, *Ideologies and Political Theory: A Conceptual Approach*. By Freeden's lights, political ideologies—patterns and systems of political thinking that construct an understanding of the political world—have often appeared to scholars as "peculiar and frequently unsavory" expressions of "distorted and power serving political thinking" and, therefore, "lag in the status stakes behind the high prestige of political philosophy, whether analytical or critical."[69] But, Freeden insists, to refuse to analyze and critique ideologies simply because they lack elegance or the high-sounding, moral purity of political philosophy is to refuse engagement with the "universe of meaning" that emerges from their world of rhetorical gestures, conceptual apparatuses, and political visions. Such a refusal makes it impossible to answer Freeden's core question: "what are the implications and the insights of a particular set of political views in terms of the conceptual connections it forms?"[70]

Several people have asked me versions of my colleague's question in the context of writing this book: why study scholars who write in a popular vein, with such clear political intent, whose methods are sometimes dubious and whose logical conclusions often do not hold water under even the most cursory of examinations? My answer to them is the same as it was then, and it is still deeply informed by Freeden's approach. I study "bad Hegelians" not because I am interested in recovering the ethical possibilities of their theories, or because I see in their work normative guidelines for a better way of imagining global politics, or because I find in their scholarship a logical coherence worth emulating. Rather, I am fascinated in following the patterns of political concepts that emerge from their "universe of meaning" because I want to know more about the implications of that universe for politics in the past, present, and future.

As my interest in political implications suggests, my choice of thinkers and authors is obviously not random. I was drawn to the "bad Hegelians" of the interwar period precisely because they were politically influential and because the theory they developed might have been (indeed, frequently was) internally incoherent, political contradictory, and philosophically dubious, but it nevertheless provided the foundation for a school of thought that would have enormous sway over a generation of international thinkers. In other words, I studied them because they were powerful and I wanted to understand how that power worked. My approach to the authors whose work I explore in this book springs from an identical concern with disclosing mechanisms and expressions of power, particularly as they manifest themselves in ideologies of liberal empire which have had (and continue to exert) enormous influence on the material lives and everyday forms of governance experienced by people all over the world.

In this regard, the thinkers I examine here can be broadly understood as public intellectuals although, as Stefan Collini, Helen Small, and other have noted, that term did not enter the vocabulary until the mid-twentieth-century.[71] The contexts in which these thinkers write and speak—and the publics to whom they address themselves—are also significantly different. Zimmern, Curtis, the members of the Round Table, and Smuts were all still riding the late-nineteenth-century wave of political theorizing that was, in Jose Harris's words, "virtually a national sport of British intellectuals."[72] As Duncan Bell points out, empire was one of the hotly debated topics taken up by intellectuals in Britain during this period and the thinkers involved in these debates were drawn from an elite class of academics, businessmen, lawyers, politicians, and journalists who often, as Bell observes, combined "several of these roles simultaneously."[73] In the early twentieth-century, the cultural traditions and institutional frameworks in which these intellectuals wrote and spoke were oriented largely around Oxford (to a lesser extent, Cambridge) and, although this was a time when intellectuals in Britain were writing to a number of "diverse publics" (in Collini's terms), the discourse of those thinkers examined in this book was aimed squarely at influencing the elite public debate in London, where it would have the most impact on imperial policy.[74] Zimmern and Curtis, both associated with Oxford, used their clout as intellectuals and their positions within an institution that was, in effect, a feeder school for imperial administration, to shape debate within those intellectual circles that mattered.[75] Even Smuts—who, as an outsider, did more to pander to the goodwill of the national newspapers in England than did Zimmern or the members of the Round Table—gave almost the entirety of his wartime speeches in London and addressed them to audiences familiar with imperial affairs, audiences he felt would do well to hear his "rough popular expression" of imperial wisdom.[76]

Kagan, Ferguson, and Ignatieff on the other hand are all (like Zimmern and Curtis) academics associated with elite institutions; however, their writing and speaking on imperial issues takes place within an entirely different public and political context. The last two decades in the United States have witnessed a dramatic expansion of the media spaces in which organized punditry is possible, as well as an explosion of possible publics to whom intellectuals can address themselves.[77] Ferguson, in particular, is exceptionally canny at taking advantage of these multiple and overlapping media spaces and publics, writing and hosting documentaries for the BBC, publishing both scholarly and popular books, and appearing as a regular commentator on television and in the pages of *Newsweek* and *The New York Times*. While Kagan and Ignatieff have never been media darlings in quite the same way as Ferguson (excepting, perhaps, Ignatieff's five-year stint as a Member of Parliament in Canada), they have both been frequent contributors of op-eds to *The New York Times* and other major media outlets. All three of these thinkers have made high profile use of their associations with Harvard and Yale and yet, all three have, at times, railed against the academy, particularly for what they see as the hegemonic mean-spiritedness of public intellectuals associated with the academic left. In 1997, in an article entitled "The Decline and Fall of the Public Intellectual," Ignatieff lamented those "tenured radicals who went into academe after 1968" who were "supposed to free the university from the conformist functionalism of American social science" but who instead set to work "erecting new stockades of conformism: neo-Marxist scholasticism, deconstruction, critical theory—the games people play when they have given up on public debate."[78] In a similar vein, Kagan made no attempt in 2011 to hide his contempt for those academics that opposed the occupation of Iraq, referring to them as "privileged people who enjoy the full benefits offered by the country they deride and detest...but lack the basic decency to pay the allegiance and respect that honor demands."[79] In sum, like their Oxford predecessors, Kagan, Ferguson, and Ignatieff take advantage of their academic affiliations to legitimize themselves but, given the breadth of media outlets available to them, are also able to reach audiences much larger and more diverse than would have been conceivable to public intellectuals in the past. They then use this expanded audience space to deride the universities with which they are affiliated—who give them employment and legitimacy—for the academy's intractable left-wing bias.

But despite differences in the political, academic, and institutional environments which shape their public discourses, each of the authors examined in this book is different from the average public intellectual found in Britain then or America now in terms of the direct influence they had and have on foreign policy and on the opinions of key power brokers. The Round Table is a particularly stark example of what this kind of intellectual power meant in the early twentieth-century. The organization was founded by Oxford graduates who had worked with Lord Milner in South Africa and came home to form a "network of semi-secret organizations," funded by Cecil Rhodes, created for the express purpose of influencing imperial policy. It was, thus, the first international relations think tank in the world; those thinkers associated with it would, after the war, form the Royal Institute of International Affairs and play a role in the creation of the Council on Foreign Relations.[80] Zimmern was also involved with the secretive Round Table, and Smuts—as a member of the imperial war council—drafted a pamphlet outlining his idea for a League of Nations that convinced Woodrow Wilson to support it. In other words, these early twentieth-century thinkers didn't just influence public opinion; they wielded fairly direct political influence. And through this influence, they were able to help ensure that the League of Nations as an institution (and the kind of internationalism it would generate) would continue to be grounded on imperialist assumptions about international hierarchy and the unequal distribution of international resources, even as it did so in the name of anti-imperialism.

In a similar vein, the contemporary thinkers analyzed here also have their fingers in a number of policy and media pies. Perhaps not surprisingly, all of them have been involved with the Council on Foreign Relations. Before he left Harvard to become a Canadian MP (only to return to Harvard in 2012), Ignatieff served on the United Nations' International Commission on Intervention and State Sovereignty. For his part, Kagan helped to found the Project for the New American Century, an organization that would have a substantial influence on the Bush Administration's foreign policy. He also helped to found the Program for Grand Strategy at Yale, which seeks to educate future world leaders in the history and practice of grand, tactical thinking. Finally, Ferguson served as an advisor to Lehman Brothers during the height of the economic boom (then bust) and was involved with John McCain's "kitchen cabinet" in 2008. In 2010, Ferguson was asked by David Cameron to participate in overhauling the history curriculum in British schools. In sum, more than any of the left-wing academics they criticize, Kagan, Ferguson, and Ignatieff exercise a certain amount of influence over policy-makers and power-brokers. Just as Zimmern, the Round

Table, and Smuts played an integral role in pushing postwar internationalism in an imperial direction, so have these three contemporary intellectuals contributed to a foreign policy consensus in America on the benefits of American leadership and global intervention upon which everyone (from the neoconservative Project for a New American Century to the liberal Princeton Project on National Security) seems to agree.[81]

Gaining greater insight into this broad consensus, this "universe of meaning" that has become common sense among so many, is ultimately both the political and critical goal of this book. Methodologically, this necessitates a fairly frequent shifting between textual and contextual analyses of these political visions, dwelling deeply in their rhetorical and narrative richness while situating them in those historical and political moments that give them shape and heft. My approach in this regard has been influenced by Quentin Skinner's analysis of political rhetoric as a legitimate lens of inquiry for political theorists interested in fleshing out the conceptual vision of canonical thinkers like Hobbes.[82] Although the authors I explore in this text are hardly canonical, they are heavily invested in shaping their own political environments, and they do this through a combination of scholarly inquiry that often purports to be interest-free while also relying on rhetorical tropes, narratives, and literary devices meant to persuade the reader by any means necessary. At the same time, the works of these authors also reflects the dense, complicated political environments in which they write, even as they strive to shape these environments into what they believe are truer portrayals of the real world.

Where I part ways with Skinner somewhat is over the question of intention. To be clear, I, more than many of his critics, appreciate Skinner's insistence that we take the intention of the author seriously when attempting to interpret a text's meaning, and that this intention can often be found "outside" the text in the ideological roil of the historical moment. This is Skinner's challenge to those interpreters who argue against what they call "the intentional fallacy" by insisting that everything important to be learned from a text arises from a sensitive reading of the text itself and not from historical, biographical, or archival context.[83] Any reading of the liberal imperialist authors explored in this book that attempted to extricate them from their historical and rhetorical context would offer us an impoverished understanding of the universe their writings both shape and reflect.

Additionally, I am attracted to Skinner's insistence on authorial intention in context for discursive and political reasons. One of the central, reoccurring themes at work in the liberal imperial narratives of deflection under investigation in this book is the insistence by these authors that the intentions of neither the British nor American states—nor the individual soldiers, colonists, and merchants acting in their name—matter in the context of telling the empire's story, or for elaborating the imperial society's liberal identity. In essence, these narratives are rife with not merely claims about the *good* intentions of imperialists, but with stories that stress a pronounced *lack* of imperial intention on the part of states and individuals, as though somehow much of the world's population ended up under British control or American influence by accident, in a "fit of absence of mind," or as the natural result of the Anglo-American love of liberty and commerce. We see this tendency not only in the substance of their historical narratives, but also in these thinkers' relentless use of the passive voice. Since the sixteenth-century, portions of the world "were absorbed" by Britain and America, cultures "were brought into contact with each other," "free trade, free capital movements, and free migration were fostered" and "the rule of law was institutionalized." And because we can never really know how the world became imperialized, and given that even when we can establish causation we know that neither Britons nor Americans ever really *intended* to behave illiberally, then it makes perfect sense, in the minds of these authors, to frame present political solutions to problems caused by empires in the past in the passive voice as well. For example, "Decisions will have to be made," Ignatieff argues, about whether or not to torture prisoners accused of terrorism.[84] But *who* makes those decisions, *who* does the torturing, and or *how* that torturing might be related to American imperial politics in the Middle East and the world are questions that simply disappear behind Ignatieff's words, obscured by the inscrutable wall of his passive voice. In response, I have made the decision in this book to avoid the passive voice whenever possible (and, although I would never admit this to my students, it is not always possible) in order to make visible the connections between the stories these public intellectuals tell about their empires and contemporary and historical acts of imperializing.

I part ways with Skinner, however, over the firm line he draws between accepting authorial utterances at face value and drawing upon other interpretive strategies to discover secondary or unconscious meaning in these utterances.[85] By contrast, like Freeden, I argue that it is possible to analyze ideology in a manner that both takes authorial intention seriously *and* calls into question the author's stated meaning, by examining texts in light of both their historical and rhetorical context and by using insights from psychology, critical theory and/ or literary criticism to theorize how these authors might displace or deflect what Freeden calls the "unconscious structural or psychological symbols that refer to further aspects of thought and conduct not apparent to the agent or the agent's society."[86] In other words, it is both fair and appropriate, to my mind, to analyze the ideology of twentieth- and twenty-first-century liberal imperialists by taking what they say at face value *while also* examining their claims in the context of the "universe of meaning" they (intentionally or unintentionally) construct. At the same time, it is important, I argue, to scrutinize the means by which their political visions and political projects structure and limit the kinds of stories these authors can tell. Thus, liberal imperialist storytellers are at all times both producers of meaning and prisoners of their own conceptual worlds, often pushed into very tight discursive corners by the difficult juggling act at the heart of their political project. There is a reason, then, that their arguments are often so profoundly tautological: the more closed-in the rhetorical walls, the tighter the circles they are forced to pace.

Strategies of Deflection and the Organization of the Book

The language I have found most useful for capturing this twofold approach to intention—the language that also supplies the organizational framework for the book—draws heavily on Mehta's brilliant conceptual term, "strategies of exclusion." Again, for Mehta, liberals, like Mill, historically excluded particular types of people from their theory's universal assumptions about the human capacity to reason and self-govern. Mehta argues that this move to exclude is neither practically necessary for liberalism as a theory nor merely a reflection of the contingent historical circumstances that influenced individual liberal thinkers. Rather, he suggests, the impulse to exclude is best understood in the context of the politically and culturally strategic *choices* that individual thinkers make about how far, and in what manner, to stray from universal principles. For Mehta, the distinction between a theory's understanding of universal human capacity and the way a theorist strategically narrows this understanding gestures toward a "space in which the liberal theorist can, as it were, raise the ante for political inclusion."[87] Mehta's work thus concentrates on the kinds of strategic exclusions that liberals employ during these moments—strategies that range from articulations of "anthropological minimums" for liberal subjects to the creation of complex notions of civilizational maturity. Mehta argues that, to the extent the distinction between universal equality and exclusion becomes associated with certain major liberal thinkers and the tradition more broadly, it also becomes possible to view it as intrinsic to liberalism—along with the space for criticism it enables.

I suggest that something similar goes on in the writings of those public intellectuals under consideration in this book. All of these authors are broadly knowledgeable about their particular empires and committed to similar sets of liberal ethics and liberal political practices. Given the historical violence and illiberalism of the imperial societies they support, each has a space, so to speak, to "up the ante" for *reflection* on this violence and illiberalism and, in the process, to imagine a different kind of politics. To the extent that they deflect attention away from the imperial state's illiberalism, it becomes possible, as Mehta might put it, to view strategic deflection as intrinsic to the ideology of liberal imperialism. It also becomes possible to disaggregate these authors' strategies from each other and theorize their strategic choices in the context of their particular circumstances, in relationship to each other, and in response to liberal imperial ideology more broadly. In sum, thinking about the rhetorical gestures of each author in terms of strategic choices—and strategic intention—enables us to look comparatively at their differences and similarities over time.

The work of Zimmern, Kagan, the Round Tablers, Ferguson, Smuts, and Ignatieff fall generally into three categories of strategic deflection The book is thus divided into three sections of two chapters each. Part One, entitled, "Strategies of Antiquity," examines the way both Zimmern and Kagan—from across a century and seemingly (in Kagan's case, that is) without knowledge of each other—developed two remarkably similar theories of the relationship between a liberal, ancient Athenian Empire and contemporary liberal British and American Empires. Both authors read their visions of Britain's and America's past, present, and future through a discourse that also effectively saves Athens from decline. Part Two, "Metanarrative Strategies," looks at the commonwealth writings of the Round Table and Ferguson's work on imperial history. Each chapter examines these thinkers' intricate construction of historical and contemporary stories that effectively sew the present empire into a metahistorical-great-chain-of-being with itself, excusing and obviating its forays into illiberalism and violence while reversing the very notion of causality, so that the empire is never responsible for creating the conditions of its own demise. Part Three, "Strategies of Character," focuses on the internationalist writings of Smuts and Ignatieff's work on international human rights, the War on Terror, and the need for a new approach to liberal interventionism that Ignatieff terms "empire lite." Employing different metaphorical and historical approaches, both men tell particular stories about their own liberal empires that consistently return to the theme of the empire's true self and its liberal character.

The organization of the book is in no way meant to imply that the three strategies do not significantly overlap in these works. All of these thinkers are, to some degree, concerned with the issue of liberal character; every one of them has a metahistorical story to tell; and we can even catch glimpses of Athens lurking in the corners of all these texts. The tripartite division of the book also in no way suggests that there aren't any number of strategies unique to each author at work here. Smuts, for instance, draws upon a philosophical understanding of holism to frame his understanding of the Commonwealth as a living organism that both resonates with other imperialists of the time and is entirely unique to his work. Ignatieff's addiction to tragedy is something we do not see in the other texts under consideration and, while all of these authors liken the empire's innocence to "sleep," Kagan's use of sleeping and waking as metaphors is far more extensive than that of the others. Both the Round Table thinkers and Ferguson play with the idea of time and causation, but in very different ways. In this same sense, the book never assumes that the strategies employed by these thinkers are unmarked by the particularities of the age. Kagan's idealist rendering of Pericles reflects his long-time status as a cold warrior, for example, while Zimmern's approach channels fifth-century B.C.E. Athens through the lens of Edwardian "English club life." Likewise, the liberalism espoused by key members of the Round Table reflects both their experiences with the progressive, pro-welfare state politics of New Liberalism at Oxford and their particular reading of English and American federalism. Ignatieff's liberalism, by contrast, owes much to the idea of tragedy in the writings of Isaiah Berlin. I explore these differences in detail in each of the chapters. At the same time, the book is anchored on the observation that, despite their differences, the arc of narrative deflection curves toward a similar end in a similar way in the work of each of these six authors, and that a critical examination of the rhetorical shape of that curve has much to tell us about the intersection of imperial deflection and imperial forgetting during these eras.

My approach throughout the book has been to theorize more explicitly how the frequently untidy bodies of thought and narrative stories that constitute liberal imperial ideology have become, as Chakrabarty puts it, "self evident to everyone" and "made to look obvious."[88] The entire book is thus, in Chakrabary's terms, a prolonged experiment in "provincializing" liberal imperialism, in making it appear less obvious. The goal of the short Conclusion, however, is somewhat different from the rest of the book and takes great inspiration from Tully's understanding of "practical philosophy." As Tully puts it in his remarkable 2002 article, "Political Philosophy as a Critical Activity," "practical philosophy" is a "form of problematization," a methodological impulse to disclose the "conditions of possibility" implicit in a "historically singular set of practices of governance."[89] In this spirit, the Conclusion is committed to briefly exploring the "conditions of possibility" that have existed, and continue to, exist alongside dominant narratives of liberal imperialism despite its deflective insistence on "who we are." Historically, such "diverse paths" (as Samuel Moyn might call them) can be found in the alternative narratives of statehood and critique that went unexplored in Britain and America after the ascendance of liberal imperialist internationalism in the wake of World War I.[90] I also consider what the loss of these "diverse paths" means for us today.

The Conclusion also briefly considers what a *reflective* rather than *deflective* approach to contemporary American imperialism might look like by reading President Barack Obama's recent comments on drone strikes, the Guantanamo Bay military prison, and domestic terrorism through the lens of Said's understanding of writing history as "counter-memory." Said describes "counter-memory" as the practice of first challenging received ideas about the imperial past "determined by the powerful" and then placing the "missing actuality back in the center of things." He goes on to argue, in *Humanism and Democratic Criticism* (2004), that a critical humanist practice grounded in "counter-memory" can pull analyses of imperialism away from the clenched jaws of liberalism's insistence that it is always the solution to its own problems. "It takes a good deal more courage, work and knowledge," Said argues, to write this kind of history than it "does to write prescriptive articles for 'liberals,' à la Michael Ignatieff, that urge more destruction and death for distant civilians."[91] For Said, writing "counter-memory" is one way to effectively integrate the violence and illiberalism of liberal empire back into contemporary narratives in a manner that is disruptively productive.

In its essence, this book aims to explore some of the key strategies that liberal imperialists use to deflect attention away from imperial violence and back toward "who we are." In the process, it takes up Said's first call to break down received assumptions about the past "determined by the powerful." It therefore assists in prying open a space where "counter-memory" can push back against liberal imperialists who seem to be constantly snapping their fingers in front of our faces and yelling, "Wake up! Don't look over there! Look at me!" In the process, I hope to contribute toward the cultivation of a political environment where it becomes more difficult, in Said's words, for "conscience to look away or fall asleep," where discussions of "who we are" become opportunities for real critical reflection about the nature and history of the "we" that imperializes, and the kinds of polities "we" could be in a world without empire.[92]

PART ONE

STRATEGIES OF ANTIQUITY

1

Alfred Zimmern's "Oxford Paradox": Displacement and Athenian Nostalgia

In a 1905 lecture entitled "The Greeks and Their Civilization," Alfred Zimmern, then a Fellow and Tutor at New College, Oxford, posed the following question to his audience: "Was Greek Culture universal or was it simple? Was it broad in its range or was it narrow?" Zimmern responded to his own query thus: "the answer is that Greek culture at its best was universal, because it was simple, and broad because it was narrow. In saying this I hope I mean something more than an Oxford paradox. Let me explain."[1]

As Zimmern's lecture unfolded, however, it became increasingly clear that the explanation he had provided was not meant to resolve the paradox implicit in his assertion that ancient Greek culture was universal in its simplicity and broad in its narrowness. Rather, Zimmern clearly believed that the paradox itself was valuable, insofar as it literally meant "something more"—something true and essential—about the Greeks. In typical Zimmern style, he spent the rest of the lecture reiterating that "something more" and ignoring the perilousness of the claim, often allowing the uniqueness of Athenian culture to stand where a philosophical explanation should. For instance, Zimmern argued that because the Greeks (or, more specifically, fifth-century B.C.E. Athenians) were so grounded in the limited environs of the city-state, and because they believed that the "civilized world was a very small place, and civilization a very simple and tangible matter," they were able to cultivate a far-ranging "sense of universality."[2] But he never described what enabled this intellectual roaming other than to stress, again and again, the genius of the Athenian *polis*. One gets the sense while reading this lecture that Zimmern desperately wanted to have his cake and eat it too; to revel in the unprecedented cast of an Athenian mind forged in this one remarkable space during this one remarkable time and yet, simultaneously, claim it as a universally true and enduring model for anyone interested in critical inquiry. "How to use the intellect," he argued, "is what we still have to learn from the Greeks and from the Greeks alone."[3]

Zimmern's paradox could be read as mere intellectual curiosity—an under-theorized moment in a never-published lecture—except for two important contextual facts about his classical scholarship and his politics that, in themselves, gesture toward the broader phenomenon at the heart of this book. First, not only did Zimmern not resolve this paradox in his 1905 talk, but he also continued to deepen and extend his claim that Athens was "universal because it was simple" throughout the book for which these lectures formed the intellectual basis, 1911's *The Greek Commonwealth: Politics and Economics in Fifth-Century Athens*. As the subtitle suggests, much of this influential book focused on exploring the political, geographical, and economic factors that coalesced in the fifth-century to produce a unique Athenian approach to life that Zimmern felt had more to offer the world than any culture since. But much of *The Greek Commonwealth* was also devoted to exploring Athens's relationship to imperial economics, colonization, and what Zimmern termed its "free intercourse" with other city-states in the Aegean and Mediterranean. In other words, Zimmern was well aware that the same Athens he described as understanding the world to be "a small place" actually developed its unique fifth-century character within an imperial context. The Athens that Zimmern described as "universal because it was simple, broad because it was narrow," was no mere isolated, provincial accident but rather, always already, an empire. The *polis* that so infatuated Zimmern was always already "Athens the city state and Athens the Mistress of the Seas."[4]

Second, Zimmern's consuming interest in fifth-century Athens was consistently colored by his longstanding concerns with contemporary politics. Like many Oxford tutors, Zimmern understood that his role as a teacher was to bring fifth-century Athens to bear on the contemporary world for his students, who would go on to become the political leaders and colonial administrators of the Empire. Arnold Toynbee would describe attending Zimmern's lectures as "one of the most thrilling intellectual experiences when I was an undergraduate at Oxford" precisely because "his interest in the Greco-Roman World...did not rule out a parallel interest in the present day world. Zimmern's example showed me that the two interests could co-exist in the same mind, and that each of them was illuminating for the other."[5] As a scholar, Zimmern understood his work on antiquity in similarly modern and instructive terms, or, as he explained to his friend Graham Wallace in 1910, that he was writing *The Greek Commonwealth* because "I want most of all to make people think about the nature of the twentieth-century."[6]

This no doubt rings almost absurdly overconfident to anyone familiar with the last one hundred tumultuous years in world history, but, for Zimmern, understanding the "nature of the twentieth-century" meant one very specific thing: developing a better understanding of the British Empire and the "unique position which it occupies and the unique possibilities that are in store for it in the world politics of the twentieth-century."[7] While he would later go on to become a scholar of international relations and a lifelong advocate of the League of Nations, in those years immediately preceding and following the completion of *The Greek Commonwealth*, Zimmern's interest in the global politics of the twentieth-century was motivated almost entirely by his desire to promote the interests of the British Empire. During this period of his life Zimmern was very much under the sway of a particular Oxford-based, liberal approach to Empire, promoted by Lord Milner and echoed in the activism of Milner's acolytes, who would go on to form the powerful pro-imperial lobby, the Round Table, in 1910. The founders of the Round Table were both undergraduates with Zimmern and some of his students at New College and he would join the group itself shortly after its initial meetings. The Round Table oriented its efforts toward the perceived need to foster a reinvigorated, more unified, British imperial politics and to promote greater cultural and political integration among the Empire's white dominions.

Where Zimmern and the members of the Round Table parted ways with Milner, Rhodes, and an older generation of imperial thinkers, however, was in their keen awareness of the ways the political environment in which they couched their liberal imperial scheme had changed since the end of the nineteenth-century. In particular, a rise in anti-imperial sentiment among leftists and liberals in Britain following the Boer War, the emergence of an explicitly nationalist, racist German imperialism during that same period, and the growth of vocal anticolonial movements in Ireland, India, and Egypt, all contributed to an environment in which the old liberal imperialist nostrums of progress and civilizational superiority were no longer as effective in convincing skeptics of the benevolence of the British imperial mission. As a result, in the course of articulating their imperial vision, Zimmern and the Round Table were forced to confront questions unique in the history of liberal imperialism. What, critics like Hobson demanded, made the British Empire any different from the German? If the British Empire was not motivated by a sense of cultural superiority, then what motivated it? If domination could not be justified in terms of race, then by what terms could it be justified? What *was* it that made the British both better able and ethically entitled to rule much of the world?

I argue in this chapter that Zimmern wrote *The Greek Commonwealth* in part to work through these questions about British imperialism. To some extent, fifth-century Athens served as a site of political displacement for Zimmern, a place where he could process the gnawing questions of British imperialism from the safety of historical distance. At the same time, Zimmern's writings about Athens were also constitutive in themselves as they contributed to his post-1910 approach to British imperialism and, by extension, the approach of the Round Table. There is, then, a spectral quality to Zimmern's Greek world in that it both reflected and refracted all of his complex and overlapping anxieties about British liberalism and the current imperial order at the same time as it laid the foundations for their solution. And finally, there is something deeply nostalgic about Zimmern's portrayal of fifth-century Athens that also reveals a similar nostalgia for the "Little England" of his imagination and a British Empire that was both at the height of its power and perilously, for Zimmern, balanced on the brink of decline.

The chapter begins with a reflection on Zimmern's career, his Burkean-liberal approach to politics, and his pre-1910 writings about the Empire. I go on to look more closely at the spectral *polis* at the heart of his Greek writings, paying particular attention to what one critic referred to as his "audacious modernity" and his strained interpretation of Thucydides as a Periclean imperialist.[8] I conclude by reflecting upon Zimmern's imperialism after the *Greek Commonwealth* and suggest that writing about Athens helped Zimmern to work out some of the nagging questions that plagued him about contemporary Britain, as well as engendering a narrative history of British imperial development that was simultaneously nostalgic and redemptive. Ironically, I conclude, throughout the course of his research on Athens and Britain, Zimmern never did resolve his "Oxford paradox." Indeed, I argue, the paradox had to remain a paradox in order to keep the question of liberal empire— rather than the effects of imperial power—at the heart of the conversation.

The Political Context of Zimmern's Athens

Alfred Zimmern was born in Surbiton (southwest London) in 1879. His parents were German immigrants, his father was Jewish, and they seemed to have worked hard to ensure that Zimmern had the most English of upbringings, sending him to Winchester College and then to Oxford in 1898.[9] Zimmern excelled in Greek translation at Oxford and in 1902 became a Lecturer and in 1904 a Tutorial Fellow.[10] He lectured in Classics at Oxford (helping to reform the Classics degree), during which time he also became involved with the Workers Education Association (WEA) and taught adult-education Classics classes on a volunteer basis. In 1909 he retired his post (much to the dismay, according to Toynbee, of his students) and went to Greece to do further research for *The Greek Commonwealth*.[11] Zimmern would never again hold an academic position in Classics and, although he would later publish a smattering of pieces on Greek topics, the majority of these (most notably, 1928's *Solon and Croesus: And Other Greek Essays*) were written during the first fifteen years of the twentieth-century.

In 1910, Zimmern returned to England, where he finished writing *The Greek Commonwealth* and continued his involvement with the WEA, and in 1912 he went to work for the Board of Education. Zimmern's sense of civic engagement at this time was clearly influenced by the New Liberal politics he inherited from Oxford—a politics explicitly evident in his support for an expanded social welfare state coupled with a simultaneous rejection of what he called the "doctrine of the class struggle."[12] Zimmern's liberalism was also tinged, interestingly, with a distinctly Burkean flavor, particularly obvious in his arguments about the importance of community.[13] For instance, in an early lecture entitled "The British Workingman," probably delivered around 1905, Zimmern painted for his audience a picture of English political liberalism that was both "more individualist" than its Continental variants but also more deeply rooted in a "sense of social solidarity."[14] In England, he argued, "Class merges into class by imperceptible gradation," and this intricate social network was wedded, through tradition and history, to liberal institutions and democratic values.[15] During World War I, Zimmern similarly described liberalism "among the English speaking peoples" as a way of life always conditioned by a deep and abiding understanding of the relationship between ethics and politics, between "the dispositions that are lovely in private life" and the "conduct of the commonwealth."[16] Zimmern's unattributed borrowing of Burke's language from *Thoughts on the Cause of the Present Discontents* (1770) in this passage illustrates just how deeply he was influenced by Burke's vision of political community. Indeed, at times like this, it is difficult to tell where Zimmern ends and Burke begins. And yet, at the same time Zimmern was crafting these arguments about the uniqueness of English liberalism, with its precious admixture of private and public life, he was also insisting, in a markedly *un*Burkean fashion, that this political approach was universally valid for all human beings at that point in history. "The enemies of liberalism," he insisted at the beginning of the Great War, "whether within or without the allied countries, are the enemies of the human race."[17]

It is for this universal liberal sentiment that Zimmern is best known among contemporary scholars. After *The Greek Commonwealth*, Zimmern turned his attention almost entirely to the establishment of the League of Nations and the study of internationalism and international relations more generally. Again, during the period after his return from Greece in 1910, Zimmern became a prominent member of the pro-imperial Round Table Society.[18] Through his Oxford connections and Round Table contacts, he landed a position with the Foreign Office during World War I, where he authored the "Foreign Office Memorandum," a document that would serve as the foundation of the plan for a League of Nations that the British Delegation took with them to Paris in 1919.[19] After the war, he became the first professor of International Relations in the world (at the University of Wales, Aberystwyth, in 1919) and eventually the first Montague Burton Professor of International Relations at Oxford in 1933. Not only was Zimmern one of the most influential members of the League of Nations Society, he also founded the Geneva School of International Studies and worked for years with various official League organizations, including the League's Committee on Intellectual Cooperation."[20] The majority of his publications for the rest of his life were devoted to subjects in international relations including *Nationality and Government* (1918), *America and Europe and Other Essays* (1929), and *The League of Nations and the Rule of Law, 1918–1935* (1936). Zimmern's impact on the evolving subdiscipline of International Relations after the First World War was so substantial that Hans Morgenthau and Kenneth Thompson referred to him as "the most influential representative of our field" during the interwar period.[21]

While an increasing number of scholars over the last ten years have drawn attention to *The Greek Commonwealth*, most (including myself) have approached Zimmern's classical work through the lens of his later international writings, often noting in particular what Julia Stapleton calls the "remarkable ease" with which Greek analogies came to Zimmern.[22] Greek examples permeated his work on international politics throughout his career and one cannot help but be struck, when one reads anything by Zimmern, by the seamless insertion of a quotation from Thucydides in the midst of an argument about German culture, or a reference to the Athenian expulsion of the Persians at Marathon in a discussion of the League of Nations. But there was nothing accidental or dilettantish about these analogies. Zimmern was not simply dropping names for dramatic effect. Rather, almost all of these analogies were meant to demonstrate the same phenomenon again and again: a likeness or even a kinship not just between Western but, specifically, between contemporary British or Anglo-American political culture and the Athens of Pericles. Thus, when Zimmern wanted to critique the Prussian understanding of the rule of law in *Nationality and Government*, he started out by negatively comparing it "with all those, whether in ancient Greece or modern Britain and America, who have preached the need for a rule, a standard, a guiding authority, as the base of the whole social scheme."[23] In 1922's *Europe in Convalescence*, Zimmern described the "slow form of social progress" which made the "young Liberals of today" so impatient by comparing it to "the same gradual, and indeed imperceptible, stages as marked the advance of modern London upon ancient Athens."[24] In *The League of Nations and the Rule of Law*, Zimmern elaborated upon the understanding of citizenship he believed undergirded the League Covenant by first comparing it, once again, to Athens, "to which the Western world owes the twin conceptions of Liberty and Law."[25]

In this chapter however, I concentrate on *The Greek Commonwealth* not just because it offers us insight into the origins of Zimmern's later internationalist analogizing. Rather, I read *The Greek Commonwealth* as an extended analogy itself, as both a troubled reflection of Zimmern's developing vision of the British Empire as well as an influence on that vision. Again, this approach differs somewhat from the way most current Zimmern scholars tend to read his classical scholarship and his particular vision of Athenian life, namely, as an intellectual prelude to his later political theory. Polly Low argues, for instance, that during the period in which he was writing *The Greek Commonwealth*, Zimmern believed "the Athenian Empire was distinguished above all by Liberty, and the Athenian mission was to spread that liberty throughout the Greek world." Low goes on to argue that, "fifteen years later," while writing about international politics, Zimmern found "that same liberty as the key to the longevity of the British Empire."[26] In Low's analysis, Zimmern was first a classicist and then an international writer, first a scholar of Athens and then of the British Empire. Paul Rich makes a similar argument in his thoughtful analysis of the relationship between interwar internationalism and imperialism in *Race and Empire in British Politics*, noting that Zimmern "saw the Hellenic civilization of the Greeks as not only laying the basis of European political thought but also acting as a model of a large scale civilized community which transcended local and national differences."[27]

Rich's and Low's assessments, however, do not take fully into consideration the extent to which Zimmern was *already* thinking about the British Empire while writing about the Athens of *The Greek Commonwealth*, and the way contemporary politics pressed in upon his vision of the fifth-century *polis*. Recently, Paul Millet has corrected this oversight somewhat by arguing that Zimmern's political involvement with the WEA, his evolving liberalism, and his understanding of British imperialism all shaped his reading of Athens.[28] But Millet relies largely upon Zimmern's postwar writings about international politics and the Empire to make his case. In contrast, I look at Zimmern's classical thought during this period in the context of those speeches and essays he wrote about the British Empire both before and immediately after *The Greek Commonwealth*. I focus in particular on two unpublished lectures Zimmern wrote around 1905, "The Seven Deadly Sins of Tariff Reform" and "United Britain," as well as a 1913 essay, "The Ethics of Empire" published in *The Round Table*. In the interstices, between 1905 and 1913, Zimmern wrote *The Greek Commonwealth* and, in the process, also puzzled through some of the lingering questions about the British Empire that his earlier lectures left unanswered.

In making this argument I by no means want to imply that Zimmern, the classical scholar and translator of Greek, was not genuinely concerned with fifth-century Athens: he spent years researching his subject and, despite his earlier words to Graham Wallas, claimed that his reason for writing the book was to "make clear to myself what fifth-century Athens was really like."[29] Indeed, Frank Turner has described *The Greek Commonwealth* as "one of the most sensitive, eloquent, evocative, and humane works ever written about Athens in this language."[30] But, as I explore below, Zimmern's overwhelming tendency to compare the ancient *polis* to modern England and the Athenian Empire with the British was difficult even for his most sympathetic reviewers to ignore. As one noted in 1912, Zimmern "is in practice excessively inclined to modernize, as when, for example, he pictures the Athenian citizen regretting that he had not stopped for a mixed drink on his way to the assembly."[31]

Zimmern was hardly alone, of course, in identifying contemporary Britain with ancient Athens. As Turner notes, the late eighteenth and nineteenth-centuries were characterized by an unprecedented "fascination for ancient Greeks" as, throughout Europe, Enlightenment scholars turned for inspiration to a European past that predated Rome and Christianity.[32] In Britain, Turner argues, debates over the Athenian constitution during the nineteenth-century and the shift during this period from eighteenth-century assumptions about the failure of Athenian democracy to a form of *polis*-worship so evident in "the effusion of Zimmern" tell the story not only of "the transformation of commentary on Athenian politics" but also "the story of the transformation of British thought itself."[33] Thus, in tandem with the move to expand the franchise in England during this period, philosophical radicals like Grote turned to Athenian democracy as an example of the "grand new idea of the sovereign People composed of free and equal citizens" that created an "energy of public and private action, such as could never be obtained under an oligarchy."[34] Toward the latter half of the century, Oxford idealists and New Liberal scholars such as T. H. Green, Benjamin Jowett, and Edward Caird also participated in revitalizing academic interest in the Athenian *polis* and championed it as a model form of political community with clear lessons for the modern, liberal world.[35] But beyond being merely instructive, Turner argues, Victorian authors also began to see themselves as direct legatees of Greek ideas and to "rationalize away fundamental differences" between the ancient world and modern-day British liberalism.[36] Hence, what Saxonhouse describes as John Stuart Mill's "absurd claim" that the "battle of Marathon . . . is more important than the battle of Hastings" is not entirely absurd if we understand that it was written during an era when public intellectuals were already preoccupied with identifying direct cultural, and even racial, connections between ancient Athens and contemporary Britain.[37] In 1850, for instance, racial theorist Robert Knox argued that not only were the ancient Greeks blonds with blue eyes but that, "it is in England and in other countries inhabited by the Saxon or Scandinavian race that women resembling the Niobe, and men the Hercules and Mars, are chiefly to be found."[38]

The fact that Zimmern's classical scholarship also reflected his thinking about the British Empire was also hardly unusual for the period. Since the late eighteenth-century, both proponents and critics of the British Empire had turned to Greece and Rome to identify lessons relevant to the contemporary imperial experience, often painting complicated and contradictory portraits of both the ancient past and the present in the process. Some defenders of British Empire found in Rome neo-republican inspiration, while others extracted from it lessons about how to avoid decline.[39] During the late nineteenth-century, imperialists used the "Greek model" to argue both for and against closer federation among Britain's settler colonies.[40] At the same time, some imperial theorists were using the example of Athens's imperial decline to demonstrate how "Oriental" diseases like malaria (which, they argued, had brought down the Greeks) could similarly endanger the British.[41] In addition, classical scholars themselves were often associated with various imperial efforts. As Phiroze Vasunia points out in his astute summation of *Classics and Imperialism in the British Empire*, Gibbon (whose massive, six-volume *The Decline and Fall of The Roman Empire* influenced many Victorian imperial thinkers) was himself a holder of East India Company bonds, while John Stuart Mill worked for the East India Company for thirty years and wrote extensively about the democratic promise of ancient Athens for Britain at the same time he argued that Indians were unsuited for democracy.[42]

The contradiction that Vasunia identifies here—between Mill's support for democracy at home and paternalism abroad—is, as he notes, the contradiction of liberal empire more generally worked, in this case, through Mill's reading of antiquity. Pro-imperial liberals like Mill used what they saw as the obvious superiority of the Greeks, and the cultural similarities (and, some asserted, the racial connections) between the Greeks and the British, to explain why Britons of today, "like the Athenians of Thucydides' fifth century narrative" ought to govern others in the name of democracy and the rule of law.[43] Zimmern's liberal imperialism similarly expressed some of the basic characteristics of this contradiction. There was no doubt in his mind that Great Britain ought to govern others, that the subject inhabitants of Britain's "dependencies" were not yet capable of governing themselves, and that the continued health and strength of the Empire was essential to the flourishing of liberal values in the world more generally.

However, Zimmern's approach to both the British and Athenian Empires was not only sympathetic to a certain English liberal take on the Empire *writ large*-it also bore the stamp of the particular kind of imperialism most prevalent during his days at Oxford, an imperialism forged during that moment when Lord Milner's vision of "imperial Union" reigned supreme among undergraduates at New College. Toward the end of the nineteenth-century and during the first decade of the twentieth, Milner tended to approach the amalgam of imperial problems with which he was particularly concerned through a spiritual lens, arguing that the only solution to what looked to him like the inevitable breakup of the Empire was to be found in strengthening the political and culture bonds of fellowship (what he sometimes called "organic ties") between England and the "white dominions" of Canada, Australia, New Zealand, and South Africa. As both a student during that period in which Milner's influence was most keenly felt at New College and the tutor and teacher of those men, such as Reginald Coupland, who would go on to form the backbone of the Round Table group, Zimmern's approach to the Empire during the early days of his academic career showed obvious signs of Milner's influence.[44]

Not surprisingly, Zimmern's two lectures on imperial topics written in 1905 were redolent of Milnerian language, beginning with Zimmern's claim in "United Britain" that he was uncomfortable altogether with the word "Imperialism" and his assertion that the lecture would deal with that more "intimate" portion of the Empire, the "union of self governing British states."[45] Zimmern went on to describe the Empire as "organic" and to insist that what "unites the Empire" was no "mechanical bond, but something spiritual."[46] Like Milner, Zimmern had an astonishing faith in "imperial patriotism" and the potential of the Empire to do good in the world. "British Imperialism," he argued, "is the greatest instrument the world has ever seen for good government. It is in fact (it is a big statement, but I make it deliberately) the greatest *political* instrument for human happiness that the world has ever seen."[47]

In stressing the political rather than military or economic unity of the Empire, Zimmern was also following Milner's repeated insistence that questions of imperial economy must be subordinate to questions of imperial politics.[48] Indeed, Zimmern's insistence on treating the Empire as a political, spiritual, and moral entity, rather than an economic unit, led him to oppose some of Milner's own political and economic positions. Milner, for instance, supported Joseph Chamberlain's movement for tariff reform, a movement which responded to the increasingly widespread fear that England was losing its industrial edge and becoming more isolated and economically disadvantaged by recasting the Empire as a self-sufficient economic block, structured around imperial preferences for Britain and the dominions.[49] In his 1905 lecture, "The Seven Deadly Sins of Tariff Reform," Zimmern opposed Chamberlain's imperial preferences but for interestingly Milner-like reasons. While sympathetic to the concerns expressed by the tariff reformers, Zimmern argued that they wrongly tried to impose on the Empire a technocratic, economic, "mechanical" solution to a problem that was more fundamentally political and spiritual.[50] "Their imperialism is bureaucratic," he argued, "it is directed, if not from Downing Street, at least from the office of the Tariff Reform League; it depends not upon a living faith in the men and women concerned but in the manufacture and adjustment of complicated machinery."[51] For this same reason, Zimmern also rejected the language that Milner had inherited from nineteenth-century thinkers like Seeley of "federation," choosing instead the "less mechanical principle of Alliance." Finally, Zimmern also railed against reducing the Empire to an entity whose sole purpose was defense and military advantage. Such a fallacy, he argued, "found its way to the pillory in the days of Aristotle." "States," he continued, may indeed be "formed for purposes of self defense," but they continue to exist "for purposes of beneficence," and while self-preservation "may render war inevitable," the "'good life' for Empires as for States can be conceived as doing without it."[52]

But Zimmern's lectures on the Empire during this time also reveal some moments of difference from Milner's position that were deeply suggestive of the way Milner's "kindergarten" (his devotees who would go on to form the Round Table) would both depart from Milner and expand upon his vision of "organic union" in response to perhaps the most pressing imperial issue of the Edwardian era: the status of the dependencies and the question of race. Unlike Milner, Zimmern and the emerging members of the Round Table were well aware that India, Egypt, and Britain's other "tropical dependencies" were too important to the financial health of the Empire to simply drop from their vision of a revitalized imperial union. They were also acutely aware of not only the rise of anticolonial nationalism in India (particularly in Bengal after partition in 1905), but of an increasingly dissatisfied sense among the huge number of educated Indian elite that the British were not taking their own stated commitments to liberal values seriously. At the same time, they were distinctly uncomfortable with the idea of a United Britain in which nonwhite subjects were given full, equal citizenship status and white citizens became the minority. And yet, at this moment after the Boer War and preceding World War I, liberal acolytes of Milner understood all too well that they were under pressure to make a case for Britain's Empire that was distinctly *not* German looking, that is, grounded in something other than racial and cultural superiority.

Zimmern's writings on the British Empire before 1910 reflected some of the deepest ambiguities and tensions regarding race and the dependencies expressed during the Round Table's earliest moments. Again, with Milner, Zimmern claimed in "United Britain" that, with regard to the political unity with which he was concerned, "I am not speaking at all of India or of our Tropical dependencies, but of the self governing portions of the Empire."[53] But India and the "Tropical dependencies" never simply disappeared for Zimmern, and at other moments in the same text he referred to them as essential parts of "United Britain." Sometimes, in this lecture, Zimmern argued that what held the Union together was a basic ethnic or cultural connection between Great Britain and her "daughter" nations, arguing that the "Empire has for the most part no past but in the English connection" and that "if it is now developing separate Nationalisms which resent English interference, it is from Englishmen and out of the character of English institutions that these instincts of independence come."[54] At the same time, Zimmern explicitly rejected ethnicity and race as unifying factors in the Empire. We know, he argued, that the Empire "does not consist solely of Englishmen, nor even of Europeans, nor even of whites," that it "includes within

it several races and languages."[55] Zimmern went on to distance himself even further from the language of race by acknowledging his own status as "an alien who,
like by far the greater number of His Majesty's subjects, has not a drop of English
blood in his veins."[56] Finally, he broadened this observation more generally by
rejecting the "fallacy" that "men of the white race have a special superiority over
and mission towards men of other races. We know that some races have capacity for colonization and government and that others have not. But we know that
some of the capable races are neither white nor European and some are incapable of both." For Zimmern, then, the "secret hinted at in the White Man's burden
resides not in race but in something else."[57]

Zimmern's inconsistencies here, coupled with his discomforted prose, suggests that not only was he vocalizing an early-twentieth-century tendency among
imperial thinkers to confuse race and culture, but that he was having a particularly difficult time identifying the "secret"—that "something else"—that made
the British Empire both "unique" and "peculiar," the "greatest instrument the
world has ever seen for the preservation of lasting peace," in nonracial terms.[58]
Zimmern's compromise haltingly located this "something else" in what he called
the "English habit of mind" or "system of life" which he described, again, in
Burkean-sounding conceptual language. Thus, Zimmern argued, those essential
characteristics that made the British so uniquely qualified to colonize the world
in a fair, just, and liberal manner sprang from their shared cultural experiences,
which constantly pressed in upon the contemporary moment, that "medley of
customs, of affections, of prejudices, of traditions, of the present rooted in the
still surviving past, of the past adapted, but never abolished, to meet the ideals
of the present."[59] For Zimmern, the origins of this "medley of customs, of affections, of prejudices, of traditions" might be distinctly *local* and English, but the
culture they produced was universal, able to generate an international outlook
that could prove the "greatest political instrument for human happiness that the
world has ever seen." There was no reason, Zimmern argued, why the combined
force "not of English men only, but all who can assimilate or feel in touch with
this English habit of mind" could not create "a decent and habitable world."[60]

Thus, at this point in his career, Zimmern seemed to believe that Englishness
was worldliness and locality, "habit of mind" not race inheritance, particularity
and universality, a broad and yet narrow vision of life that was both bound by tradition and, in a profoundly liberal sense, ripe for voluntary adoption by "all who
can assimilate or feel in touch" with it. Not only was the English "system of life"
there for emulation by the non-English, Zimmern argued, it also recognized the
unique needs and desires of "self-respecting nationalities" and never imposed its
way of life on anyone. By contrast, Zimmern was quick to argue, in "The Seven
Deadly Sins of Tariff Reform" that it was the German Empire, not the British,
who "crushed" small states "out of existence altogether."[61] By Zimmern's lights,

the British had developed an approach to empire that somehow never "quenched the national aspirations" of is subjects even, apparently, as it was quenching the aspirations of nationalists in India, Ireland, and Egypt at that very moment.

Zimmern also insisted that the British had never really set out to become imperialists and that they weren't even naturally very inclined toward it. After claiming that the British Empire was the "greatest political instrument for human happiness that the world has ever seen" Zimmern quickly interjected:

> I do not know why this should be so. It is one of the mysteries of the British character. The British race is neither very keen witted nor very imaginative nor very sensitive. It is perhaps, on the whole, the most unintelligent race, certainly it is the most illogical, that is now playing a big part on the world's stage.[62]

In this sense, Zimmern both argued that there was nothing special about the English "race" while simultaneously giving legitimacy to the idea that there *was* something special, something distinct about English people that made them particularly good imperialists, something that just happened to overlap with British "character." At the same time, and somewhat confusedly, Zimmern seemed to feel that it was important to stress that the British had not actually really *intended* to create a global empire, that it was just an accident that a people so illogical and insensitive should happen to have stumbled upon something so great and universally compelling.

At the end of Zimmern's 1905 lectures on the Empire, we are left with a variety of unanswered questions. We do not know what it is exactly about the British "habit of mind" that makes them particularly good at creating a peaceful global order when they are so dispositionally opposed to it. We are not clear about the relationship between the dependencies and the "Imperial Union" writ large and it is not at all obvious if the Indians and Egyptians could either adopt an English "habit of mind" if they wished or develop their "self respecting nationalities." Most importantly, despite Zimmern's claim to be concerned with "the present rooted in the still surviving past," we have no clue about the historical process that enabled a small-minded, liberal people to become the leaders of a globe-spanning Empire upon whose shoulders world peace had now come to rest.

It was while grappling with these deeply contentious and contradictory reflections on the British Empire that Zimmern began to research and write *The Greek Commonwealth*. Through this process, Zimmern worked out the historical backstory behind the liberal British Empire's rise to dominance by telling it—and reimagining it—through a narrative of fifth-century Athenian development that was both distant from, and yet comparable to, modern Britain. And while he never resolved the "Oxford paradox" (universal and simple, broad and narrow) at the center of both imperial narratives, he did refine his portraits of the Athenian and British imperial forests to the point where the paradox itself became less obvious through the trees.

We Athenians

Initially published in 1911, *The Greek Commonwealth* (Zimmern's first book) would go through five different editions and establish his career as a classical scholar. Again, as Zimmern explained in the 1911 Preface, his purpose in writing the book (and the reason for which he spent a year in Athens in 1909) was to "make clear to myself what fifth-century Athens was really like."[63] This irked some classical scholars such as Gilbert Murray, who once accused him gently of making "too light of the value of your subject" and treating "the Greeks as a lot of funny little people who are quite amusing to study—not as the great pioneers and achievers that they really were."[64] But for a Hellenist like Zimmern, there was no greater tribute to the enduring relevance of Greece than a project whose goal was to explore both the grandiose and mundane economic, social, and political conditions that led to the flowering of the Athenian *polis*. Zimmern's innovation in this text was to draw together classical sources and recent anthropological and archeological discoveries into one descriptive and entertaining narrative aimed at painting the richest and most detailed portrait of fifth-century Athens yet written.

At nearly five hundred pages, *The Greek Commonwealth* begins with a loving description of the geography of the Attic peninsula, spends most of its time looking at the nature of social, economic, and political life in Athens, and ends with a short chapter on the Peloponnesian War up to Thucydides's Melian Dialogue. At times, the book reads almost like a travel log in its pithy descriptions of the Athenian market, the agricultural environment, forms of economic exchange, the day-to-day interactions of the populace, and even the weather. Reviewers in 1911 and throughout the 1920s and 1930s were genuinely impressed with the historical detail Zimmern brought to his descriptions and the warmth of his prose, although some did express a clear discomfort with the "popular," almost "novella like" style of the book.[65] Over the course of the years and many new editions, critics tended to take issue with two outstanding features of Zimmern's analysis: his "rather roseate view of the motives animating Athens before the Plague" and his "excessive" inclination to modernize.[66]

To call Zimmern's attitude toward Athens "rather roseate," is, in fact, a radical understatement. For reasons I will describe in detail below, his understanding of "what fifth century Athens was really like" took Thucydides's version of Pericles's

Funeral Speech at face value as an accurate description of a sublime political society, in perfect equipoise, beloved by its citizens and neighbors. As testament to this fact, Part Two of the book is organized into chapters with headings drawn from, as Ehrenberg put it, "inexact" readings of the political concepts central to the Funeral Speech, culminating in Chapter Eight, "The Idea of Citizenship," which consists solely of Zimmern's own translation of the speech, as if Pericles's observations simply spoke for themselves.[67] In Zimmern's mind, the "Athenian community during the Periclean time, must be regarded as the most successful example of social organization known to history."[68]

This basic strategy of seeing Athens almost entirely through the eyes of Pericles as Thucydides presented him, in a version of the Funeral Speech that Zimmern himself translated, colored the way Zimmern read almost every aspect of Athenian life. "For a whole wonderful half century," he maintained, Athens was "the richest and happiest in the recorded history of any single community" where "Politics and Morality, the deepest and strongest forces of national and of individual life, had moved forward hand in hand toward a common ideal, the perfect citizen in the perfect state."[69] Zimmern argued that this "common ideal" was made possible by the genius of Athenian democracy; the way the *polis* drew forth a deep patriotism from its citizens while at the same time ensuring that individuals continued to use their reason independently. Fifth-century democracy demanded, he argued, that citizens engage in "active public work" but never required the sublimation of the private into the public.[70] In fact, what made Athens truly brilliant for Zimmern (and what made his analysis of it unique among classicists at the time) was the sheer number of small societies, organizations, and private hobbies that together constituted the vibrant civil life of the humming *agora*. For Zimmern, the richness of Athenian civil society, coupled with the centrality of public-spiritedness and the clear divide between public and private life, made it possible for Athenian citizens to reconcile their primordial love for family and city with a rational, civic love for the laws and institutions and, thereby, to transform patriotism into the practicalities of life in a thriving democracy. These cultural and political practices of everyday life meant, Zimmern argued, "Athenians took to politics as easily, and were as politically gifted, as any community in history."[71]

Zimmern's idealized Athenian vision raised two obvious problems for his critics, the first of which he seemed to be well aware as he wrote the book. One gets the sense, as one reads *The Greek Commonwealth*, that Zimmern understood that making an argument about the perfection of Athens also required him to devote considerable time to explaining and then downplaying those characteristics that made it less than perfect to early-twentieth-century, liberal-minded readers: namely, the status of its many metics (resident noncitizens) and slaves. Thus, in contrast to both eighteenth-century notions of Athens as provincial and xenophobic, and to the reality of autochthonous citizenship in the fifth-century, Zimmern argued forcefully that, aside from the fact that they could not be citizens, there was still a level of "democratic equality" between Athenians and aliens that arose, conversely, from the fact that most foreigners "appreciated Athenian excellence" and were happy to live as well-treated non-citizens. By Zimmern's lights (and in a revealing slide into the present tense), Athens was a bustling, cosmopolitan metropolis that "welcomes workers from all the world and has adapted her institutions to their needs" and whose citizens were committed to a kind of fifth-century, liberal multiculturalism.[72] Slaves, too, Zimmern argued, were largely happy with their lives. Fifth-century Athenian citizens (unlike later Athenians or the "Southern Planter" in America) treated their slaves well, according to Zimmern, allowing each individual slave to "become assimilated in spirit and appearance to the world of free men around him."[73] Greek slave owners believed, Zimmern maintained, that they had a duty to teach slaves (who were largely barbarians and therefore more childlike and not as accustomed to self mastery as the Athenians) how to become more like Athenians. Thus, slaves themselves treated their temporary bondage as a form of tutelage, where an individual could "gradually learn to lay aside . . . the dull compelling scourge, and to make his appeal to a worthier, or, at the worst, a steadier class of motives." [74]

Some critics were not only dissatisfied with Zimmern's long and complicated dance around Athenian hierarchy, they were also irked by the way Zimmern explained Periclean politics in modern political-theory terms. Ehrenberg, for instance, was completely unsatisfied first with Zimmern's translation of Periclean ideas into English and then with his choice to use these terms as titles for each chapter in the section of the book on Athenian politics. For Ehrenberg (who, a bit viperously, called Zimmern's translations "completely appalling") it just "purely and simply does not make sense that 'Efficiency or the Rule of the Magistrate' embodies the idea of *eu zēn* [to live well] and just as little that 'The Rule of Religion' is declared as *sōphrosynē* [moderation]."[75] But, it also just "does not make sense" that Zimmern would begin this section not with a quotation from an ancient commentator, but from Burke's description of friendship among Roman senators in, again, *Thoughts on Our Current Discontents*. "*Idem sentire de republica* was with them a principal ground of friendship and attachment, nor do I know any other capable of forming firmer, dearer, more pleasing, more honorable, and more virtuous habitudes."[76]

Both the odd translations to which Ehrenberg took exception and Zimmern's decision to frame the Politics section through Burke make considerably more sense, however, if we remember that Zimmern wrote *The Greek Commonwealth* not merely to demonstrate "what fifth-century Athens was really like" but also, "to make people think about the nature of the twentieth-century." In other words, Zimmern used modern political theory to describe Athens not simply because it was the only conceptual language he had but, rather, because his ulti-mate goal was also to tell a modern story about English political culture. For his part, Ehrenberg was convinced that there was something more going on with Zimmern's description of the *polis*. Anyone who writes a book like this, Ehrenberg argued, and then uses "the exceptionally English, untranslatable word 'commonwealth'" in the title has "has set himself a much larger topic than to speak of 'politics and economy in fifth-century Athens.'"[77]

In fact, in addition to the title, Zimmern only used the word "commonwealth" four times in this text: in an early discussion of Solon, in reference to the British Empire, in a quotation from Burke he attributed to Aristotle, and most notably, in paragraph forty-three of his translation of the funeral speech where Pericles remembers the sacrifice made by the Athenian citizens whom the community was laying to rest. "So they gave their bodies to the commonwealth," Zimmern's translation goes, "and received, each for his own memory, praise that will never die."[78] Zimmern's decision to translate the Greek word *koine* ("common") as a noun was not an unheard of choice for the time, but it was more rare and had very specific political implications. In other words, this same sentence is often translated to suggest not that Athenian men gave their bodies to an entity *known as* the commonwealth but rather, through their sacrifice, *in common*.[79] Zimmern's translation clearly has Pericles evoking not only a *common act* but also a *common political object* that made this sacrifice coherent. Moreover, Zimmern's choice of the word "commonwealth" (rather than *polis*, "common good," or "common weal") had specifically English connotations insofar as it resonated with the seventeenth-century commonwealth tradition. Perhaps not surprisingly, given the specifically English implications of the term "commonwealth," Zimmern's translation of the Funeral Speech bears an uncanny resemblance to that of Hobbes, who also referred to "commonwealth" in his 1628 rendering of *The History of the Peloponnesian War*.[80]

Why use a word deeply embedded in the English political tradition to describe the fifth-century Athenian *polis*? Because, again, Zimmern's goal in this text was not only to tell a story about Athens, but also to tell a story about mod-ern England—and this story was explicitly Burkean. Thus, in the sentence imme-diately preceding the "*Idem sentire*" portion of the quotation (which Zimmern does not cite), Burke clarified that the subjects of his observations on friendship were, in fact, the "greatest patriots" in the "greatest commonwealths." The politi-cal object for which Athenians gave their lives in the Funeral Speech looked, to Zimmern's mind, like a commonwealth in the most Burkean of senses, popu-lated by freedom-loving individuals who found their love for the community in the "little platoons" of civic and private life. "Greek patriotism," he argued, "fused the emotions of school and family, of inheritance and early training, of religion and politics, all the best of boyhood with all the best of manhood into one passionate whole."[81] In Zimmern's mind, it was precisely this *"Idem sentire de republica"* ("sameness of feeling about the republic") that made the Athenians among the "greatest patriots" in the "greatest commonwealths."[82] This slippage between Athens and England is even more apparent in a lengthy paragraph on page 72 which Zimmern began with a quotation from Aristotle's *Politics* ("The city is the highest form of association and embraces all the rest") and then, halfway through, switched to quoting Burke's *Thoughts on the Cause of our Present Discontents* ("to bring the dispositions that are lovely in private life into the service and conduct of the commonwealth') as though he were still quoting Aristotle. This is the same quotation from Burke (also unacknowledged) that he would later use to describe the "liberalism" of "English speaking peoples" in *Nationality and Government*. It is almost as if, for Zimmern, Athens and England, Aristotle and Burke, were reaching out to each other across time toward the same political and ethical goals, the same "habit of mind" or "system of life."

And yet, Zimmern's Athenians were never simply reverential Burkeans, comfortable with the hierarchical distinctions of traditional aristocratic life. Rather, Zimmern took great pains to stress their very modern-looking liberal sensibilities, particularly their appreciation for individual merit, their desire for free movement and free trade, and their work ethic. We can see these liberal attributes best in those moments when Zimmern used Sparta as a kind of Janus-faced foil for Athens. On the one hand, he argued that when Pericles insisted in the Funeral Speech that Athenians found "time for both public and private work" he had pictured in his mind the distinction between Athenians and "the lordly Spartans who spend their mornings drilling and their afternoons, after the unappetizing meal which the Helots have brought in to them from their farms, hunting or boxing or making themselves beautiful."[83] In his vision, Athenians were no leisured loafers, lounging around the *agora,* waiting to cast their next votes in the Assembly. Rather, they were active, self-made men, busily doing work the "lordly" Spartans reserved for slaves. On the other hand, Sparta also grafted beautifully onto another Edwardian enemy of liberalism: the centralized state that might do well at organizing a war machine but, at the same time, brought all minds down to the same, sluggish, Prussian level. In contrast, Zimmern argued, Athenian society was "so arranged ('organized' is too deliberate a word) as to make the most and the best of the human material at its disposal. Without any system of national education, in our sense of the word, it 'drew out' of its members all the power and goodness that was in them."[84] Thus, without even thinking about it, without "organizing" institutions like a national education system to bang its citizens into shape, Athenians were able to work together to create a functioning society full of joyful people living their lives with "independence of spirit, in contrast to the stolid conscientiousness of the Spartan."[85] In sum, Sparta (with her overweening state and her "slow minds") reflected back an Athenian *polis* that was distinctly liberal in both its rejection of aristocracy *and* its freedom from the centralizing policies of, for instance, unified Germany or, very soon, the Soviet Union. It was thus arranged without being organized and its people both free individuals and committed patriots. These were the most outstanding attributes, by Zimmern's lights, of the "liberal-minded democracy of Athens."[86]

Zimmern's contention that Athenians were "liberal minded" also, of course, highlights the second outstanding feature of the book with which his critics took exception. In fact, as soon as it was released, critics were marveling at not only Zimmern's fondness for translating Periclean Athens into modern English political-theoretical terms, but also at his relentless comparisons between fifth-century Athens and modern Britain more generally—what one reviewer referred to as his "audacious modernity."[87] There appeared, in fact, to be literally no minutiae of ancient Greek life that Zimmern did not think it possible to compare to contemporary Edwardian England, from its economic practices, to its cultural and class assumptions, to its politics. Hence, Zimmern argued that the relative equality of the *polis* and the public nature of its debate resembled British "club life."[88] He also insisted that that the Greek city-state was "like an English college," and that the distinction between "gentle and simple" was present in both the Athenian and English attitudes toward their aristocracy (distinguishing both from the "feudal societies on the Continent.")[89] Zimmern's other mundane parallels included contrasting the attitudes of an Athenian cobbler and a London clerk toward their holidays, the Athenian sense of belonging to the English understanding of national belonging, and the average "capital wealth" of Attica to the "total wealth of the United Kingdom."[90] In the end, even when Zimmern was alluding to contemporary examples in order to demonstrate the differences between the ancient world and the modern, he still assumed that Britain and ancient Greece *were comparable*, that, despite their internal variations, each society spoke to a similar core set of experiences and values, that they were in some way mutually comprehensible across time.

But Zimmern's "inclination to modernize" did not stop there. Not only did he relentlessly compare Athens to England, the book also brims with historical parallels between the fifth-century Athenian experience of their empire and the British imperial experience, particularly its rule in India. This set of comparisons makes sense if we consider that Zimmern became involved with the Round Table in 1910, when he returned to England from Greece to finish the book, and that members of the Round Table at that time were involved in a heated debate about the inclusion of India in their developing vision of a united British Empire—a debate inflected by questions about British identity, fears about the end of civilization, racial superiority, and the limits of democracy.[91] That Zimmern was consumed with the Indian question as he wrote *The Greek Commonwealth* can be seen in two distinct and overlapping trends present in the book: one inchoate, and the other explicit. On the one hand, the book spends a considerable amount of time distinguishing between what Said has called the "imagined geography" between Western and "Oriental" culture, or, between what Zimmern identified as the developing democratic, liberal sensibilities of the ancient Greeks and the static culture and politics of Eastern despots. Zimmern did this, again, by comparing ancient and modern forms of Asian authoritarianism. For instance, in contrast to the Persians, Zimmern argued, the watchword of the alliance between the Athenians and the Ionians "was not Defense but Freedom."[92] The emerging imperial politics of the Athenians were thus driven by a simple pursuit of ideals, rather than the accumulation of riches so common to Persian tyrants, whom Zimmern rather slyly refers to as "Moguls"—a term that was not in use before the Middle Ages and certainly not in Ancient Greece.[93] At the same time he was lauding the liberal sensibilities of the Athenians, however, Zimmern was also quick to associate later, internal challenges to Greek life with Asian influence. For instance, Zimmern suggested that Plato's work should be understood in light of the Egyptian "or, as some think, the Indian" influence on his philosophy.[94]

On the other hand, the book is overburdened with explicit historical parallels between the fifth-century Athenian experience of empire and the British rule in India. For instance, when Zimmern wanted his audience to understand the importance of teaching ancient Greek "as a means of training the young" he turned to the "analogous attempt" to use English as the language of education in India.[95] To illustrate the process whereby Athenian currency became standardized in the Empire, he drew upon the circulation of currency in the "Indian native states."[96] When Zimmern discussed taxation in the Athenian Empire, he did so by drawing parallels between ancient forms of tax collection and the British government's taxation policy in Bengal.[97]

The net effect of this persistent vacillation between the ancient Greek and the modern British imperial examples is to emphasize for the reader the extent to which Athenian and British experiences of both political life and empire were comparable, despite their historical remoteness from one another. In this sense, it is no wonder that Zimmern spent so much time minimizing the role of slavery in Athens; if Athens then was like Britain now, and if Britain now was liberal then, then Athens must be shown to have never really been illiberal. At the same time, the problem that drove Zimmern to downplay the reality of ancient Athenian slavery also confronted him with regard to Athens's empire: how to explain the fact that a society that was so perfectly conscious of liberty, so opposed to "organized" politics, so nominally committed to equality, could behave toward other city-states in ways that looked coercive and illiberal? When, for instance, the Athenians exacted tributes by force or manufactured regime changes in their tribute-paying allies and dominions, weren't they behaving, in effect, like "lordly

Spartans"? This is, of course, the classic question of liberal imperialism: how to explain, in the present or the past, why a liberal society would behave toward its empire in a manner that seemed to violate its liberal principles.

Zimmern responded to this problem by writing an historical narrative of Athenian imperial development before the Peloponnesian War aimed at proving that not only was Pericles's description of the *polis* correct, but his seemingly self-serving analysis of Athens's Empire was true as well: Athens treated her allies and colonies as "free partners in the Empire"; these colonies and allies (at least initially) recognized the innate moral and political superiority of Athens's laws; and, more importantly, Zimmern insisted, just as Athenians did not approach their daily lives with an organized "conscientiousness," neither did they develop their Empire this way. The Athenians were, in this sense, both accidental and inspired imperialists.

Zimmern constructed this narrative in part from the limited textual and archeological information available about Athenian economic practices in the early fifth-century. Thus, he argued, because early-fifth-century Athens needed grain to sustain it, the state and its citizens logically looked for trading partners beyond the Attic peninsula and established these throughout the Aegean. While the impetus for Athens to look beyond its city walls might have been material, however, Zimmern cautioned the modern critic to remember "the lofty objects for which her riches were deliberately sought," namely, the sustenance and improvement of the best city.[98] He went on to argue that because the "arrangement" of the *polis* produced independent, freedom-loving citizens, these early Athenian explorers avoided creating trading monopolies but, rather, looked to establish "access to free intercourse and power to mingle and exchange with other nations."[99] It was only natural, then, that Athens would enter into an alliance with other city-states to expel the Persians—an event, Zimmern argued, that marked the simultaneous birth of Western political culture and the first cohesive act of the nascent "PanHellenic confederacy."[100] As the strongest and most perfect polity, Zimmern insisted, it was also only natural that Athens would then take center stage in the Delian League, leading to its eventual dominance as an economic and military power.

Because it was a "model state," argued Zimmern, it was obvious that Athenian customs would come to dominate the region. Thus, he maintained, no compulsion was ever used to ensure the standardization of the *drachma*, because its clear superiority as a currency ensured its inevitable adoption by all. Athens simply allowed competing currencies to "circulate side by side" and then watched the drachma rise to the top, just as the British now did, Zimmern claimed, in "the Indian native states."[101] Likewise, as the dominant military power, it was simply more convenient for the Athenians to take over all military defenses in the alliance, just as the "acknowledged excellence of the Solonian laws and institutions" made it logical for Athens to set the standards for all commercial treaties between members of the Delian League.[102]

Zimmern's point about the rise of Athenian power is most evident in his unremitting use of the word "gradual," which appears throughout the book, but particularly in his discussions of empire. Athens's transformation from city-state to empire was slow and effortless, the result of incrementally accumulated economic and political ties coupled with a natural genius for governing, plus the acknowledged excellence of its polity. "Athens had gradually formed herself," Zimmern argued, "whether her pupils liked it or not, to be 'an education to Greece.' The process was so gradual, and the control so wisely exercised that the allies could not easily put their hand on any particular cause of complaint."[103] Athens, argued Zimmern, through no fault of its own and, in fact, because of the superiority of its political life, became an empire. "Like other great things," Zimmern argued, "the Athenian Empire was the child of necessity, and its creators did not know what they were doing."[104] By Zimmern's lights, the Athenians did not sit down and plan on becoming imperialists, they just accidentally and gradually evolved into the role because their society was so economically and socially free, so patriotic and yet liberal and open minded, and overall, because they were just too preoccupied with the work of trading and building up their city to notice the web of Panhellenic connections they were weaving. Thus, "the men of these two generations of empire-building were not conscious of any wickedness," Zimmern argued, they were simply "too busy with their work."[105]

But, Zimmern maintained, this accidental, "unconscious" moment of Athenian Empire-building did, eventually, come to an end. Toward the middle of the fifth century and after years of gradually coalescing as an empire, the Athenians, with the help of Pericles, woke up from their unconscious colonizing, declared themselves to be imperialists, and rose to the occasion with aplomb. Once again, Zimmern chose to frame this moment of realization through a comparison with the British imperial experience, arguing that, in response to the "plain facts" of the imperial situation and in contrast to those "Little Athenians" who wanted to dissolve the Delian League, most mid-century Athenians understood that "Athens could no more step back than most Englishmen feel they can leave India. She had woken up to find herself an Empire and was resolved to play the part."[106] Just as Seeley had argued in 1883 that Britain had "conquered and peopled half the world in a fit of absence of mind" so Zimmern now claimed that the Athenians, like their later British brethren, had been driven to empire by the union between their finer attributes and the unintended accumulation of circumstances that accrued while they slept—circumstances which now compelled them to claim the mantle of imperial leadership. With the help of Pericles they developed an approach to empire based on a "new imperial ideal of freedom" that sprang from "considerations of mutual interest" with Athens's tribute-paying allies in the east and in the extension of commercial relation-ships with cities in the west.[107] Like the British, the Athenians managed inadver-tently to develop principles of governance unique to themselves that they then accidentally brought into the world through their Empire that, in practice, also proved enduringly right for others. Athenian imperial culture was the Oxford paradox: universal and simple, broad and narrow.

For Zimmern, Periclean imperial policy—particularly Athens's expansion in the west—was clearly and transparently about free trade rather than power, more about "free intercourse" than the domination of other Greeks. The prob-lem (which Zimmern seemed to sense) with this claim is that it contradicted Thucydides, Zimmern's primary historical source on the Athenian Empire, who did not describe Athenian imperial expansion during this period in these terms and, in fact, argued in I.1.23 of *The History of the Peloponnesian War* that the "real reason for the war" was the "growth of Athenian power and the fear which this caused in Sparta."[108] While Zimmern never directly addressed Thucydides's causal claim in Book One, he clearly responded to it in other parts of the text, and he did so in three different ways.

First, in the section of the book devoted to a discussion of Athenian impe-rial expansion in the west, Zimmern chose to focus on historical events that Thucydides *did not* speak of in *The History* to demonstrate that, while Sparta might have perceived Athens as aggressive, these impressions were false. For example, Zimmern argued that the "most important record of the nature and extent of Athenian designs is the scheme for the colonization of Thurii."[109] Actual historical evidence about Thurii's founding is scarce and most authors (including Zimmern) still rely on Diodorus's account of events.[110] Key for Zimmern was the purportedly "PanHellenic" plan for the colony, which he argued embodied the open, cosmopolitan qualities of Athenian culture that had become more explicit as its empire grew throughout the mid-fifth-century. According to Zimmern:

> The new colony was not to be an offshoot of Athens on the old City
> State lines. It was to be a PanHellenic settlement under the influence of
> Athens, a permanent embodiment of her new ideal of the blessings of
> free intercourse.[111]

Hence, while the development of the empire in the east might have been "grad-ual," Athens's westward expansion was done conscientiously, based on the les-sons the Athenians had learned as initially reluctant imperialists about freedom of trade and intercourse. Thus Thurii, for Zimmern, "embodied the new imperial ideal of freedom" articulated by Pericles insofar as it was explicitly based on the blessings of free trade, open to new ideas, multicultural, and remarkably liberal in appearance.[112]

Zimmern certainly was not the first openly pro-Periclean scholar of fifth-century Athens to dwell on the idealism supposedly evident in the founding of Thurii, but he is somewhat unique for his time in declaring it the definitive example of Periclean and Athenian imperial intentions in the west.[113] But making such a claim also required that Zimmern not only dwell on material not covered by Thucydides, but also ignore other imperial actions on the part of Athens during this period that Thucydides similarly did not discuss in detail, and which deviated from what later critics like Mason Hammond would describe as Zimmern's "rosy view of the early Pericles." As an example, Hammond pointed out in his 1948 essay "Ancient Imperialism: Contemporary Justifications," that Zimmern avoided talking about Pericles's "attempt between 454 and 446 B.C.E. to build up a land empire, an attempt ended by the so-called Thirty Years' Peace with Sparta."[114] Rather, Zimmern's concentration on, and valuation of, the founding of Thurii seems a clear attempt, if not to prove Thucydides wrong about the "real cause" of the war, than at least to demonstrate that Spartan fears about Athenian power and imperial ambition in the west during this period were unjustified.

Second, Zimmern's portrayal of Thucydides as an historian, an Athenian, and a political interpreter of events was temporally complicated in the sense that it asked the reader to accept *some* of the things Thucydides said as true or as reflections of his true feeling about Athens based upon when he wrote them. For instance, in "Thucydides the Imperialist," a lecture written around 1905 and later republished in 1928's *Solon and Croesus*, Zimmern argued that Thucydides was "old and embittered" when he wrote much of *The History*. But Zimmern, who was influenced by his teacher Wilamowitz on this point, argued that toward the end of his life Thucydides rediscovered the love for the Athenian *polis* that he had experienced in his youth and that he wrote "The Funeral Speech" during this period.[115] Zimmern maintained that Thucydides then "deliberately inserted" the speech where he did in the text "to point the contrast between Athens before and Athens after the plague and the war fever."[116] For Zimmern, the Funeral Speech offered readers a more accurate portrayal of Thucydides's real view on Athens than his analysis of Athens's expansion in the west, the incident at Melos, the Sicilian invasion, or any other moment in Thucydides's narrative of the war and its causes. Zimmern encouraged his readers to "re-imagine" for themselves "the Thucydides of 434, before the outbreak of the war, in all the ardor of his youthful enthusiasm" as a way of gaining "better insight into much that was written by the old and embittered Thucydides of 405."[117]

At the same time, Zimmern not only argued that the Funeral Speech offered readers better insight into Thucydides's true feelings about Athens, it also gave them a real glimpse into Pericles's own mind. In other words, because Thucydides the historian returned to his youthful enthusiasm about Periclean Athens toward the end of his life, he was able to drop the hopelessness and cynicism that Zimmern felt infected much of the rest of the text, and report accurately on what Pericles said and thought. Zimmern was neither dogmatic nor naïve enough to insist (as Donald Kagan later would) that Thucydides's speeches in general— and the Funeral Speech in particular—were absolutely accurate accounts of Pericles's speech. Indeed, he argued, Thucydides would deliberately "insert" certain phrases into Pericles's mouth to make a point and also observed frankly that "the speech which Pericles delivered" was not "the kind of speech usually given on such occasions."[118] But at the same time, he argued that there was "no reason to doubt that Thucydides had heard his hero speak, most probably more than once, over the city's fallen soldiers," and that the speech itself embodied a fairly seamless entwining of both Pericles's actual words and Thucydides's true feelings about Athens. We can thus hear in the speech, according to Zimmern, the timbre of "two great spirits at once": Pericles's voice "coming through, a little faint and thin after the lapse of years" and "the deep tones of the historian."[119]

In sum, for Zimmern, Thucydides's rendering of Pericles's description of Athens and the Athenian Empire was a more accurate reflection of what Pericles actually believed (and Thucydides thought was true) than Thucydides's descriptions of other parts of the war, including his account of the Thirty Years Peace and the events that let up to the onset of hostilities. For Zimmern, this included those portions of the Funeral Speech that seem deeply ironic in their exaggerated portrayal of an enlightened *polis* that was the "the exact opposite of the rest of mankind" in "doing good" for its neighbors and allies. Additionally, Zimmern seemed to argue, because we can trust this less "embittered" Thucydides more than his other self, Pericles's claims in the Funeral Speech should also be viewed as a fairly accurate representation of the actual goals of the Empire during the Thirty Years Peace. In a sense, Zimmern wanted his readers to trust the Thucydides who heard and later recorded the Funeral Speech more than the Thucydides who claimed to have discovered the "real cause" of the war.

Third, in contrast to those readers over the centuries who have read Thucydides as either a critic of democracy or a critic of the negative effects of imperialism—or, at the very least, a certain type of aggressive *archē*, or dominion over others, and the hubris that accompanies it—on democracy, Zimmern believed that Thucydides *was* an imperialist and a supporter of Periclean democracy and did not necessarily see a conflict between these two modes of political life.[120] By Zimmern's lights, the history of the Peloponnesian War according to Thucydides was a cautionary tale not about what happens to good democracies when they become empires, but rather, about what happens to liberal democracies that do not adequately wake up and theorize their empires. The story, in Zimmern's telling, goes something like this: Athens became an empire initially, without thinking about it, through the actions of its vibrant citizens, who "felt free within themselves, free and lighthearted and confident and incapable of doing wrong."[121] Because they felt so free and confident, according to Zimmern, these citizens "had neither the leisure nor the desire, any more than eighteenth-century Englishmen, to invent an imperial theory of their own."[122] Pericles developed a theory for them and began putting it into practice in the years leading up to the war. Pericles's vision died, however, in the face of what Zimmern described as "plague and war fever."[123] The word "fever" here creates an equivalency in Zimmern's narrative between the war and the plague by naturalizing them both, transforming the war into just another disease that suddenly descended upon an otherwise healthy body. Neither the plague nor the war, it seems, were caused by Athenian or Periclean actions. Rather, both simply happened, catching the Athenians unawares, and killing the Periclean vision in the process.

In *The Greek Commonwealth*, Zimmern argued that while the Athenians prior to the plague had neither the "leisure nor the desire" to invent their own imperial theory, "Thucydides, writing when most of what was mortal in their work had already crumbled into dust, invented one for them."[124] After the fact, after the war and the decline of morals at Melos and the horror of the Sicilian expedition, Thucydides came up with the theory of how the Athenians *should have* behaved as an empire in retrospect—and it looked, for all intents and purposes, exactly like the vision Pericles had articulated before the plague. In other words, at a moment "when Periclean imperialism, like Periclean patriotism has vanished forever," according to Zimmern, Thucydides resurrected it as, if not a way forward, then a lesson for future generations. This is truly the lesson that, for Zimmern, made *The History* a "possession for all time" and the lesson he believed Thucydides meant for his audience to take away from his work. At the moment of crisis, Athenians *should have* embraced Pericles's imperialism (as Thucydides presented it) and, if they had, they could have stopped the decline of the *polis*, solidified the Empire, and instantiated Athens as a permanent "Education to Greece."[125]

That Zimmern thought Thucydides both supported Pericles's vision of the empire *and* expanded upon or shaped it through his own rendering is abundantly clear in both *The Greek Commonwealth* and the furiously less coherent "Thucydides the Imperialist." Sometimes Zimmern simply declared that Thucydides "was, after all, but a Pereclean."[126] At other times, he conflated their imperial visions, while also making it clear that Thucydides was inventing his own version of Pericles's message through his rhetorical silences. [127] For example, "What sort of conception," Zimmern asked, "did Pericles, and the young Thucydides, have of the Athenian Empire?":

> We are familiar now-a-days with the contradiction between Imperialism and Nationalism, between the conceptions of Little England or Little

> France and the conception of the British Empire or the French Empire. Was there any such contradiction in the minds of Pericles between Athens the city-state and Athens the Mistress of the Seas? The most extraordinary thing about the Funeral Speech is that there is no such contradiction… About Athens as an Imperial state Thucydides lets Pericles be significantly and ominously silent.[128]

Zimmern interpreted the "significance" of Thucydides's decision to "let" Pericles be silent as evidence that Thucydides (although we are not certain about Pericles) believed that there was, or should be, no contradiction between Athens the perfect, liberal, free, democratic polity and Athens the "Mistress of the Seas." As further proof that Thucydides thought this to be so, Zimmern recalled Pericles's hyperbolic claim that "We secure our friends not by accepting favors but by doing them."[129] "What an amazing statement it is that Thucydides has put in Pericles' mouth!" Zimmern expounded; he then went on to recount the obvious fact that a democratic Athens had grown wealthy thanks to the tribute of its "friends." Zimmern's point here seems to be that Thucydides put into Pericles's mouth what he believed to be true and enduring about the Athenian Empire: namely, that Athens gave to the world far more than anything its allies could achieve on their own.

Clearly neither Zimmern nor his Thucydides were interested in how the post-plague Athenians might have learned the imperial lessons of Pericles. Rather, they seemed satisfied to look back, with longing nostalgia, on the glory that was fifth-century Athens while imagining the unfulfilled possibilities that its Empire presented for a different kind of Greek world. Zimmern never told his readers much about what that world might have looked like, except for the brief glimpse of Pericles's "imperial ideal of freedom," embodied in the initial hopes for the "PanHellenic" Thurii. The greatest clue, however, of what Zimmern would have liked for Athens can be found in the title of the book itself. Again, the "exceptional, untranslatable English word 'commonwealth'" appeared only a few times in the text and only once in reference to Athens. Why, then, would he choose this word as the title for a book *about* fifth-century Athens? Moreover, why would he entitle a book about Athens *The* Greek *Commonwealth?* The answer, I argue, is that Zimmern's title choice expressed a profound act of wish fulfillment, a not-fully-worked-through conviction that *if only* the Athenians had listened to Pericles, they not only could have saved the culture of the *polis*, but they could have also moved beyond the "city state model" and transformed themselves into an education for a Pan-Hellenic Greek community, united by Burkean principles of the "best commonwealth," the patriotic love of hearth, home, nation, and liberty for which Pericles's fallen soldiers had given their lives. The secret that the Athenians ultimately failed to grasp, for Zimmern, was to extend the principles of commonwealth beyond the *polis* and into the world.

It was Rosebery, of course, who first coined the term "Commonwealth of Nations" in the 1880s to describe the British Empire, although the idea gained very little traction during the first decade of the twentieth-century, and it did not appear in Zimmern's work on either the Athenian or British Empires before *The Greek Commonwealth*. It should come as no surprise, however, that Zimmern stumbled upon it in 1910, when he returned to England and reconnected with Curtis, Kerr, and the other members of Milner's "kindergarten," who were in the mist of developing a "theory of commonwealth" as a response to the "imperial problem." Perhaps, like his Thucydides, Zimmern rediscovered his Periclean imperial roots only at the end of his project, when the majority of the text had been written. Thus, in a deeply nostalgic way, the title *The Greek Commonwealth* simultaneously conjured up images of what Athens *had been* at the height of its pre-plague glory, mourned its loss, and reminded Zimmern's readers of what it *could have been* had its citizens woken up earlier and truly become "an education to Greece." At the same time, the title suggests that another international commonwealth, the British Commonwealth, had a fighting chance at making the Periclean dream a reality.

Conclusion: Displacement and Nostalgia

That Zimmern wrote *The Greek Commonwealth* in part to help him think through some of the historical and conceptual instabilities of his narrative approach to the British Empire is abundantly evident not only in the book itself (with its excessive use of analogies and its constant reference to English political culture and British imperial experiences), but also in Zimmern's writing on the British Empire and Commonwealth shortly after the book came out in 1911. Prior to *The Greek Commonwealth*, Zimmern's essays and lectures on Empire suggested that he had not yet intuited how to articulate the backstory behind his assertion that the character of the British people made them particularly adept at global leadership despite (or maybe because of) the fact that they were so dispositionally opposed to either thinking through an imperial plan or conquering others. Additional, lingering questions in these early writings also include: How did a liberal and independent people, so seriously disinclined toward the construction of grand metatheories of governance, become imperialist in the first place? What exactly was the relationship of the "medley of customs, of affections, of prejudices, of traditions, of the present rooted in the still surviving past" to the present that Zimmern identified as essential for understanding the nature of the British Empire at the turn of the twentieth-century?

One sees a certain amount of displacement, in a basic psychoanalytic sense, in Zimmern's reading of the fifth-century, a shift or unconscious redirection of the imperial narrative he wanted to tell about Britain away from Britain itself, whose actual history of violence and domination would make a socially conscious, pacifist-oriented, liberal defender of empire like Zimmern uncomfortable. A detailed telling of Britain's imperial past simply cut too close to the liberal bone for Zimmern in a way that would have forced him to wrestle with his vision's obvious historical contradictions. At the same time, there was something more at work in Zimmern's displacement than a basic Freudian desire to avoid discomfort. In this sense, it was not only Zimmern's historical understanding of the British Empire that could not stand up to a head-on confrontation with its imperial past; his political theory was similarly incapable of weathering this kind of challenge.

To clarify, by using the language of displacement in reference to political theory, I mean something other than what contemporary theorists like Bonnie Honig suggest when they make a case for the "displacement of politics in political theory."[130] For Honig, republican, liberal, and communitarian political theorists are often made uncomfortable by the messiness of actual politics, the way the agonistic barbs of democratic practice are difficult to disclose and resolve. From Kant to Sandel to Rawls, Honig argues, political theorists have responded to this discomfort by displacing politics onto administration, bureaucracy, or hermetically sealed visions of political spheres which "close down the agon." One can see something similar in Zimmern's analysis: the violence, materialism, and naked use of power implicit in actual imperial practices made him uncomfortable and propelled him to theorize a peaceful, liberal, imperial space free from the jousting bombast of power politics. But, as a liberal whose politics were also attached to habits and cultural traditions in a deeply Burkean way, Zimmern's displacement is far more complicated than that of a Kant or Rawls whose ideal political spheres are already detached from the warp and web of lived political life. Unlike Kant and even Rawls (despite his dour nod to the wars of religion and *modus vivendi*), Zimmern, the Burkean liberal, needed an historical, cultural, and social location for the liberal polity he most admired. The Athenian *polis*, with its limited historical sources and sketchy archeological information, enabled Zimmern to see what he wanted to see (a liberal utopia) and then make a case that this is what fifth-century Athens "was really like." The paucity of information on Athenian imperial development—Diodorus's date slippages, Thucydides's silences—allowed him to do the same with the Empire. At the same time, in Zimmern's analysis, Athens was never entirely remote from contemporary Britain, as his relentless analogies and comparisons suggest. Ancient Athens and contemporary Britain were practically *one and the same* polity for Zimmern, occupying similar spaces in time but at different moments, always just slightly out of phase with each other. Displacing Britain's imperial past onto Athens thus provided Zimmern with both the safety of historical distance and the nearness of political kinship; it allowed him to talk about Britain and Athens as if they were the same yet different.

But at the same time, it is important to remember that Zimmern was not simply displacing the British Empire onto Athens as a way to circumvent having to think about uncomfortable contradictions within British liberalism in the context of empire. Rather, Athens itself served as a kind of staging ground for Zimmern's theories about the British Empire upon which he displaced his thoughts about the modern Empire not only to avoid its difficult history, but also to provide narrative alternatives to that history. Thus, Zimmern's work on the *polis* and the Athenian Empire allowed him to process his evolving narrative of British imperial development in a way that avoided addressing historical details, and yet enabled him to assert a fully formed theory of these details in the present. In this sense, instead of actually dealing with the myriad political complexities of British imperialism in the eighteenth-century (where, for instance, contradicting claims of an "empire of liberty" coexisted alongside practices of slavery), Zimmern could turn his attention to the Athenians, who coincidentally, "like eighteenth century Englishmen," were liberals who did not have time to think about developing metatheories of empire. From Zimmern's perspective, like eighteenth-century Englishmen, the Athenians simply forged ahead into the world, armed with their ethic of liberty and their patriotic love of the *polis*, and blithely proceeded with the business of trading and forging links with other city-states. With the onset of the war with Persia, they were naturally thrust into a leadership position, and their central role in the Delian League came about largely as the result of "gradual" developments in their imperial strength. Thus, they created their empire unconsciously and spontaneously, in contrast to the "stolid conscientiousness of the Spartan," through the exercise of their finer attributes in the world plus an accumulation of circumstances. Through this process, it became apparent that the political values developed in the little *polis* were truly best for everyone in the Empire. Therefore, Zimmern argued that Thucydides and Pericles alike believed that "Both in public and in private, by her free self-governing institutions and the high personal character of her citizens, Athens was an education to Greece."[131]

Thus, by the time Zimmern was ready to mount an historical defense of the British Empire in his 1913 article, "The Ethics of Empire," he had already worked out the contours of this approach—the basic framework of the story—through Greece. Before I begin to talk about this article in greater detail, however, it is important to note that while I am not alone in my claim that Zimmern wrote "The Ethics of Empire," the question itself is not entirely settled.[132] All of the articles in the early editions of *The Round Table* were authored anonymously, although it is often possible to discern who penned which articles by their styles and their placement in the journal (for instance, Kerr, the editor, always wrote the first article for each edition). My argument that Zimmern wrote "The Ethics of Empire" is based on two key observations, substantive and stylistic as well as historical. First, the style of the article is quintessentially Zimmern. While it expressed many of the same sentiments as those of other Round Table members (particularly in its insistence that the bond between citizens of the Empire was moral and spiritual rather than economic), it begins its argument with a quotation from Burke on the morality of politics. One of Zimmern's signature rhetorical traits during this period, as we have seen, was to frame his argument in terms of Burke's ideas, either by quoting him directly or, often, by simply folding Burkean conceptual language into his own prose. It is the only article published during the first three years of *The Round Table* to mention Burke's political philosophy. It is also the only article written in these first three years to explicitly suggest that the British Empire ought to learn from the "rich civic life of Ancient Athens," a life that "made life worth living to the humblest citizen."[133] Finally, the argument in "The Ethics of Empire" is remarkably similar to the argument in his 1914 essay "German Culture and The British Government," in which he makes similar use of Burke to argue for the unique "nature of the British Commonwealth" and the "character of its citizenship and ideals."[134]

Second, the article was written at precisely the time when Zimmern was most involved with the Round Table and its powerful "London group". It resembles his writing style so closely that, when researching the organization in 1948, the American historian Carroll Quigley wrote to Zimmern to ask if he had written it or knew who had. Zimmern's reply to this question is revealing. He claimed not to remember who wrote the article "but could easily recognize the style."[135] In answering this way, Zimmern seemed to be playing the same game of evasion he had been playing with Quigley for several years. Quigley himself was an ardent opponent of what he argued was an elitist, Anglo-American foreign policy establishment, embodied in the Royal Institute of International Affairs (at Chatham House) and its American sibling, the Council on Foreign Relations, both of which he claimed (correctly) had their foundations in the quasi-secret society of the Round Table. His book on the subject (written in 1949 but published posthumously in 1981) sought to link these current organizations to both the Round Table and to earlier secret societies organized by Milner and Rhodes. By the time he talked with Quigley, Zimmern had rejected both the Round Table and Chatham House (because of their stance on the League of Nations), but he was remarkably worried both about being associated too closely with the group itself by Quigley *or* of alienating its founders. Quigley recalled that when he asked him why he had continued to affiliate himself with the Round Table after he officially resigned in 1922, Zimmern responded by insisting that "I continued to cooperate with them because I had to do so if I wanted to do anything in foreign relations.

They were so powerful that it was necessary to cooperate with them in order to do anything." "Later," Quigley noted, "he said to me 'if you publish anything of this I shall have to deny it all.'"[136] Zimmern was clearly paranoid about giving Quigley any information that could be traced back to him and, over the years, the tone of Quigley's queries grew increasingly exasperated with what he saw as Zimmern's intentional obfuscation. Indeed, at one point he all but accused Zimmern of lying to him, noting that "I think that if you reconsider your objections to my manuscript on the basis of this new evidence it will be clear that your desire to restrict the membership of the Secret Society to the Round Table Group is no longer tenable, and that my effort to tie into the Society persons like Miss Shaw, Garrett, and Maurice Hankey can now be regarded as valid."[137] In sum, given Zimmern's evasiveness on the subject in general, and given that Quigley himself could so easily recognize his style in "The Ethics of Empire," it is both likely that Zimmern wrote the document and hardly surprising that he would deny having done so.

Again, the article itself began with a quotation from Burke and went on to argue that the "development of the British Empire teaches how moral conviction and devotion to duty have inspired the building" of its structure.[138] He then addressed those critical of this assertion: "Opponents of Imperialism," he argued, "are wont to suggest that the story will not bear inspection, that it is largely a record of self-aggrandizement and greed." But this is to misunderstand, he maintained, the primary motives and qualities of the main characters of this story—that is, the plucky Englishmen who went forth into the world, propelled by their strength of character:

> It is true the Elizabethan pioneers recked lightly of aggression and plunder, for they were combatants in the life and death struggle against Spain. It is true that in the seventeenth and eighteenth centuries the expansion of Britain in east and west was governed by interests of commerce; but it is also true that with the assumption of responsibility economic ambition was subordinated to the moral ends of the political government. The gradual transformation of the East India Company from a trading corporation into an instrument of government shows clearly how, when the Empire was once in being, the interests of wealth yielded place to those of law. Commercial and strategical motives led England to Egypt, but her policy there was directed to the reform of abuses and maintenance of rights. The men who have labored most enduringly at the fabric of Empire were not getters of wealth or plunderers of soil. It was due to their strength of character and moral purpose that British rule in India and Egypt has become the embodiment of order and justice.[139]

Understanding the British Empire, for Zimmern, meant understanding that while the British never intended to become imperialists, and while their motives might at times have been aimed at commerce, it was English character exhibited through the actions of striving English citizens that propelled the Empire toward a higher moral purpose, just as the "high personal character" of the Athenians, brought out by the wisdom with which they educated their citizens, had "gradually" transformed Athens into a model city. Zimmern went on to argue, in "German Culture and the British Commonwealth," that English education did something similar for its young people by "gradual leading-out" the "unfolding, expanding" of their "mental and bodily powers," helping them to become "not soldiers, or missionaries of culture, or pioneers of Empire, or even British citizens, but simply human personalities."[140] In other words, like the Athenians, the British were not educated to think consciously about imperializing but, rather, to be human, and partakers in a humanity that now made them particularly fit for empire.

The fact that this "gradual" transformation had already taken place through Britain's ancient Athenian proxy meant that Zimmern felt no need to fill in the historical details made invisible by the wide curve of his passive voice, a voice that soothingly reassured its readers that "economic ambition was subordinated to the moral ends of the political government." Everyone knew that, despite the "aggression and plunder" of the Elizabethans and the commercial interests of the seventeenth- and eighteenth-century explorers, the British had never meant to become imperialists, just as the Athenians had never meant to be anything other than themselves. All of the paradoxes implicit in the current predicament of being a liberal society that conquered others, in developing a form of governance that was uniquely English and yet universally valid, seemed to disappear beneath Zimmern's assertion that all of this was incidental to the original lack of intention—the original, liberal push into the world propelled by the weight of Athenian and British character.

Zimmern's displacement thus spoke not only to his need to avoid the discomfort of the present imperial moment, but was also constitutive of that moment. We understand better, after reading Zimmern on Athens, what he believed lay behind the "surviving past" of the British Empire: the enduringly liberal character of its citizens who never meant to become imperialists but were thrust into being so by circumstances beyond their control. In his mind, what Zimmern believed Thucydides believed Pericles wanted for Athens was also precisely what needed to be done in England in 1913; conservatives, liberals, socialists, nationalists, and Little Englanders alike needed to wake up, look around them, and embrace the Empire for the good of all that was sacred about Englishness and about liberalism in general. In retrospect, Zimmern argued through Thucydides, once the Athenians had unintentionally accumulated their Empire and the

Greek world had become both a better place and dependent upon their continued hegemony, they *ought to have* seriously embraced their imperial duty with a strength of conviction that could have carried them through the "plague and war fever." In a sense, Zimmern presented his readers with a Thucydidean/Periclean solution to the problem of liberal empire that would have required Athenians to act in ways that seemed antithetical to their nature; to bring what had been created spontaneously into real time, to bring "conscientiousness" to what had been for so long remained unintentional and unconscious.

With regard to the British Empire in 1913, Zimmern urged his audience to think seriously about the project of strengthening the bonds of "union" within the Empire that would, in the process, make it more possible to improve life within the domestic realm of England itself. "The social problem in these islands," he argued, "like those in India and the dominions, demand for their solution, the efforts of a united Empire."[141] As with his Pericles, there was no contradiction between "Little England" and the British Empire, between Athens the city-state and Athens the Mistress of the Sea. "The creed of the so-called Little Englander," he argued, "is the dying relic of an effete political philosophy within the field of domestic legislation."[142] True social reform and real liberalism, Zimmern insisted, lay in embracing imperial unity between the dominions, the dependencies, and the Mother Country. Additionally, gone was any unease Zimmern might have expressed earlier with regard to the inclusion of India and the dependencies in this explicitly ethical vision of imperial order. In other words, while Zimmern's earlier works on empire were unclear about the status of the nonwhite dependencies in a newly United Britain (including them in one moment, explicitly excluding them in the next), the vision of empire he cultivated in 1913 solved the contradiction by refusing to acknowledge it in the first place. Thus, in the place of any explicit discussion of the status of India in the Empire stood precisely the kind of silence that Zimmern argued allowed Pericles to negotiate the contradiction between Athens and the Empire, the kind of silence that would tolerate no unease about promoting a vision of the Empire as a liberal whole grounded in an actual politics that entailed differences in the status of citizens, subjects, and slaves. Rather than parse the question, Zimmern simply spoke of India *as if it were* already a coherent part of an organic, imperial union that included England and the dominions. Again, "The social problems in these islands," Zimmern argued, "like those in India and the dominions, demand for their solution the efforts of a united Empire."[143] To his critics—those anti-imperialists who would compare the British Empire to the German—Zimmern replied by defiantly insisting, as he had with the Athenians, that some forms of national character are simply incorruptible: "To any man acquainted with the character and interests of the Mother Country and the dominions, the suggestion that a united Empire would use its strength in aggression against other nations is simply unthinkable."[144] Britain, like

Athens, was essentially liberal and the character of its people was liberal. For it to behave any other way was impossible.

And yet, Zimmern had to contend in *The Greek Commonwealth* with the fact that Athens did fall, that between the "plague and war fever," and despite the best of Pericles's intentions and his demands for an explicitly, theorized "Pan Hellenic" empire, the *polis* as it had been in its prime collapsed. With Thucydides, Zimmern was clearly also crushed by Athens's imperial decline, its move away from Periclean sensibilities toward a crude understanding of imperial power for imperial power's sake. One gets the sense in his 1913 article that he felt similarly anxious about the British Empire. Faced with internal critics on the right and the left acting in concert with the Germans and all who represented both the extremes of state-oriented nationalism and the factionalism of class politics, the British Empire, he implied, could be toppled at any moment by both enemies from without and bad policy from within, generated by ideologues who failed to attend to "situations of fact."[145] *Not* attending to the facts—that is, not waking up and embracing the duties that were entailed in running an empire— could mean, for Zimmern, that all that was valuable and worth saving about the British character and liberalism itself could die just as it had in Greece: "Political liberty had its birth in ancient Greece, but dissolved in the Greek city state into political anarchy," Zimmern argued. The only remedy was to do what the Greeks had failed to do: to create closer union between the dominions and dependencies that composed the British Commonwealth, thus strengthening the "Empire as a whole."[146]

On one level then, Zimmern's nostalgia for a lost Periclean vision fueled the explicit contemporary lesson—the "possession for all time"—that he hoped to teach modern Britons. On another level, however, Zimmern's nostalgia was more internally complicated than this, both in regard to modern Britain and Athens. Thus, not only was Zimmern nostalgic for the Athenian *polis* and the Periclean Empire that could have been, he was already nostalgic for the end of Britain's imperial innocence. In this sense, for Zimmern, translating Britain's imperial past into liberal terms required that he tell a developmental narrative of the Empire, one in which the English were accidental imperialists who, because of their natural liberal proclivities toward trade and exploration, had blithely stumbled into a project of global significance whose vital relationship to world order they were only now, at the beginning of the twentieth-century, fully coming to grasp. But there is something in Zimmern's repeated turn to the language of reality and obligation, both in his 1913 article and in his work over the next several years, as well as something in his overemphasis of the need to "recognize responsibility," create "constructive solutions," and "develop a clear knowledge of the facts" that suggest a kind of mournful longing for an idyllic childhood that must be put aside when adult responsibilities press in. In the end, the amount of time Zimmern lingered on Burke and the exceptional qualities of the English commonwealth in this essay, coupled with his abrupt turns to the language of responsibility, suggests that he accepted that the reality of empire must be embraced, while pining for more innocent times before "the facts" made it necessary for liberals like himself to have to think about such things.

However, there is something even more complicated at work in Zimmern's nostalgic attitude toward British liberal innocence than first meets the eye. The fact that Zimmern felt nostalgic for a political moment—that temporal state in which English liberals had not yet come to terms with their imperial responsibilities—and then declared it over, invented that moment as the object of nostalgia precisely as it mourned its passing. In other words, in declaring innocence dead, Zimmern also breathed life into the idea that such a state had once existed. Again, in Zimmern's imaginary, the English developed their liberal sensibilities locally, among the little platoons, and the Empire flowed outward from their innocent liberal curiosity thrust unknowingly into the world. This suggests that a coherent liberalism existed in England *before* the emergence of its Empire. However, just as Zimmern's beloved fifth-century *polis* was always, already an empire, so was the liberal England of Zimmern's fantasy—with its patriotic citizens and their tenacious drive for free trade—always already in the process of becoming an empire. Liberalism and imperialism in Britain, as so many recent scholars have argued, were birthed in the same historical moment, driven by so many of the same economic and political impulses that is difficult to posit which came first.[147] But by first lamenting the loss of an innocent-of-empire sensibility, and then requiring his audience to man up to the realities of Empire, Zimmern's nostalgia *created* the rhetorical object that he now declared it necessary to abandon. In order to stage a moment in which guileless English liberals looked around in dizzying surprise at the Empire they had created while busy doing other things and then uncomplainingly took on the burden of being imperialists, there had to have been a time before, a time made real by the very act of declaring it over.

But again, just as Athens played a critical role in Zimmern's displacement of British imperial history, so too did Athens play an important role in the productive push of his nostalgia. In this sense, it is perhaps best to understand Zimmern's attitude toward Athens and the Athenian Empire as a form of not just "proleptic nostalgia" (in Baucum's sense), but *retroactive* proleptic nostalgia. Like Baucum's tourist, Zimmern captured moments from the lived world of Athens's past in his descriptions of the details of everyday life: the turn of the crooked street, the feel of the sunshine, that moment when the citizen pauses to regret "he had not stopped for a mixed drink on his way to the assembly." And implicit in this historical tourism is Zimmern's assurances, through his constant use of analogies, that Athens was familiar to the modern Englishman, that its institutions and way of life were not just comprehensible but profoundly recognizable and only slightly out of temporal phase. For Zimmern, Athens was England, and England was Athens, and if it was possible to feel nostalgia for Athens, it was also possible to feel nostalgia for the contemporary moment of imperial naïveté as it ebbed toward its inevitable closure. It was thus possible to "evacuate the present" with all of is discomforting, niggling contradictions between Little England and the British Empire. At the same time, Zimmern's nostalgia was also piercingly redemptive. In other words, Athens might have fallen, but it *could have been saved* had it listened to Pericles and become a true "Education to Greece." The era of England's naïve imperialists may be gone, Zimmern argued, but it could also *be saved* in part through the concerted desire of its subjects to embrace a unified form of imperial governance. And in the process, Athens could also be redeemed.

Zimmern's thinking on Athens and Britain was thus caught in a loop of temporal simultaneity that played out across much of his early writing on Greece, empire, and internationalism. In this view, Athens was Britain now and Britain was Athens then, and the moment to save both Empires was always right in front of us. This approach to imagining and salvaging both the imperial past and present would not only have a deep impact on the way Round Table thinkers couched their own emerging vision of the "Commonwealth of Nations," but would soon be echoed in the way Cold War and post-Cold War theorists of Athens like Donald Kagan made their case for the significance of Athens and Thucydides to the contemporary world.

For all of the redemptive qualities of his imperial vision, however, for all the ways it held out Athens as ultimately reclaimable through Britain, Zimmern never did resolve the "Oxford paradox" at the center of both his thinking on antiquity and his belief in a United Britain. Nowhere is this more obvious than in a 1916 letter Zimmern wrote to John Hobson responding to Hobson's acerbic conclusion that British liberal imperialists were simply deluding themselves by imagining that the British Empire was fundamentally different from the German, or that the British possessed "special genius for government" that made their form of empire more humane. Zimmern answered with stunningly honest opacity that the British imperial project was different from the German and that it ought rightly to be viewed as "an attempt to work out not national or racial but universal and fundamental principles, which are not regarded as right because they are British but have been accepted and worked out and constantly modified by Britain because they have been tested and found enduringly right."[148] Zimmern's return to the passive voice here ("are regarded," "have been worked out") only barely concealed the deeper paradox still at work in his thinking about both Athens and Britain: that the "fundamental principles" of liberalism which Zimmern believed were developed by, and deeply reflective of, the British also just happened to be enduringly right for everyone, including people in communities who had substantively different visions of the political. Simple and universal. Narrow and reluctantly (but sufficiently) broad. But there is a reason why Zimmern never resolved his own paradox. Quite simply, the paradox *must remain* a paradox, calling forth explanation but never fully explaining, because the question about Athenian and British imperial domination must remain open. How, Zimmern asked again and again, did such a simple people come to such awesome responsibility? Such a question invited endless circularity—the Empire is an attempt to work out fundamental principles that are not regarded as right because they are British, but because they have been found to be right—and endless inquiry. Keeping the paradox unresolved thus, by necessity, meant keeping the imperializing society permanently at the center of reflection. What fell out of the picture was anything that the colonized, the dominated, and the unwilling recipients of an imperial education might have to say. Keeping the paradox alive meant that the arguments of the critics—the Mytileneans and the Melians, the Indians and the Irish—could only be registered as the high-pitched, background whine of the eternally incomprehensible and the radically ungrateful.

Falling in Love with Athens: Donald Kagan on America and Thucydides's Revisionism

Let me say that our system of government does not copy the institutions of our neighbors. It is more the case of our being a model to others, than of our imitating anyone else.

—Pericles's Funeral Speech, Thucydides's *History of the Peloponnesian War*

Scholar of ancient history and Yale professor Donald Kagan is best known for his numerous works on Athens, Thucydides, and the Peloponnesian War, and for the wealth of analogies he draws between this period and contemporary America—analogies that invariably serve to justify neoconservative foreign policy objectives. Indeed, Kagan's relentless championing of the Peloponnesian analogy over the last forty years has been so influential in some circles that in 2003—five months after the American invasion of Iraq—Irving Kristol credited Kagan (along with Leo Strauss) with making Thucydides's *History* "the favorite neoconservative text on foreign affairs."[1] Douglas Murray concurred, arguing in 2006 that, "Spurred on by Professor Donald Kagan...as well as by Strauss, neoconservatives drew, and continue to draw, inspiration for their attitudes to conflict from the ancients, in particular from Thucydides."[2]

Occasionally over the last forty years, however, Kagan has expanded his direct analogizing to include examples from modern history and, on those occasions, he has invariably turned to Britain's experience just before or between the World Wars. Thus, Kagan argued in a 1987 piece for *Commentary* magazine:

The lessons of the two world wars provide useful analogies for the world today. Once again we see two great antagonistic powers, one largely content, the other plainly dissatisfied. Like Great Britain before the two wars, the United States is a contented power, concerned lest a newly risen rival destroy a satisfactory equilibrium and threaten its safety. It is more similar to the earlier Britain which, though it had lost ground relatively since its peak in the 19th century remained the richest and most powerful nation in the world...[3]

Thirteen years later, in a book Kagan coauthored with his son, the historian Frederick Kagan, he pushed the analogy forward in time so that America in the present paralleled Britain during the interwar period: stymied by appeasement, and blithely unaware, in the Kagans's minds, of the danger posed by Nazi Germany. "After World War One," they argue, "Great Britain found itself in a situation very similar to the one in which we live today.... The British believed then, as we do now, that no storm was on the horizon and none could appear before they were able to respond. They were wrong."[4]

In 1987 and 2000, Donald Kagan argued that America's takeaway lesson from an examination of Great Britain at these two moments—right before World War I and between World Wars I and II, when the British Empire was both supremely powerful and yet on the verge of decline—ought to be a widespread recognition of the "the importance of vigilance" and "preparedness." The United States should buckle down, according to Kagan, increase its defense spending, and commit itself fully to bearing the inescapable burden of ordering the world. In this sense, Kagan understands his British analogy as an explicit refutation of what he argues has been the near-total ascendency of "revisionist" accounts of the period that draw significantly different lessons for American foreign policy in the present: lessons that urge the state toward "greater caution, a willingness to bargain" and "a greater willingness to understand the point of view of nations late in coming to power on the world scene."[5]

Kagan's British analogies are fascinating, I argue, for a variety of reasons but, first and foremost, because of the very fact that he is so drawn toward this period as a point of comparison in the first place. It is both ironic and hardly surprising that Kagan imagines America now to be experiencing something similar to Britain then, given that his overall interpretation of fifth-century B.C.E. Athens during the period leading up to the Peloponnesian War bears such a stunning resemblance to the vision developed by Alfred Zimmern in *The Greek Commonwealth* in 1911. Despite notable differences in their domestic and international political agendas, Kagan and Zimmern both read Periclean Athens through not only rosy but also decidedly modern lenses, as the paramount example of a distinctly liberal society, uniquely capable of democratic debate and reflection. With Zimmern, Kagan believes that Athens never had expansionist intentions in the west but, rather, that its imperializing was of a Panhellenic nature. Like Zimmern, Kagan challenges traditional ways of reading Thucydides that stress the incompatibility between Athenian democracy and empire. Finally, Kagan uses the experience

of Athens it the preservation of freedom throughout
the world l leadership. Even more importantly, like
Zimmern tand that not only must America take on the
burden o t must do so even though it never intended
to be exp , even though its empire was the accidental
result of freedom and free trade, and, therefore, even
though i or creating the worrisome conditions of the
current i his political project, I argue, that most shapes
and colc :ship, particularly his lifelong quest to counter
Thucydides's claim that the growth of Athenian power, and subsequent Spartan
fear, was the "real reason" behind, or true "cause" of, the Peloponnesian War.[6]

However, Kagan's understanding of a strengthened American hegemony
looks distinctly different from Zimmern's vision of the British Commonwealth.
Kagan's is a much more hawkish approach to American foreign policy; he insists
that not only must America embrace a proactive form of military and political
engagement, but it also must do so from the perspective of permanent, wary
vigilance. Britain failed to protect its empire, Kagan argues, because it appeased
undemocratic, illiberal regimes. Such regimes are to be attacked head on by
the liberal hegemon (Britain then, America now) willing not only to fully fund
its military but also to invade rogue states and replace their governments with
democracies amenable to free market liberalism. The opportunity to do precisely
this presented itself in 2003 when Kagan and the rest of his cohort of neoconservative intellectuals associated with the Project for a New American Century
(PNAC) were able to convince the Bush administration to invade Iraq in the
name of "regime change." That same year, Kagan published *The Peloponnesian
War*, in which he made the case that Athens might have emerged triumphant
over Sparta had it been more willing to commit troops to the Sicilian expedition.

Critics of the way Kagan reads neoconservative politics into his classical
scholarship tend to focus on these more bellicose counterfactual claims and,
in so doing, largely ignore those portions of his scholarship that resemble
Zimmern's—namely, his prolonged infatuation with the period before the outbreak of the Peloponnesian War in 431 B.C.E., as well as the nostalgic vision he
paints of Athens as a thoroughly modern, liberal democracy. By contrast, political theorists who do focus on this portion of Kagan's narrative tend to restrict
their analysis to his unabashed "*polis* envy," while historians have pointed to
Kagan's argument about the period and wondered at his many methodological
ellipses and his reliance on counterfactual posturing.[7] But such investigations
rarely tie these interpretive or methodological critiques to an analysis of Kagan's
support for a form of liberal imperialism grounded in a preemptive American
foreign policy. This chapter brings together these two streams of critique and
argues that we cannot truly understand Kagan's imperialist blustering over

Iraq/Sicily unless we read it against the backdrop of his reading of fifth-century Athens and his historical narrative of the Thirty Years Peace—a narrative that, like Zimmern's dream of the democratic Athenian Empire, exonerates Athens/Britain/America from responsibility retroactively for creating the conditions for conflict in the first place while simultaneously declaring them to be thoughtful, self-critical societies, intuitively committed to reflection and critique.

Section One of the chapter looks closely at the intellectual climate of the Cold War that shaped Kagan's approach to antiquity and examines his growing relationship with American neoconservatism and his writings on war and foreign policy. The next section examines Kagan's refutation of Thucydides, and Section Three interrogates the complexities of this reading in light of the analogies he draws between Athens, Britain, and America. The chapter concludes by dwelling briefly on the irony of the fact that, despite their political differences, Kagan and Zimmern's ideological commitment to a liberal imperialism fundamentally at odds with itself pushed them toward developing readings of antiquity that were not only remarkably similar, but which further the self-absorbed amnesia that makes real critical reflection on America's role in the world so difficult today.

Intellectual Climate

Donald Kagan is Sterling Professor of Classics and History at Yale where he has been teaching since the early 1970s (also serving as dean from 1989–1992), and is the author of over fifty books and articles dealing primarily with classical history. His most notable contribution to the study of ancient Greece is a four-volume, often beautifully written, history of the Peloponnesian War that Kagan published over a period of twenty years (1969–1987). He is also the author of 2003's self-described "new history" of the war (a condensed version of his earlier works), 2009's *Thucydides: the Reinvention of History,* and countless articles and chapters in edited volumes on the subject.[8] Kagan's writings about Thucydides and the war are not limited to works devoted to classical scholarship, but also appear in both his own and others' volumes on the history of war and international politics such as *The Making of Strategy: Rulers, States, and War,* edited by Williamson Murray (1994) and his own book, *On the Origins of War and the Preservation of the Peace* (1995).[9] In a 2005 article reflecting on Kagan's academic career, Barry Strauss noted admiringly that over the years, Kagan's expertise on questions of war and strategy in antiquity spilled over into a more general interest with "the history of strategy, from Vegetius to Clausewitz and from Sun Tzu to Mao." Kagan, according to Strauss, "is also an observer and frequent writer on contemporary strategy, which makes him unusually sensitive to the realities of power."[10]

Like Zimmern, Kagan is an inspirational professor who has, throughout his career, brought issues of contemporary politics and foreign policy to his teaching of the classics. Strauss remembers the intensity of Kagan's public presence at Yale in the 1970s, his status as an "advocate of freedom of speech, gadfly, scholar, author, editor, raconteur, political commentator, sports fan, film buff, and family man, and one of the most popular and highly regarded teachers on campus."[11] Throughout his career, Kagan has used his charismatic public presence to advocate for a distinctly neoconservative agenda, one that supports civil rights but is vehemently opposed to the identity politics of the new social movements of the 1960s and 1970s. In 1969, after nearly ten years in the History Department, Kagan left Cornell (along with his colleague Allan Bloom) because of the university's decision to concede to some of the demands of student protestors, a decision that Kagan saw as form of appeasement in the face of tyranny. "For the first time," he described later, "I understood what happened in Nazi Germany."[12] Kagan also identified this time at Cornell with his own ideological shift to the right, arguing that watching "administrators demonstrate all the courage of Neville Chamberlain had a great impact on me, and I became much more conservative."[13] While at Yale, Kagan has become one of the academy's most ardent defenders of Western "Great Books" programs in colleges and universities, and in 1979 he cowrote a conservative text book, *The Western Heritage*, which has since been described as "old fashioned" in its excessive attention to Athenian politics, yet nevertheless has been reprinted ten times.[14] Kagan is also a vocal critic of multicultural education, literary theory, postmodernism, and what he identifies as the leftward sweep of the professoriate more generally. Finally, as the father of two well-known neoconservative activists—the historian Frederick Kagan and historian and foreign policy commentator Robert Kagan—Kagan has effectively established his own neoconservative dynasty.

In addition to publishing articles and op-eds in *The New York Times, Commentary, The Wall Street Journal,* and *The Weekly Standard,* Kagan has been active in foreign policy circles for years and in 1997, along with Dick Cheney, Elliott Abrams, Francis Fukuyama, and Paul Wolfowitz, helped to found the PNAC, an organization dedicated to the idea that the end of the Cold War required an expansion, rather than a retraction, of American military spending. According to the group's founding documents, increased military spending was necessary because "we need to accept responsibility for America's unique role in preserving and extending an international order friendly to our security, our prosperity, and our principles."[15] The PNAC argues for a proactive and preemptive approach to foreign policy, an imperial vision of the world that requires the United States to actively intervene in (rather than merely contain) states whose illiberal politics threaten American security. Along with Gary Schmitt and Thomas Donnelly, Kagan coauthored one of the PNAC's first reports in 2000,

"Rebuilding America's Defenses: Strategy, Forces, and Resources for a New Strategy," in which he argued that "America should seek to preserve and extend its position of global leadership by maintaining the preeminence of U.S. military forces" in order "to preserve and enhance this 'American peace.' "[16]

Not surprisingly, around this time, PNAC intellectuals like Kagan associated with universities also set about founding academic programs to develop in future political leaders the strategic sensibilities necessary for preserving and extending American global leadership. In its statement of purpose, Yale's Brady Johnson Program in Grand Strategy (whose twin academic stars are Kagan and John Lewis Gaddis) identifies the program's *raison d'être* as the need to "revive the study and practice of grand strategy" which it does "by devising methods to teach that subject at the graduate and undergraduate levels" and "by training future leaders to think about and implement grand strategies in imaginative and effective ways."[17] Like its sister programs at Duke, Texas, Columbia, and Temple (all funded largely through the donations of right-wing philanthropists like Roger Hertog), the program seeks to educate future leaders in the grand sweep of imperial strategy.[18] Given Kagan's involvement, it is hardly surprising that the syllabus for its foundational course, "Studies in Grand Strategy," divides the class into two teams, Athenians and Spartans.[19]

Like Zimmern, Kagan is well know for the way he has, for decades, drawn upon analogies from antiquity to illustrate contemporary life and examples from contemporary life to illustrate the world of antiquity. These analogies often go far beyond merely demonstrating the similarities between different forms of strategic thinking, as Barry Strauss would have us believe, and instead paint a fairly seamless connection, at times, between ancient Athens and contemporary America. "In their rational and secular approach," Kagan argued in *Pericles of Athens*, "in their commitment to political freedom and individual autonomy in a constitutional republican and democratic public life, the Athenians of Pericles' day are closer to the values of our era than any culture that has appeared since antiquity."[20] And yet, while Kagan never shies away from making these kinds of analogies in his work, he also understands that not everyone is going to find them convincing. At times, Kagan seems almost defensive about his approach, and many of his historical works include introductory moments where he stops to address himself to those people who might find his presentism troubling. "I have often drawn historical analogies between situations in the fifth-century B.C.E. and modern events," he notes in the Introduction to 1969's *The Outbreak of the Peloponnesian War*. But, he quickly insists, "I have used them appropriately and with due caution" and in full awareness of the "danger of such analogies."[21] Kagan leaves to speculation what these dangers might be but, over the years, critics have either found these analogies extremely troubling or simply unhelpful. As Ronald Stroud put it simply in 1971, "Kagan's parallels between ancient and modern history will be for most readers a matter of personal taste."[22]

Neoconservative readers sympathetic to Kagan's larger worldview, however, have been drawn to his analogies in much the same way that Toynbee once drank in Zimmern's conviction that ancient Greece had much to teach students of contemporary politics, "that the two interests could co-exist in the same mind, and that each of them was illuminating for the other."[23] In this sense, Kagan's greatest contribution to the evolution of the neoconservative foreign policy agenda, according to neoconservative authors Irving Kristol and Douglas Murray, has been his relentless championing of Thucydides's *History of the Peloponnesian War* as a text of enduring relevance for international politics. But, Murray stresses, it is important to grasp that neoconservatives do not read *The History* "in order to learn how to act in the world" but, rather, as "a text that supports their instinctive beliefs in foreign policy" which, according to Murray, include an assumption that patriotism is a good, that world government is to be rejected, and that leaders should distinguish between friends and enemies.[24] These three assumptions are hardly controversial, nor do they give us much insight into how neoconservatives draw their imperialist vision of the world from this potentially limiting set of ethical tenets. What is revealing here is Murray's contention that Thucydides does not offer neoconservatives policy prescriptions for how to more effectively imperialize but, rather, support for their "instinctive beliefs" about foreign policy. The irony, of course, is that programs that focus on Grand Strategies claim to look to the past for instrumental reasons, precisely "in order to learn how to act in the world," or in the program's own description of itself, to "think about and implement grand strategies." Murray's words, however, suggest that there is something deeper at work in neoconservative interpretations of Thucydides, something they are intuiting about the text that goes beyond a belief in patriotism, a rejection of world government, and a policy that distinguishes between friends and enemies. Rather, they are drawn to Kagan's absolute belief in the rightness of the Athenian cause and the similarities between Athens and America, both as liberal polities and liberal empires.

Understanding Kagan's political vision of the Athenian Empire, his interpretation of Thucydides, and his approach to the Peloponnesian War, requires some exploration of the intellectual environment that shaped his reading of antiquity. Kagan began, and then extensively developed, his particular approach to classical history during a period in which Thucydidean scholarship in American political science and international history was dominated by the parallel concerns of realist International Relations (IR) scholarship and Cold War politics. As IR solidified into its own coherent subdiscipline in Britain and America during the interwar period, proponents of the emerging school of realism, such as Hans Morgenthau, turned to the history of political thought in Europe in order to locate a "tradition" for their cohering approaches. Over time, Thucydides would become the foundational figure in the new, realist IR canon, a trend that can be seen today in the innumerable textbooks that refer to Thucydides as the founder or "father" of realism, and the IR collections that begin with what realists see as the first expression of the realist doctrine in history, the Melian Dialogue.[25] *The History* is a "possession for all time," according to these scholars, because of Thucydides's cynical view of human nature, his treatment of peoples as collective units of action, and his basic inclination in support of, as Morgenthau put it, "interest defined as power."[26]

By contrast, Kagan's work has always been sympathetic to the position taken by scholars and policy makers influenced by Cold War politics. As historian W. Robert Connor remembers the 1950s, "For me, and I believe for many other students of the classics in my generation, Thucydides possessed an immediate applicability."[27] The timelessness of Thucydides's work, argued these thinkers, lies in the contrast he painted between a liberal, democratic, spontaneous yet disciplined Athens (apparent in Pericles's Funeral Speech) and cautious, overtrained, socialist, goose-steeping Sparta. In the eyes of these readers, the allegorical qualities of the Athenian-Spartan relationship mapped perfectly onto the polarized nature of the American and Soviet spheres of influence and highlighted both the superiority of the American way of life and the need for American global leadership, while also serving as a warning to all free peoples to remain permanently vigilant or suffer the fate of Athens. As Louis J. Halle of the Department of State's policy planning staff noted in his 1952 article for the *Foreign Service Journal*, "The present in which our country finds herself, like Athens after the Persian War, called upon to assume the leadership of the free world brings him [Thucydides] virtually to our side...It seems to me that since World War Two, Thucydides has come still closer to us so that he now speaks to our ear."[28]

The key moment in *The History*, for these Cold War readers, was Thucydides's recounting of Pericles's Funeral Speech and his rich description of Athenian democracy in the context of its benign and educative empire, something Cold War scholars also saw in America and its relationship with those states most firmly tucked under its spheres of influence. Toward the end of his life, Zimmern himself, now having abandoned his hopes for a hegemonic British Commonwealth uniquely able to bring democratic peace to the world, similarly shifted his analogical allegiances to America. "Athens," Zimmern argued in a 1951 essay, "Our Greek Augustan Age," "was a Great Power, a democratic Great Power." "The American people," he went on to insist:

> have now picked up this thread of Ariadne, the thread of a large scale democratic power, thus challenging the axioms of the sages of European political and social science.... Europeans today are rubbing

their eyes in astonishment that a world power of this unexampled character should have actually come into being and should be exerting a predominant influence in world affairs from China to Peru. They have hardly even begun to ask themselves how and why this phenomenon has come about. It seems too good to be true. Perhaps we can help them to overcome their astonishment by sending them back to the fifth century—to Herodotus, to the Persae of Aeschylus and to the Funeral Speech of Pericles.[29]

What made Athens great, according to Zimmern, was its unique ability to be both a Great Power and a democracy—a blessed and rare feat in the history of the world and something that, after the decline of the British Empire, the United States alone now seemed capable of achieving.

On a policy level, one can see how realist concerns with interest-driven, power-oriented interstate relations often neatly overlapped in practice with the Cold Warriors' ideological commitment to American global leadership. Both sides, for instance, accepted a deeply polarized vision of international politics and the need to maintain a militarily alert American state. One can also see how these approaches could diverge spectacularly, as they did during the Vietnam and Iraq Wars, when many realists accused the Administrations of privileging ideological orthodoxy above American strategic interests.[30]

Such divisions also reflected these thinkers' interpretations of Thucydides in ways that went beyond mere emphasis. In other words, at its core, the difference between realist and Cold War readings of *The History* turned on more than the realists' almost exclusive focus on the Melian Dialogue or the Cold Warriors' fascination with the Funeral Speech. Rather, these thinkers disagreed on the correct interpretation of Thucydides's stated purpose in writing the text itself: his claim that the "real reason" for the war was the "growth of Athenian power and the fear which this caused in Sparta."[31] For realists, Thucydides's assertion that the "real reason" for the war was Athenian expansion simply reflected his commitment to, in Keohane and Nye's words, an "overall power model" of international politics that took the unified state's lust for power as the sole moving factor behind all international conflict.[32] As multiple IR scholars and political theorists have argued over the years, this realist account of *The History* unnecessarily flattens and strategically bloats Thucydides's work, glossing over his complicated judgments about the moral character of particular generals and demagogues, his support for Pericles, his irony, his situated reading of *hegemonia*, his concern with leadership, his passionate and detailed descriptions of the horrors of war, and his consistent troubling of the relationship between the democratic *polis* and imperialism.[33] And yet, all of these critiques aside, Thucydides's conviction that the growth of Athenian power caused the war remains perfectly compatible with a limited realist account of *The History* as a text primarily concerned with power politics.

For Cold Warriors like Kagan, Thucydides's claim presented a more fundamental political and interpretive problem, particularly after the fall of the Soviet Union. If Athens was liberal and democratic and Athens was America, and if Athens caused the war by overreaching, then how—in the absence of sclerotic, authoritarian Sparta/Russia as a credible threat to world order—was it possible to reconcile Athenian/American claims to be liberal and freedom-loving with an aggressive foreign policy that not only denied freedom to others, but did so in a manner that went so far beyond protecting their spheres of influence that it produced unsalvable fear in their rivals? Kagan and his vision of a Cold War Thucydides thus came up hard against precisely the problem of liberal imperialism. If, to Kagan's mind, Pericles's Athens was based on celebrating individual autonomy within the community by rejecting "the leveling principle pursued by both ancient Sparta and modern socialism which requires suppression of those rights," then under what conditions could Athens or America justify suppressing those rights for Melians or Iraqis?[34] Kagan's solution to this problem was (and is) a combination of complementary impulses that, in some moments, resemble Zimmern's approach almost in its entirety and, at the same time, solve questions that Zimmern's analysis of Thucydides left unanswered.

Proving Thucydides Wrong

One of the most enduring themes of Kagan's work on the Peloponnesian War over the last thirty years has been his insistent challenging of Thucydides's claim that Athenian overreach caused the war. More philologically-oriented scholars (during the 1950s in particular) attempted to understand Thucydides's famous assertions in Book I.23 by interrogating the three Greek words that he uses for "cause."[35] Kagan, however, is less interested in close questions of translation. Rather, the central, motivating argument most apparent in all of Kagan's writings on Thucydides, from 1969 to 2009, is not that scholars have not adequately grasped Thucydides's meaning, but rather that Thucydides got it wrong. In other words, the Peloponnesian War may indeed be a "possession for all time" but not, argues Kagan, because Thucydides discovered the definitive, structural cause of the war, an argument that realists have embraced. Rather, Kagan maintains that Thucydides's goal in writing *The History* was actually to challenge the dominant opinion of the time and change "our way of looking at the matter generally."[36] In particular, Kagan argues, there is strong evidence to suggest that, at the time Thucydides was writing his history, Athenians held Pericles responsible for the war. Thucydides's goal, argued Kagan, was to resuscitate Pericles's actions and turn the dispute over the "causes of and responsibility for the war" against the Athenians, to "show that the common opinion was wrong in all major respects," that "Pericles was not responsible for the war but rather deserved praise for recognizing that it was inevitable and making intelligent plans to face it accordingly."[37] Thucydides's objective in *The History*, then, is to demonstrate, according to Kagan, that Athens was no longer a democracy in the period leading up to the war, that it had abandoned its principles in favor of imperial aggression, and that it refused to listen to Pericles, its most wise leader, and therefore got exactly what it deserved after Pericles's death: namely, the bullying, autocratic antihero of Thucydides's story, Cleon.

In contrast, as Kagan argued in 1988, "my own work for the past two decades has largely been to recover those forgotten and contemporary opinions and to compare them with Thucydides' own interpretations" and, at the same time, to read Thucydides's work "carefully and selectively" for what he omitted, for what Zimmern would call "silences."[38] Kagan's inquiries regarding the Thirty Years Peace have aimed, overall, to shed light on the "interesting dispute" over the "causes of and responsibility for the war." For Kagan this means demonstrating first, in contrast to Thucydides's assertions, that Athens during this period both was thoroughly democratic and, second, that it was neither aggressive nor expansionist in its imperial intentions, and thus posed no threat to Sparta.

Kagan addresses the first issue by arguing that Thucydides was an elitist who was intensely dubious throughout *The History* about the ability of the Athenian *polis* to collectively make and act on the kinds of wise tactical choices that Pericles exhorted them to embrace in his Funeral Speech and through his policy of withdrawal and retrenchment. For political theorists interested in Athenian democracy, whether or not Thucydides's skepticism about the *polis* ought to be read as a condemnation or dismissal of democratic politics more generally, or as an extended observation on an imperial democracy in decline, remains one of the most enduringly fascinating and enigmatic aspects of *The History*.[39] In Thucydides's words, during this period, "in what was nominally a democracy, power was really in the hands of the first citizen."[40] Thucydides shows us, time and time again, the way a largely silent *demos* moves from thoughtful reflection to swinish blood lust, from acceptance to rejection of Pericles, from the Mytilenean Debate to the Melian Dialogue.[41] Moreover, *The History of the Peloponnesian War* has also been read as an examination of the relationship between the demands of Great Power politics in the external world, and the maintenance of democracy based on equality within the *polis*.[42] More specifically, Thucydides's work also provides readers with a sustained examination of the effects of imperialism on a democracy—a position most apparent in Thucydides's decision to have his least favorite Athenian (Cleon) taunt the people of Athens for their unwillingness to sentence the male population of Mytilene to death.[43] Thucydidean scholars, including Cornford and Romilly, have suggested that Thucydides cast a skeptical eye on the possibility of marrying Athenian democracy to an excessively militaristic empire, and that the text ought to be read as a warning against imperial hubris.[44]

Over the last forty years, from *The Outbreak of the Peloponnesian War* through *Thucydides and the Reinvention of History*, Kagan has rejected Thucydides's claim that democracy in Athens during this period was in decline. While he admits that Athenian democracy was limited to only a fraction of the city's population (by autochthony and the exclusion of slaves and women), he frequently dismisses concerns with these exclusions (as he does in *Thucydides*) as "parochial and anachronistic." Kagan then goes on to insist that Thucydides was incorrect in his assessment of Athenian democracy. Kagan's methodology here, again, has been to "recover those forgotten and obscure contemporary opinions" about Athenian democracy in order to shed light on the veracity of Thucydides's claim. In particular, he pays attention to the writings of elitist Athenian critics of Periclean Athens, who were confident in their assertion that it was a democracy, as well as critics like the "Old Oligarch," the unknown author of an antidemocratic pamphlet written after Pericles' death.[45] "So far as we know," Kagan concludes, "Thucydides was the only ancient writer to suggest that Periclean Athens was anything but a thoroughgoing democracy."[46]

Having established that Athens was thoroughly democratic, Kagan proceeds to counter Thucydides's claim that Athens caused the war through imperial aggression. In the spirit of Zimmern, Kagan turns to historical events that Thucydides does not address in his *History*—first and foremost, the founding of Thurii. Kagan explores Thurii most extensively in Chapter Nine of *The Outbreak of the Peloponnesian War* ("Athens and the West: The Foundation of Thurii), but refers to it throughout his works both on the Peloponnesian War and political history more generally, including *Pericles of Athens*, and *On the Origins of War and the Preservation of the Peace*. In all of these texts, Kagan argues, like Zimmern, that the Athenians actively recruited people from all over Greece to colonize Thurii, and that this demonstrates definitively both their lack of expansionist intentions for the west and their sense that Thurii was to benefit the entire region rather than Athens alone. Kagan spends considerably more time on this point in 1969's *The Outbreak of the Peloponnesian War* than did Zimmern, largely because he is compelled to address the fact that, in the intervening years, scholars such as Victor Ehrenberg and Theodore Wade-Gery had questioned the pacific intentions of the Athenians in Thurii, turning to mounting numismatic evidence as proof that Panhellenism was simply a cover for Pericles' real desire for "powerful expansion and imperialism."[47] By contrast, Kagan dismisses this evidence and continues to argue that Thurii remains an example of Pericles's policy of "peaceful imperialism," even suggesting that Pericles's eventual refusal to intervene in the war between Thurii and Taras similarly highlights his underlying commitment to a "policy of peaceful Panhellenism and nonintervention."[48] Kagan argues that Thurii's eventual turn from Athens can be considered a foreign policy failure only if we assume that Pericles "intended the colony as a spearhead for Western imperialism, but we have seen that there is no basis for such an assumption."[49]

Reviewers over the years have questioned both Kagan's reading of Thurii and the extent to which he exaggerated its Panhellenic qualities,[50] while others have used Kagan's fascination with the founding of the colony as an example of his "carelessness" and his readiness to "flesh out our skeletal tradition through assertion."[51] But regardless of its accuracy, the argument for a Panhellenic Thurii plays an essential role in the one-two punch of Kagan's message. In other words, from 1969 until today Kagan has insisted that, during the period leading up to the Peloponnesian War, Athens was thoroughly democratic and that it had no imperial designs on the west but, rather, that its imperial expansion was peaceful and Panhellenic. The implication of these two arguments working in tandem is that the account of the Athenian Empire expressed by the Athenian delegation at Sparta in Thucydides's *History* was absolutely correct: according to the Athenians, "We did not gain this empire by force."[52] While Kagan acknowledges in *Pericles of Athens* that Athenians often maintained their empire by military means after the war with the Persians and the creation of the Delian League, he insists there was very little they could have done about this. Kagan accepts Pericles's own assumption that the Athenians needed the Empire to become the kind of "education to Greece" that they were meant to be and that this was "an empire different from any other that had ever existed."[53] The Athenian Empire during the Thirty Years Peace was, in effect, uninterested in domination according to Kagan, and committed, rather, to education and freedom of trade. When it imposed its will on its colonies it did so by replacing oligarchies with democracies (as it did Boeotia), in contrast to the Spartans.[54] When it did expand, during this period, it did so in a manner that Kagan describes as Panhellenic. Kagan's two-pronged approach here thus allows him to have his cake and eat it too; fifth-century Athens was not expansionist but, even if it was, its liberal-democratic ethos assured that it was an empire of a good, Panhellenic sort. It was, as Zimmern described America in 1951, a "large scale democratic power."

Kagan's analysis of Thucydides, however, also solves some of the logical problems that Zimmern's interpretation leaves hanging. Zimmern's account, for instance, asks us to believe Thucydides sometimes but not at other times, to assume that some of his descriptions (the Funeral Speech) were accurate reflections of his feelings about Athenian imperialism, while others (the Melian Dialogue) were not. Kagan addresses this problem of when and when not to believe Thucydides in three ways. First, in an ironic turn, given his conviction that Thucydides is a "revisionist" historian, Kagan reads the speeches in *The History* literally, as factual reflections of what the participants actually said. This puts Kagan at odds with Thucydides himself, who famously explained his own approach thus:

> In this history I have made use of set speeches some of which were delivered just before and others during the war. I have found it difficult to remember the precise words used in the speeches which I listened to myself and my various informants have experienced the same difficulty; so my method has been, while keeping as closely as possible to the general sense of the words that were actually used, to make the speakers say what, in my opinion, was called for by each situation.[55]

Generations of Thucydides scholars have interpreted these words to mean that we ought to exercise caution when reading the speeches and avoid interpreting them as accurate representations of what the political actors in each instance were really saying. As Romilly notes in her reflections on the Mytilene debate, "We cannot discover what resemblance there was between the ideas expressed in Thucydides and those put forward in real life by Cleon and his opponent."[56] Much more commonly, political theorists and historical interpreters of Thucydides have argued that he, in Saxonhouse's words, "allowed his characters to make speeches" in order to make broader points about the war itself, international politics, democracy, imperialism, or the effects of human nature on politics more generally.[57] In 1911 Zimmern himself made a similar observation, noting in his analysis of the Funeral Speech that Pericles's claim that "we secure our friends not by accepting favors but by doing them" was an "amazing statement" for Thucydides to "put in Pericles' mouth!"[58]

Kagan resolutely rejects this reading and instead insists that Thucydides' claim to keep as "closely as possible to the general sense of the words that were actually used" qualifies the latter half of the sentence, in which he admits to making "the speakers say what, in my opinion, was called for by each situation." For Kagan, Thucydides is simply arguing that his speeches represent as close an approximation to reality as can reasonably be expected and that "we are obliged to accept the essential authenticity of the speeches reported."[59] Kagan argues that questions of interpretation, then, should focus not on the authenticity of the speeches or upon ferreting out their meaning *vis à vis* what we believe to be Thucydides's larger arguments but, rather, on where Thucydides chose to place them in the text and on his strategic deletion of speeches where historical record would suggest such speeches ought to be. Kagan thus reads Thucydides literally for what he says and then speculates about what he does not. For example,

Kagan wonders, why does Thucydides supply his readers with an account of the speeches made by the Corcyrean delegates to Athens in Book I, but then does not record any of the Athenian Assembly's responses? Kagan speculates that this is because to do so would have revealed that "most Athenians did not think that war was inevitable," a point of view which Thucydides contested.[60]

It is precisely in Kagan's attempts to fill in these ellipses—these moments of quietude in *The History*—that we again see his second approach to establishing Thucydides's veracity: his use of the limited and fragmentary pieces of evidence that exist about the war not written by Thucydides and his heavy reliance on speculative accounts of what political actors might have been thinking given these pieces of evidence—what one reviewer described in 1983 as Kagan's tendency to try and "do more than is genuinely possible for the ancient historian."[61] For instance, Kagan wonders, why did the Corinthians, "whose hatred of Athens dated back for two decades," side with the Athenians during a meeting of the Peloponnesian League over the invasion of Samos? This must have been, according to Kagan, because they "understood the signal sent by the Athenian action at Thurii" to mean that Athens was not aiming to expand its imperial power in the west.[62] Kagan then uses this as further proof that Athens did not behave aggressively during the Thirty Years Peace, and that Spartan and Corinthian fears were unfounded.

Third and finally, Kagan's speculative tendencies are not limited to imagining what political actors might have been thinking or doing that led to known historical outcomes. He also asks frequently about what might have happened if these political actors had done things differently. Kagan is very clear, for instance, that if we analyze the peace treaty that established the Thirty Years Peace "without preconceptions," we can see that it contained elements within it necessary for a lasting peace.[63] Nothing—least of all, according to Kagan, Athenian imperialism—made the war inevitable, and one of his longstanding scholarly goals is to take this lack of inevitability seriously and think speculatively about what might have been done differently to not only avoid but, eventually, to win the war. Kagan argues in *On The Origins of War*, for instance, that the Athenians might have deterred Corinth had they been less hesitant in their use of force at Sybota. "Perhaps a full offensive and defensive alliance such as the Corcyraeans proposed would have convinced the Corinthians that Athens was serious," he suggests.[64]

As with his use of contemporary analogies, Kagan frequently acknowledges his methodological dependence on speculation and counterfactuals in the introductions to his works on ancient history. For example, he notes in his Introduction to 1987's *The Fall of the Athenian Empire* that "More than one able and sympathetic reader of my earlier volumes has been troubled by my practice of comparing what took place with what might have happened had individuals or peoples taken different actions and by my penchant for the subjunctive mood, or what is sometimes called 'counterfactual history.' "[65] Kagan gives several reasons for his use of counterfactuals. First and foremost, argues Kagan, Thucydides used them himself throughout *The History*, for example, when he speculates on what might have happened if the Athenians had listened to Pericles early on in the war. Kagan also argues that any history which is more than chronology must rely on some form of speculation and that his use of counterfactuals simply serves to "put the reader on notice" that whatever follows is a judgment rather than a statement of fact. Putting the reader "on notice" about authorial interpretation then loosens up precisely that move in Thucydides's *History* that most troubles Kagan: his revisionist attempt to convince generations of readers that Athenian power made war with Sparta inevitable. Rather, argues Kagan, counterfactuals help avoid "the excessive power of the *fait accompli*, making it clear that what really occurred was not the inevitable outcome of superhuman forces but the result of decisions by human beings and suggesting that both decisions and their outcomes could well have been different."[66]

It is Kagan's repeated suggestion that "what really occurred" not be understood as the "inevitable outcome" that has most irritated his recent critics, particularly since the publication of 2003's *The Peloponnesian War*. Written during the invasion of Iraq, right about the time Kagan was most involved with the group of neoconservative thinkers largely responsible for the construction of the Bush Doctrine, these critics have rightly identified an underlying politics in the speculations at work in this book. Kagan begins his "new history" by making a claim about its uniqueness; the book is meant to borrow heavily from Thucydides, he argues, but "is designed to meet the needs of readers in the twenty-first century."[67] "I have avoided" he goes on to insist, "making comparisons between events in it and those in later history, although many leap to mind, in the hope that an uninterrupted account will better allow readers to draw their own conclusions." But one of the conclusions that continually leaps most clearly to mind in reading this book is that the Athenians could have won the Peloponnesian War if they had been more aggressive and willing to take more military risks. Kagan condemns Nicias as a traitorous, self-interested coward whose unwillingness to at first really commit to the mission, and then to let it go, ultimately led to its failure. Observations like these are what prompted Anne Norton to express absolute disbelief at Kagan's analysis in her 2004 book *Leo Strauss and the Politics of American Empire*, particularly at his conviction "that earlier scholars and public intellectuals have read Thucydides wrong and that the Athenians failed only in not being imperial enough."[68] Daniel Mendelsohn's 2004 *New Yorker* review even more succinctly expresses the politics at the heart of Kagan's speculative, counterfactual account. Kagan's book, according to Mendelsohn, "represents the Ollie North take on the Peloponnesian War: 'If we'd only gone in there with more triremes,' he seems to be saying, 'we would have won that sucker.' "[69]

Norton and Mendelsohn concentrate their critiques on Kagan's contentious, counterfactual observation that the Sicilian expedition could have been won had the Athenians listened to the more hawkish elements in their midst. Both comment on the way Kagan has turned traditional readings of *The History* as a story of Athenian hubris and overreach into a perversely counterfactual lesson on what happens to hegemonic states that refuse to act more imperially. Both note the astonishing lack of interest Kagan shows in the Melian Dialogue, a moment in the text where Thucydides's poignantly demonstrates, through speeches, the arrogance of the Athenians, now drunk on war and imperial power. Thucydides's brief description of the casual manner in which the Athenians put all the men of the island to death and sold the women and children into slavery suggests just how far their moral standards had fallen since the Mytilenean Debate.[70] For Kagan, however, the Melian Dialogue serves no didactic purpose, and he refers to the incident itself merely as "the outlet [the Athenians] needed to express their energy and frustration."[71] His few references to the slaughter on Melos are largely couched in the passive voice (e.g. "the entire male population of Melos and Scione were wiped out") as if it were the inevitable result of the war, rather than the decision of an Athenian Assembly who clearly no longer experienced the doubt about slaughter they had in the Mytilenean Debate.[72]

Kagan's use of the passive voice here, his casual dismissal of the Melian incident as a *fait accompli*, runs directly against his own desire to avoid the "excessive power of the *fait accompli*" and to challenge those interpretations of history that deny human agency. For this reason, and for many others, it can be safely argued that one of the primary reasons that Kagan uses counterfactuals is not to open up historical interpretation to alternative meaning but, as Norton and Mendelsohn have accurately identified, to justify a particular kind of foreign policy in the present. But while accounts such as Norton's and Mendelsohn's are correct in their interpretation of Kagan's political agenda, they only identify half of it: the part that focuses on reading the need for American military aggression through the Sicilian expedition. Because of this, they are never actually able to put this agenda in a broader context, as is evident in the somewhat baffled tone both authors adopt. How, they marvel, can Kagan believe this? How can anyone believe such a blatantly political attempt to sew the Sicilian expedition to what Mendelsohn calls "a uniquely twenty-first-century project of preemptive war"?

In order to contextualize Kagan's argument about the Sicilian expedition, we must view this argument in light of those qualities that make his definitively not a " uniquely twenty first century" project, qualities that underlie the reason why neoconservatives believe *The History* reinforces their "instinctive beliefs" about foreign policy. The complex rhetorical power of Kagan's work lies not only in his counterfactual assertion that the Athenians could have won the Peloponnesian War, but also in the assumption that they bear no responsibility for creating the conditions that led to the war in the first place. In stark contrast to Thucydides, Kagan argues for a narrative of the events leading up to the war that insists that Athenian power did not grow between 445 and 435 B. C. E, and which casts the Athenians as guilelessly unaware of the way their greatness instilled fear in others (although he admits that they were "not without guilt" and that they could have behaved with "less arrogance and harshness toward Potidaea and Megara.")[73] Thus, behind the bluster over Sicily, behind the blithe dismissal of Melos, behind Kagan's claim that Americans have something to learn from the Athenians' harsh treatment of their generals, lies an assumption about Athenian/American imperial innocence and intention that exempts it, eternally, from the blame for causing wars to break out.[74] And as Zimmern's reading of Athens should make abundantly clear, such analyses are not without precedent in the long and convoluted trajectory of liberal imperial history.

We Sleeping Athenians

At the heart of Kagan's career-long aim to prove that Athens was not responsible for the outbreak of the Peloponnesian War lies a deep and abiding sense that the Athenian *polis* looked, for all intents and purposes, like us. For Kagan, ancient Athens was not only democratic, it was a liberal democracy in a familiar, modern sense insofar as it enabled and fostered individual freedom within the context of a civic community that took the equality between members seriously. In essence, like Zimmern, Kagan takes Pericles's Funeral Speech at face value, as a true reflection of fifth-century Athens. The Athenians, for Kagan, solved the puzzle that has plagued all other liberal democracies since: how to balance democracy and individuality, liberty and communal feeling, equality and merit. And while his analysis of Athens occasionally troubles this understanding of the *polis* by noting the presence of contention or quibbling factions within the Assembly, for the most part Kagan's presentation of Athens is of a polity whose overall identity—its very essence—serves as an enduring model for all time, or in Pericles's words, as "an education to Greece." Indeed, for Kagan, Periclean Athens achieved the status of liberal society at its most copacetic. Again, this was a polity that "reconciled the tension between liberty and equality by rejecting the imposition of equality by state control (as in Sparta)."[75] Rather, it "exalted the individual within the political community" and "limited the scope and power of the state, leaving enough space for individual freedom, privacy, and the human dignity of which they are a crucial part. It rejected the leveling principle pursued by both ancient Sparta and modern socialism which requires a suppression of those rights."[76] According to Kagan, Athens had solved liberalism's most persistent ideological knot (the tension between freedom and equality), and had done so without a centralized state. Thus, Pericles had every reason, in Kagan's analysis, to ask the audience listening to his Funeral Speech to "fix your eyes every day on the greatness of Athens as she really is" and "fall in love with her."[77]

Critics of Kagan's nostalgic vision of the Athenian *polis* have rightly noted, as does Saxonhouse, the way it flattens "the complexity of ancient democracy" so that "any theoretical significance is lost."[78] Additionally, even sympathetic readers like Orwin are made somewhat uncomfortable by the easy, ahistorical elision Kagan makes between ancient Greek and modern liberal democracy.[79] It is also, perhaps, not coincidental that while Kagan has always been sympathetic to Athenian democracy, he became even more effusive in his praise and deepened the intensity of his comparison with the publication of *Pericles of Athens and the Birth of Democracy* in 1991, right at the moment when the precipitous decline of the Soviet Union brought the Thucydidean Cold War puzzle to the fore with furious intensity. Again, if, for Cold Warriors like Kagan, liberal-democratic Athens was America and Thucydides said that Athens caused the war and eventually its own demise by behaving aggressively, how does one explain and justify the need for continued American military hegemony now that America's unipolar power looks less anti-Soviet and more blatantly imperial? During the Cold War, Kagan resolved this puzzle by fashioning and refashioning the two imbricated and complementary arguments discussed above: a) Thucydides was wrong and Athens did not behave like an expansionist empire, thereby causing the war; and b) Thucydides was wrong and Athenian democracy was not in decline during this period but, rather, had perfected a form of liberal democracy unparalleled in human history. The absence of the Soviet Union/Sparta as a credible threat after 1990 simply exacerbated Kagan's desire to emphasize, again and again, the liberal credentials of the last superpower standing.

Thus, the narrative thrust of Kagan's collective work on the Thirty Years Peace urges readers to reject the first half of Thucydides's famous contention regarding the cause of the war but to accept the second. The real cause of the war lay in the Corinthians' intransigence and the fact that the Spartans "allowed their war party to frighten them with unfounded alarms of Athenian aggression."[80] In other words, the war was caused not by the "growth of Athenian power," but rather by the entirely unfounded fear of the Spartans. In Kagan's view, Spartan fear was unjustified and without factual merit. Kagan's contentious observations in his 2003 book that Athens (America) ought to have behaved more aggressively in Sicily (Iraq) makes considerably more sense if we understand that, for Kagan, the polity that voted to slaughter the Melians and launch the Sicilian expedition was ultimately responsible only for being itself. Democratic, commercial polities like Athens and America evoke unjustified fear in others—Sparta, Russia, Iraq, China, India—by virtue of being liberal democracies with benign Panhellenic empires. As Kagan argued in reference to the British before World War I, some great powers are simply "content" and others plainly "dissatisfied," and there is no causal relationship between external circumstances and the state of the state's being.

Like Zimmern's understanding of the Greek Commonwealth, Kagan's reading of Athens as a liberal empire relies heavily on a form of historical (and rhetorical) displacement. In this sense, Kagan's methodological tic of making broad political generalizations about Athens from limited evidence (which has so annoyed his critics) has allowed him to fill the void left by the refusal of neoconservatives to understand America's current precarious predicament in light of the history of its foreign policy decisions. In other words, the historical plane of American foreign policy since World War II is crowded with evidence of military invasions, assassinations, wars, support for dictators, and the systematic underdevelopment of the former colonized world. The Thirty Years Peace, by contrast, suffers from the same paucity of sources and archeological information that plagues all of the "skeletal tradition" that is classical history; it is this absence of evidence that allows Kagan ample room to paint his picture of Athenian superiority and Athenian innocence with a wide, hagiographic brush. Kagan acknowledges that the lack of information on the period requires him to rely heavily on counterfactuals and speculation. In addition, he is quite open about the way he uses analogies from better-documented historical periods (particularly from European experiences in the First and Second World Wars) to fill the historical gaps in his narrative of the Peloponnesian War. As he notes in the Introduction to *The Outbreak of the Peloponnesian War*, "I have been much impressed by the illumination a close study of the origins of that war [World War One], so copiously documented, can provide for an understanding of the outbreak of the Peloponnesian War."[81] Thus, when looking for an explanation of why the Corinthians decided to capture Corcyra even though they knew the Athenians would most likely intervene, Kagan turns to the period following the Sarajevo assassination of 1914, when Germany urged Austria to attack Serbia. Just as Germany underestimated the willingness of the British to get involved in the conflict, so the Corinthians underestimated the Athenians.[82] Kagan's stated purpose in using this analogy is to help us understand the way "states" rarely behave with prudence. However, the underlying lesson here (which is difficult to miss) is that Athens in the fifth-century and Britain before the Great War are comparable because both were great democratic powers who, in the end, would not be pushed by the political machinations of tyrants, even when such machinations appeared not to affect them directly. In this twisted, temporal inversion, Kagan uses insights from the First World War to interpret the Peloponnesian War in order, in the long run, to reflect on contemporary American global power. Ironically then, like Zimmern, Kagan displaces his own liberal imperial polity onto Athens, and he does so through the lens of Zimmern's own historical moment.

This displacement of America onto Athens (often via Britain) lies at the heart of Donald Murray's claim that neoconservatives see their "instinctive beliefs" about foreign policy reflected in Thucydides's *History*. The underlying instinct about the world that neoconservatives share and that they find in the pages of *The History* is, Murray argues, a basic "moral clarity" in an "age which regards moral clarity as suspect," a sureness about America's role in the world at a time when "the world is adrift."[83] What is so astonishing about Murray's claim here is that, for centuries, scholars have read *The History* as anything *but* morally clear. From Hobbes to Cornford to Lebow, thoughtful people have grappled with Thucydides's work with fascination, and have made distinctly different arguments about what lessons we are meant to draw from its pages. Is this a book about imperial hubris? Is it a condemnation or celebration of democracy? Does it describe, as the realists insist, how people and states really act in the world, or is it a morality story, as the Cold Warriors argued, about the conflict between a free and unfree society? The only way to get moral clarity from Thucydides is to read him exclusively through Kagan's dream world of Athens in the years leading up to the war, before the Spartans without-and the "defeatists" within-brought the dream to an end.[84] This vision of Athens neatly squares the circle between democracy and empire in a way that adds an element of moral clarity to an otherwise morally ambiguous war and a morally ambiguous imperial past while, at the same time, assuring neoconservative readers that ancient Athens was then as America is now. In other words, the "instinctive beliefs" that neoconservatives find validated in Thucydides's work are actually Kagan's "instinctive beliefs" about what Athens was then and who we are now, and reflect his flattened, polished, terrifyingly clear portrait of a polity that now suffers not for acting aggressively, but simply for being more perfect than its neighbors.

It is out of this most fundamental of instincts that the rest of Kagan's foreign policy objectives tumble—objectives that when read back onto the Sicilian expedition strike Norton and Mendelsohn as almost obscene. By Kagan's lights, the sad irony of international politics for great democratic powers like Athens and America is that the very liberal qualities that make them great in the first place, and inspire fear in "dissatisfied" states like Sparta and the Soviet Union, also make them less prepared to fight wars (as, he argues, was ultimately true for Pericles) and more likely to employ "moderate foreign policies aimed at deterrence" rather than make the sacrifices that preemptive invasions require.[85] Liberal democracies value open debate, open debate breeds self-doubt, and self-doubt can lead to widespread defeatism, or a movement to direct resources away from military preparedness and toward education and welfare. The problem with revisionist historians such as Thucydides, argues Kagan, is that they confuse the side effects of being a great liberal democracy with the cause of the war. Thus, he grouses in his positive 1999 review of Niall Ferguson's book on the First World War, *The Pity of War*:

> Democratic, commercial nations, like Britain then and the United States today, typically resist the facing of reality for as long as they can—until, at last, they are driven to fight wars they have failed to deter and find costly and difficult to win. Then, if they survive, they can count on revisionist historians to explain how they need never have fought at all, if only they had been more tolerant and understanding.[86]

Ultimately for Kagan, because they induce fear in other states, because of their tendency toward deterrence rather than aggression, and because their citizens often disagree about the efficacy of military spending, liberal democracies sow the seeds of their own demise.

It is at this point that Kagan's love for liberal democracy, the temporal layering of his narrative, and his political agenda come into full-blown conflict. Kagan's readings of the Peloponnesian War, the First and Second World Wars, and America's War on Terror insist that "democratic, commercial nations" are not responsible for creating the global economic and political conditions that render the world so dangerous and, in Murray's words, "adrift." In this sense, no one is to blame for our current condition. But, at the same time, "democratic, commercial nations" are also supposed to be, by Kagan's lights, particularly self-aware. Indeed, in those moments when he is adamantly defending the "Western tradition," Kagan argues that it is precisely this ability to engage in free debate about issues of major importance to the polity, and then critically reflect on its future direction, which make Western civilization great. In this spirit, the first critical theme he highlights in the Introduction to the 2007 edition of *The Western Heritage* is the "capacity of Western civilization from the time of the Greeks to the present to transform itself through self-criticism."[87] But, given this quality, how do we explain the failure of so many people—in the past and in the present—to see the immediacy of the danger posed by the way their liberal democracy generates jealousy in other societies? How do self-critical, self-aware polities miss issues of such magnitude?

Kagan has, occasionally, sought answers to these questions in modern history but, when he has done so, he is confronted with the very quality of modern history that draws him to it as a supplement for antiquity in the first place: the fact that it has been "so copiously documented." Thus, while revisionist historians may, by Kagan's lights, in their temerity have gotten the reasons for the First and Second World Wars all wrong, they have largely not done so through speculation and counterfactual analysis (Niall Ferguson being one of the obvious exceptions), but rather through close examination of the same historical records and multiplicity of opinions and critiques about Britain's role in the war and the world to which Kagan himself has access. In comparison to the nearly blank slate that is Periclean Athens, opinions on the causes of the two major wars of the twentieth-century stand cheek to jowl on the academic landscape, rendering it much more difficult to paint the picture that Kagan has in his mind's eye.

Because of this, Kagan's few attempts to look to Britain directly as an analogy for contemporary America—rather than looking through Britain to better understand Athens in order to better understand America—have relied heavily upon rhetorical strategies that empty that analogy of historical content by wiping the historical slate clean, so that Kagan can write upon it more effectively. A particularly potent example of this strategy in action is Kagan's decision to title his 2000 book on Britain and America *While America Sleeps: Self Delusion, Military Weakness, and the Threat to Peace Today*, and to use the metaphors of sleeping and waking to frame the work's central argument. Kagan and his son Frederick wrote the book with the intention of using Britain's experience during the interwar era as a warning to Americans today; the title is an homage to Winston Churchill's 1938 collection of speeches entitled *While England Slept* and John Kennedy's published thesis, *Why England Slept*. The central argument of both of these earlier books, according to the Kagans, was that England's narcoleptic unwillingness to "face realities" in the 1930s prevented it from making an assault on Germany earlier, which could have prevented, or shortened, the war. The Kagans make a similar suggestion about America today, noting in their concluding section (entitled, "America, Wake Up!") that warnings that "England was sleeping came too late to do any good. We hope that this one comes in time. America must wake up, look realistically to its position in the world and to its defenses. It must strengthen its alliances by demonstrating its willingness to bear its inescapable responsibilities."[88]

The metaphors of sleeping and waking serve a similar purpose for the Kagans as they did for Churchill and Kennedy. On the one hand, the trope of sleep suggests that the citizens of the great, democratic, imperial state (Britain then, America now) have simply not been paying proper attention to the realities of the world, or that they have made errors in judgment because they were not fully alert. But, on the other hand, in the context of both states' imperial pasts, sleep implies a kind of innocence, a blissful unawareness that one's actions have consequences. In this sense, Britain then and America now are populated with liberally minded citizens, blithely bumbling into the world in support of free trade, the expansion of markets, and the taming of uncharted wilderness. Sleeping suggests that these actions were spontaneous, never thought through, never explicitly committed to the bigger project, never originating (like the German or Japanese Empires) in a fevered commitment to a fatherland. Sleeping works particularly well as a metaphor in this sense because, as Halbwachs suggests, "the person who sleeps finds himself during a certain period of time in a state of isolation which resembles, at least partially, the state in which he would live if he were in contact with no society."[89] For Halbwachs, sleep thus provides the perfect example of those instances when an individual has no need for collective memory. But the Kagans' use of sleep is more complex than this. Not only does it seem to insist that America now and Britain then are populated by individuals making decisions locked in their own mental worlds, it also suggests, perversely, that they were/are making these decisions collectively. Sleeping implies that while citizens of democratic, commercial nations may have simply been going about their own business, these individuals were going about it together, that everyone was napping at the same time and that this—this collective sleep—in effect, is what makes them a people in the first place.

But the trope of sleeping serves another rhetorical purpose for the Kagans: it not only implies a lack of intention and a common endeavor, it also absolutely requires that America wake up before Britain did, that it come to grips with its hegemonic status and assert its leadership more forcefully in the world before it is too late. In both the British and American examples, waking up also suggests a break with the innocence of the past and a willingness to acknowledge that some peoples are simply intractably committed to the destruction of our liberal state out of sheer, jealous, ill will. Waking thus presses up against the possibility of pausing for a moment to reflect on the imperial state's past. Rather, it implies immediacy, a call to action, and a clear sense that a price must be paid for stopping to think after waking up, that decisions must be made before one's feet even hit the ground. By the Kagans' lights, any kind of committed reflection on what the American state might have done in the recent or remote past to attract the ire of the rest of the world amounts to dithering, to revisionist history aimed at making us all feel bad about who are. Kagan thus wants America to express its "willingness to bear its inescapable responsibilities" but sneers at the possibility that "bearing" such responsibilities could entail "taking" responsibility.

Ironically, in this critical sense, sleeping and waking, as rhetorical devices, also resist precisely the kind of political life that Kagan claims to find so moving about democratic, commercial nations and, in particular, that he finds in fifth-century Athens, which he insistently evokes as not only the "first and sharpest break" with the unthinking authority worship of all previous societies, but also as the most enduring source of "inspiration and instruction" for contemporary democracies.[90] Thus, Socrates famously claimed in *The Apology* that if the Athenians were to strike him dead "then you could sleep on for the rest of your days unless the god, in his care for you, sends you some one else."[91] Generations of scholars, most notably Leo Strauss, have interpreted Socrates's chiding of the

Athenians in this moment as a reflection of his broader critique of democracy, his sense that the Athenians were motivated by an unthinking reliance on tradition, and that it was his job, as gadfly, as "gift of the god to the city," to wake them from their somnolent torpor.[92] But Kagan defiantly does not want to believe that fifth-century Athens was a place where people fell asleep en masse. By contrast, he finds something immensely appealing in what he sees as the roil and ruckus of a vibrant and alert Athenian world. For Kagan, Athenian society was governed not by the "guided and controlled movement that Socrates sought," but rather, by a political ethic that did not seek to impose a "single form of life upon the people from on high" and which allowed for all the "unpredictability" that accompanied politics in a free democratic city.[93] Socrates himself, Kagan argues, understood this about Athens. While he "surely rejected democracy as a good form of government," Kagan argued in a 1988 letter to *Commentary*, Socrates "was not its fanatical enemy who would die, even in part, as 'a political ploy' against it. He lived under its laws for seventy years and never left Athenian territory except to fight bravely in defense of his democratic homeland."[94] In other words, Socrates understood, according to Kagan, that the Athenian commitment to reasoned self-reflection and critique made him the gadfly that he was. Athenian political culture encouraged the efflorescence of men like Socrates and it demanded, according to Kagan, that its citizens abandon "the use of faith, poetry and intuition" and rely instead on their reason. "The Greeks," he argued, "exposed everything they perceived—natural, human, and divine—to the searching examination of the logos."[95] They were thus, according to Kagan, always awake.

The problem here is that, in his own historical moment, Kagan loathes both sustained critique of American foreign policy and the multiple gadflies who engage in it, people he characterizes as doubters and defeatists. The "fashionable assaults on patriotism" issuing from the halls of the American academy, Kagan argues, are not thoughtful reflections, they are "failures of character." "They are made by privileged individuals who enjoy the full benefits offered by the country they deride and detest—its opportunities, its freedom, its riches—but," Kagan opines, "who lack the basic decency to pay their country the allegiance and respect that honor demands."[96] What Kagan seems to demand of contemporary Americans, therefore, is precisely the kind of reliance on faith and intuition that he insists the Greeks, in their wisdom, abandoned. We moderns, by contrast, are to take it at face value that ours is a polity worth dying for.

In the end, it seems that what Kagan wants most of all is the veneer of rational self-reflection without any of the self-doubt or messy internal critique that such self-reflection generates. What is most important to Kagan is that we understand ourselves to be the kind of polity that "exposes everything...to the searching examination of logos" without actually doing so, to look like a society always under the endless trial of self-justification without actually exposing the polity to the rigors of critique. In this same vein, in *While America Sleeps, On the Origins of War*, and in countless op-eds and interviews written over the years, Kagan makes it clear that what he wants most of all from his students, readers, and the American public more generally is to understand the importance of looking to history for instruction and guidance in making difficult foreign policy decisions. At the same time, Kagan wants the lesson of history to always be the same: that "countries like Great Britain, when they were the number one liberal state in the world, and the United States" generate ire in less-satisfied states just by being who they are, and that the Spartans of the world will always step in to make trouble if these liberal states give in to what comes most naturally to them—critique, debate, and deterrence.[97]

The beauty of Kagan's fifth-century Athens as an analogy—in comparison to Britain before and during the World Wars—is that its remoteness allows it to do the rhetorical work that holds together these conflicting strands of thought. The fact that we know far less about Athens than we do about twentieth-century Britain means that Kagan can fill up his rhetorical vessel with almost whatever he wants, both in terms of descriptions and lessons, and then claim that, across time, we are like them and they are like us. If we understand America as Athens, we have no need to reflect on (much less apologize for) our state's imperial past, because we simply already are the kind of polity that engages in widespread, critical reflection. In this way, Kagan's Athens is a palimpsest on which critique and patriotic loyalty, imperial expansion and imperial innocence, the past and the present, are layered so they appear to be one single expression of democratic freedom parading through history. It is this basic circularity, this hermetically sealed vision of two polities joined at the hip across time—the ancient answering all the questions for the modern—that lies at the core of neoconservative "instinctive beliefs" about what makes Thucydides's *History* a "possession for all time."

Conclusion

In some ways, the fact that Kagan and Zimmern would end up producing such similar accounts of Athens and Thucydides is surprising, given that it is not at all clear that Kagan has ever read Zimmern. Indeed, Kagan's one mention of Zimmern appears in the final pages of *Pericles of Athens*, where he refers to him simply as a "distinguished British classical scholar" before approvingly quoting from the preface to the 1915 edition of *The Greek Commonwealth*. Like Zimmern, Kagan agrees, "Greek ideas and Greek inspiration can help us today, not only in facing the duties of the moment, but in the work of deepening and extending the range and the meaning of Democracy and Citizenship."[98] But Kagan pulls this quotation not from *The Greek Commonwealth* itself but from Frank Turner's chapter on Zimmern in *The Greek Heritage in Victorian Britain*. Additionally, as we have seen, Zimmern was a New Liberal, a civil servant, and a vocal supporter of the emerging welfare state in England, and in his work on both the Greek and the British Commonwealth we can see the growing interest in liberal internationalism that would eventually make him one of England's most undaunted champions first of the League of Nations, and then the United Nations. Kagan, by contrast, while libertarian in some of his sensibilities about social policy, has consistently advocated for a neo-conservative vision of the state that wants to limit its capacity domestically while expanding military spending. Kagan's foreign policy vision is also far more hawkish and cynical than Zimmern's, and his few mentions of either the League of Nations or the United Nations are dismissive at best and derisive at worst.

On the other hand, the similarities between Kagan's and Zimmern's readings of Athens are hardly surprising at all, given that both men supported a vision of liberal imperialism that was fundamentally at odds with itself. In this sense, displacing the modern American polity and the British Empire (and their foreign policy entanglements) onto Athens allows Kagan and Zimmern to resolve two deeply contradictory views of the liberal imperial polity. On the one hand, it enables them to explain how a democratic polity could be both imperialist and bear no responsibility for any of the ire of its neighbors. On the other hand, it gives them the descriptive language to imagine the liberal democratic *polis* in essential terms, as always being just what it is and just who we are—a society engaged in the trials of internal critique—even when the possibilities for debate and critique have been all but foreclosed. Those who question whether or not the liberal state's imperial policies are in its best interest, or those who urge us, in Kagan's words, toward "a greater willingness to understand the point of view of nations late in coming to power on the world scene" are as inscrutable to Kagan and Zimmern as they were to Pericles. Athens is, as Pericles intoned, a model to others, and from these others we have nothing to learn. In the end, the best thing we can do for ourselves and the world is to fix our eyes on Athens/Britain/America in all her greatness, "as she really is," and fall in love with her, all over again.

PART TWO

METANARRATIVE
STRATEGIES

3

The Round Table's Story of Commonwealth

In 1916, after reading Lionel Curtis's *The Commonwealth of Nations*, imperial critic John Hobson wrote Alfred Zimmern and explained that he found the entire book marred throughout by the "assumption that Britain had developed a special genius for government, and that what Lowell called 'the Anglo Saxon idea' was of universal validity; this may be true, but in the present stage of human affairs it ranks formally with the claim of Prussianism."[1] In this single sentence, Hobson neatly summarized both everything Curtis and the pro-imperial organization he led, the Round Table, hoped to achieve with the publication of *The Commonwealth of Nations*, and the one thing they hoped most to avoid. In other words, central to Curtis and the Round Table's imperial vision was a fundamental belief that the British *did* have a "special genius for government" and that Anglo-Saxon culture *was* of universal validity. At the same time, they insisted upon what Curtis referred to as the "profound antagonism" between the British and German Empires.[2] British imperialism was not really about imperialism at all: it was about the expansion of liberty. German imperialism, on the other hand, was simply imperialist.

But while Germany loomed large in the minds of the Round Table in the years leading up to and during World War I, it was hardly the only anxiety they associated with the complex bundle of issues often referred to simply as the "imperial problem." The simultaneous rise of Russia, Japan, and America as world powers highlighted, for the Round Table, how much the British military was overextended and its economic ascendency endangered. Rebellion within the dependencies and the growth of nationalist movements throughout the Empire suggested surging levels of dissatisfaction with imperial rule—dissatisfaction often framed in the very language of liberal freedom that the Empire claimed to espouse. Finally, the self-governing dominions were moving in an increasingly national (rather than Empire-centered) direction and, as a result, were bearing few of the financial costs of imperial defense. Part think tank, part research group, part secret social club, and part lobbying outfit, the Round Table was created in 1909 to address these and other issues associated with an Empire that resembled, in Andrea Bosco's and Alex May's words, "the sun at noon," perched at "the moment of its greatest radiance but also the beginning of its rapid and inexorable decline."[3] Led by the efforts of the group's General Secretary, Lionel Curtis (also known as "the prophet" by fellow members), the Round Table devoted much of its activity in the years leading up to the war to a process of fact-finding, communal and individual research, multiple meetings, and the creation of countless drafts for review, ultimately culminating in the private circulation of *The Project of a Commonwealth* in 1915 and the publication of the same text (rechristened *The Commonwealth of Nations*) a year later.[4] At 706 pages, *The Commonwealth of Nations* was meant to lay out, in baroque detail, the theory and historical context behind the Round Table's political plan for strengthening and restructuring the British Empire in the twentieth-century.

The Round Table was hardly alone during this period in expressing grave concern over the future of the Empire. Other worried, pro-imperial organizations devoted to discovering a solution to Britain's "imperial problem" in the period between 1900 and 1914 included the Royal Colonial Institute, the British Empire League, and the Society of Comparative Legislation, as well as a number of "cross party discussion groups" such as the Rainbow Circle and the Coefficients, whose members devoted themselves to drawing out connections between a domestic, liberal agenda and the project of imperialism.[5] The Round Table was also not alone in its celebration of Anglo-Saxon uniqueness. As Peter Mandler notes in *The English National Character*, the years leading up to World War I were like "the summer of 1848 all over again" in the sense that many people in Britain were turning away in disgust from the perceived corruption of Continental politics and back toward a nostalgic appreciation of all that was upright, provincial, and unique about Englishness. According to Mandler, this "newly defensive sense of uniqueness," was significantly "different from the expansive, assertive, sense of the Victorians" and suggested "a retreat not only from 'world civilization' but also from the civilization of the Empire."[6]

What made the Round Table somewhat unique among both pro-imperial and pro-English groups at the time was its attempt to combine Englishness and imperialism, to "refashion empire," in Mandler's words, not as a project "of British power but of British culture, a community rather than an empire."[7] But while Mandler is correct in his observation that one of the primary goals of the Round Table was to establish the cultural uniqueness of the British Empire, this goal also went hand in hand with what he identifies as a more Victorian "expansiveness," a sense that, in Hobson's words, " 'the Anglo Saxon idea' was of universal validity." The goal of the Round Table in *The Commonwealth of Nations* was to demonstrate not only the cultural uniqueness of the British Commonwealth but also to prove that this uniqueness was universally applicable and that it embodied the movement of history toward something that looked like "world civilization." Nearly thirty years after writing *The Commonwealth of Nations,* Curtis would recall his approach to the Commonwealth thus:

> I developed the theme that while the Greeks had achieved the city commonwealth, England had made an immense advance in achieving a national commonwealth; but this was by no means the end of the process of development. The next step in the history of mankind must be the creation of an international commonwealth.[8]

In this narrative, the British Empire/Commonwealth was both unique and the vehicle for a greater idea as it worked its way toward world historical ends.

This chapter looks closely at the complicated rendering of commonwealth at the heart of the Round Table's publications during the period leading up to and during the Great War. It does this by interrogating the political project that shaped the Round Table's approach to empire and the metahistorical narrative Curtis, Philip Kerr, and the other members of the Round Table developed to speak to the complicated and contradictory desires and goals that made this project so fraught. These desires and goals tended to cluster around the group's feeling that, unlike Germany, the British Empire was liberal and democratic at its core even when it did not appear to be so, even when it appeared to look (in Hobson's sense) "Prussian." With Zimmern and Kagan, the Round Table responded to this complicated set of political criteria by constructing an historical narrative that consistently drew the reader's attention away from the Empire's acts of imperializing (which might remind people of German aggression) and back toward the liberal, democratic character and nature of the Empire itself—back toward "who we are." They did this through two interrelated rhetorical strategies: first, they rechristened the Empire as the "British Commonwealth," and spent a considerable amount of time theorizing the term. Second, they situated this idea of commonwealth in history in a way that naturalized the Empire's origins, emphasized its unique Anglo-Saxon culture, explained its universal relevance, justified the continued exclusion of nonwhite subjects from political representation, and rendered the Empire the logical solution to its own misdeeds.

The Round Table was arguably the most powerful and long lasting of the pro-imperial organizations formed in Britain during this era. Not only is its journal published to this day, its members would play a key role in formulating Prime Minister David Lloyd George's war policy and developing the response of the British government to the founding of the League of Nations. Shortly after the war, these same members formed the Royal Institute for International Affairs (Chatham House) and played a not-insignificant role in the creation, at the same time, of the Council on Foreign Relations in America. Both of these organizations would have a considerable impact on the foreign policies of the two countries for the next half a century and provide, in Inderjeet Parmeer's words, "critical forums for the more respectable 'liberal' elements within the US and the UK to map out a new world order."[9] Because of this influence, scholars have paid considerable attention to the logistics of the group's intellectual foundations.[10] However, because the actual policy proposals inherent in the commonwealth project—primarily the creation of an imperial parliament that would redistribute the political, financial, and military burden of the Empire among the self-governing dominions—were never realized, these same scholars have tended to pay scant attention to the actual content of the *Commonwealth* writings.

By contrast, I argue in this chapter that even though the specifics of the group's approach to commonwealth were never instantiated in imperial policy, *The Commonwealth of Nations* deserves close attention because the political theory and elaborate historical narrative of empire developed therein helped to lay the ideological groundwork for an approach to world order in which formal imperialism could effectively masquerade as internationalism. During the interwar period and well into the 1960s, this vision of world organization—with its particular "mechanisms of exclusion" (to use Anthony Anghie's phrase)— was most apparent in the League of Nations' Mandate System and the United Nations' Trusteeship Council, both of which officially extended formal imperialism in the name of internationalism long after processes of decolonization had been set in motion.[11] These same basic impulses live on in the official and unofficial discourses of international cooperation and global governance in which deep economic and political inequalities between the Global North and South are masked through a language of formal equality. The *Commonwealth* writings should be approached, I argue, as one of the first and most elaborate expressions of an imperialism that cannot say its name, an imperialism recast to look tolerant, liberal, multicultural, pacific, and universal while actually remaining aggressive, partial, and exclusive. The Round Table vision of the world strategically emptied imperial history of its uncomfortable content, insisted that Anglo-Saxon culture was always both particular and universal, divorced democratic participation from democracy, and rendered imperialism as the eternal answer to the questions generated by empire.

This chapter begins by looking more closely at the historical context that framed the Round Table's approach to Commonwealth, paying particular attention to the way the group responded to the nagging specter of Prussianism, the increase in imperial criticism at home and colonial nationalism abroad, and the strategic need to avoid racial language. The second section of the chapter examines how the word "empire" had, by this period, developed, in Rosebery's words, a "disagreeable association," and then focuses on the Round Table's development of the "idea of commonwealth" in response to this negative association.[12] The chapter moves on to examine how Curtis located this notion of commonwealth in a complicated metahistorical narrative that linked ancient Athens to the Saxons and then to the British Commonwealth in a fashion that both occluded and justified acts of illiberality, violence, and exclusion in the British imperial past, reversed the causal relation between the problem of empire and its imperial solution, and transformed the notion of democratic citizenship into a theory of formal submission. Finally, the chapter concludes by looking at how the Round Table's commonwealth vision provided an ideological template for recasting twentieth-century imperialism as benevolent internationalism, thus formally extending imperial power relations into an era that triumphantly declared the age of empire dead.

An Imperial Problem

Described by Richard Higgott and Diane Stone as "something of a forerunner to the modern think tank," the Round Table was founded in Britain in 1909, emerging out of the transplanted remains of Lord Milner's "kindergarten," the group of young Oxford graduates he had recruited to join him in South Africa when he served there as High Commissioner after the Boer War.[13] Educated largely in the idealist, New Liberal and neo-Hegelian tradition of New College and Balliol, the "kindergarten" (including Lionel Curtis and Robert Henry Brand) returned to England brimming with ideas about the future of the Empire and with the desire to create an organization to address these ideas. Shortly thereafter, they were joined by Phillip Kerr and Dougal Malcolm and formed an organization they christened the Round Table, whose activities were funded throughout its existence by significant contributions from the Rhodes Trust.[14] Other Oxford graduates and Milner enthusiasts (most notably, Edward Grigg, Ramsey Muir, and Alfred Zimmern) were drawn early on to the group, whose express purpose was to provide "a medium of mutual information on Imperial affairs."[15] In 1910, Curtis and Kerr traveled extensively to Canada, Australia, New Zealand, and South Africa to recruit followers to Round Table affiliate groups in the dominions and, upon returning to England, threw themselves into the project of further developing, articulating, and consolidating the group's overall approach to the "imperial problem." Kerr did this primarily by dedicating himself to the publication and administration of the group's in-house journal, *The Round Table*, while Curtis began researching and writing what he referred to gravely as the "fundamental report upon which everything depends" and the "basis of the whole movement," a text meant to reflect and encapsulate the Round Table's *raison d'être*.[16] As Arthur Steel-Maitland once joked, "the issue of this book is something so momentous that it is debated as though the whole world were hanging on it."[17] This was an organization that took itself very seriously.

The process by which the group developed the texts that John Kendle refers to as the "closest the movement came to defining its aims" was labor intensive, time consuming, and often quite secretive.[18] Curtis would write and then cir-culate drafts (sometimes referred to as "eggs") for discussion among a limited number of Round Table members (described in the introductory note to the first internally circulated memo as a "few friends"), who would then make com-ments on these drafts, which would then become lengthy memoranda that were distributed for comment to Round Table societies throughout Britain, New Zealand, Canada, and South Africa, before being returned to London for further discussion among the core group.[19] Despite extensive comments from Round Table affiliate members throughout the Empire, it was Curtis, Kerr, and their immediate circle (known as the "London group") that shaped the direction of the Round Table's major publications during this period, and Curtis's name that finally appeared as sole author of all three *Commonwealth* publications.[20] Thus, whatever the Society's proclamations to the contrary, these publications bore the distinct imprint of Curtis, the London group, and the experience of Oxford and Milnerian New Liberalism that most of them shared.

At the heart of the Round Table's concerns about "imperial affairs" was their general, typically Edwardian conviction that the rise of Germany, the US, and Russia as competing imperial powers, the increase of unrest in the colonies and the rise of anticolonial nationalism, and the movement of the dominions toward independence, threatened the Empire's coherence as an overburdened metro-pole struggled to finance the defense of an increasingly stressed edifice. The set of questions that preoccupied the Round Tablers focused on how the future Empire might be recast to address these concerns. What was the Empire to look like in the coming century? What would be the relationship of the British state, the dominions, and the dependencies to each other? How was imperial foreign policy to be developed and the military maintained? How was it to be financed? Never did they speculate about the legitimacy or necessity of the Empire itself; that the Empire was a positive force in the world and that its demise would wreck civilization was never questioned. Rather, in Curtis's words, the "kindergarten" had "imbibed two leading ideas" from Milner while in South Africa. "He made us feel," noted Curtis in a 1931 letter, "that the greatest contribution we could make to the world at large was to maintain the British Empire and develop it on the right lines. The other was that we could only discover the right lines of devel-opment by continuous study."[21]

On a policy level, the Round Table's suggestions for reforming the Empire did not differ significantly from the Federationists of a generation earlier. With Seeley, they also envisioned the British Commonwealth as a single, globe-spanning state in which the self-governing dominions played an important role, departing from the Federationists only in their call for the creation of an imperial parliament which would meet regularly to discuss issues of foreign policy and to determine the "taxable capacity of each member state."[22] The basic shape of this approach was influenced by Milner's turn-of-the-century understanding of the need to further consolidate the Empire as an "organic union." As discussed in Chapter One, Milner was the predominant influence on a generation of young Oxford imperialists, and all of the Round Table's founders, in Kendle's words, drank "deeply at Milner's ideological well."[23] Like Milner, they tended to stress the liberal, voluntary character of the Empire; were uncomfortable with the word "Empire" itself; and often couched their expressions of "organic union" in distinctly spiritual terms.[24]

For Milner, the nature of this spiritual bond was rooted in a basic race patriotism and in a faith in the liberal, freedom-loving attributes of Anglo-Saxons throughout the colonies—a view that ultimately led him to approach the nonwhite dependencies as, in Richard Symonds's words, "a temporary excrescence."[25] In other words, despite, or perhaps because of, his time in Egypt and South Africa during moments of nationalist uprising and racial violence, Milner's vision for the Empire of the future favored a union of self-governing, white Anglo-Saxon states over retention of the nonwhite dependencies, a vision that reflected the thinking of the imperial Federationists of his generation. Seeley, for instance, suggested in *The Expansion of England* that the "great burden which is imposed by India on foreign policy" would someday become too much for a consolidated "Greater Britain" to bear.[26] The majority of the time, however, both Milner and Seeley dealt with the disconnect between their theory of a unified Anglo-Saxon "Greater Britain" and the continuing occupation of India and the other dependencies by simply omitting them altogether from their discussions of "organic union."[27]

By 1910, Milner's disciples clearly felt that they could no longer avoid the question of India and the entire issue of the relationship of the dependencies to the Empire and, as a result, they developed a slightly different attitude toward race (and toward the nature of the spiritual bond that united the Empire) from that of the Federationists that preceded them. Despite the fact that, as Paul Rich notes, they spent a considerable amount of time in South Africa crafting a plan to maintain racial distinctions between a newly unified white population and the majority Africans, Round Tablers tended not to be as committed to dogmatic racial patriotism as Milner, perhaps because racial attitudes (particularly among liberals) in the England they returned to in 1909 had changed somewhat as a result of the Boer War and the rise of racial segregation in both the American South and the newly unified South Africa.[28] More importantly, liberal supporters of empire were increasingly aware during this period that they had to distinguish British imperialism from its racialized, German counterpart. Curtis, Kerr, and other Round Table members thus made a conscious effort to identify Germany with racial intolerance and Britain with an open-minded attitude toward what Kerr described in 1910 as "racial individuality" and a desire to give "liberty to racial characteristics."[29] With some notable and vocal exceptions, most of the key Round Table activists of this period supported Kerr's understanding of what Rich has referred to as a "blunted form of multi-racialism."[30]

Unlike Milner and Seeley, the Round Tablers were also not so sanguine about the economic loss of Britain's nonwhite dependencies, particularly India, without whom, according to Kerr, "we sink to the level of a trade competitor with Germany and the United States."[31] Marxist economic theorists have long observed that India's economic significance during this period was not confined to the mere production of raw materials and the creation of investment opportunities and markets. Rather, as Marcello de Cecco argues, between the years 1890 and 1914, India played "the role of a protagonist of the international settlement system: her trade surplus with the rest of the world and her trade deficit with England allowed the latter to square her international settlements on current account."[32] In essence, India generated the economic resources that allowed Britain to maintain itself during this period as the hegemonic monetary and financial power in the world. What Seeley and Milner had either ignored or imagined as too burdensome or as mere "excrescence," the Round Table saw as essential to the future survival (and continuing superiority) of the Empire.[33] Thus, while fifty years later Enoch Powell would accuse the Round Table of not understanding that the British Empire was "overwhelmingly an empire of India," it is clear from reading their memoranda, correspondences, and writings before the war that they were acutely aware that India was key to the future of British power.[34]

At the same time, however, the most influential Round Table members were also troubled by anticolonial nationalism in India and the dissatisfaction expressed by educated Indian elites at the slow pace of imperial reform. If, as Kerr in particular argued, Indians were to be wholly excluded from representation in the proposed imperial parliament, they would interpret such exclusion as a form of racial prejudice. Summarizing Kerr's position nearly fifty years later, S. R. Mehrotra noted, somewhat tongue-in-cheekily, that this assumption of racial prejudice would "wound their [the Indians'] *amour proper* and shake their faith in the good intentions of Britain... they will invoke the solemn pledges of equal rights and privileges repeatedly given to them in the past. Their demand will be supported by liberal opinion at home."[35] Add to this the fact that, as

Round Table members would almost obsessively observe, Indians comprised over three-quarters of the entire British imperial population, and the question of India's representation in the "imperial union" simply could not be ignored.[36] In Zimmern's words, "one cannot nowadays have a political philosophy, as earlier thinkers did, which excludes the problem of India and other 'dependencies' from consideration."[37] Whatever course of action the Round Table ultimately decided upon, its key movers and shakers believed, in the years leading up to World War I, that Indian intellectuals and activists, and their supporters in Britain, had to be mollified and the issue of Indian representation in the proposed imperial parliament at least entertained.

To complicate the picture further, the majority of Round Table members who supported some kind of Indian representation in an imperial parliament were, at the end of the day, no less racist than Milner. Curtis and Kerr's writings before, during, and after the war are peppered with references to "child," "dependent," "subject," and "less developed" races. While Curtis and Kerr just assumed that black Africans required autocratic European governance in perpetuity because of their complete lack of civilization, they also maintained that "in India and even in Egypt," nonwhite subjects demonstrated a loud and lingering "incapacity" to secure civilized governance for themselves.[38] In addition, Round Tablers were also extremely worried about the looming question of population growth. From their multiple graphic representations of both the global and imperial population by race that appear from their earliest memoranda and throughout the *Commonwealth* publications, one gets a sense of the Round Table's almost palpable fear that both white Anglo-Saxon imperial subjects and white populations more generally were on the decline.[39] Observing the "crisis" of Indian labor in South Africa during the years leading up to Gandhi's organization of mass protests, Curtis argued in a 1907 letter to Kerr that "in the coming centuries the greatest reservoir of Indian races will be opened and allowed to deluge the whole of the Im[...] inions and submerge the white community."[40] Nearly [...] still arguing that this issue of population and internal [...] problem for the Empire because during "the period [...] was absorbing multitudes of Asiatics and Africans" [...] seeing an "increase of its ruling race," but instead, [...] rgely diverted to the territories it had lost," namely

In sum, this generation of Oxford liberals sympathetic to Milner's vision was caught between a rock and a hard place. The position of India in the Empire and the sheer vastness of its population convinced them, in Duncan Bell's words, of "the practical impossibility of permanently disenfranchising the majority of the imperial population."[42] At the same time, their racism and their fear of nonwhite ascendency compelled them to deny the dependencies equal status in their developing notion of an "organic union" organized around a democratic, imperial parliament. Simultaneously, their anti-Germanism forbade them from expressing this denial of equal status on the grounds of racial or cultural superiority. Finally, in light of their concern about the way their plans would be received by Indians should they feel they were being denied the liberal rights they had so long been promised, even a nineteenth-century "leading strings" approach to imperial independence (one that promised autonomy somewhere down the line) appeared to be no longer possible in its uncomplicated form—as sovereignty permanently forestalled. Rather, there had to be something more to the Round Table's logic, something that could both include India in the notion of "organic whole" in the present while still excluding its wholesale participation in governance for the foreseeable future. Round Tablers were thus forced to come up with a theory of organic union that imagined its centripetal force—its "spiritual life" in Milner's terms, it's "actuating principle" as Curtis called it—in terms of something else, something less German-sounding than "race," something that both gestured toward universal liberal notions of equality and autonomy while practically denying these rights to most people.[43]

As Oxford New Liberals sympathetic to idealist state theory, the Round Tablers were faced with yet another rhetorical hurdle as they struggled to articulate the group's vision. Members of the London Group in particular gravitated toward imagining imperial union through the lenses of T.H. Green's account of the state as a coherent, universal, and democratic community, where the linkages of mutual duty and affection bound citizens to one another. From their various comments on the early memoranda, it is clear that Round Tablers hoped that once imperial citizens understood the relationship between duty, freedom, and statehood more correctly, their sense of loyalty to the imperial state would then trump all other political attachments and pull scattered imperial populations toward a moralized colonial center.[44] At the same time, the Round Tablers were well aware that, unlike Green and an earlier generation of Oxford theorists, they were articulating their centripetal, duty-bound vision of imperial statehood in a political context rife with charges of "Prussianism." While their understanding of Germany as an aggressive, nationalistic state bent on racial domination through imperial expansion is obvious in their publications from 1910 onward, the Round Table's desire to avoid these charges became almost histrionic during the summer of 1914.[45] Hobson's claim that Curtis's state theory was "indistinguishable from Prussianism" illustrated precisely the kinds of accusations they were hoping to avoid.[46] Thus, as with most idealist, state-oriented, vaguely Prussianist-sounding theories in the years leading up to 1914, the Round Table's vision required clear Angloification. One of the group's main goals, argued Grigg in 1914, was to clarify for readers why this particular rendition of the Empire should be treated as a "distinctive *English* method of government."[47]

From the Round Table's earliest document for circulation, 1910's "Green Memorandum" (also referred to as the "original egg") and throughout the pages of *The Round Table's* first volume, Curtis, Kerr, and others were engaged in a fierce rhetorical battle to distinguish the British idea of imperial statehood from that of the German, insisting on what they identified as a "profound antagonism between the two systems."[48] Central to this assertion was the Round Table's conviction that the German state was intensely totalizing while the British state had been, and remained, predicated on a commitment to individual liberty. Over the centuries, the difference in these "national characteristics," in Kerr's words, resulted in two very different approaches to empire on the part of the Germans and the British. On one side, argued Curtis, the German Empire had been consolidated through "forcible conquest and annexation" and the procurement of treaties which were "rendered possible only by a previous display of force."[49] On the other side, Kerr described an organically evolved British Empire that had developed through the "unconscious working" of the "intense spirit of individualism" that ran throughout its history.[50]

The problem for the Round Table in 1910, however, was that the actual imperial entity they were so committed to both salvaging and describing looked, in most respects, not like an organic whole brought together through the slow accretion of individual actions but, rather, like an increasingly fissiparous, ad hoc collection of geographically scattered communities whose now common political present had been cobbled together out of the sometimes violent, often state-sanctioned, trading and monopoly creating practices of the past three hundred years.[51] As early as 1905, before the Round Table was founded, Zimmern described this disconnect but, undaunted, offered what would become the organization's stock response to the conundrum it created. Empires like the British, Zimmern argued, "may have been formed by accidental or by purely economic causes," but "unless they are maintained by sentiment they remain inorganic agglomerations and do not grow into organic empires."[52] Part and parcel of the Round Table's mission was thus to find ways to generate the kinds of imperial "sentiment" about a non-German form of a British imperial state that would allow the Empire to, in essence, become more "organic": that is, more like it actually was. As Dougal Malcolm put it, the goal of *The Commonwealth* writings was to demonstrate how "organic union *can be effected* and what the essentials of such union are."[53]

Of course, the very idea of "effecting" organic union was fraught with the strain between intentionality and authenticity, between design and nature, between the group's instrumental desire to literally invent a form of political organization that had not existed before—a new and improved British imperial union—and its concurrent desire to prove that this organization was preexistent. The Round Table responded to this disconnect between nature and intention in a number of different ways. On a symbolic level, by referring to the group's various drafts and memoranda as "eggs," they rather ingeniously naturalized their own process.[54] On a more substantive level, Round Table stalwarts (Kerr and Curtis in particular) insisted that the Empire constituted a single, organic political community precisely because its "actuating principle"—its commitment to liberty and democratic governance—had conditioned its growth from the beginning *even when* it did not seem to reflect these values and *even though* it did not currently look like an organic whole. This, in effect, meant claiming (as had Milner) that the Empire was *something other* than an Empire, because, as Grigg put it, the "word Empire is historically associated with autocracy, the absolute rule of one individual, whereas the distinctive institution within the British Empire, and the secret of its power, is the democratic commonwealth."[55] In the years leading up the Great War, theorizing the nature of this commonwealth and writing it back into imperial history became the Round Table's almost singular obsession.

A Commonwealth Solution

While the word "commonwealth" appeared in some of the Round Table's earliest private memorandums, it was not used to describe the Empire as a whole (as opposed to the autonomous "Commonwealths" of Australia and South Africa) in the pages of *The Round Table* until the summer of 1914, a year before the publication of *The Project of a Commonwealth*.[56] And yet clearly, from early on, the Round Table devoted much of its effort—its endless meetings, the production of memorandum, its weekend-long "moots"—to theorizing and modifying what they termed the "principle of commonwealth." Curtis, for instance, began his comments on the "Strawberry Memorandum" (Draft of Section III of *The Commonwealth of Nations*) by attempting to first summarize the group's "philosophical position" on the nature of the state, arguing that in its most stripped-down form, a state resembled little more than force, "a social organization which claims a sole and absolute right to dispose of the lives and property of its subjects and to exact their unlimited obedience." Beyond this, he argued, states took two shapes in the world: despotic states (which he associated with Asia and in which, he argued, the claim to authority "is formulated by a single person") and commonwealths (the "Western and higher form"). In terms pregnant with the Greenian and Oxford New Liberal promise that freedom and duty could be dialectically reconciled within a well-run civic community, Curtis described commonwealths as institutionally superior states governed by a liberal commitment to freedom of expression and movement, where the rule of law reflected public opinion rather than the will of an autocrat, and where citizens participated freely in maintaining the common good not out of fear but because of a shared commitment to each other and to the polity as a whole. For Curtis; "In a Commonwealth every citizen has a duty to every other citizen, viz., to recognize him as an end in himself and not as a means to an end."[57] Duty and freedom were ineradicably connected principles in the commonwealth, argued Curtis, because in it, "all citizens who are fit to do so share in enacting the laws" to which they are required to submit.[58] To be free, in this sense, required following the free laws of the commonwealth which reflected the general will of the people, rather than the desires of a single autocrat. The commonwealth idea thus embodied, in Kerr's words, the basic "Western ideas of self-government and liberalism."[59]

According to Curtis, the commonwealth also embodied a kind of spiritual cohesion that transcended the civic realm. In a commonwealth, he maintained, the bond between citizens and the state was familial, almost sacred:

> The quickening principle of the state is a sense of devotion, and adequate recognition somewhere in the minds of its subjects that their own interests are subordinate to those of the state. The bond which unites them and constitutes them collectively as a state is, to use the words of Lincoln, in the nature of *dedication*. Its validity, like that of the marriage tie, is at root not contractual but sacramental.[60]

As the term "quickening principle" would suggest, Curtis's organicism in this context extended beyond the metaphorical. In its most pure form, he argued, the commonwealth was a single, natural entity with an ability to grow and to evolve that was "at its best when able and free to adapt its own structures to conditions as they change, in accordance with its own experience of those conditions."[61] Freedom, in this sense, implied a kind of radical social freedom—the freedom of the state as a literal body politic—to change and expand its principles into the world. Indeed, according to Curtis, this desire for change, this striving outward with freedom in hand, was innate to the commonwealth's life process. "Freedom," he argued, "like the principle of life in the physical world, is inseparable from growth. Commonwealths are the corporeal frame in which it is incarnate, and they cease to flourish when they cease to extend the principle that inspires them in an increasing degree to an ever widening circle of men."[62] A threat to the growth of the commonwealth was thus a threat to freedom generally.

That Curtis and his colleagues would strike upon the word "commonwealth" in the first place was hardly surprising. Both pro and anti-imperial public intellectuals, from Little Englanders to Federationists, from Bernard Shaw to Goldwin Smith, had been referring to the Empire as a "Commonwealth of Nations" since Rosebery first coined the term in 1884.[63] It was Curtis and his Round Table cohorts who would make the connection explicit and popularize the term as a substitute for "empire." As Curtis recalled in 1937, he and the other members of the kindergarten had originally chosen the word because they were "hunting for a good Anglo-Saxon word to express the kind of state for which it stood," and "naturally lit upon the word 'Commonwealth.' "[64]

Curtis's caginess about the origins of the term "Commonwealth of Nations" is understandable if we consider the Round Table's desire to frame the growth of the Empire as a gradual and organic process of historical evolution. Curtis clearly wanted to characterize this process not in derivative terms (as part of a general, late-nineteenth/early-twentieth-century framing of imperial politics) but as a kind of excavation, a reaching back through time toward the Empire's authentic origins. This probably also explains why Curtis would excise other, more contemporary influences from both his early theorizing on commonwealth and from his recollections of the period. In particular, Curtis rarely acknowledged that the Round Table's project was in any way inspired by the work of late-nineteenth-century imperial Federationists with whom Milner would have been so familiar.[65] While scholars such as Daniel Gorman argue that Curtis "drew heavily on the campaigns of the imperial Federationists of the 1880's and early 1890's," this conclusion is not at all obvious from Curtis's writings.[66] Rather, Curtis more often eschewed such connection, insisting in his later recollections of the period that the only "federalist" he and the other members of the kindergarten were thinking about while they were in South Africa was Alexander Hamilton.[67]

But Curtis and the Round Table had another, more compelling reason to avoid connections with the Victorian Federationists. Like Milner, most of these earlier thinkers understood their vision of a federated Empire or "Greater Britain" in distinctly national and racial terms, as one coherent ethnic community united by a "common blood."[68] By contrast, Curtis and the Round Tablers argued that the Empire was comprised of "many lands and many races."[69] Indeed, as Curtis argued on the first page of the Introduction to *The Commonwealth of Nations,* the "essential difference" between the two largest empires in the world (the Chinese and the British) was that the "people of China are one race" while nations "in the British Empire, on the other hand, are comprised the people of every gradation in the human scale."[70] Curtis's words here suggested two key facts about the way the Round Table conceptualized the Empire. In contrast to the Federationists, they understood it as essentially diverse and multicultural. At the same time, they visualized the differences between the "many lands and races" in gradational terms with white Anglo-Saxons occupying the top tiers of a racial hierarchy. However, given the situation in Germany, they were no longer able articulate this conviction of supremacy with the same alacrity as had the Federationists.

In some ways, the Round Table's theory of commonwealth responded to the racial tension in their project by sometimes embracing a basic Victorian conception of universal liberal progress. As with nineteenth-century liberal imperialists like Mill and Macaulay, the Round Tablers understood the Empire in universal terms as a form of governance "good for all men, white or dark."[71] With the Victorians, the Round Tablers's notion of universality was also accompanied by a firm conviction that the needs and rights of human beings in the Empire might be universally grasped, but that the universality of these foundational principles in no way implied equality of status among imperial subjects. In fact, the Round Table was quite clear that the Empire represented a "vertical section of humanity in which all levels have some place," and that the majority of its imperial subjects occupied a large, lower swath of that vertical section.[72]

At the same time, the "principle of commonwealth" differed from the nineteenth-century, liberal imperial vision in some subtle but important ways that clustered around the desire of the Round Tablers to distance themselves from an empire based on imperialism, that is, on the "process or policy of establishing or maintaining an empire."[73] According to Uday Mehta, nineteenth-century liberals like the Mills understood the use of force through the logic of civilizational improvement. This logic, as Chakrabarty and other critics of liberal imperial historiography have argued, imagined time in such a way that Europeans were always located at the front of an historical march toward progress while nonwhite civilizations were stuck, lagging somewhere near the end. As Chakrabarty puts it, such perceptions consigned "Indians, Africans, and other 'rude' nations to an imaginary waiting room of history."[74] Under these conditions, any expressed desire on the part of colonized people to deviate from the path of progress dictated by the colonizer was understood by imperialists to mean obduracy—a stubborn, childish insistence on sticking to tradition for tradition's sake—and required a response of active, forceful, unsticking. As Mehta explains, societies confined to the "waiting room of history" that refused to follow the correct path to progress must be coerced along that path by "some other agency," with "the key to that room."[75] For Mehta, the process by which backward or stalled civilizations were to be brought up to speed thus "turns on a force external to those civilizations."[76] The use of force for good was essential, argued Mehta, for the entire temporal project of liberal empire to function.

Because they associated imperial force with the Germans, in the years leading up to 1914, Round Tablers were increasingly unwilling to talk about the Empire as a polity that imperialized. "Shallow observers," Kerr noted in 1910, "have frequently described British foreign policy as one of calculated aggression. Nothing could be further from the truth."[77] It was the Germans, Kerr countered, who reveled in a spirit of aggression and sought to force their cultural superiority on other nations. By contrast, he insisted, an "aggressive and expansive policy is contrary to the whole spirit of England," and this was true, he argued, both "within the boundaries of the Empire" and without.[78] In essence, Kerr and his colleagues were committed to theorizing an Empire in which military force, violence, and the suppression of dissent were incidental to the endeavor in which the Empire was engaged. The "principle of commonwealth" helped them to make this argument by insisting that the Empire (or Commonwealth of Nations) existed for the common good of all its parts and that all its parts were common. Hence, rather than imagining the Empire as a foreign body imposing its will upon recalcitrant societies under its tutelage, the language of commonwealth evoked a sense of these societies (particularly India) as junior partners in a greater endeavor being gently prodded toward adulthood by senior members of the community. In this vision, there was nothing *externally* coercive in the relationship between India and the British Empire, because the body engaged in tutoring was already a body to whom India belonged and for whom it felt sentimental and familial connections. As if to drive this point home, Curtis argued often in *The Commonwealth of Nations* that the Commonwealth could evolve faster toward its unifying goals and strengthen the bonds of "organic union" between its members by expanding responsibility for taking care of the dependencies to the dominions, just as families do with younger children. For Curtis, "the filial sense is strongest in children who have been called upon early to share the responsibilities of the family life."[79]

Curtis made this argument for the "filial" nature of the Commonwealth by bringing together two, sometimes mutually exclusive, approaches to the study of the relationship between English and British character and then making one serve the purpose of the other. As Baucum and other have argued, debates about the relationship between English national and British imperial identity already had a long and storied history in Britain before the Round Table entered the fray in 1910.[80] In the course of articulating their visions of Englishness, historians, philosophers, and social commentators such as Edmund Burke and E. H. Freeman had, since the seventeenth-century, often framed their accounts of Anglo-Saxon freedom *against* "Britishness," and "in reaction," as Linda Colley puts it, "to the Other beyond their shores."[81] Significantly, thinkers like Burke and Freeman were likely to be *anti-imperial* in their politics.[82] Even fans of Anglo-Saxon freedom who did support the Empire (such as the Federationists) usually restricted their notions of union to Britain's white, settler colonies, whose inhabitants they imaged as cultural brethren.[83]

Round Tablers wanted to do something different. They wanted a universal theory that was also specifically Anglo-Saxon in origin, and they wanted to tell a story of Anglo Saxon exceptionalism that would tie their evolving vision of commonwealth to a particular English form of liberty that was distinctively superior to that of the Germans. But their political project was made more internally complicated by this very endeavor: differentiating themselves from Germany meant championing English culture—but the problem with Germans, according to the Round

Table, was their obsessive concern with championing German culture. Given this difficulty, the Round Table put forward a theory of English exceptionalism in which there was no contradiction between English liberty and British imperial expansion, and where the Empire had always been, and would always be, a humble and yet capacious form of political community capable of speaking to the cultural and political needs of people "of every gradation in the human scale." As early as 1910, Round Tablers like Kerr clearly understood that making an argument for a British Commonwealth that was exceptional yet universal, peaceful yet expansionist, grounded in English freedom but international in its scope, required extensive historical revision. Kerr hinted at this when he argued:

> It is within the British Empire that the spirit of individualism has grown to its full maturity. Of all the Teutonic peoples the Anglo Saxon alone have been free from the cramping necessity of subordinating their development to the exigencies of war. Scarcely ever have they heard the drums of war in their homes, for nature has provided in the Channel a better defense than walls of steel..... The unconscious working of this intense spirit of individualism runs through the whole history of the Empire. It is the keynote of the long struggle of the people first within the feudal barons and later with the crown, and when after two revolutions, the victory was won, the constitution which enshrined the liberties of the British people were transplanted to America, Africa, and Australia.[84]

In this brief, explanatory story, the history of the British Empire unfolded from a channel-protected Anglo-Saxon love of liberty, to the struggle against feudalism, to the rest of the world in a kind of long, natural swoop, tied together by the tight, inscrutable knots of the passive voice (e.g. "were transplanted") and utter silence with regard to India and Asia. The metahistorical narrative at the heart of the *Commonwealth* texts was, on a most basic level, written to fill in these historical gaps and silences. And yet, the story that emerged from the pages of *The Commonwealth of Nations* was no less opaque, elisional, and passively constructed than the one Kerr told briefly in 1910. It was, however, more detailed, and therefore took on the shape of epic truth, a robust portrait of the British imperial character.

Historicizing and Naturalizing the Commonwealth

The approach to history taken by Curtis and the Round Table in *The Commonwealth* writings can best be described as explicitly metahistorical. In this sense, the Round

Table not only engaged in a lengthy process of transforming, in Hayden White's terms, the "chronicle" of Empire into the "story" of Commonwealth, but it also cast the emergence of this Commonwealth in history as the coming to fruition of a single, unifying, and redemptive theme over time. History itself, Curtis argued in markedly Hegelian terms, was the overall logic that made sense out of past events, that imbued the movement of time with purpose, and that shone "with an ever-increasing light upon things which are yet to be."[85] For Curtis and the Round Table, the "principle of commonwealth" in history was both real and rational. Indeed, many Round Tablers spoke about the idea of the British Commonwealth as they imagined it to be as if it was *more* real than the Empire in its current, rumpled, frayed state. For these thinkers, the true Commonwealth was simply being hidden from view by the contemporary cluster of world events, a situation that ought to compel all well-intentioned people throughout the Empire to commit themselves fully to making its indwelling nature manifest. In Kerr's words, "one might say, that which is in future to be made apparent does already exist behind the veil of non-appearance, and moves our minds to action."[86]

That Curtis and the other Round Tablers involved most intimately with the construction of the *Commonwealth* writings would speak with such obviously Hegelian inflected overtones is hardly surprising, given the idealist legacy of the Oxford school that so influenced their generation.[87] But the idealist or metahistorical quality of this narrative also dovetailed particularly well with the political objective of the group, to square the circle between their support for a hierarchical, racialized Empire and their enthusiasm for a holistic account of democratic commonwealth. Reading the history of the Empire as the slow unfolding of the idea of commonwealth over time enabled the Round Table to account both for moments when the Empire seemed to depart from that ideal and, at the same time, to insist that even though the Empire did not yet resemble its vision of organic union, it still was, and had always been, what it was meant to be from its inception: a liberal democracy bouncing blithely along history toward its brilliant future. Most of all, it gave the ad hoc, historically contingent character of Britain's actual imperial history a narrative arc—what White calls "emplotment"—a beginning, a middle, and a presumed end.[88]

The Round Tablers were also influenced by a number of contemporary approaches to the study of English and imperial history which they often synthesized with stunning alacrity. For example, many of the members involved in writing the *Commonwealth* texts were drawn to the Anglo-Saxon model of political development championed by E. H. Freeman and William Stubbs and by the racial history of Woodrow Wilson. John M. Hobson cunningly refers to this as the "Aryan/Teutonic relay race" approach because of the way its adherents imagined progress as the transference of liberal notions of freedom and democratic equality from one "member of team Teuton" to the next, the handing-off of the baton of liberty from the ancient Germans to the Anglo-Saxons, from the British to the Americans.[89] Curtis took the relay race one step further (or backward) by combining it with Zimmern's rendering of the Athenian Empire as a precursor to the British Commonwealth, thus explicitly linking Zimmern's original idea to yet another, earlier nineteenth-century tradition of establishing first Teutons, then Anglo-Saxons, as the racial progeny of the ancient Greeks.

Curtis began his narrative account of "how and why the British Commonwealth came to exist" not in England but in ancient Greece where, he argued, we first find "people who differ not in degree but in kind from those of Asia because they are no longer dominated by habit"; people who had purged their minds of theocratic cobwebs and entered fully into the project of construct-ing a "Greek Commonwealth" enlivened not by the desire of subjects to please a single ruler, but rather by a "sense of mutual enthusiasm—of duty to each other" experienced by free citizens.[90] It is of course hardly surprising, as Chapter One explains, that Curtis would turn to fifth-century B.C.E. Athens, given the role Athens played in the political imaginaries of nineteenth-century liberals and imperialists (particularly at Oxford) and given the fact that one of their own, Zimmern, had published *The Greek Commonwealth* in 1911 right at the moment when the Round Table was fishing about for an alternative model for Empire.[91] Conceptually, however, there are a variety of other reasons why the Athenian *polis* proved such an important starting point for the Round Table's narrative of Commonwealth development. First, associating the British Empire with the "essential condition of the principle which inspires the commonwealth" and then locating that principle in Athens allowed the Round Table to insist that in the deep background of the Empire—fused into the cells of its political DNA— was a polity which had already successfully reconciled individual freedom with a patriotic love of the city in a manner that was "completely organic" rather than marshal.[92] In Athens, Curtis argued, "the use of force to constrain the obedi-ence" of citizens was "unnecessary" because all citizens understood their con-nection to each other in patriotic and personal terms grounded in both a rational commitment to a polity whose laws they helped shape, and a deeper connection to other citizens through bonds of traditional loyalty. This was also precisely a point that the Round Table wanted to make about the British Commonwealth. As Zimmern put it in 1914, the British Commonwealth, was comprised of the "organic union and free activity of its several national members" whose "patrio-tism has been built up, not by precept and doctrine, but on a firm foundation of older loyalties."[93] At its base then, back at its pre-founding in Athens according to the Round Table, the British Commonwealth was conditioned by a set of politi-cal relationships that made force unnecessary. By this logic, whenever the British Empire behaved in a fashion that looked aggressive it was the result of external circumstances antithetical to its nature.

The Athenian *polis* was rhetorically useful to Curtis and the Round Table in other ways as well. In particular, it provided them with a language that helped them reconcile universal citizenship and deep inequality in one body politic by recasting the commonwealth's democratic credentials not as a reflection of its existing levels of political participation, but in terms of its *potential* for democratic inclusion. The idea of commonwealth that thrived in ancient Athens, Curtis argued, assumed that "a certain number of citizens are capable of formulating public opinion in light of experience," a number which expanded as the commonwealth developed and matured.[94] For the Round Tablers, the Athenian *polis* was always defined by this potential, this capacity "to adapt its own structures to conditions as they change." Such a society, argued Curtis, "travels in the direction of democracy as naturally as the theocratic principle travels toward despotism."[95] The Athenians, in this vision, were democratic because they were traveling toward democracy, just as the British Commonwealth was democratic because it was traveling toward a more inclusive future. Likewise, the Commonwealth was always defined by what it would potentially be rather than what it currently was, by the fact that, back at the beginning of Western civilization, it had been making its way toward Britain.

The teleological story of Athens's journey toward the fulfillment of the "principle of commonwealth" was, for the Round Table, both tragic and redemptive. The Greeks, Curtis argued, had invented the idea of the democratic commonwealth but "in a form too slight and delicate to survive" outside of the *polis*.[96] The "tragic paradox" of Greek history, according to Curtis, was the Athenians' failure to grasp the fact that they could expand the ambit of those citizens "fit" to rule beyond the city-state and potentially create an international commonwealth through their empire. Thus, Curtis continued, "it was precisely during these years that Athens was creating the ideal city-state patriotism" and it was "just at the same time as she was thus perfecting the idea of a commonwealth" that she was "failing to grasp the idea of a wider Imperial Commonwealth."[97] After Athens's decline in the fifth-century, according to *The Commonwealth of Nations*, the Romans incorporated the history of the Athenian Commonwealth into their Empire, where it finally "vanished" as they expanded into the east and eventually succumbed "to the Oriental idea of theocracy."[98] But all was not lost. The idea of commonwealth was "sleeping not dead" and reemerged in England during the period of the Saxon kings, coming to fruition with William the Conqueror, ultimately blossoming into the "wider Imperial Commonwealth" of the British Empire, thus fulfilling the promise of Athens on an international scale.

Curtis and the Round Table established the historical connection between Athenians and Britons by fusing several nineteenth- and early-twentieth-century schools of thought. On the one hand, Curtis simply reiterated the general intellectual *zeitgeist* that bundled Anglo-Saxon culture together with that of ancient Athens through a series of rhetorical linkages. Nineteenth-century authors, for example, would often connect the two cultures simply by evoking them at the same time (as did Thomas Carlyle), or by asserting their shared ideals, the "unbroken history," in Freeman's words, between the "earliest days of Greece" and the "most modern days of England."[99] On the other hand, Curtis also combined several popular turn-of-the century racial theories, arguing first that the ancient Greeks were themselves the descendants of Teutons who had "branched southwards and settled in the peninsula which bears their name."[100] Curtis was influenced here by the contemporary writings of archeologists and classicists such as William Ridgeway and John Myres, who claimed to have found archeological proof that the original inhabitants of the Attic peninsula were a "fair-haired race" that had migrated "from the shores of the Northern Ocean."[101] The "primitive customs" of these original, Teutonic inhabitants favored independence, a general disinclination toward autocracy, and a tendency to be moved more by persuasion than force. Curtis then combined this understanding of an ancient Teuton migration south with the Saxon migration west, thus fusing two other popular approaches to British history at the time. The first was found, again, in the writings of Freeman and Stubbs, who both pinpointed the origins of English constitutional principles in the purportedly democratic impulses of the Saxons. According to these thinkers, the Saxons brought democratic traditions to England (embodied in their folk or town "moots") from the forests of Germany, which were then sewn into the fabric of English politics. Freeman and Stubbs both located the Teutonic, democratic impulses of the Saxons in the continuity and incorruptibility of both the linguistic and racial characteristics of the English people over time, people who were, in Stubbs's words, "of German descent in the main constituents of blood, character, and language."[102] These "constituents" ensured that, despite Britain's history of monarchical power and feudalism, the democratic nature of English political governance had remained embedded in the cultural and racial knowledge of the polity. Because of this, argued Freeman, "the continuity of our national Assemblies has never been broken."[103]

But despite a deep admiration for Athenian democracy—which in Freeman's case entailed a formidable knowledge of ancient Greek and a firm belief in a "long history of civilized man which stretches on in one unbroken tale from the union of the towns of Attica to the last measure of progress in England or in Germany"—neither Freeman nor Stubbs ever made the case for a racial tie between the Saxon and ancient Greek peoples, other than to note a general "philological" similarity between the two groups.[104] Curtis's innovation here was to join the theory of Saxon democracy with that of the original Teutonic migration into Greece through an interpretation that leaned heavily on an approach that Myres termed "Historical Geography."[105] As Zimmern described it, "Historical Geography" assumed that "neither an individual nor a nation can be properly understood without a knowledge of their surroundings and means of support."[106] For Curtis, geography explained the gaping historical lag between the rise of the Athenian *polis* and the emergence of the English Commonwealth. In this rendering, while the Teutonic clans of Northern Europe may have possessed the racial and cultural impulses so essential to the founding of the Greek Commonwealth, their geographic location in northern Europe prevented them from establishing similar commonwealths outside of Greece. Because, he argued, "Northern Europe was not so divided into pockets," as Greece, the Teutonic tribes that remained there after the decline of Rome "could not collect, solidify, and develop the *esprit de corps* which is the necessary basis of the organic state," and "in the absence of physical frontiers the only bond by which the tribes could be united in a state was by race, not locality."[107] Thus, according to Curtis, early on, the absence of clear geographic boundaries meant that the Teutons in Germany developed a predilection for racial theories of statehood based on feudal hierarchies with a tendency toward internecine conflict and imperial sprawl. By contrast, once "Roman civilization" in Britain was "displaced by the custom, language, and religion of the Germanic invaders," argued Curtis, the natural Teutonic predisposition for liberty and commonwealth could blossom given that England, like Athens, was isolated by water.[108] Thus, Curtis argued, it was in England, not in "Germany itself that the Teutonic tradition of freedom was able to take root and reproduce once more the principle of government which first blossomed in Greece and almost vanished in the Roman Empire."[109]

By making this argument, Curtis and the Round Table combined and reiterated preexisting nineteenth-century racial theories about England's origins, but with a slightly unique set of ends.[110] First, they established something that Freeman and Stubbs had not: they both linked England to German or Teutonic principles of democracy, and then definitively distinguished between English freedom and the moment when Germany went wrong and swung toward authoritarianism and racial orthodoxy. Secondly, they linked England racially and culturally to the Greek idea of commonwealth, skirted the authoritarian (and, ironically, racialist) theory of German statehood, and transformed the British into the redeemers of Greece and the British Commonwealth into the next logical step in the movement of world history. In other words, from this racial story they were able to extract a distinctly universal or, in Mandler's words, "world civilizational" conclusion. Yes, the English were linked to the Greeks through racial ties but, over time, they had managed to do something which the Greeks (and the Germans) had both failed to accomplish: they expanded the institutions of the commonwealth "in a form which transcended the narrow limitations imposed upon it, as the ancients believed, by Nature herself" to encompass the entire nation. The expansion of this national English Commonwealth into the British Commonwealth happened organically over time in a manner that allowed the British to reconcile the "tragic paradox" at the heart of the Athenian Empire.[111] And they did this in the name both of all that was unique about England, and all that was universal about international commonwealth.[112]

The Round Table's theory of commonwealth thus naturalized the history of the Empire by transforming history itself into a developmental process of a racial polity "travelling toward democracy" where the political "growth" of the commonwealth, "like the principle of life in the physical world," unfolded in such a way that in the end it became universally valid. Casting the theory of commonwealth in terms of one reoccurring "body of principles" and then conflating this reoccurring "body of principles" first with the English Commonwealth and then with the Empire assumed that, at its core, this was a polity shaped by its principle commitment to liberty, democracy, and the rule of law, even when this appeared not to be the case.[113] Taking a page from Freeman and Stubbs, Curtis told the history of the English Commonwealth as if these principles were *always the same*—despite the fact that English history was as replete with tyrannical monarchs and civil war as it was with democracy. The fact that the majority of English subjects were themselves unable to participate in fashioning the general will that made the laws and determined their execution throughout most of English history (indeed, that full male suffrage was not achieved until after World War I) could not touch the overall fact of its democratic substance. The English Commonwealth had always been *essentially* democratic because its internal impulses were always traveling toward democracy.

In their approach to the English Commonwealth, Curtis and the Round Table's emphatic and overwhelming emphasis on "who we are"—over and against any historical phenomena or events that might challenge the fixity of that identity—had an enormous impact on their approach to England's imperial history broadly construed. According to this narrative, the English Commonwealth, whose "insular character" had always been one of "the ruling facts of its history," was eventually compelled overseas during the early modern period.[114] In order to preserve the "civilization for which she stood" in an era of increasingly limited resources at home and competition from abroad, the England, like Rome, set out for "distant continents" from which "she drew the wealth which enabled her to maintain the supremacy at sea which was the condition of her existence."[115] Once pushed into the international arena, according to Curtis, "the wealth and daring of an island race, inspired by the enterprise and patriotism which free institutions beget" enabled England to establish successful colonies and trade routes throughout North America and Asia and thus counterbalance the advantage of "continental kings" with their "vastly superior numbers."[116] The difference between the Roman and the British Empires, argued the

Round Table, lay in the ability of the British to gradually, over time, expand from an insular island commonwealth into an international commonwealth inclusive of large sections of the world's "non European races" and "admit them without, like the Republic of Rome, destroying its own character as such."[117] Hence, at the core of the Round Table's narrative rested the basic belief that no matter how much it expanded, no matter how much geographic and human space it encompassed, no matter how diverse its inhabitants, the basic character of the British Commonwealth stayed the same.

The implication of this reading of imperial history is profound. If the British Commonwealth has always been motivated by its character—its "actuating principle," or who it really was—and if this character was always grounded in a basic commitment to individual freedom, the rule of law, democracy, and civic patriotism, then every act of imperial expansion throughout its history must flow from that set of principles and nothing else. By this logic, the trading practices of individual British citizens, the military actions of chartered companies, and the processes of direct or indirect rule by the imperial state itself that might, in retrospect, *appear* to have violated these principles could not have played a central role in making the Empire what it was by 1914. Through this set of lenses, violence, slavery, occupation, and famine are all rendered incidental to the character of the imperial state. In his description of the East India Company's violent history in South Asia, for instance, Curtis argued that, early on, the English had been merely trying to engage in "legitimate trade" in the region and only when that path to legitimate trade was blocked, by tyrants of both a Continental and Oriental persuasion, were they unfortunately forced to turn to violence. In such instances, argued Curtis "however pacific the intentions of the London merchants, their right to navigate the Indian seas had to be asserted by powder and shot."[118]

The conviction that British trading companies had a "right" to navigate the Indian seas, much less a right to trade with anyone they wanted, anywhere in the world, obviously predated the Round Table. Since it was first articulated by legal theorist de Vitoria in the sixteenth-century (reaching a particularly virulent apex during the Opium Wars and the Scramble for Africa), the notion of a cosmopolitan "right" to free trade has functioned particularly well as what Tully terms the "Trojan Horse of western imperialism," the guiding ideological justification for global capitalist expansion throughout the modern era.[119] What made Curtis's explanation of English expansion slightly different from this "right" to free trade, broadly construed, was the extent to which he attached the British impulse toward free trade to the liberal, democratic *oeuvre* of the "principle of commonwealth." The "wealth and daring" of the British, argued Curtis, originated not only in their impulse toward liberty and their natural predilection toward individualism, but also from the "enterprise and patriotism which free institutions beget." From the perspective of *The Commonwealth of Nations*, what mattered most about British imperial history, and about the transformation of the English into the British Commonwealth, were the essential qualities of a polity just being who it was in the world. Thus, from the earliest participants in the Atlantic trade to the London directorate of the East India Company to the twentieth-century rubber barons, the story that Curtis and the Round Table told of public and private British imperial development was one not of persistent *good* intentions on the part of individuals and companies, but of these same individuals' and companies' *lack* of any intention at all. They were just Englishmen, doing what they were bred to do, moved by the "capacity for adaptation which the principle of the commonwealth imparts" to expand their search for economic sustenance beyond their island borders and, when their natural right to this expansion was challenged, being forced by circumstances to behave violently or in a manner that might look, from the outside, like expansionism.[120] The British, in this narrative, were never imperialist with intent. They were simply being who they were.

The Round Table's constant telling and retelling of the story of the British Commonwealth's liberal-democratic identity (from the Greeks, to the Teutons, to the English, to the world) did more than inoculate it against charges of violence or illiberalism arising from specific historical sets of events, such as the way it secured the Indian seas by force, or the manner in which the East India Company created the conditions for the famine in Bengal, or the state's violent suppression of the Mahdi army at Omdurman. Rather, reconceptualizing the British Empire through the "corporeal frame" of the British Commonwealth smoothed over more long-term and systemic practices of imperial exploitation that, by 1914, many liberals and socialists were beginning to associate with the expansionist impulses of imperial capitalism. Take, for instance, the historical connection between slavery and the expansion of British trade and colonialism in the Atlantic. As Kenneth Morgan argues, even if today some debate lingers about the direct contribution of the capital amassed by the slave trade to British economic growth in the years prior to 1800, there is no doubt that slavery, and the "sugar-slave nexus," had "an important, though not decisive, impact on Britain's long term development between the late Stuart and the early Victorian age."[121] And yet, from reading *The Commonwealth of Nations*, one would assume that the institution of modern slavery (much less the complicity of British traders in its expansion) was something that the British had only accidentally stumbled into and which they tried to get out of faster, and with more compassion, than any other European state. Curtis devoted a scant paragraph in the voluminous *The Commonwealth of Nations* to a discussion of English slavery, noting merely that the "slave trade with America was an important source of English wealth and the philosopher John Locke did not scruple to invest in it." And yet immediately after making this admission, Curtis deflected the argument away from English traders:

> There is no European race which can afford to remember its first contact with the subject peoples otherwise than with shame and attempts to assess their relative degrees of guilt as fruitless as they are invidious. The question of real importance is how far these various states were able to purge themselves of the poison and rise to a higher realization of their duty towards races that they were called by the claims of their own superior civilizations to protect. The fate of that civilization itself hung upon that issue.[122]

Curtis's slight tipping of the hat to two hundred years of British involvement in the slave trade was ideologically wily for a number of reasons. First, it reduced Britain's slave history to a brief, and eminently excusable, moment of "first contact" with peoples who were already "subject." Second, it dismissed any attempt to "assess" guilt as "fruitless" and "invidious." Finally, and perhaps most importantly, it almost immediately diverted the readers' attention away from the long-term involvement of Britain in the slave trade by switching the focus of analysis. The "question of real importance," according to Curtis, was not the slave trade per se but Britain's success in purging itself of the "poison" of slavery in comparison to other European states, as if slavery were simply a natural contagion that the British were better at curing than their European counterparts. In one brief moment, Curtis rendered the experiences of millions of African people peripheral to the English experience of their own pained coming to terms with illiberalism.

By Curtis's lights, their "legal habits" and commitment to the rule of law ultimately "prevented the British ... from lapsing into principles the negation of those which underlie their constitution."[123] In this profoundly tautological vision of the world, even when they behaved illiberally the British Commonwealth could not be illiberal because their nature prevented it. Of course, Curtis acknowledged, there "were serious gaps" in the smooth extension of the rule of law over time (the existence of slavery being one of them) but, ultimately, the reliance of the British on slavery and the slave trade for hundreds of years (much less the continued existence of legal slavery in the British-held portions of Nepal, Burma, and the Sudan into the 1920s) simply did not count as much in Curtis's narrative as did the Commonwealth's essential nature.[124] By Curtis's reckoning, the "type of citizen" produced by England's commitment to the rule of law administered colonies better than other European states, and was the "ultimate reason why native races have on the whole fared better under British rule than any other."[125] Widespread recognition of this administrative capability also explained why "the myriads should have acquiesced" to British power in the first place.

The two rhetorical tropes that Curtis relied on most heavily to convey this sense of inevitability and acquiescence were his constant and unrelenting use of the passive voice in his discussion of British expansion into areas other than North America and the dominions and, like Zimmern, an overreliance on the word "gradual." Thus, according to Curtis, with the opening of the high seas, "partitions which had ever divided the families of mankind *were rapidly* breached" just as the "races of Africa *are transplanted* wholesale to the Americas."[126] The British, in Curtis's estimation, never seemed to actually set out to breach these partitions (which were never as rigid as Curtis describes) nor transplant Africans to America. Indeed, Curtis never really explained the exact nature of their role in these endeavors at all. Rather, the British—trailing behind them all the institutional, cultural, and racial qualities implicit in the idea of commonwealth— emerged from these pages almost as bumbling, innocent bystanders who just happened to get caught up in historical events and, by the sheer magnetic pull of their ideals, drew people into their imperial circle. After this initial contact, argued Curtis, the Commonwealth "gradually" extended its growth outward, into the rest of the world. This, for Curtis, was the natural coming to fruition of the commonwealth ideal "gradually extended, now by one community, now by another, but chiefly by the community founded in the dark ages by Teutonic invaders of the British Isles" to the whole world.[127] By this logic, because they were representative of the "type of citizen" produced by the Commonwealth, the financial directors and agents of the East India Company were gradually compelled to accept the "task of territorial administration" in India because no one else was as qualified and then, by a "series of steps," the British Government eventually "assumed control of this powerful corporation."[128] Missing from Curtis's narrative were any subjects of history who did not cohere to the gradual thesis; rebels in India, protestors in the Parliament, or supporters of the Company committed to extending its charter such as Mill.[129] Rather, in Curtis's relentlessy passive voice, control of the government "was gradually strengthened until at length the Company was expropriated and its charter cancelled."[130] In this way, Curtis's history ensured that everything that might make current liberal supporters of empire uncomfortable about the actual historic and contemporary "process or policy of establishing and maintaining an empire" fell out of the Empire's purview, somewhere just beyond the margins of *The Commonwealth of Nations*, never fully representative of who and what the British Empire truly was.

The British Commonwealth described in *The Commonwealth of Nations* was like a black hole that pulled all historical events—all the practices of imperialism that involved force or annexation or expansion or violence—into its gravitational orbit, leaving behind only a trail of their essence and at times (as with slavery) a whiff of regret. When an historical event or institution was simply too violent, illiberal, or sustained to ignore, Curtis would briefly acknowledge it and then move on to the more relevant story of commonwealth development that guided his narrative. At other times, Curtis's use of the passive voice made it seem as though the rapid growth of European imperial expansion from the seventeenth- through the nineteenth-centuries was just something that happened, a greater force of nature caused by the instability that inevitably resulted when the "isolated races of mankind" are "rapidly brought into touch."[131] That they *had* to be "brought into touch," and that Britain had to expand, was something that Curtis never questioned, just as he never asked himself how the "races of mankind" on the receiving end of European expansion might have experienced this contact. Rather, in this vision of imperial history, whenever civilizations with different visions of the world came into contact with each other, conflict and instability ensued, and the British (ever intrepid in their desire to truck and trade and spread their institutions) fell into the fray with the rest of the Continental powers. It mattered not, Curtis argued, that the British had gone into India and elsewhere with the idea of making a profit. Quoting approvingly and at length from *The Times's* 1910 special collection of articles entitled "India and the Durbar," Curtis noted that while there "is little substantial evidence of high initial moral purpose of a far reaching kind," on the part of the British "there can be no doubt that it existed in varying and often obscure form almost from the very beginning. In a race with the traditions and the ideals held by the English it is bound to be early manifested and to import some infusion of unselfish beneficence into their acts."[132] In this version of imperial history, the "character of the English counted for more in the long run than the material purpose which first took them to India."[133] The British in India were beneficent not with intention but simply by being themselves.

Casting Britain's imperial past as a story of preexisting conflict caused by the inevitable meeting of the "isolated races of mankind" that the English just happened to stumble upon, order, and gradually transform into an international commonwealth was also a particularly useful rhetorical strategy for the Round Table at this moment because it reversed the causation involved in this unfolding of imperial events. The British Empire emerged from the pages of *The Commonwealth of Nations* as the *solution* to international instability and conflict—both historical and contemporary—rather than one of its primary causes. For Curtis, "the composition of the British Empire," was "a practical attempt to supply the solution" to the "magnitude and the delicacy" of the problems raised when civilizations at different levels of development and with different political visions came into touch with one another.[134] The current "structure" of the Empire, Curtis argued, its status as a "paramount state," was the direct result of its efforts, throughout its existence, to negotiate and contain the international conflicts generated by the expansion of European markets. In other words, the very composition of the British Empire was a response to conflict and overreach on the part of other states or its own accidental interruption of isolated societies rather than its overreach, its imperializing, or the expansive and violent economic practices of its chartered companies. The effect of this backward causality was twofold. Not only did it transform British imperial expansion into a response to problems outside of its control, it also posited the Empire as the eternal answer to the question in the past, present, and future. More and better Empire, in this sense, was always the solution to the "imperial problem."

Finally, framing their vision of the Commonwealth in history as an entity representing "all the races" of human society spoke to one of the most internally contradictory aspects of positing the Commonwealth as a response to the "imperial problem" in 1914. On the one hand, it suggested that, unlike the Germans, the British embraced, rather than rejected, their multicultural character. It suggested that their Commonwealth bound together "the diverse families of mankind" and that the British were particularly adept at governing this kind of diversity not because of their inherent racial superiority but because, as a particularly attuned race, they had stumbled upon a fairer, more open political culture and a better way of shaping citizens.[135] In this sense, just as the Empire was the solution to the problems generated by Empire, so were the sensibilities inherent in the British as a race the solution to both the conflicts generated by the interaction of the "isolated races of mankind," and the racism of the Germans. The Round Table made this point through a complicated chicken-and-egg approach to British racial history, both insisting that the English had inherited their commonwealth sensibilities through their racial and cultural connections to the Greeks (via the Saxons) *and* that the "peculiar temper" of the British—their concern with individual rights, civic patriotism, and the rule of law—was the result (rather than the cause) of the Commonwealth's institutions, "the product of the system rather than of the race."[136] Anyone, by this logic, even Prussians, could benefit from the salutary effect of English institutions, because, in Curtis's words, there was "no reason to suppose that Austrians bred in England could not acquire it to the same degree" as the English themselves.[137]

On the other hand, at the same time Curtis suggested that the institutional sensibilities of the British could be learned by members of other races and cultures, his conception of the Commonwealth as multiracial and multicultural also reaffirmed the group's equally firm belief in racial difference and racial hierarchy, even as it stressed its holistic and comprehensive quality. All of the *Commonwealth* texts unfailingly describe the diversity of the Empire in terms of the "gradations" of the races grouped by their capacity to exercise political responsibility. For Curtis, the seeming "paradox" of the British Commonwealth in 1914 was that it was "based upon principles" which were "unintelligible to the majority of its subjects."[138] However, Curtis and his Round Table colleagues believed this paradox to be ultimately reconciled through the idea of

commonwealth itself which, they argued, was perfectly capable of expressing all that was bright and hopeful about liberty, the rule of law, and democracy while simultaneously administering the majority of the Empire through
means that they themselves described as despotic. Because sovereignty in the
Commonwealth "had passed once for all from the Crown to Parliament, or
rather to the voters who elect it," the British could not rule India in a manner
that did not reflect this basic democratic character:

> The allegiance of the people of the United Kingdom and of all its depen-
> dencies is due to the same paramount authority. All of them are citizens
> of one comprehensive state, and that a state in which autocracy has
> been finally discarded and government consciously based on the prin-
> ciple of the commonwealth. *However despotic the power of the Viceroy,*
> and however prone the Oriental to regard such power as evidence of
> divine authority, that power is in fact derived from the British parlia-
> ment not by virtue of its sovereignty over the United Kingdom, still less
> by virtue of its sovereignty over India, but by virtue of its sovereignty
> over the greater state of which both are integral parts.[139]

In Curtis's estimation, once "native inhabitants were actually incorporated in the
fabric of the Commonwealth," they became "integral parts" of a whole whose
authority sprang not from the despotic power it exercised, but from its democratic institutions. They were "citizens of one comprehensive state."

Curtis's notion of citizenship here was at odds with traditional liberal and
democratic uses of the term at the same time it embraced them. Along with most
of the major figures in modern European political theory, Curtis argued that
(in contrast to monarchical, feudal, and authoritarian modes of governance) a
democratic commonwealth was defined by the way its laws reflected the "public
opinion" generated by citizens rather than the individual will "of an autocrat to
command the unhesitating obedience of his subjects."[140] Where Curtis departed
from democratic theorists however, was in his refusal or reluctance to link citizenship to equality of representation. In other words, most theorists of citizenship throughout modernity have accepted some version of T. H. Marshall's claim
that citizenship "is a status bestowed on those who are full members of a community. All who possess the status are equal with respect to the rights and duties
with which the status endowed."[141] Theorists and statesmen (from the Levellers
to the American Founders) who did not believe in the inherent equality of all
people to govern simply distinguished between those who met the criteria for
citizenship and those who did not.[142] In other cases, when the foundational principle of a country's constitution or legal doctrines insisted on the equality of
all people, but the ruling elite did not feel like including certain people in the

citizenry, they could use local or informal methods of exclusion or intimidation to keep these people from exercising the political rights of citizenship.[143]

The approach of Curtis and the Round Table to the issue of Commonwealth citizenship was somewhat different. While Curtis clearly believed that there was a certain equality inherent in citizenship, this equality arose not from the equal participation by citizens in making the laws, but, rather, from the duty each individual citizen owed equally "to every other citizen" and to "the laws of the Commonwealth."[144] According to Curtis, *all* of the individual members of the dominions and the dependencies were equally citizens of the British Commonwealth, and all of them were equally constrained by their mutual duty to each other to submit to its laws, because these laws were the reflection of democratic public opinion rather than the will of an autocrat. This, he argued, was the "fuller and more rational conception of the ultimate foundations upon which the duty of obedience to government rests."[145] However, Curtis made it clear that while all individuals in the Empire were equally citizens, united by their sense of "mutual responsibility" toward each other and a duty to submit to a government guided by public opinion, they were not all equally entitled to participate in shaping this public opinion. "The principle of commonwealth rests upon mutual responsibility, but such responsibility is seldom distributed equally," Curtis concluded in regard to India. "It rests with those that have more knowledge rather than with those who have less, on the strong rather than the weak."[146] Thus, all citizens were equally required to submit to law because that law reflected the general will but the general will did not need to be produced generally.

Curtis's distinction here was subtle but ingenious. Along with similar nineteenth-century liberal theories of civilizational development, his approach to citizenship effectively gestured toward a universal principle while backing away from the implication of that universalism, thus practically allowing the Round Table to express a commitment to the kind of democracy that arises from citizen government, while actively excluding three-quarters of its citizens from governing. Strategically and ideologically, the approach to citizenship developed by Curtis allowed the group to argue that because Indians were *already* fully incorporated in the Commonwealth and because the Commonwealth was *already* constitutionally democratic—indeed, democratic by nature—then right now, at this moment, Indians and the citizens of the Empire's other dependencies *were also already* fully realized democratic citizens. This understanding of Commonwealth citizenship pushed well beyond the rhetorical utility of Macaulay's desire to some day, in the far distant future, create "a class of persons, Indian in blood and colour, but English in taste, in opinions, in morals, and in intellect."[147] Rather, Curtis and his colleagues maintained by this logic that because Indians were full citizens of the Commonwealth they ought, as such, to commit themselves fully to the cause of the Empire *right now*, not at some future moment when they became more like the British or were given more political responsibility.

This does not mean that Curtis and the Round Table shrunk from the language of forestallment. Like their nineteenth-century counterparts, they were only too happy to insist that some day, the majority of nonwhite people in the dependencies would be capable of exercising the responsibility of governance by participating with the dominions in an imperial parliament— but that day was not today. To Curtis's mind, "as surely as day follows the night the time must come when, as knowledge spreads in India, the aureole which envelopes and sanctions its authority will be dispelled." Indians, he argued, would be someday granted more political authority in the Commonwealth as the "habits" of democracy that flowed from closer association with Anglo-Saxon political culture were allowed to "penetrate and disturb Oriental society."[148]

At the same time, the Round Table also used the language of forestallment to its advantage by threading that language through the eye of potentiality, insisting that the Commonwealth's democratic potential in the future meant that its character was fundamentally democratic in the present. Thus, by Curtis's lights a "commonwealth is a living thing. It cannot suffer any part of itself to remain inert" and therefore to fructify, indeed to *stay alive*, it must continually expand the ambit of governing to an ever-widening circle of citizens, "who are fit for government." [149] In the words of one Round Table member in yet another one of the group's internally circulated memos, the principle of commonwealth was "the principle to which British political development has always striven, and is still striving to realize."[150] In teleological terms, the very fact that its ends were democratic, that it was traveling toward democracy, meant that it was also democratic *right now*, and so to refuse to obeys its laws amounted not only to rebellion but also to a basic refusal to grasp the requirements of democracy. As Curtis put it, in a commonwealth where all citizens who were fit to "share in enacting the laws" did so, to resist those laws "would prove unfitness."[151] Thus, because the true essence of the Commonwealth—the "essential condition of the principle" upon which it rested—was democratic, any citizen member of this body who refused to obey the law demonstrated his unpreparedness for law making. The "further development" of representative institutions in India, Curtis thus concluded, would depend upon how much enthusiasm Indian citizens showed, in the present, for the Commonwealth, how well Indians lived out their "sense of their duty to their fellow citizens and realize it in the practice of daily life."[152] Curtis's theory reiterated, in a new and improved form, the down-the-rabbit-hole quality of the kind of liberal imperialism articulated by Mill, which insisted that Indians were yet incapable of enjoying self government because they did not understand how to properly submit to the law.[153] Mill's account, however, never actually explains the relationship between obedience and autonomy, except through a rather loose account of the "habits" necessary for self-control and, hence, self-government. Curtis's vision, by contrast, suggested that the hundreds of millions of imperial subjects in the dependencies *were already* citizens of a democratic society. Rebellion, revolt, or protest, in this context, appeared to be not merely obdurate and barbarian: it amounted to a kind of cognitive dissonance, the senseless evisceration of a political body made whole by the road down which it traveled.

Conclusion

Curtis and the Round Table wrote the *Commonwealth* texts not merely to define their goals; they wrote them to lay out an entire world vision in its long, fantastical context. Conditioned from its inception by Teutonic, and then Saxon, notions of freedom, Curtis argued, the "principle of commonwealth" grew from an idea limited to the Athenian *polis* to the folk moots of England, and from the English nation to the Commonwealth of Nations, an organization embracing "a quarter of mankind."[154] The key to solving the "imperial problem," as they explained it, lay in the willingness of imperial citizens in Great Britain and throughout the dependencies and the dominions to affirm their faith in the "essential condition" of commonwealth that was their legitimate inheritance, and to find inside the true chrysalis of the "one international State" they both were already and were always meant to be. The choice, as the Round Table saw it in the years leading up to and during the Great War, was not between a politics that favored English liberty over the despotism of Empire, or an approach to national character split between Anglo-Saxon culture and an incoherent imperium whose majority occupants were neither white nor English. The choice—or non-choice—lay between becoming a true Commonwealth or watching the world fall prey to less moral imperial powers like Germany.

The beauty of the "principle of commonwealth" for the Round Table was that it allowed them to speak two languages at once. By Round Table logic, there was something uniquely virtuous and broad-minded about Anglo-Saxons as a race, but this uniqueness made them profoundly capable of ushering in the universal idea of international statehood. Whereas the German Empire was aggressive for the aggrandizement of its own culture, all imperial action on the part of the British—in the past, present, and future—was guided by the sensibilities of freedom and democracy that shaped the polity. Its forays into violence or aggression—either in a short- or long-term context—were either understandable as self-defense, or the product (like slavery) of a more general sickness. As the "corporeal frame" in which freedom was incarnate, the Commonwealth was incapable of acting in a manner that was unfree. Likewise, all of its citizens benefited equally from the democracy that gave the Commonwealth shape, even when they could not participate in creating its laws. The Commonwealth was always freedom and democracy to all people, even when it was not.

From a pure policy perspective, all the effort of the Round Table to generate this sublimely circular idea—its years of meetings and memos and research—ended in spectacular failure. The imperial parliament it envisioned was never convened, and the British Commonwealth that emerged from decolonization was unified by neither the patriotic loyalty nor the political connections that the Round Table once imagined possible. But the Round Table's impact on global politics has been far more long lasting than this initial observation would assume. During the war, Kerr and Curtis parlayed their understanding of imperial citizenship in the dependencies into a more fully developed notion of "trusteeship," an approach to governing "backward" people couched not in the name of a single state, but rather as a sacred trust of the universal goals implicit in the British Commonwealth experience. Once popularized by the Round Table, these ideas were to have a profound impact on first Jan Smuts, and then Woodrow Wilson, and help lay the foundations of the League of Nations' Mandate System and later the United Nations' Trusteeship Council.[155] But perhaps more importantly, after the First World War, at the moment when they realized that the time had passed for making explicit arguments in support of imperial politics (even in the name of a "principle of commonwealth"), Curtis, Kerr, and others decided that it was necessary to make "tactical changes" in their self-presentation. [156] They thus joined together to form Chatham House, a think tank that remained devoted to furthering the goals of the Round Table but did so by articulating these goals through a professed interest in "international", rather than imperial, relations. With its American cousin, the Council on Foreign Relations, Chatham House helped to lay the groundwork for a language of both international relations and global governance that—in the spirit of the Commonwealth writings—consistently posited the democratic sensibilities of Britain and America as beyond reproach, and promoted a vision of world order in which the formal equality of states masked deep inequalities between the world's peoples. The Round Table's commonwealth ideal thus set the stage for the kind of postimperial imperialism that would first come to fruition in the League of Nations (through the deflective strategies of Jan Smuts) and which has continued to rear its colossal head ever since, most recently, in the metanarrative vision of Niall Ferguson.

The Empire Whisperer: Niall Ferguson's Misdirection, Disavowal, and the Perilousness of Neoliberal Time

The punch line ladies and gentlemen is that, yes, there are lessons from history, we all know that, but Americans have to learn that the history they need to learn from is not necessarily their own... In all of world history, there have been roughly 86 empires. This, I make the calculation very roughly, is the 86th. But it will not be an enduring empire and its achievements will be little to boast of, if it does not sooner or later learn from the successes and the failures of the last great Anglophone empire, the British one.[1]

—Niall Ferguson, *Is the U.S. an Empire in Denial?*, 2003.

Civilizations, as I have endeavored to show in this book, are highly complex systems, made up of a very large number of interacting components that are asymmetrically organized... A small input to such a system can produce huge, often unanticipated changes—what scientists call "the amplifier effect." Causal relationships are often non linear, which means that traditional methods of generalization from observation (such as trend analysis and sampling) are of little use.[2]

—Niall Ferguson, *Civilization: The West and the Rest*, 2011.

When Niall Ferguson made the first observation above in the fall of 2003, the United States was in its sixth month of a military occupation of Iraq. For Ferguson, it seemed perfectly obvious that not only did the United States "resemble" and "exceed" the "last great Anglophone empire" when it came to "military capability and economic resources," but that the Bush security strategy itself mimicked the British Empire's rhetorical and ideological commitments.[3] "President Bush's ideal of freedom as a universal desideratum," Ferguson argued in 2004's *Colossus: The Price of America's Empire*, "rather closely resembles the

Victorian ideal of 'civilization.' "[4] Because of these similarities, Ferguson encouraged his American audience to abandon their sense of exceptionalism and actively imagine their state as the heir apparent to the British Empire. Later in the summer of 2003, as he reflected on what already had gone wrong in Iraq, Ferguson chastised the Bush administration for its "failure to learn from history."[5] In particular, he argued in 2008, the Administration and the American people had not adequately learned the appropriate lessons from Britain's capacity to "rule the world" with a population that amounted to no more than "2.5% of humanity at that time."[6] Unlike their British counterparts, who believed in the extensive and expansive project of empire, Ferguson argued, Americans suffered from a chronic unwillingness to put "boots on the ground" and an incapacity to tolerate the rest of the world's ire, an unwillingness to accept that "being hated is what happens to dominant empires."[7]

However, the second quotation that begins this chapter, from Ferguson's 2011 book, *Civilization: The West and the Rest*, seems to contradict his earlier exhortation that the American people learn from history. After nearly ten years, two hugely unpopular and expensive wars, an ongoing fiscal crisis, and a change of administrations, Ferguson's earlier suggestion that contemporary Americans learn to mimic the "last great Anglophone empire" is considerably more muted or, at least, more opaque. The central, far more grandiose, question that motivates *Civilization* is not what "lessons for global power" might America learn from the British Empire, but how was it that "the West" (which Ferguson makes no bones about identifying primarily with Britain and America) came to so successfully dominate the world for the last five hundred years, and how might this civilization be saved from its own decline and from the rise of "the Rest"? Ferguson's response to the first question relies on a highly selective historical explanation of the "six killer apps" (competition, science, property, medicine, consumption, and work) that led to the rise of the West in history.

His response to the second question, however, is much less clear, given the questions he raises in the same text about the possibility of drawing historical conclusions at all. Civilizations are, he argues, "complex systems" that more closely resemble "a Namibian termite mound than an Egyptian pyramid."[8] While elsewhere Ferguson substitutes "Great Powers and empires" or just "empires" for civilizations, the point of his inquiry is the same: globe-spanning political, economic, and military powers resemble forms of organization that occur in nature which, because of their internal complexity, deflect ordinary academic analyses, including historical analyses, that rely upon causal claims.[9] Ferguson also insists that in the case of complex systems, "causal relationships are often non-linear."[10] It would almost seem to follow that in the absence of linearity, any kind of historical inquiry that observes the past and then argues that some events—or clusters of events, ideological formations, or economic, military, and political structures acting in particular ways or in concert—might have had an influence on the course of history is doomed to failure. How, then, does Ferguson expect his readers, both academic and popular, to draw conclusions from the past and save the West? Does he want us to learn from history or not?

The answer is yes. And no.

This chapter examines Ferguson's fraught political project and the deeply conflicted approach to the past it has engendered. What makes this project unique among most foreign policy plans hatched by public intellectuals in America since September 11, 2001, is not only the reach of Ferguson's influence, but the extent to which he has eschewed the language of American hegemony and demanded an explicit, triumphalist revival of the word "empire" itself, with all that it implies. In Chapter Three of *Colossus*, "The Case for a Liberal Empire," Ferguson poses the question for himself thus: "Might it not be that for some countries some form of imperial governance, meaning a partial or complete suspension of their national sovereignty, might be better than full independence, not just for a few months or years but for decades?"[11] Ferguson responds in the affirmative and turns to the historical example of the British Empire to demonstrate why this is so.

Such a return has also prompted Ferguson to promote a very particular reading of the British Empire's past, a reading that his critics have long observed resembles a form of Swiss-cheese history, riddled with strategic omissions. As Pankaj Mishra notes in his concisely brilliant 2011 review of *Civilization*, Ferguson not only skims over the violence of the Empire's past, he also "suppresses or ignores facts that complicate his picture of the West's sui generis efflorescence."[12] In addition, as the media outcry over Ferguson's misleading account of Barak Obama's presidency suggests, Ferguson does not simply suppress facts: he intentionally misinterprets them as well.[13] I argue in this chapter, however, that while these observations about Ferguson's omissions are absolutely correct, they do not provide us with a complete picture of both *why* Ferguson suppresses or misinterprets information and *how* such ellipses fit into the broader ideological push of his political vision. To paint that picture, we must also look at both the political and methodological imperatives behind Ferguson's particular approach to writing metanarrative, and the way this approach both resembles and differs significantly from liberal imperialist authors of one hundred years ago,—the way he both is and is not, in Mishra's words, a "retro rather than revisionist historian."[14]

In some important ways, not only have the intellectual and political circumstances in which Ferguson writes his metanarrative changed significantly from those of the Round Table, but the type of liberalism he espouses also looks distinctly different as well. Ferguson is a neoliberal with a very specific understanding of the kind of integrated global economy that he believes is best for the world. His metanarratives are written with an eye not only to reading this global economy back into the history of the British Empire, they are written with the urgency of someone who imagines time and history itself in financial terms, as always on the brink of collapse. History is not cyclical, Ferguson intones, and it is not moved by the dialectic or the grand march of ideas. A more appropriate analogy for the historical condition of our current moment, he argues, can be found in "the old poster, once so popular in thousands of college dorm rooms, of a runaway steam train that had crashed through the wall of a Victorian railway terminus and hit the street below nose first. A defective brake or a sleeping driver can be all it takes to go over the edge of chaos."[15] Ferguson constructs his metanarrative in part to reaffirm the faith of Americans in the story of Anglo-American ascendency that they need to hear in order to keep the imperial engine from driving over the edge into financial and political ruin. His work is thus predicated on all sides and at all times by deep-rooted anxiety, by a fear of imperial decline, despite his protestations to the contrary. "Don't call me a 'declinist'," he angrily asserts at the beginning of his 2011 article for *Newsweek*, "America's 'Oh Sh*t!' Moment." "I don't believe the United States—or Western civilization, more generally—is in some kind of gradual, inexorable decline."[16]

But while decline for Ferguson may not be gradual or inexorable, it is a constant presence in his work, and it conditions the very kind of history he can tell. In this sense, his work and his political project very much resemble that of the Round Table. Like the Round Table, Ferguson must maintain the fiction that the imperial state is primarily about liberalism, even when it is behaving in a racist or illiberal fashion—although, being unable to dismiss fifty years of anti-imperial history and entire groups of people as "child races," he has less leeway to do this. He speaks to this necessity not merely by omitting those historical realities that do not fit his overall Anglophilic vision, he also acknowledges these moments and then either misdirects his readers' attention or disavows these realities. In both cases, these tactics serve as a form of rhetorical deflection that occlude the violence of imperial history and the experiences of the colonized by constantly bringing the liberal character of the imperial state back to the center of the analysis. The story of stories that runs through all of Ferguson's narratives, like that of the Round Table, always seems to be reaching out to its audience, pleading "Don't look at them! Look at me! Look at me!"

The chapter begins by looking more closely at Ferguson's political agenda, his historical methodology, and his theory of sped-up financial time, and then analyzes how these work together to shape and constrain the kind of metanarrative he can tell. The second half of the chapter then turns to a close reading of Ferguson's works on empire, and interrogates the various strategies of forgetting that make up his sweeping metanarrative of Anglo-American triumphalism across time, focusing in particular on the way he omits alternative stories, misdirects his readers to look elsewhere, and disavows the Empire's illiberal history in order to prove its liberal nature. The chapter concludes by considering the irony of the fact that while Ferguson may proclaim a nostalgic connection to the British Empire of the Victorian era, his own metanarrative echoes the more petulant and defensive qualities of those imperial historians writing in 1914, at the very moment when, according to Ferguson, the Empire itself was showing signs of being a "weary Titan."[17] Thus, while the story Ferguson tells bears the unmistakable marks of a distinctly neoliberal project, it also harkens back to a period in British history when denial, forgetting, and fear of decline transformed what could have been a moment of real reflection on imperial power into a continuation of Anglo-American domination with a new face.

History as a Political Project: Anglobalization, Financial Time, and Crises of Confidence

Niall Ferguson is currently the Lawrence A. Tisch Professor of History at Harvard University, a senior research fellow at Jesus College, Oxford, and a Senior Fellow at the Hoover Institute at Stanford. He has written multiple books on both financial and imperial history including *The Pity of War: Explaining World War I* (1999), *Empire: The Rise and Demise of the British World Order and the Lessons for Global Power* (2003), *Colossus: The Rise and Fall of the American Empire* (2004), *The Ascent of Money: A Financial History of the World* (2008), and *Civilization: The West and the Rest* (2011.) Over the years Ferguson's work has evolved from academic analyses based on original research that focused on particular historical moments, to sweeping metanarratives that make huge claims about historical phenomena over time and which are based almost entirely on secondary sources. Every time Ferguson produces a book this tendency becomes more pronounced. *Civilization*—with its span of five hundred years, limited list of secondary sources for citation, but extensive-looking bibliography—which claims to have captured the essence of Western civilization in "six killer apps," is the most outstanding example of Ferguson's methodology to date.

This move away from serious historical scholarship has also paralleled Ferguson's transformation into a popular historian and public intellectual who has had a profound influence on the world of finance, politics, and media culture. Niall Ferguson is a weekly columnist for *Newsweek* and a contributing editor for Bloomberg TV, has produced seven major television series for the BBC, and in 2004 was named one of the one hundred most influential people in the world by *Time* magazine (beating out Tony Blair). He served as an investment management consultant to the hedge fund GLG Partners (founded by Lehman Brothers), was a member of the board of trustees of the American Academy in Berlin, the Museum of American Finance, and the New York Historical Society, and advised merchant bank Kleinwort Benson. Ferguson has also played a direct and indirect role in shaping educational, fiscal, and foreign policy in both Britain and America. In 2010, for instance, he was invited by David Cameron and other Conservatives to participate in overhauling the history curriculum in British schools.[18] Ferguson has also advised major political figures in the United States—he served on John McCain's unofficial "kitchen cabinet" before his bid for the presidency in 2008—and was one of the many conservative intellectuals who urged the Bush administration to some of its most important foreign policy decisions during his first term in office.[19] In addition, Ferguson's status as a Harvard professor has allowed him significant sway with the American Right during a decade that has seen a significant decline in intellectual conservatism. As Michael Lind caustically put it in 2011, "in an era when the conservative movement is symbolized by lightweights like Glenn Beck, Ann Coulter and Jonah Goldberg, rather than William F. Buckley Jr., George Will and Irving Kristol, even Niall Ferguson can be mistaken for an intellectual."[20]

Ferguson, then, is different from the elite members of the Round Table insofar as he works his influence from both behind closed doors and in the popular media. But his imperial sensibilities are in key ways more similar to those of the Round Table than they are to most contemporary historians or foreign policy pundits, particularly in the way he exhorts an explicit and reinvigorated embracement of an American imperial state that looks like the British Empire at the end of the nineteenth-century. Ferguson's overall political project is to establish a continuity of liberal imperial sensibilities across time that unites one set of imperial practices (the British) with another (the American) in much the same way the Round Table worked to weave the same coherent thread of a liberal commonwealth through Athens, England, and the British Empire. Additionally, Ferguson often articulates his vision in cultural terms that parallel those of the Round Table, arguing since the 1990s that the British Empire was, overall, a beneficial form of economic integration and liberal global governance, and that these institutions emerged out of its Anglo-Saxon inclinations toward liberty, democracy, and free trade—inclinations that live on in the global economic and military practices of the United States today.

What most differentiates Ferguson's imperial vision from that of the Round Table, however, is the nature of his liberalism. While members of the Round Table represented a variety of different political positions, its key architects and authors (Zimmern, Curtis, etc.) were primarily influenced by T. H. Green's New Liberal approach to the state and social welfare. They argued that the state ought, however paternalistically, to help alleviate the suffering of the poor and level the playing field for its citizens through the creation and maintenance of social services and public programs both in the metropole and throughout the Empire.[21] And while all of them were deeply committed to a broader notion of "free trade," they were somewhat divided on the subject of tariffs.[22] Ferguson, by contrast, has described himself as a "confirmed Thatcherite" with a basic faith in the benefits of limited government, deregulation, and increased global economic integration.[23] However, what makes Ferguson a neoliberal (of the same shade as Reagan and Thatcher) and not just a libertarian is the extent to which he believes in an interventionist state with a sizable military and security apparatus to ensure the conditions for capital's profitability, even as he insists on the benefits of shrinking the social state. This also makes Ferguson a neoliberal of a particular ilk. For Marxist geographer David Harvey, one of the most self-contradictory elements of neoliberal ideology is its explicit avowal of limited statehood (particularly a belief in the diminished capacity of the state to regulate capital) coupled with an unwillingness to admit to the increased role they imagine for the state in the "reorganization of international capitalism" and in reinforcing the "ground rules" for economic competition (particularly property rights) in formerly colonized or "developing" states.[24] Rather, neoliberals tend to emphasize the informal imperialist institutions of the World Trade Organization, the International Monetary Fund, and the World Bank, thus effectively masking their support for a strong security state, stripped of its social capacity, whose primary purpose is to enforce the rule of law, private property, and free trade at home and abroad. The terrorist attacks of September 11, 2001, however, created an ideological environment in which it was possible for some supporters of neoliberal globalization to come out as explicitly pro-imperialist, often by joining forces with the neoconservative interventionists associated with the Project for a New American Century, who held sway over the Bush Administration. Ferguson used his emerging influence as a public intellectual writing in a popular vein with a growing influence on both the financial sector and the American Right to lead the charge of these neoliberal imperialists.[25]

But even before the events of September 11, 2001 freed some neoliberals from the shackles of informal imperialism, Ferguson was making a name for himself as an economic historian who understood the neoliberal benefits of empire. Ferguson himself has consistently maintained that it is his cognizance of the role of state power in the creation of global markets that differentiates his work on empire from those of other economic historians who are, like him, interested in a contemporary neoliberal project. As he argued in an early 2001 panel discussion entitle "Globalization in Interdisciplinary Perspective":

> Economic historians... tend to pay more attention to the ways government can facilitate globalization by various kinds of deregulation... than to the ways it can promote globalization more actively. It is only relatively recently that we have come to understand the importance of political institutions—the rule of law, credible monetary systems, and

transparent fiscal systems—in encouraging cross-border capital flows. Little work, by contrast, has been done on the way globalization can be imposed by the use of force. "Empire" is the concept that seems to lurk between the lines of a number of the preceding chapters, which have perhaps discussed the economic globalization of the eighteenth and nineteenth centuries with too little regard for the remarkable political globalization brought about by the European empires in the same period.[26]

Ferguson thus believes that economic historians should be viewing the British Empire through neoliberal eyes as the creator and champion of an earlier form of economic globalization. In contrast to most critics of Ferguson who, like Mishra, argue that Ferguson "set aside" his "expertise in economic history" when he became "an evangelist-cum-historian of empire," I suggest that Ferguson's imperial histories actually emerge out of his ideological commitment to global economic integration in the past, present, and future.[27]

Ferguson makes this point explicitly in the "Introduction" to *Empire*. "There are already several good general histories of the British Empire in print," he notes generously. "My aim has been not to replicate these but to write the history of globalization as it was promoted by Great Britain and her colonies— 'Anglobalization', if you like."[28] His penchant for catch phrases aside, by using the word "globalization" (which first emerged in the pages of economic journals in the 1960s, but did not gain broad currency within international relations and finance discourse until the late 1980s) in this context to refer to both a contemporary and earlier form global capitalism, Ferguson signals that he is both a retro and *retroactive* historian, willing to not only mimic the bluster of Victorian imperialists but also read the neoliberal project back into British history.[29] The British imperial mission, by Ferguson's lights, emerged out of a desire to convince reluctant states to deregulate their economies and establish a liberal rule of law to protect private property, thereby encouraging "cross-border capital flows." The fact that this was accomplished by force, occupation, and extended periods of formal and informal rule is beside the point for Ferguson. With their gunboats, he insists, the British "imposed superior economic institutions wherever they ruled" and this was "on balance a good thing."[30]

One is almost tempted, in an instance like this, to feel a certain amount of relief at Ferguson's candor, at his willingness to admit that behind the beneficence of the British Empire lay state power, and that this power was absolutely necessary to establish the international economy of the modern world. But, as we shall see in the next section, the grand sweep of Ferguson's metanarrative—his persistent reassertion of the "overall" and "on balance" portion of the imperial story—consistently draws the reader's attention away from the actual violence inherent in the state force required to maintain an empire. Violence and state power are present in Ferguson's narrative, but they are largely unarticulated, lurking in the background in the passive voice. Because of the British Empire, Ferguson insists, "free trade, free capital movements, and free migration were fostered. The rule of law was institutionalized."[31] The violence behind this fostering and institutionalization remains oblique.

At the same time, Ferguson's neoliberal conception of the world does more than shape the content of his historical inquiries: it also frames the way he understands the organization of social and economic entities more generally as "complex systems" and this, in turn, shapes and conditions the very kind of history that he can tell. Of course, anyone familiar with the political-economic theory of the grandfather of neoliberalism, Frederick Hayek, will immediately recognize Ferguson's notion of "complex systems" from Hayek's 1967 essays "The Theory of Complex Phenomena" and "Notes on the Evolution of Systems of Rules of Conduct." In these essays, Hayek set aside his previous commitment to a social and economic theory of equilibrium for an analysis that described social, political, and economic entities as "complex systems" enlivened by the "twin ideas of evolution and spontaneous order."[32] But while Hayek may have invented the language of "complex systems" and "spontaneous order," complexity theory only really caught on with economists and social scientists after the founding of the privately funded Santa Fe Institute in 1984. The Institute's mission ever since has been to bring together economists, mathematicians, evolutionary theorists, physicists, and theoretical biologists to further develop complex systems theory and bring its insight to the realms of economics, politics, natural science, and even, Ferguson himself notes gleefully in the conclusion of *Civilization*, "metahistory."[33] Scholars at the Santa Fe Institute thus helped lay the groundwork for a systemic and ecological understanding of human organization that has, over the last three decades, had substantial effects not only on economic theory more generally, but on the development policies and practices of non-governmental financial institutions such as the World Bank and the International Monetary Fund.[34]

In order to understand Ferguson's reading of complex systems, it is perhaps best to take his suggestion that causation is nonlinear seriously, by starting from his latter works and moving backward, focusing particularly on the conclusion of *Civilization*, a 2010 article for *Foreign Affairs* titled "Complexity and Collapse," and several other pieces written around the same time. In "Complexity and Collapse," Ferguson argues, "Great powers and empires are, I would suggest, complex systems made up of a large number of interacting components that are asymmetrically organized."[35] To "understand complexity," Ferguson recommends that his readers examine how natural scientists use the concept. "Think of the spontaneous organization of a million ants or termites which allows them to construct complex hills and nests," Ferguson argues, going on to note that political and economic systems develop similar forms of spontaneous organization and that they are continually adapting to their environments—often despite a "lack of central control."[36]

Ferguson maintains that a "complex system" like a Great Power, or an empire, or the international financial system they help to maintain, might "look like it is in equilibrium and economists are trained to think of it as being mostly an equilibrium" but, this is not in fact the case.[37] Rather, these systems "operate somewhere between order and disorder—on 'the edge of chaos.' "[38] As Ferguson goes on to explain:

> Whether the canopy of a rain forest or the trading floor of Wall Street, complex systems share certain characteristics. A small input to such a system can produce huge, often unanticipated changes—what scientists call the 'amplifier effect.'... Meanwhile, causal relationships are often nonlinear which means that traditional methods of generalizing through observation (such as trend analysis and sampling) are often of little use.[39]

Thus, because there are so many imbricated variables at work in a complex system, because its organization is spontaneous and decentralized, because it exists on the edge of chaos, even the smallest input can cause it to "go critical." Historians who imagine that "history has rhythm," Ferguson argues, or believe they can see predictable patterns in the rise and fall of empires and civilizations, simply fail to capture the extent to which complex systems always exist on the verge of disaster. History itself, Ferguson suggests, is not cyclical, patterned, or predictable, but rather "arrhythmic—sometimes almost stationary but also capable of violent acceleration."[40] Additionally, as Ferguson suggests here, complex systems make it difficult, if not impossible, to establish causal relationships, because these relationships are themselves "often nonlinear." In contrast to those places in these texts where Ferguson uses natural phenomena to help explain the way that complex systems function, he never offers a single example of what a "nonlinear causal relationship" might look like, natural or otherwise. Does cause and effect work backward for Ferguson in some instances? Does time not flow in a single direction in a complex system?

Leaving these questions aside, Ferguson's theory of history (in which complex systems are always on the brink of chaos and crisis) uncritically reflects the way neoliberal economists such as Andrew Haldane also use complex systems theory to explain the current global financial crisis. Haldane maintains that the financial crisis may be usefully compared to the outbreak of diseases like the SARS epidemic—and the global public health response—because both are "manifestations of the behavior under stress of a complex, adaptive network."[41] For his part, Ferguson's descriptions of financial systems "under stress" vacillate between examples drawn from nature and technology. When he is not arguing that the global economy resembles a "Namibian anthill" he is comparing it to an "over optimized electrical grid" where seemingly small phenomena, like defaults on subprime mortgages in the United States, can produce a "surge" capable of tipping "the entire world economy into a financial blackout."[42] The utility of these kinds of comparisons for neoliberals are obvious. On the one hand, in the long tradition of liberal economists since Adam Smith first coined the term "invisible hand," such analogies have worked to naturalize the capitalist economy and its processes, so that questioning its current formulation is tantamount to questioning the existence of anthills or infrastructure. On the other hand, insofar as the "complex system" approach resists long-term explanations, it makes it possible for neoliberal economists to avoid structural analyses that might challenge their orthodoxy and, instead, insist that all critical work focus on identifying what Ferguson calls the "proximate triggers of a crisis."[43]

Ferguson's insistence that we focus all of our critical efforts on understanding complex global phenomena in light of short-term "proximate triggers" is especially evident in his analysis of the debt crisis. In the conclusion to *Civilization* and in a number of different articles and opinion pieces published since 2010, Ferguson has argued that two of the proximate causes of the financial crisis that began in 2008 are the mass defaulting on subprime loans in the United States and an overall increase in consumer debt. What is never entirely clear from any of Ferguson's economic arguments is the source of the housing crisis and the rise in consumer debt. According to Ferguson's analysis, "American profligacy" would seem to have blossomed out of the ether, part and parcel of a generalized cultural malaise, too deeply embedded within the web of the system's internal complexity to identify.[44] By contrast, Harvey locates the origins of the increase in consumer debt within much deeper and longstanding trends in the cyclical nature of capitalism: specifically, in the wage repression of the 1970s.[45] Ferguson, however, is patently uninterested in either cyclical or structural analyses that try to explain "proximate causes" as anything other than spontaneous triggers inherent in a complex system's life on the edge. Looking for deeper causes in the oh-so-fuzzy past of thirty years ago is ludicrous, in Ferguson's opinion. Blaming the debt crisis on "deregulation under U.S. President Ronald Reagan," he argues, "is about as plausible as blaming World War One on the buildup of the German navy under Admiral Alfred von Tirpitz."[46]

The beauty of complex systems theory for a scholar as intrigued by the fast-paced world of finance as Ferguson is that this theory not only dovetails with the way neoliberals naturalize the economy, it also can be used to describe everything—from anthills to empires, from economics, to politics, to history—so that all of time (the past, present, and future) becomes financial time: sped up, chaotic, short term, and always on the brink of collapse. It is this conception of time that he has in mind when Ferguson suggests "History is not just how we study the past; it is how we study time itself."[47] It is also a conception of time that presses against any and all long-term or causal explanations of the current world order.

And yet, Ferguson's emphasis on limited causal explanations, the challenges of nonlinear time, and the centrality of complexity has certainly not led him to reject all causation as narrative closure, nor is he drawn in a post-structuralist direction to look (as did Foucault) at the past with an eye to identifying "ruptures," "discontinuities," and "disjunctions."[48] Ferguson not only dismisses postmodernism (interestingly, because he thinks it rehashes "idealist nostrums"), he also derides the work of the critics and practitioners of "narrative history," like Hayden White, who argue that historical narrative is never "merely a neutral discursive form … but rather entails ontological and epistemic choices with distinct ideological and even specifically political implications."[49] Ferguson identifies this approach to history—the kind that understands the historian's primary role in terms of the need "to impose a narrative order on the confusion of the past"— with what he calls a "creeping subjectivism."[50] Such theories go too far in the direction of rejecting scientific understandings of history altogether. Ironically then, despite the fact that he believes history to be nonlinear, complex, chaotic, and guided by no overriding structural concerns, Ferguson still insists that it is possible to write an account of the past that provides a reasonably accurate picture of what did and did not happen, and generates lessons for what is to come.

"Some theorists of complexity," Ferguson argues, "would go so far as to say that complex systems are wholly nondeterministic; meaning that it is impossible to make predictions about their future behavior based on existing data."[51] Ferguson disagrees, arguing that complex systems are, in fact, amenable to some kind of critical analysis. He thus insists that developing an "understanding of how complex systems function is an essential part of any strategy to anticipate and delay their failure." However, given the temporality at work in Ferguson's vision, it is not immediately clear how the canny observer is meant to develop such an understanding in the first place. Ferguson suggests that because complex systems exist on the edge of chaos, the only thing that we can possibly "understand" about them is: a) that they are complex and b) that crises can be triggered by the smallest proximate causes. In logical terms this is tautological. In temporal terms, what Ferguson describes here is a tyranny of the present, a sense that the world is moving all around us in ways too complex to grasp and that everything is happening right now, in this moment of near crisis.

What, then, is the concerned historian to do? It would seem that historical observations about past empires and past crises would be the last thing we ought to dredge up to help us understand complex systems, much less to "anticipate and delay their failure." But Ferguson makes a positive case for historical inquiry anyway, albeit history of a particular and peculiar kind. Long before he began to talk in the language of complex systems, he had been gravitating toward an approach to historical inquiry guided by the insights of complex system theory's older cousin, chaos theory. As Ferguson explains in a review of Mark Buchanan's *Ubiquity: The Science of History, or Why the World is Simpler than We Think* for *Nature* magazine in 2000,

> As a historian, what I liked about chaos theory was the way it reconciled the manifest unpredictability of history—its apparent chaos—with the reality of determinism, in the sense of meaningful causal relationships. Rather, the multiple equations at work in history were nonlinear. So teleological philosophies of history such as that of Marx could be consigned to the rubbish bin without the need to retreat to the idealist position of idealist philosophers of history."[52]

In other words, Ferguson is drawn to chaos theory in history (what he sometimes refers to in glib Ferguson fashion as "chaostry") because it allows him to imagine the past in complex, chaotic, and interrelated ways without, apparently, dispensing with causation altogether.

But there is something markedly disingenuous about Ferguson's nod to causation, given that the temporal logic at work in his understanding of economic crises and complex systems imprisons the would-be critical historian in the present moment, and makes the genuine study of causation impossible. What emerges most clearly from Ferguson's ruminations on historical methodology is the clear sense that his gestures toward causal logic are largely performative rather than internally coherent. Ferguson knows the story he wants to tell (of consistent, Anglophone liberal imperialism over time) and, in the process, knows that he wants to consign a generation of Marxist historians like E. P. Thompson and Eric Hobsbawm (who ground their historical analyses in the evolving relationship of social, ideological, political, and material forces over time) "to the rubbish bin." At base, Ferguson's real problem with these thinkers is both their method *and* their conclusions. "At once materialist in conception and romantic at heart," he writes in the Introduction to *The Cash Nexus: Money and Power in the Modern World, 1700–2000* (2001), "an entire library of history has been based on the assumption that there was something fundamentally amiss with the capitalist economy."[53] Ferguson's goal when writing imperial history is to provide a more positive accounting of global capitalism; he does this, in part, by rejecting Marxist methodology and insisting instead that developments in some spheres (e.g., the growth of industrial capitalism) cannot really be said to have had effects on other spheres (e.g., the rise of class consciousness, an increase in urban poverty, the destruction of native industries in the colonies). But at the same time, Ferguson is perfectly aware that he cannot tell the kinds of historical stories he wants to tell and have people take him seriously as anything more than an imperial mythmaker if he were to jettison causation altogether. His response to this conundrum has been to affirm his belief in causation, but then, to turn around and argue that, because of the chaotic nature of history, only certain, narrow types of causal claims are actually worth our investigative efforts. In the process, he develops a methodology that excludes just about every historical approach but his own.

Nowhere does Ferguson explain this approach to history-as-chaos in more detail than in the introduction to the collection of essays he edited titled *Virtual History: Alternatives and Counterfactuals* (1999). The book itself is dedicated to counterfactual readings of various historical events (e.g., what if Britain had stayed neutral in World War I? What if the Nazis had won?), and Ferguson writes the Introduction with an eye to justifying these accounts to a skeptical academic audience used to reading counterfactual histories as science fiction or, in E. H. Carr's words, as "parlor games." In the process, he introduces the notion of historical chaos arguing that the world is "condemned to increasing disorder by entropy," that the events historians study were originally "stochastic" (that is, sporadic and non-deterministic), and that the behavior of the material world itself is "governed by non-linear as well as linear questions." In the face of this great, temporal uncertainty, Ferguson claims, the search for "universal laws" of history becomes ludicrous. The world is "not divinely ordered nor governed by Reason, the class struggle, or any other determinist 'law,'" Ferguson argues, in one fell swoop dismissing almost every approach to history that scholars have ever taken.[54] Because history is chaotic and we cannot know how it works, any theory that attempts to understand long-term trends through structural or philosophical analyses becomes "determinist" in its search for certain fixed, historical outcomes. Marxist and Idealist approaches to history are both driven by a teleological desire to reach inevitable conclusions, according to Ferguson, who makes no attempt to distinguish between different variants of Marxist and Idealist history. Because their eyes are so fixed on the long-term horizon they will, by necessity, miss the most important causal effects in history that are, Ferguson argues, almost always proximate and local. Scholars who stress historiographical theories that emphasize large material or social processes, or philosophers of history who see the past and the present in terms of cyclical movement, miss, to Ferguson's mind, the main point.

Given these constraints, Ferguson continues, "the most historians can do is to make tentative statements about causation with reference to plausible counterfactuals, constructed on the basis of judgments about probability."[55] Simply put, Ferguson allows that historians may look at the immediate environment in which an historical event took place and make limited causal claims based on an informed understanding of the alternatives available, and then imagine alternate scenarios about how things might have been different had these alternatives been explored. Ferguson argues that this approach can more closely approximate what actually happened at a particularly critical historical moment because, by focusing on the multiple options that existed at that moment, a counterfactual analysis can tell us which "alternatives were seen at the time as realistic."[56]

In practice, Ferguson is more likely to reverse-engineer counterfactuals in his work than study past events with the kind of laborious attention to detail he describes in *Virtual History*. For example, as he posits in the Introduction to *Colossus*, many people assume that empires always engender violence, and thus that the presence of American troops in the Middle East has made the world a more dangerous place. "One way to test such arguments," he argues, "is to ask the counterfactual question: Would American foreign policy have been more effective in the past four years, or if you prefer, would the world be in a safer place today—if Afghanistan and Iraq had not been invaded?"[57] Ferguson then proceeds to explain why, in his judgment, the world would not be a safer place. Of course, one of the beautiful qualities of counterfactuals is that there is no way to prove Ferguson wrong. Counterfactuals are, despite Ferguson's language of testing, ultimately untestable. As we will see in the next section of this chapter, such untestable "it could have been worse" propositions remain central, reoccurring tropes in all of Ferguson's historical works giving them, at times, the slightly off-kilter feel of auguring in reverse. At the same time, Ferguson continues to claim throughout his writing that counterfactual analysis offers readers a more compelling, more "realistic," understanding of the past.

One would think that if Ferguson truly believed in the process he describes in *Virtual History*, his books would all consist simply of extended "what if" stories centered on very local, proximate causes. In contrast, his actual accounts of the British Empire, the American Empire, and the rise of Western civilization itself are, like the Round Table's histories, sweeping in their scope and radically expansive in their claims about the constancy of the liberal, Anglo-American spirit over time. Ferguson speaks to the obvious disconnect here between his methodological commitments and his narrative conclusions by arguing, in part, that he also draws upon a few other acceptable approaches to writing history in a chaotic and complex world. In addition to focusing on counterfactuals, he argues in the Introduction to *Civilization*, historians are correct to mimic the way social scientists have devised "covering laws" or general statements about social, political, and economic phenomena "that appear to cover most cases." At the same time, he maintains, historians ought to also commune with the dead by "imaginatively reconstructing" the experiences of those individuals for whom we have documentation "in the way

described by the great Oxford philosopher R. G. Collingwood."[58] Between counterfactuals, "covering laws," and imaginative reconstructions, Ferguson argues, it
is possible for historians to gain the kind of insight that allows them to discern, in
Collingwood's words, "the tiger in the grass."

But clearly there is something more going on in Ferguson's historical writings for which counterfactuals, covering laws, and reconstructions alone cannot
account. This "something more" emerges most clearly in those moments when
Ferguson argues explicitly for a return to history curricula that offer students
in the English-speaking world a coherent "grand narrative of Western ascent,"
rather than the "unconnected fragments" of history he insists they are currently being fed in school. On one level, it seems simply baldly hypocritical that,
given his explicit perorations on the complexity—nigh incoherence—of history, Ferguson would now turn around and demand *connected* stories. In this
light, Ferguson's insistence upon grand narratives so shortly after condemning
the possibility of coherence altogether appears crass and opportunistic, a cynical thumbing of the nose at all historical inquiry that tell stories he dislikes. On
a more complicated level, however, Ferguson's tendency to both call for and
tell sweeping metahistorical narratives is also the result of the epistemological
dilemma generated by his self-undermining view of history as chaotic financial
time. This dilemma is most apparent in the convergence of two major themes
that thread their way through his writings: first, an obsession with British and
American "crises of confidence" and, second, a conviction that complex systems
on the verge of chaos can be pushed over the edge by even the perception of
weakness or failure.

Ferguson has long been interested in the way a loss of collective confidence
on the part of imperial peoples can lead to military and fiscal crises that can bring
down an empire. For instance, in *The Pity of War* and in the counterfactual story
he tells in *Virtual History*, "The Kaiser's European Union," Ferguson dwells on
the impact of the Boer War on the English imperial psyche. The Boer War, he
insists, "undermined" British self-confidence and awoke "anxieties" about "the
cost of maintaining Britain's vast overseas imperium" which then led the Foreign
Office to abandon isolationism in favor of détente with other imperial powers.[59] Missing from Ferguson's analysis of the period is any explanation of why
the Boer War might have caused these anxieties (e.g. its excessive violence, its
expense.) Ferguson addresses neither the discursive and political texture of the
anxieties themselves nor the context in which they arose—for instance, the fact
that Liberals were torn on the issue of whether or not to pursue the war, that
Labour opposed the war while Fabians supported it, and that it led to both a
rejection of and increase in domestic jingoism.[60] In Ferguson's mind, the Boer
War was experienced in identical ways throughout British society, as a generalized loss of confidence in the imperial mission.

As he has moved on to writing broader imperial histories, Ferguson's concern with "crises of confidence" (in the past and present) has become more acute. Before the 1920s, he argues in *Empire*, the British "had been remarkably good at not 'wembling'—at taking their empire seriously."[61] But, he continues, "a generation was cracking," there was increasing "loss of faith," a niggling sense of doubt, "a creeping crisis of confidence in empire" that manifested itself in the debates and literature of the period.[62] By the time he wrote *Colossus* two years later, Ferguson had neatly transferred his concern with this malady of the national imperial psyche into an epoch spanning, transatlantic syndrome, arguing that America's "fragile self image" might prevent it from embracing its "cryptoimperial role with self-confidence."[63] Pro-imperial articles from the period send the same message, urging Americans to stay confident in their empire, stay the course in Iraq (despite recent revelations of the atrocities at Abu Ghraib), and not give in to "sagging morale at home—the traditional Achilles heel" of American imperial power.[64] In none of these instances—historical or current, British or American—does Ferguson imagine that, in a democracy, widespread debate about the nature, cost, morality, and future of empire might be a positive thing in and of itself, much less, produce a more thoughtful foreign policy. Crises of confidence are always, for Ferguson, both a sign that there is something fundamentally amiss in the psyche of the imperial nation and a serious threat to its future.

But why, for Ferguson, is this necessarily the case? The answer, I suggest, lies in the second powerful and reoccurring theme in Ferguson's work: how the "nonlinearity of fiscal history" means that imperial and financial powers can collapse quickly with little warning. As he explained in a 2010 Niarchos Lecture, Great Powers live in the shadow of the "suddenness with which things can go wrong in the realm of public finance and from there, to the realm of geopolitics."[65] At times in his books, articles, and lectures, Ferguson tells this story as he does in this lecture: a financial crisis triggers a geopolitical crisis that triggers the collapse of an empire. At other times, Ferguson insists that *any* kind of crisis (financial, political, cultural, or collectively psychological) can contribute to the collapse of an empire—although he still imagines the process of imperial decline and collapse in terms explicitly borrowed from the breakneck speed of the financial world. In "America's 'Oh Sh*t!' Moment," for instance, Ferguson insists that the most "striking feature" of all civilizations and empires in the past has been the "speed with which most of them collapsed, regardless of the cause."[66] He argues that the Roman Empire did not "fall sedately," but rather, quickly over the course of a few years, as did the Ming Dynasty and the Soviet Union. "This process," he proceeds to tell his readers, "is a familiar one to students of financial markets. Even as I write it is far from clear that the European Monetary Union can be salvaged from the dramatic collapse of confidence in the fiscal policies of its peripheral member states. In the realm of power, as in the domain of the bond vigilantes, you're fine until you're not fine—and when you're not fine, you're suddenly in a terrifying death spiral."[67]

Whether bond markets or empires, Ferguson's vision of a world defined by Great Powers always just one step away from "terrifying death spirals," conditioned on all sides by "nonlinearity" and chaos, once again would seem to betoken the futility of historical analysis altogether. Yet for Ferguson, any inkling of skepticism on the part of academics within these Great Powers—any outward sign of an epistemological faintness of heart, as it were—only speeds up the downward spiral. As he notes again and again throughout his work on financial and imperial history, when it comes to collapse, the very perception of weakness (in either the imperial power itself or its financial stability) can cause a complex system to "go critical." In the realm of "political entities," he argues, "the role of perception is just as crucial" as it is in the financial world "if not more so. In imperial crises, it is not the material underpinnings of power that really matter but expectations about future power."[68]

Ferguson thus ends *Civilization* with both a warning and a call for redemptive history. A complex, adaptive, imperial system can fall over the edge into chaos and crisis when a "critical mass of constituents loses faith in its viability," that is, when enough people stop believing in the mission of Western forms of free trade, the rule of law, scientific enlightenment, and representative government.[69] This "package" of Western goods "still seems to offer human societies the best available set of economic, social, and political institutions," Ferguson notes soberly. But, he continues, the big question now facing the West is "whether or not we are still able to recognize the superiority of that package."[70] Given the decline in Great Books programs at colleges and universities and the "modular" (rather than "narrative") form of history that most children in England and America are taught these days, it is hardly surprising, Ferguson argues, that so few young people seem to believe in the project of Anglobalization. Today, he argues, the biggest threat to the West is posed "not by the rise of China, or Islam, or CO_2 emissions but by our own loss of faith in the civilization we inherited from our ancestors" by our own "pusillanimity—and by the historical ignorance that feeds it."[71]

Ferguson's mission in *Civilization, Colossus, Empire*, and indeed almost everything he writes, I argue, ought to be understood as an attempt to rectify this historical ignorance by providing readers with metanarratives intended to restore their faith in the superiority of their own civilization and ameliorate any doubts that the imperial state to which they belong has ever engaged in anything worthy of critique on its own terms. In other words, despite his constant claim to be writing "realistic" accounts of the past and the present, despite his insistence that his historical methodology is limited and focused on proximate causes, and despite his repeated conviction that Western liberal values are good for everyone in the world, Ferguson writes history in order to reconstruct liberal faith in the specific imperial locations where he senses it might be lost, in order to keep the train that is Anglo-American global domination from going over the edge. There is a deep taint of cynicism and instrumentality in this approach, an almost faux-Nietzschean mendacity in the manner with which Ferguson self-consciously constructs a metanarrative of "Anglobalization" over the centuries, transforming the violence of imperialism and colonial capitalism into what Priyamvada Gopal has described as a "poisonous fairytale" of "a benign developmental mission."[72] Ferguson's goal, in this sense, is to fortify neoimperial domination through a rekindling of imperial faith, by telling us the histories we need to hear to believe in who we are now.

Ferguson's recent critics dwell, sometimes apoplectically, on the factual misrepresentations in his stories—but in so doing, they lose sight of the basic imperial-discursive dynamic at work in the project that I have just described. For instance, a number of journalists and public intellectuals have lambasted Ferguson's 2012 articles in *Newsweek* on President Obama for what these authors argue are outright falsehoods. Rather than make a "straightforward case against the current administration," argues Matthew O'Brien of *The Atlantic*, "Ferguson delves into a fantasy world of incorrect and tendentious facts. He simply gets things wrong, again and again and again."[73] James Fallows, Paul Krugman, and Noah Smith make similar arguments, each carefully taking on several of Ferguson's assertions and demonstrating the extent to which each is divorced from reality. There is a note of bafflement in the tone of these responses, genuine wonder that Ferguson the scholar, the academic, would, for instance, willfully misrepresent the statistics produced by the General Accounting Office rather than simply offer a different, more dire, interpretation of these statistics. In O'Brien's words, "bluster" and "untruths" are things "we expect from our politicians, not our professors."[74]

What confuses critics like O'Brien is Ferguson's unwillingness to make a "straightforward argument," or at least an argument that seems to arise out of facts with a thesis and a conclusion, a beginning, middle, and end, something that we recognize as academic. O'Brien argues that this is a level to which only the recent Ferguson has stooped and he bemoans the loss of the scholar of yesteryear, a man whose "early academic work was as good as his punditry is bad." "It's a shame," O'Brien continues, "that Niall Ferguson wasn't the Niall Ferguson who wrote the *Newsweek* story." Others, like Eric Zuesse, have noted quite rightly that "this type of deceit (or else 'convenient-ignorance') on the part of the British-now-American Ferguson is nothing new" and that Ferguson has made misrepresentations part of his stock and trade for years.[75]

Mishra agrees with this latter interpretation, arguing that, as in his other books, "a vast bibliography trails the main text of *Civilization*, signaling the diligent scholar rather than the populist simplifier." But, Mishra goes on to point out, such an appearance of diligence serves to mask the fact that Ferguson is suppressing and omitting facts and voices that might challenge his overall vision. For instance, Ferguson argues that in the Ottoman Empire "Jews and Christians were tolerated" but that their status "was closer to that of Jews in medieval Europe—confined to specific areas and occupations and taxed at a higher rate."[76] The fact that Ferguson's sole reference for this claim (the notoriously Orientalist Bernard Lewis) has been refuted on this point by a majority of Ottoman historians seems not to trouble Ferguson in the least.[77] At other times, Ferguson simply resorts to intentional misreading in order to maintain the purity of his fiction. For example, one of the reasons Marxism failed to capture the imagination of so many workers, he argues in *Civilization*, it that Marx's prescriptions, such as the creation of a "community of women (wife swapping)" were "singularly unappealing" to workers."[78] Of course Marx supported no such thing and referred to a "community of women" in *The Communist Manifesto* in the context of critiquing bourgeois attitudes toward women as commodities. Marx equated what Ferguson calls "wife swapping" with prostitution and exploitation.[79] One can either assume here that Ferguson has never read *The Communist Manifesto* or, given his claim to have such intimate knowledge of Marxist perspectives on economic history, that he simply felt no qualms about misrepresenting its argument if it served the purpose of restoring our faith in liberal capitalism.

And yet, as this next section explores, Ferguson's strategically elliptical approach to history is just one among several rhetorical devices he uses to construct a metanarrative meant to restore our faith in Anglobalization—a metanarrative that, in the end, looks more like what Foucault called a "prayer to the god of just causes" than history.[80]

Ferguson's Imperial Metanarrative: Omission, Misdirection, and Disavowal

When Ferguson compares America today to "the United Kingdom roughly a century ago" he means this comparison to evoke far more than power politics.[81] Rather, in *Empire*, *Colossus*, and *Civilization*, Ferguson ultimately wants his readers to understand that Britain then and America now were and are so successful precisely because they share a common set of economic, political, cultural, and institutional practices that make the form of global hegemony they exercise exceptional in very particular ways. It is this common set of practices that makes the "Anglobalization" of the British identical in many respects to the kinds of international power and forms of economic integration that the United States pursues today, argues Ferguson, even if the majority of Americans and their policy makers refuse to see these similarities or to call their state an empire. The problem with Americans, Ferguson insists, is that they simply do not understand the kind of empire he is describing. Britain then and America now both embody, Ferguson insists,

> a liberal empire... one that not only underwrites the free international exchange of commodities, labor and capital but also creates and upholds the conditions without which markets cannot function— peace and order, the rule of law, non-corrupt administration, stable fiscal and monetary policies—as well as provides public goods.[82]

Ferguson's histories are thus aimed, first, at writing this particular liberal identity back into the history of the British Empire. His second aim is to then marry this identity to America, both historically and in the present. In the end, the stories of British and American imperialism coalesce into one coherent narrative about one coherent form of liberalism and its development over time.

Despite the differences in their liberalisms, Ferguson's project is, in many ways, conditioned by many of the same political and historical anxieties that plagued the Round Table in 1914. Like the Round Tablers, he is deeply worried about the future of Anglo-American domination: his unsettled references to Europe's "demographic decline" and the rise of "illiberal" China as a world power resemble the Round Table's excessive concern with population statistics before the Great War.[83] Like the Round Tablers, Ferguson has to make these arguments in a manner that speaks to critics of America's empire today and Britain's power in the past by stressing the universal appeal and ultimate fairness of Anglobal, liberal institutions while, at the same time, stressing the need for continued American economic, political, and military domination. Ferguson must thus spin his story of Anglo-Saxon/American superiority in a manner that both sounds universal and can comfortably embrace the long-term exclusion of most people in the world without sounding racist. In sum, Ferguson's historical-imperial worldview must argue for an overall Anglobal hegemony that is currently dominant but also imperiled, while exhorting American and British liberalism in universal terms that are actually exclusive, while all the while avoiding charges of illiberality and racial hubris. A tall order indeed.

It is perhaps not surprising, then, that the imperial story Ferguson tells closely resembles the metahistorical yarn of the liberal Anglo-Saxon commonwealth spun by the Round Table. The master narrative at work in *Empire*, *Colossus*, and *Civilization* explains the success of a particular constellation of cultural and institutional phenomena sometimes associated with "the West" more generally but in reality, for Ferguson, closely adhering to the outline of the British Empire and its former colonies. This metanarrative contains, Ferguson concedes, "many smaller tales or micro-histories within it" but these stories are chosen selectively, so as not to challenge the main thrust of the story of stories: that Great Britain not only shaped the modern world into the global economy of today but that the world is better off today precisely because British imperialists forced open societies in Asia, Africa, and the New World to "free trade," the rule of law, and fair political institutions. The seamless transfer of political, cultural, and economic traditions from one imperial society to the next (from Britain to America) is Ferguson's own version of the "Anglo-Saxon relay race" so prominent in the work of the Round Table.[84] As with the Round Table, this relay-race approach to metanarrative stands alongside and supplements the equally powerful push of the idea of progress (what Tully refers to as the "western legitimating narrative of universal development") by claiming that the institutional values that drive it are both good for all people and particular to Anglo-Saxon culture.

Ferguson's imperial narrative is thus, in key respects, rife with contemporary iterations of the kinds of contradictions that haunted the Round Table and liberal imperialists more generally. On the one hand, he proclaims his commitment to freedom—that is, freedom of movement, freedom of trade, freedom of speech, and free political practices embodied in parliamentary institutions.[85] On the other hand, the free movement of capital also simultaneously requires the imposition of order on an otherwise chaotic world so as to uphold "the conditions without which markets cannot function." This in turn necessitates the coercive power of a political entity like the state (or a trans-state association like empire) capable of enforcing this "peace and order" and "the rule of law." Without such an entity, all hard-working individuals would be subject to the perennial harassment of what Locke described as the "quarrelsome and contentious," those who have, with their actions, put themselves outside of the liberal order. For Ferguson, the modern equivalents of these renegades who cannot be reformed include both the global yet singular threat of "radical Islam" as well as third-world governments who "no matter how persuasive the arguments for economic openness" continue to peevishly "cling to their tariffs."[86] In other words, anyone who engages in "internationalist, revolutionary, and anti-capitalist-rhetoric" that is more often "of the left than of the right."[87]

Early proponents of economic liberalism like Smith were perfectly willing to admit that governments were instituted for the express purpose of containing the "quarrelsome and contentious," the un-propertied rabble.[88] Governments could do good, according to Smith—they could promote the public welfare and make the commonwealth safe for commerce—but he was always clear-eyed about the original purpose of government: to make the commonwealth safe for those with capital stock from those who had none. By contrast, for all Ferguson positions himself as an economic realist, he is never willing to make this admission, and it is in this unwillingness that the ideological impulse behind his meta-narrative becomes most apparent. Even as he talks about the need for strong states and for imperial power, even as he concedes that the necessity of opening up markets may require violence, even as he notes that sometimes economic integration does not work out well for all people, Ferguson still insists that the underlying purpose of both the British and American Empires has always been—"overall" and "on balance"—to spread fair and secure forms of governance and economic organization based on universal principles of liberty. In their essence, the British and American imperial states were and are, according to Ferguson, grounded on the liberal values of freedom and the rule of law, always committed to "Anglophone economic and political liberalism."[89]

In his equation of political and economic freedom here, Ferguson echoes one of liberalism's most elisional qualities, what G. A. Cohen has termed the "unreflective association of ideas" where the "market economy is *ipso facto* a free society."[90] But this act of elision is more difficult for Ferguson than for the liberal and libertarian thinkers that Cohen critiques precisely because Ferguson's association of these ideas requires that he ignore not just the fact that political freedom can mask the un-freedom of capitalism (as Cohen argues) but that, in the context of empire, political freedom itself must be denied to some for the express purpose of maintaining the "free" economic order. Remarkably, there is no moment in Ferguson's work when he pauses to observe obvious tensions between the imposition of a liberal rule of law or free trade regime on colonized people and their freedom to live, trade, or work in the fashion they choose. Rather, as a retrohistorian of both empire and finance, Ferguson has long argued that economic freedom, direct political control of some peoples by others, and state and military policies oriented toward "encouraging cross-border capital flows" are mutually reinforcing phenomena, a fact about which he believes the British were more forthcoming than Americans are today.[91] In this respect, Ferguson's vision fits neatly into the long and storied imperial tradition of transforming what Tully describes as the "massive dispossession and restructuring" involved in forcing slave labor, then wage labor, private property, market organization, and capitalist trading practices on the non-West into a gift of civilization.[92]

Additionally, Ferguson's narrative frequently relies on a strained counterfactual form of argument that briefly acknowledges the negative impacts of the British Empire on colonized peoples and economies, but then immediately interject an "it could have been worse" statement. For instance, Ferguson will happily argue that, "the British Empire proved that empire is a form of international government that can work—and not just for the benefit of the ruling power."[93] Yet proof for this claim lies in his counterfactual intuition that, while in reality, the "benefits" of imperialism might not have been spread evenly between the colonizer and the colonized, the "alternatives to British rule represented by the German and Japanese Empires were clearly far worse."[94] One senses a keen but familiar fatalism in Ferguson's imperial ideology, a fatalism similar to the way Round Table thinkers, other liberal imperialists, and even liberal anti-imperialists like Hobson all accepted that the colonization of the entire globe by Europeans was inevitable, that there were more or less humane ways of doing this, and that denizens of the British Empire were lucky to have been colonized by a liberal state rather than the Germans. Ferguson uses a similar logic today with his dire warnings about "tyrannous and toxic" Chinese imperialism.[95] You may not like American imperial domination, he implies, but it could be worse—it could be China. Whether or not this kind of statement is true (and it very well could be) such "it could be worse" statements serve the very real rhetorical purpose of silencing discussions about alternatives to British and American imperialism in the past, present, and future.

Importantly however, the political and intellectual environment in which Ferguson writes differs in two meaningful ways from that experienced by the Round Table. First, between the Round Table's rise to prominence and Ferguson's leap into imperial history lie nearly a hundred years first of ascending anticolonial movements, the dissolution of the formal British Empire, and the emergence of 120 new states.[96] Ferguson still has to answer the very liberal problem at the heart of liberal imperialism—how does one reconcile the denial of political freedom for some with an expressed commitment to liberal freedom for all, and identify which people are to be excluded from the practices of liberal democracy? But, unlike the Round Table authors, he cannot do this by using the language of race. Thus, even as they were arguing that they were not racist like the Germans, and that anyone could become a citizen of the British Commonwealth regardless of race or ethnicity, Round Table authors in 1914 still grounded their arguments about imperial citizenship in a racist and Orientalists terminology no longer available in its uncensored form to Ferguson. Second, the intellectual context for historicizing the British and American Empires also shifted significantly after World War II as an increasing majority of academics, from both the West and the postcolonial world, called into question the long-term benefits of imperialism and brought to light the intensity of the violence necessary to sustain it. In sum, both scholarly and popular opinion since decolonization weigh heavily against precisely the kinds of pro-imperial history that Ferguson wants to write.

Ferguson has gone to great lengths to insist, again and again, that he is not a racist, to the point of threatening to sue the London Review of Books over Mishra's review of Civilization because, he argues, Mishra "made a vile allegation of racism against me."[97] He has also, occasionally, acknowledges both the traditional biases of his field and the complexity of imperial history itself.

In *Empire*, for instance, he concedes that what British historians once dismissively referred to as "anarchy" in India during the 1740s could more accurately be described as "internecine warfare," a "struggle for mastery in India no different from the struggle for mastery in Hapsburg-dominated Europe that had been raging since the seventeenth-century."[98] Ferguson's gesture here appears to arise from a desire to correct the longstanding tendency of imperial historians to portray the colonized world as an incoherent, primordial soup. Note, however, that the comparison is with Hapsburg Europe, not Britain, suggesting an affinity for the pre-liberal, authoritarian tendencies of squabbling nationalities rather than self-motivated individuals—even, perhaps, for empire. For Ferguson, what existed in India before British occupation was not anarchy but an ailing imperium. At other times, Ferguson seems to have absolutely no problem engaging in outright Orientalism, as long as this is balanced by a nod to those persons from the non-West who he believes agree with him. Thus, while *Civilization* frequently dabbles in Orientalist language (describing the Sultan Osman as presiding "indolently over a decadent Ottoman Empire"), Ferguson offsets such utterances by evoking those "ardent and eloquent defenders of Western values today whose ethnic origins are very different from mine—from Amartya Sen to Liu Xiaobo, from Hernando de Soto to the dedicatee of this book," his second wife, the anti-Muslim activist Ayaan Hirsi Ali.[99]

More often than not, however, Ferguson has negotiated the contemporary discursive environment on race and empire by relying upon both strategic omissions of the colonial and racial other and on rhetorical acts of misdirection and disavowal that deflect the reader's attention away from imperial illiberalism or violence. For instance, Ferguson often employs a kind of Orientalism by proxy that still reiterates Said's "imaginative geography" between East and West without sounding explicitly racist. As Mishra rightly notes, Ferguson's histories are full of strategic silences, ellipses, and a carefully orchestrated understanding of when to dip down from the overall temporal flow of the narrative to touch upon historical or factual specifics that highlight the point he is making, while ignoring the voices of colonial historians and intellectuals with strikingly different understandings of the West from his own.[100] What is most notable about this kind of pro-imperial discourse for Said is how totalizing its understanding of the West is, "how all enveloping its attitude and gestures, how much it shuts out even as it includes, compresses, and consolidates."[101] Ferguson himself acknowledges, in the Introduction to *Civilization*, that his method requires "shutting out" certain subjects, which he describes as a form of improvisation. Always aware of his critics, he addresses himself directly to "those who will complain about what has been omitted" from his analysis. "I can do no more," he goes on to argue, "than quote the idiosyncratic jazz pianist Thelonius Monk: 'Don't play everything (or every time): let some things to by... What you don't play can be more

important than what you do.'"[102] In Ferguson's case this is absolutely true. What
he chooses to omit is often more important than what he includes—but not
in the way he imagines. Rather, when coupled with those stories that Ferguson
deems it appropriate to relate, his strategic silences reveal a great deal about the
ideological impulses at the heart of his approach to history.

For instance, Ferguson uses personal stories in *Empire* and *Civilization* in a
way that occludes indigenous perspectives that do not support his overall story
while, at the same time, encouraging his readers to associate the Anglophonic
empire with the actions of individuals capable of self mastery and of forging a life
for themselves in the wilderness—in essence, as both the creators, and deserv-
ing recipients of, liberal institutions. Ferguson does this by occasionally halting
his narrative of Anglo-American triumphalism mid-stream to tell the story of
a single individual or family. In the spirit of Collingwood's exhortation to find
"historical knowledge" in "the re-enactment of a past thought," Ferguson's work
offers his readers countless biographical vignettes of colonists, economic entre-
preneurs in Africa, and low-level functionaries in India, all complete with names.
These are the people (including several close Ferguson relatives) who contributed to the Empire's expansion on an everyday level. We learn about the travails
of Ferguson's Great-Aunt Agnes in rural Canada, the cultural adjustments of
Third-class Magistrate Evan Machonochie in India, and the indignity suffered
by indentured servant John Harrower in Virginia, all of which serve to person-
alize what otherwise might remain an abstract account of the British imperial
state, its navy, and its great men.[103] However, we are almost never privy to a single
account of an ordinary nonwhite imperial subject, except for the occasional brief
discussion of an indigenous elite or future nationalist leader, all of whom are
British educated. Native thinkers who might have had a different understanding
of European domination are simply absent; sometimes the quietude of these
voices is so stark it startles. Thus, in *Civilization*, Ferguson moves with lightning
speed in the same paragraph from a discussion of the way Locke's theory of
property transformed all Native American lands into *terra nullis* to the story of
two scrappy, English colonists in Carolina who benefited from this expropriation. Ferguson makes no attempt to follow the life story of an individual member
of the Piedmont or Cherokee tribes who were summarily uprooted from their
land. The imperialized remain undifferentiated masses, acted upon rather than
actors, the silent objects of liberal ordering.[104]

In essence, Ferguson's metanarratives are as shaped just as much by what
they include (in a Saidian sense) and how they include these things as they are
by what they shut out, by holes and silences. Moreover, beyond the simple and
inspiring stories of white pioneers that fascinate Ferguson, his metanarratives
also specifically address imperial wrongdoing and violence. However, Ferguson
grapples with instances of imperial illiberalism in a way that recuperates these

moments for the Empire and, in the process, confronts the obdurate presence of the un-liberal in a way that smoothes it back into the unruffled sheen of the Anglobal endeavor. In this regard, Ferguson's pro-imperial narratives differ from those written by imperial historians in the mid- to late nineteenth-century. As described by Bill Ashcroft, these scholars often wrote as if the Jamaican rebellion "had never occurred." This was not merely "convenient forgetting of an uncomfortable event," Ashcroft argues. "Imperial history," he continues, "could make no place for this scandal without undermining its own premises."[105] Ferguson, by contrast, confronts the Jamaican rebellion and Britain's response—and many other moments of imperial uprising and violence—as a perverse way of reaffirming the Empire's liberal premises. In a sense, his approach to these events can be seen as an exaggerated version of the Round Table thinkers' belief that they could not simply ignore some of the more egregious illiberal acts of the British Empire in history if they wanted to salve the consciences of otherwise sympathetic liberals. But unlike the Round Tablers, Ferguson cannot, after two generations of critical imperial history, brush off something like the Atlantic slave trade, as the Round Table did, by simply mentioning it and then turning quickly to the "question of real importance"—namely, how the British had worked to rid themselves of the "poison" of slavery. Ferguson, by contrast, clearly feels that he has to confront the criticisms of those who can still "work themselves up into a state of high moral indignation over the misdeeds of the European empires" by engaging these misdeeds.[106]

Ferguson accomplishes this in two ways. One tactic amounts to a basic rhetorical act of misdirection that often looks, for all intents and purposes, just like the Round Table's quick move from violence and slavery to absolution. Ferguson, however, couples this with a more bombastic, self-referential claim to transparency and forthrightness. From very early on in *Empire*, for example, he assures us that he will not shy away from the egregious acts of violence committed by the imperial state. "I have endeavored," Ferguson argues in the Introduction, "not to select so as to flatter. Slavery and the slave trade cannot and are not to be disclaimed, any more than is the Irish potato famine, the expropriation of the Matebele or the Amritsar massacre."[107] Similarly, in the Introduction to *Civilization*, immediately after minimizing the critiques of those who get "worked up into a state" over the memory of imperial "misdeeds," Ferguson declares, "Misdeeds there certainly were, and they are not absent from these pages."[108] So we understand that Ferguson is not going to spare us any of the gory details of imperial history. But almost in the same breath as he acknowledges the reality of colonial violence, Ferguson directs the reader's gaze elsewhere, toward moments when the imperial state fostered decent government, the rule of law, and functional economies. Yes, famine and violence were not good things—but, overall, empire was. The fact remains, argues Ferguson, that "no organization in history has done more to promote the free movement of goods, capital and labor than the British Empire in the nineteenth and early twentieth centuries. And no organization has done more to impose Western norms of law, order and governance around the world."[109] Ferguson thus asks his readers to look at the illiberal acts of the British Empire in history and then immediately deflects attention away from those acts back to the Empire's liberal endeavoring.

Ferguson also misdirects his readers by, again, turning these moments of illiberality and violence into counterfactual questions. Yes, the effects of the Opium Wars (which Ferguson dispenses with in one paragraph in *Civilization*) might have been economically devastating to the Chinese, but were they any more devastating than the "retarding effect of political monopoly in East Asia?"[110] Sure, colonial violence in Africa might have been excessive, but would Africans have been better off if they had not been colonized? It is simply unconvincing, he asserts in *Colossus*, to "blame all the problems of the developing world today on the malign after-effects of colonial rule."[111] Counterfactuals, in this sense, like the move redirecting the reader's gaze toward colonial good governance, consistently call the character, identity, and good intentions (or lack of intentions) of the imperializing society back into the center of the analysis in a way that blots out the actual effects of colonial capitalism and imperialism. The relevant question becomes not what actually happened, but what *might* have happened if colonization had never occurred; in Ferguson's words, "The question is not whether British imperialism was without blemish. It was not. The question is whether there could have been a less bloody path to modernity."[112] And with the smooth, unprovable logic only really possible in a counterfactual universe, Ferguson concludes that there was not.

Ferguson also tacitly acknowledges illiberalism and violence in the history of the British Empire through a profound form of self-conscious disavowal. I use "disavowal" here not in the colloquial sense of the word as the simple action of repudiating, denying, or refusing to acknowledge a person or event. Rather, the kind of disavowal I am thinking of in this case resembles the psychoanalytic use of the term that Sibylle Fischer explores in *Modernity Disavowed: Haiti and the Cultures of Slavery in the Age of Revolution*.[113] As Fischer notes, scholars of psychoanalysis define disavowal as "a refusal to recognize the reality of a traumatic perception."[114] Fischer finds this way of conceptualizing disavowal useful for analyzing the particular qualities of the silence endemic to European accounts of the Haitian revolution because it stresses the fact that, in the process of disavowing, something is also being acknowledged. "As Freud explains," argues Fischer, "disavowal exists alongside recognition; 'Whenever we are in a position to study them [acts of disavowal] they turn out to be half measures, incomplete attempts at detachment from reality. The disavowal is always supplemented by acknowledgement.'"[115] Ferguson's approach to the violence of liberal imperialism and colonial capitalism in the history of "Anglobalization" works as a kind of explicit or self-conscious form of disavowal, insofar as he often acknowledges the imperial state's slip into illiberality (that "which must not be seen") before disavowing and, in the process, refusing to "recognize the reality of the traumatic perception." That which disturbs the premises of the liberal empire is always there in Ferguson's analysis, both when it is named and in Ferguson's attempts to thrust it just beyond our peripheral vision.

Fischer's approach to disavowal is even more useful as a lens through which to view not only the over-determined character of the imperial atrocities that Ferguson is forced to recognize, but also the kinds of discursive strategies for reinstalling a firm identification of imperialism with liberalism that this recognition makes possible. Fischer understands disavowal in a Foucaultian sense as both silencing and producing other discourses, as generative of "further stories, further screens, that hide from view what must not be seen."[116] In a similar vein, I argue that by acknowledging and disavowing moments of violence and illiberalism in the history of the British Empire, Ferguson transforms these moments into sites for the production of a metahistorical, Anglophone liberal character. What made the British Empire's acts of imperial violence so different from those of the French, Dutch, Belgian, and later, German and Japanese Empires, he argues, was that the British acts were accompanied by a constant, nagging, sometimes barely audible, but always present liberal conscience. Thus, he maintains,

> whenever the British were behaving despotically, there was almost always a liberal critique of that behavior from within British society. Indeed, so powerful and consistent was this tendency to judge Britain's imperial conduct by the yardstick of liberty that it gave the British Empire something of a self-liquidating character. Once a colonized society had sufficiently adopted the other institutions the British brought with them, it became very hard for the British to prohibit that political liberty to which they attached so much significance for themselves.[117]

And yet, while it may have been "very hard" to prohibit political liberty in the colonies, this is precisely what the British imperial state did in its everyday practices of colonial governance and its more flamboyant forays into repression in Amritsar, Omdurman, and Iraq. Ferguson acknowledges these practices, but not in order to better understand their impact on the colonized. Rather, he explores them as a way to reaffirm and lament the psychological pain that they caused British policy makers and colonial administrators, thereby seeing and not seeing such instances, avowing and disavowing them, at the same time. In the process, Ferguson establishes the Empire's liberal sensibilities as constant over time.

In other words, the very fact that the British state's response to its own illiberal behavior is one of anguish proves its qualitatively liberal nature in spite of—or indeed because of—its actions. Ferguson's suggestion, then, that the "self liquidating" nature of the Empire made it "hard" to act imperially is not meant to explain imperial hesitancy or even to justify the imperial state in retrospect but, rather, to reinforce its liberal character across history.

This experience of liberal guilt played out across numerous stages spread throughout the Empire is a recurring motif in Ferguson's work. The early white settlers of Australia, he claims, were "liberated" through the act of immigrating. But when these settlers began to behave toward Aboriginal people in ways that would now be considered genocidal, they were restrained by the more liberal-minded impulses of colonial administrators in London, raising the uncomfortable question: "How could an empire that claimed to be founded on liberty justify overruling the wishes of colonists when they clashed with those of a very distant legislature?"[118] Similarly, when white planters brutally suppressed black Jamaicans in 1865, the result was a face-off between the "liberalism of the center" and the "racism of the periphery," a confrontation that ultimately led to direct rule of the island designed to "protect the rights of black Jamaicans."[119] In these instances, the tensions between the liberal center and a racist periphery resulted in policies that depleted the political power of white settlers and increased the power of the central government in London. In other cases (such as the Boer War, the imperial state's explicit support for the slaughter of the Mahdi Army, and the violent suppression of the Mau Mau Uprising) the central government might have been plagued by guilt but, in the end, sacrificed its liberal political principles in order to maintain the kind of order that liberalism demanded.

Thus, according to Ferguson, while we can see the British Empire's essentially liberal nature in the spread of its democratic institutions and notions "of property, law, and governance" throughout the imperial world since the 1770s, it is the perennial conflict between the Empire's true liberal nature and the imperial state's coercive but necessary denial of liberal principles in the colonies that really prove its liberal credentials and inflect *Empire*, in particular, with an almost masochistic quality.[120] Ferguson's insistent reiteration of the anxiety produced by the clash between liberal values and coercive action in the history of the British Empire reinforces the perception that the Empire was ultimately *about* liberty. The tragic element of this narrative lies in the fact that the liberal Empire was consistently forced to make decisions which, because of who it was in its very essence, would inevitably cause it pain. Good imperial governance, for Ferguson, was all about accepting the pain as a necessary part of the endeavor, while being aware that the pain itself was there to remind the Empire of its true identity. In other words, "I know that I am human because when I put my foot in the fire to stamp out the blaze it hurts me," or, "I know that I am a liberal because when I am forced to act illiberally I suffer." In this self-referential, insistently productive, form of disavowal, that which is too painful to be seen *must* be seen (at least briefly) because the "traumatic perception" provides the necessary foundation for reaffirming the suffering liberal imperial self.

In sum, Ferguson strives to inoculate himself against the charge that he is presenting a whitewashed version of a British Empire without blemish by frequently pointing out the imperial state's use of coercion and violence against its largely nonwhite subjects in the colonies. At base, although this rhetorical strategy superficially acknowledges imperial racism, it depersonalizes colonized subjects, misdirects the reader by pointing toward the Empire's liberal identity, argues that it could have been worse (it could have been German), and, ultimately gestures toward imperial violence in a way that disavows that violence and, in the process, reinstantiates the Empire's liberal *modus operandi*. The net effect of his narrative strategy is to transform the Empire into a fixed version of itself, a smooth liberal egg, bobbing through history on a wave of activity produced by countless white, British citizens whose life stories and personal ambitions stand in stark contrast to the timeless, silent, despotic inclinations of the colonized, an imperial culture buoyed by its pained self-awareness of what it must do to be itself.

Once Ferguson has dismissed the charge that he is presenting a biased story of imperial history and has used the British Empire's violent past to reiterate its liberal intentions, he can proceed to the real purpose of *Empire*, *Colossus*, and *Civilization*: to craft a triumphalist metanarrative of Anglobalization that connects the liberal qualities of British global power to contemporary America and reaffirms our faith in this social, political, economic, and cultural hegemony at a time when we are perched on the edge of crisis, one negative perception away from tumbling into the abyss. In all of these texts, Ferguson aims to establish a clear linkage between British and American global leadership. "Like the United States today," he argues in *Empire*,

> Great Britain was very ready to use its naval and military superiority to fight numerous small wars against what we might now call failed states and rogue regimes... like the United States today the Victorian imperialists did not act purely in the name of national or imperial security. Just like the American presidents of recent decades have consistently propounded the benefit of economic globalization... British statesmen a century ago regarded the spread of freed trade and the liberalization of commodity labor and capital markets as desirable for the general good. And just as most Americans today regard global democratization on the American model as self evidently good, so the British in those days

aspired to export their own institutions—not just common law but ultimately also parliamentary monarchy—to the rest of the world.[121]

I quote at length here not merely to demonstrate the astounding similarity across time that Ferguson establishes between the British and American imperial missions, but also to emphasize the particular temporal flashpoint of his nostalgia. The imperial moment Ferguson emphasizes here is the "Victorian" Empire, the mid- to late-nineteenth-century period of world-straddling brashness whose most stunning visual image is the 1892 *Punch* cartoon of Rhodes the Colossus "bestriding" Africa.[122] Americans today have much to learn from this period, argues Ferguson, and from their "more self-confident British predecessors."[123]

Ferguson's mission in these texts is not just to outline the shape of this imperial self-confidence in order to establish it as a model for imitation, but also to explore precisely what happens when self-confidence is transformed into doubt, when liberal imperialists lose their bold willingness to violate the liberal policies of the Empire in the name of "Anglophone economic and political liberalism." This is particularly important for Ferguson because it is precisely the lack of self-confidence in the institutions and culture of the West that can send the complex imperial system into a "death spiral" from which there is no escape.[124] Ferguson turns to the history of the British Empire not only to prop up contemporary Americans' faith in the superiority and longevity of their culture, but also to demonstrate what happens to liberal empires when the widespread, manly embracement of what must be done (embodied in Rhodes's campaign in Sudan) falters as a cultural norm. From the turn of the nineteenth-century onwards, but especially after World War I, he argues, "British attitudes flipped over from arrogance to anxiety."[125] He goes on to make it clear that arrogance—with its brash desire for improvement and infinite will to succeed—was eminently preferable to the whining of toadying liberals who cringed at the slightest massacre, liberals no longer ready to accept the violence that comes with putting down nationalist rebellions. And, he adds, after Asquith's election in 1906, the increasing presence of these people in both government and popular and intellectual culture resulted in the emergence of two fatal characteristics that would ultimately shatter the imperial armor: doubt and squeamishness.

Ferguson's last chapters of *Empire* are devoted almost entirely to the enervating stench of doubt during this period. Indeed, he repeatedly describes Britons' attitudes toward their Empire in the postwar period as mired in "doubt," a "crisis of confidence" equal to a "loss of faith that ultimately went hand in hand with loss of faith in God."[126] Smarmy intellectuals of the time such as E. M. Forster and Evelyn Waugh severely "damaged" the Empire through their mocking portrayals of priggish colonials, thus adding to this overall culture of anxiety.[127] The "collapse of British self confidence" during this time, Ferguson argues, led to "hand wringing" and "second thoughts" about the use of force to put down rebellion, which ultimately made the Empire appear weak.[128] Ferguson contends throughout these chapters that the British now "lacked the stomach" for repression, that they had "lost their ruthless determination," that the mood had changed "from self-righteousness to remorse."[129]

For Ferguson, this lack of determination, the rise in self-doubt, and a new unwillingness to buckle down and do the right thing regardless of the blood involved ultimately killed the Empire, not nationalist rebellion or world war, much less some sudden realization that liberal principles of democracy should be extended to the colonized. Self-doubt weakened the Empire to such a degree, Ferguson contends, that by the time World War II came around it was all the British could do to fight off the world-dominating ambitions of other empires, those not based on liberty but on total domination. Wasting away from self-doubt, the British rallied just enough strength to engage in this "collision" between their Empire (grounded as it was in "some conception of human rights") and the Japanese and German Empires, which "regarded alien races as no better than swine."[130] In fighting the war, the British Empire "did the right thing" but was unable to recover from the blow. Even in defeat, however, Ferguson cannot help portraying the Empire in terms utterly overdetermined by a masochistic desire to take on the pain of the world for its own good—indeed, for its very redemption. "This was the Empire's Passion," he argues, "its time on the cross. After this, could it ever be resurrected?"[131] The answer, of course, is that it was, that the redeemer was found in a newly hegemonic American state that ably took the baton of Anglophone liberty from the British, although in a manner that was rarely as explicit about its imperial intentions as Ferguson would like. But just as Christ suffered for our sins, Ferguson implies, so must this new empire also be willing to suffer by violating its own liberal premises in order stave off the infinitely more illiberal imperializing of China, or the chaos of a world where "radical Islam" takes refuge in the failed states of the postcolonial era.

Conclusion

As I have shown in this chapter, Ferguson takes the history of the British Empire and squeezes it through a metanarrative conditioned on all sides by the dire necessities of financial time and the fixedness of liberal character such that two, and only two, options for the contemporary world emerge as possibilities: Americans can either embrace the pain of violating their own liberal values in the name of "Anglobalization," or watch global politics descend into the chaos of an empireless world from which there will be no return. Ferguson cautions that this must be done boldly, with neither qualms nor queasiness, in the name of liberal order. It is no surprise, then, that he ends *Empire* with an excerpt from "The White Man's Burden." The United States, he concludes, has already "taken up some kind of global burden just as Kipling urged."[132] The key to its success now lies in its willingness to shake off denial, squeamishness, and guilt, and embrace the violence that comes with such painful responsibility.

While more subdued in its explicit exhortations of American Empire than *Empire* or *Colossus*, as a text, *Civilization* captures perfectly the marriage of Ferguson's neoliberal sense of time with his imperial nostalgia. In the fast-paced world of financial time, in the split second it takes for the train to fall over the edge into the abyss, Ferguson assures us that there is no time for reflection on foreign policy, military intervention, the history of imperialism, or the costs and benefits of global economic integration. In Ferguson's conception of the world as a complex financial system, the frantic pace of time ramps up the pressure to commit, to act, and never doubt the superiority of Anglobal domination because, in Thatcher's famous words, "there is no alternative." At the same time, Ferguson's avowal and disavowal of the atrocities committed by the British and American Empires reflects and distorts a contemporary political culture where we are bombarded on a daily basis with images of poverty, atrocity, and disaster (e.g. Abu Ghraib, Syria, Hurricane Katrina) without ever once being asked to consider how American imperializing, American foreign policy, or neoliberal economics might have contributed to these catastrophes. All we can do, in such moments, is act, and that action must be based solely on a metanarrative of Anglophone greatness because all critique is doubt, all doubt is pusillanimity, and pusillanimity leads to the "terrifying death spiral."

Ironically, Ferguson may be nostalgic for the pitiless bravado of the Victorian Empire, but his kind of metanarrative has far more in common with those pro-imperial historians like the Round Table authors who wrote precisely at the moment when, to Ferguson's mind, the dominant culture of the Empire in Britain turned decidedly away from brashness to fear, from acceptance to critique. Thus, when Ferguson argues it is "fast becoming conventional wisdom that the power of the United States today closely resembles that of the United Kingdom roughly a century ago," he is actually more on the mark than he realizes. Ferguson, the retrohistorian, may try very hard to capture the insouciant tone of the nineteenth-century historians, but his discursive tactics—his metanarrative, his misdirection, his disavowal, his racist non-racism—look eerily familiar to those used by anxious liberal Edwardians fretting about the possibility of decline. And while it may be easy to look back today at the writings of the Round Table and dismiss them as hopeless propaganda, in their time, members of the group were able to take the vision they developed and convert it into a discourse of liberal internationalism that would successfully extend official colonialism until well after World War II and enable the processes of informal imperialism to blossom through the language of colonial "mandates." In other words, Round Table scholars took what could have been a moment for real reflection on imperial politics and transformed it into a reaffirmation of domination.

Ferguson's liberal neo-imperialism poses similar hazards today. It is easy to look at his bluster, his wild departures from academic norms, his occasionally huge publicity blunders, and simply dismiss him as a hapless media hog, an anxious nostalgic, hopelessly out of touch with the world, undeserving of our sustained scholarly attention.[133] From this perspective, Ferguson's myriad historical inaccuracies, his extensive silences coupled with a dearth of credible citations, make academic critique of his work appear like little more than shooting fish in a barrel. But Ferguson is no average public intellectual and, as I have endeavored to show in this chapter, the problems with his work amount to far more than a simple lack of attention to historical fact. Ferguson wields significant rhetorical power over popular media culture in both Britain and America and advises some of the world's biggest financial firms in part because the BBC, *Newsweek, The New York Times,* and the editors of *Foreign Affairs* believe him to be a legitimate historian. Indeed, even in the midst of the scandal surrounding his homophobic remarks about John Maynard Keynes at an investment conference in 2013, the media never once stopped referring to Ferguson as a "Harvard Professor" and many were quick to conclude that, despite the momentary ugliness, all had been forgiven back at Cambridge, where momentarily scorned Ferguson was welcomed back into the academic fold with open arms by everyone but the most intransigent leftists. As the George Mason University's *History News Network* put it in a screaming headline, "Niall Ferguson's Harvard Colleagues Support Him, but Not LGBT Historians."[134]

Thus, under the cover of academic legitimacy—with, evidently, only queer historians dissenting—Ferguson is able, through his television documentaries, books, articles, and countless public appearances a year, to proselytize for a return to an imperial triumphalism that will no doubt contribute to extending the life of the American Empire long after it is economically, environmentally, and politically sustainable, particularly if he has the ear of future Republican presidential candidates as had in the past. He does this, again, by constructing a metanarrative most notable not merely for what it forgets and omits, but also for what it remembers and memorializes in the process of forgetting and forging a liberal identity. In this way Ferguson positions himself as the Empire Whisperer of the early twenty-first century, the man who sits alongside the imperial society as it perches on the edge of chaos, calmly encouraging us not to jump but to believe in ourselves by believing in his vision of who we are. Don't look over the edge into the terrifying death spiral, he says soothingly, holding out his hand in our direction. Don't look down. Look at me.

PART THREE

STRATEGIES OF CHARACTER

Empire's Handyman: Jan Smuts and the Politics of International Holism

The Attempt to form empires or leagues of nations on the basis of
inequality and the bondage and oppression of the smaller national
units has failed, and the work has to be done all over again on a new
basis and an enormous scale.
—Jan Smuts, *The League of Nations: A Practical Suggestion*

Of all the contradictory statements made by South African statesman, nationalist, internationalist, and Commonwealth activist General Jan Smuts in his 1918
pamphlet, *The League of Nations: A Practical Suggestion*, none seem more jarring
than those about empire. In the course of his argument, Smuts claimed that the
war itself was brought about by the rapacious overreach of grasping European
empires, and that the League of Nations ought to constitute a completely new
approach to international relations. Old empires, argued Smuts, formed "on the
basis of inequality and the bondage and oppression of the smaller national units"
have failed and that, in the face of the mass destruction wrought by the First
World War, "the work has to be done all over again on a new basis and an enormous scale."[1] The League of Nations movement was essentially an anti-imperial
movement, Smuts argued, insisting that old "legal concepts of imperialism,"
would now be abandoned in "the new world of Freedom."[2] However, at other
points in this same text, Smuts maintained that the functions of the League
would not differ significantly in practice from those of an empire, and that the
League was in fact the "reversionary," "successor," and "real live active heir to the
former Empires."[3] In the course of the pamphlet, Smuts argued that old empires
had "been liquidated," that they had "all broken down," leaving only the League
of Nations to pick up the pieces.[4] But as one reads on it becomes apparent that
Smuts was thinking only of the Germans, Hapsburgs, and the Ottomans: he
remained entirely silent about the overseas empires of the rest of Europe and
the United States, not to mention the imperial ambitions of Australia and New
Zealand in the Pacific and those of his own state, white dominated South Africa.

In a dizzying set of inversions, deflections, and silences, Smuts thus established the League of Nations as an anti-imperial, imperial endeavor.

The only extant empire that Smuts mentioned in this pamphlet was the British Empire and it, for Smuts, was no ordinary empire. Rather, the British Empire embodied precisely the sort of polity upon which he believed the League of Nations ought to be modeled. In the British Empire, according to Smuts, we find an "embryo league of nations," a "lesser league already existing," and the "nearest approach to the League of Nations" in the present world.[5] And yet the British Empire that Smuts imagined as a precursor to international governance bore only a vague resemblance to the actual British Empire, historically or during his lifetime. Rather, this was an alternative narrative of empire that brought together seemingly contradictory rhetorical imaginaries about its nature, its historical trajectory, and its most defining qualities, and folded them into one holistic expression of an organic international community.

This chapter looks closely at Smuts's vision of the British Empire, its relationship to his philosophical holism, and to his influential proposal for a postwar League of Nations. As one of the leading figures in the generation that followed the late-nineteenth-century makers of modern imperialism—a generation that, Mark Mazower argues, "sought to prolong the life of an empire of white rule through international cooperation"—Smuts was able to successfully push to the ideological fore a vision of a League of Nations grounded on a particular reading of the British Empire. [6] In Smuts's terms, what made the Empire such an excellent model for international organization was not its capacity to expansively bring civilization to the rest of the world, but rather, its very constitution as an internally variegated, complex, and well-ordered association of "more or less equal Governments."[7] Smuts's understanding of the Empire and his plan for a future League of Nations thus reconciled colonialism with internationalism in a manner that gave imperialists in Britain and America precisely what they were looking for at precisely the right moment.

While in many ways Smuts's organic conception of the Empire resembled that of the Round Table, his vision improved upon it for the purposes of imperialist internationalism by speaking directly to two tensions left unresolved by the Round Table's theory of commonwealth. First, the Round Tablers were insistent in their conviction that the Commonwealth was not, ultimately, based on force. But, at the same time, they understood the Commonwealth (like the earlier Federationists) as one coherent, international state and defined states themselves (even commonwealths) as organizations that claim "a sole and absolute right to dispose of the lives and property" of their subjects and "to exact their unlimited obedience." Smuts's vision (and the international organization to follow in its wake) abstracted the empire from the idea of statehood altogether, thus removing it from assumptions of force and making it sound more palatable to both liberals interested in postwar internationalism and European, American, and dominion governments which bristled at the idea of a "world state."

Second, the Round Tablers were never able to entirely resolve the question of whether or not the dependencies, particularly India, should be included in a formal imperial parliament. Despite their fixation with imperial unity and their insistence that imperial citizenship applied equally to all throughout the Commonwealth, they still depended upon a language of eventuality and forestallment, one that suggested full political membership to nonwhite imperial citizens somewhere down the civilizational road. Smuts's theory, by contrast, eliminated the need for a language of forestallment altogether by retooling the liberal conception of progressive history (so central to the thought of nineteenth-century theorists like Mill and Edwardian liberals alike) such that international hierarchy became a permanent feature of the new, liberal internationalist order and seemed perfectly compatible with an international ethic of sovereign equality. In essence, Smuts solved liberal imperialism's temporal problem, at least temporarily.

Thus, in contrast to many accounts of Smuts's internationalist writings and activism which draw a distinction between his seemingly expansive, international idealism on the one hand and his parochial, South African-focused racism on the other, I argue that Smuts's internationalism was, from the very beginning, shot through with a cynical rejection of liberal universalism. His was a political vision born out of a fear of declining European racial power that sought not to justify political exclusion in the name of liberal progress but, rather, to reconcile the two, or, in Bill Schwartz's brilliantly concise summation, "to devise a politics—a conception of civilization—in which the truths of white supremacy could conform to the requirements of a liberal, neighborly, and inclusive imperial ideal."[8] In the end, Smuts retooled the liberal Empire to save the liberal Empire from the problems generated by the liberal Empire and, in the process, ushered in both the extension of formal imperialism into the age of internationalism and set the stage for the informal imperialism that followed. Not for nothing did his Boer critics in South Africa and his liberal fans in Britain refer to him as "Empire's Handyman."[9]

The chapter begins by exploring the political context in South Africa and in the Empire that so profoundly shaped Smuts's imperial vision, focusing in particular on the way his presentation of himself as a "barbarian from the outer marches of the Empire" led him to a position of influence (particularly among English liberals) during the First World War. The second section focuses on an under-researched aspect of Smuts's work, his philosophical holism, and makes a case for reading his internationalism through this lens.[10] Section three follows the threads of Smuts's philosophy through his 1917 speeches and his hugely influential 1918 pamphlet, *The League of Nations: A Practical Suggestion*. The conclusion examines the long-term impact of Smuts's internationalism, particularly his influence on the League of Nations and his sway with Woodrow Wilson. In the words of Wilson's secretary of state, Robert Lansing, Smuts's assertion that the League should be "the heir of Empires" in an era when "imperialism was no more…sank deep into the mind of the President and impressed him with the wisdom of Smuts."[11] Finally, the chapter ends with a brief observation of the deeply wrought global inequality that Smuts's holistic form of deflection continues to sustain, most distressingly, in the contemporary reemergence of a language of mandates and trusteeship.

The Racist Darling of Liberal England

Understanding both Smuts's imperial vision and the impact of his brand of internationalism on the creation of the League of Nations requires examining the particular role that South Africa played in his politics, as well as the unique position he held in the collective British liberal imperial psyche during and shortly after the Great War. Born to wealthy Afrikaner farmers in 1870, Jan Christian Smuts left South Africa and was educated at Cambridge in the early 1890s, where he was considered an exceptional student with an astonishingly wide range of intellectual interests—most notably, German idealist philosophy, which he honed while studying in Strasbourg in the summer of 1894. Legal scholar F. W. Maitland (who maintained that Smuts was not only first but "brilliantly first" in his law Tripos, or honors degree) noted a little sadly in an 1894 letter to Smuts that he supported his decision to abjure scholarly life for the practice of law because "I am always hoping that some day Cambridge will turn out a great Romanticist" who was also legal scholar and he felt that Smuts could be that man.[12]

When he left Cambridge, Smuts returned to South Africa to practice law, participate in politics, and eventually to serve as a commander in the Boer War (1899–1902). In 1900, during the war, Smuts wrote a scathing account of the British in South Africa entitled *A Century of Wrong* which he began by noting how ironic it was that he, a "friend and supporter" of Cecil Rhodes and Alfred Milner, a defender of the "cause of the progressive Briton against the Conservative Boer" who had been actively seeking "the establishment of a progressive Liberal Administration in Pretoria," would now be writing such a text. "I am almost the last man in the Empire," he insisted, "who could be regarded as an authorized exponent of the case of the Boers."[13] One can see here precisely the role Smuts would establish for himself vis-à-vis the British public (and British liberals in particular) during World War I; the consummate outsider-insider who fought for "progressive

Britain," for the Empire's truest self, even when the Empire failed to respect its own liberal principles, such as during the Boer War. Smuts played up this image of himself while in Britain by referring to himself coyly as a "barbarian from the outer marches of the Empire," a humble South African soldier simply commenting on what was right and true.[14] At the same time, Smuts's image as a liberal crusader from the provinces was shored up by his lifelong friendships with English liberals and radicals like J. A. Hobson and L.T. Hobhouse and with a number of feminist and pacifist women, including Emily Hobhouse and Alice Clark.[15] In a 1917 interview, Edward Marshall referred to Smuts as "a democrat of democrats, a man for the second time involved in the great struggle for ideals which in human life is wagered against human life with freedom as the ultimate stake."[16] Throughout the war the British press would present Smuts precisely in this light, as the savior from the fringes, an imperial patriot concerned with higher ideals with "no particular axe to grind and no interest—save that of the Empire—to push."[17]

But Smuts's presentation of himself as the ultimate champion of liberal values and his own long-term and enthusiastic support for the Empire was not interest free—indeed, Carroll Quigley has described him as a "devious opportunist" whose concern for both liberalism and the Empire flowed from both his personal ambition and his political agenda for the newly unified—and deeply segregated—South African state.[18] At base, Smuts was motivated throughout his career by his deeply held racist fears that whites in South Africa, and Afrikaner culture in particular, would not survive the "shadows and darkness" of Africa without support from Britain.[19] Smuts's experiences with armed Africans fighting for the British in the Boer War seemed only to have exacerbated his overwhelming sense that whites were an imperiled community living among barbarians. "Perhaps," he wrote to his wife in 1901, "it is the future of our little race to be sacrificed on the alter of the world's Ideals; perhaps we are destined to be the martyr race which must redeem our sordid money age from the charge of absolute worldliness and selfishness."[20] Smuts's speeches and writings about South Africa, before and during World War I, are filled with an equally dire sense that white civilization in Africa was on the verge of collapse both from a decline in white birth rate and from an influx of South Asian labor. "South Africa as the home of a white race is young yet," Smuts argued in a 1903 letter to the Labour Commission, in which he begged them to block immigration from China and Asia, arguing that "the introduction of Asiatics on the scale contemplated by its advocates will probably seal its [South Africa's] fate forever."[21] Throughout his career, Smuts couched his fear about the potential decline of white hegemony in South Africa in terms of racial and civilizational uniqueness. As he wrote in a letter to Gandhi, "racial legislation" was not the same thing as "color prejudice" because it was concerned not with oppression but preservation. How, Smuts argued with Gandhi, "will you solve the difficulty about the fundamental differences of our cultures? Let alone the question of superiority, there is no doubt that your civilization is different from ours. Ours must not be overwhelmed by yours."[22]

Smuts saw three clear solutions to the problem of white decline which—after Louis Botha's election as Prime Minister in 1906 and Smuts's own occupation of a number of different cabinet positions—he was strategically placed to bring to fruition. The first was to restrict immigration from India, repatriate Chinese workers, and help to shore up racial segregation through a series of Native Affairs Acts that laid the groundwork for the segregationist state in South Africa during the interwar era, and earned him the reputation as one of the fathers of apartheid. The second was to push for greater "racial" unification between the two white communities in South Africa through top-down forms of state-making, which did not always win him favors from English speakers or Afrikaner nationalists, particularly after he and Botha violently put down a strike by white miners in 1914.[23] But for Smuts, white unification was absolutely necessary to combat what he saw as the onslaught of African and South Asian population expansion. And for Smuts, this kind of integration demanded a real fusion of British and Afrikaner "races" into one nation state, rather than a federated system shaped along cultural and linguistic differences. As he argued in a 1909 speech before the Transvaal Parliament, "you have these races [British and Afrikaner] who live side by side in every Colony of South Africa, and they are already fusing and being fused under the existing form of the Colonial Constitution under which they live...Any attempt to keep up racial distinctions through such a distinction as was made in Canada need not be made here, and indeed, cannot any longer be made."[24] And as an historical example of such a fusion, Smuts not coincidentally turned to Britain. "The results of that union between England and Scotland...had been that from two petty kingdoms, Great Britain has become the mistress of the world, very largely as a result of that far reaching step that was taken when two countries were united under a unified form of government."[25]

Not surprisingly then, the third solution that Smuts identified early on for the preservation of whiteness in South Africa entailed redefining and shoring up the link between a unified, white South African nation and the British Empire. Smuts frequently framed South Africa's role in the Empire in terms similar to those he used to pitch himself to English liberals, as a naïve but upstart "barbarian" nation from the fringes, invigorating an empire currently experiencing the malaise that flows from self-doubt. This particular narrative fused South Africa's own imperial ambitions in Africa with the broader goals of the British by claiming that South Africa's goal was to civilize the continent "from the South" after Rhodes's failed "attempts at civilization from the North."[26] And yet even as he made these claims, Smuts was careful not to alienate himself from the British imperial mission more generally by always referring to these previous attempts not as British or even as Rhodes's efforts, but as efforts that "we" made as a civilization and an Empire. For Smuts, unified white South Africa was the scrappy child of Britain come to maturity, ready and willing to offer energy and guidance to an empire itself overrun by brown and black people by attempting to create a European swath through the "black pool of Africa."[27] Cementing South Africa to the Empire thus entailed, for Smuts, fostering a dual narrative in which white dominions like South Africa were given greater autonomy to engage in their own projects of colonization, but in which they still remained bound to the greater purpose of the British Empire in the world.

By 1914, both Smuts and Botha agreed that cementing South Africa to the Empire entailed full support by the South African Union for Britain's war effort. Smuts led a campaign by white South African troops in South West Africa in 1915, and was then asked by the British to command the campaign in East Africa as well, during which time he was named a lieutenant general in the British army. In 1917 he was appointed to the British War Cabinet and spent the remainder of the war in London organizing the air defense, participating in the Imperial War Conference, traveling to Egypt and Palestine, advising on questions of Irish home rule, and giving influential speeches in which he both elaborated his evolving understanding of the British Empire as a commonwealth, and laid the groundwork for his vision for the League of Nations.

Ironically, Smuts's enthusiasm for the war often brought him into conflict with not only Boer nationalists, but with the multitude of liberal and radical acquaintances in England whose friendships he had assiduously cultivated and maintained, often since his Cambridge days, right through his international-ized conflict with Gandhi, his suppression of striking workers, and his role in the passage of the 1913 "Native Land Act," which dramatically reduced the right of black South Africans to land ownership.[28] While in England, however, Smuts was apparently able to smooth over these conflicts and once again por-tray himself to liberal supporters like Hobson, the Hobhouses, and Clark as, in the words of former Cape Colony Prime Minister Merriman, an "ardent young liberal."[29] Part of Smuts's mystique was his ability to cultivate the image of him-self as the ultimate concerned outsider bearing the conscience of the Empire, whose lofty speeches about freedom, equality, and the rights of small nations throughout 1917 and 1918 made him, in Saul Dubow words, the "darling of British liberals and nonconformists."[30] In his excellent chapter on the South African general, Schwarz argues that Smuts was able to do this because of his brilliant capacity to present himself as someone whose experience as a white South African gave him insight into race relations unavailable to white Britons, and who could therefore "speak the truths of race."[31] At the same time, Schwarz argues, Smuts worked hard to distinguish between the white supremacists of South Africa and America and the "extremist" humanists in both countries who wanted complete racial integration.[32] Through his careful self-presentation,

Smuts simultaneously declared integration and supremacy to be extremist and positioned himself as a measured liberal, walking a solemn path between two unacceptable alternatives.

As Dubow concludes, Smuts's stunningly prolix ability to deflect liberal attention from the racial politics of the man behind the curtain finally came to a crashing halt many years later when, during the first meeting of the UN General Assembly, the delegate from India, Vijaya Lakshmi Pandit, assailed Smuts for South Africa's treatment of its Indian minority by throwing Smuts's own language of universal human rights in his face.[33] Prior to that moment, however, Smuts was able to successfully portray himself to many liberals in Britain and America as a visionary idealist, a supporter of liberal internationalism, and a man who stood up for the rights of small nations yet remained committed to the liberal project of the British Empire as the prototype of a new internationalism.

After his death in 1950, Smuts apologists sought to resuscitate his image not by excusing his racism but, rather, by acknowledging precisely the contradiction noted by Pandit in 1946—between Smuts's professed love for the liberal principles of human rights and international organization and his support for racist politics at home—and then portraying this as a tragic, but understandable flaw in his character, completely distinct from his liberal impulses. As Marks notes, many sympathetic biographers chalked up Smuts's racism to "instinct," to a kind of subconscious impulse learned in childhood that dogged someone who would otherwise be a liberal man with the best of intentions.[34] Indeed, one comes away from reading the Round Table's 1950 eulogy to Smuts with the distinct sense that race in South Africa was an annoyance, a mere externality to Smuts, a cross which he only reluctantly bore and which liberals from Europe and America simply could not understand.[35]

Other sympathetic portrayers of Smuts's legacy have turned to his philosophical holism to help smooth over uncomfortable tensions in his life and work. One of the clear goals of F. S. Crafford's biography of Smuts, for example, was to establish a consistency of purpose behind Smuts's various political endeavors, by tying them all to his holistic approach to philosophy and the world. For Crafford, what looked like contradictions between Smuts's liberal internationalism and South African racism were actually reflections of discrete moments in the process that Smuts described as "whole making." In Crafford's mind, Smuts's holistic philosophy of life demanded that

> Small units must needs develop into bigger wholes, and they in their turn again must grow into larger and ever-larger structures without cessation. Advancement lay along that path. Thus the unification of the four provinces in the Union of South Africa, the idea of the British

Commonwealth of Nations, and, finally, the great whole resulting from the combination of the peoples of the earth in a great league of nations were but a logical progression consistent with his philosophical tenets.[36]

As Crafford presents them, Smuts's politics were consistent over time because his philosophy was consistent over time. Smuts simply had not yet gotten around to figuring out how to integrate black Africans into this logical progression but he had it in his sights; they too eventually would become part of the "great whole" that made up the League of Nations and then the United Nations. Hancock made a similar argument in his three-volume account of Smuts's life, maintaining again and again that Smuts's approach to politics was guided at all times by a "passion for synthesis" and a commitment to "whole making" on a greater and smaller scale.[37] In good time, this synthesis would include all people of all races in the world.

I argue below that Crafford and Hancock correctly identified Smuts's holism as an integral part of his political vision, even if the impulse to do so sprang from both men's obvious desire to excuse his contradictory life. In fact, Smuts's holism allowed him to sustain contradictions much greater than those that adhered to his particularly ugly vision of a racially segregated South Africa—contradictions that arose from the liberal imperial project more generally. In sum, Smuts's holism facilitated the development of a political language that could effectively assuage liberal fears of racial and imperial decline within the context of a brave new world guided by the principles of international cooperation and national self-determination.

Smuts's Holism

Until the end of apartheid, aside from the occasional sympathetic portrayal by his biographers (and their clear desire to salvage Smuts's reputation as a liberal internationalist), most scholars writing about Smuts's political life ignored his philosophical writings altogether, while most supporters and proponents of Smuts's holism eschewed discussing his politics. "Holism" (a term Smuts coined) enjoyed a certain cachet in both scholarly and popular circles throughout the twentieth-century, principally among philosophers concerned with systems theory or process philosophy (including Quine), psychologists interested in "holistic" approaches to personality, New Age acolytes searching for synthetic theories of nature and spirit, and environmental theorists interested in developing holistic accounts of the natural world.[38] The end of apartheid, however, witnessed a more general reassessment of Smuts's political legacy in South Africa and has spurred a number of scholars (primarily but not exclusively South Africans) to critically reexamine his holism in the context of his politics.[39]

Smuts's philosophical project was, on its face, grandiose in the extreme. It involved developing a theory of everything that could explain the world (science, nature, politics, psychology) through the interaction of two fundamental life forces: a synthesizing, ordering, and controlling force he described as holism, and the growing, changing, developing force of evolution. In his magnum opus on the subject, 1926's *Holism and Evolution*, Smuts concluded that that the universe was comprised of a series of wholes which were distinct and which, like concentric circles, embodied the totality of the universe. The process of evolution ensured that these wholes (comprised of organisms, plants, animal species, individuals, social groups, and entire peoples) were constantly moving toward greater inner complexity, while the ordering process of holism worked to synthesize all the conflicting elements involved in evolution and push the emerging wholes—and the totality of which they were a part—toward perfection. In other words, for Smuts, the whole was always much more than the sum of its parts.

Smuts became interested in philosophy and began developing the method and ethic that he would later call holism while at Cambridge and while studying philosophy and German literature in Strasbourg in the summer of 1894. Setting aside his biographer's observation that Smuts was simply a natural holist whose native "passion for synthesis" sprang from his earliest experiences on his father's farm, Smuts appears to have been most deeply influenced during this period by British Idealism, with its particular emphasis on the reconciliation of the individual and the community through a domesticated notion of spirit.[40] While eventually receiving a degree in law, Smuts wrote widely outside his field and published numerous essays on philosophical topics. His early essay, "Law, A Liberal Study," claimed to harmonize "the subjective with the objective" or "the law of freedom" with "the whole."[41] Smuts also wrote several pieces that expanded on this relationship between the whole-making movement of the world and "biological phenomena," culminating in an unpublished 1895 manuscript, "Walt Whitman: A Study in the Evolution of Personality." Smuts's goal in this manuscript was to marry Darwin and Hegel through what he termed a "synthetic application of evolution" to the study of human personality, using Walt Whitman as an example of a fully evolved, "great mind."[42] He did this by first elaborating Hegel's notion of the "Idea" as "that immanent activity or life principle which, in the absence of external interference or impediments, will perfectly realize the potency or capability of a thing."[43] He then went on to combine Darwinian and Hegelian insights into what he called a "synthetic application of evolution" to the study of human personality.[44]

After the Boer War, Smuts went on to develop these concepts further in a never published, 1910 manuscript titled "An Inquiry into the Unification of the

Whole."[45] The idea of the whole, to Smuts's mind, was not merely "arithmetical" but, rather, could be understood in a "concrete sense" as a "single dynamic, organic, psychic agency underlying, penetrating, and indeed, forming all subjects and objects of experience."[46] He described the movement of the whole in the world as "the psychological process of growing experience," the "evolutionary development of the universe," and the "formulation of universal laws of a physical character."[47] In this sense, Smuts took the Hegelian contention that "the real is the rational" quite literally by insisting that the whole was not only spiritual and metaphysical, it was found in the very life processes of nature, and was, in this sense "the taproot of all reality." The goal of the philosopher, scientist, and politician alike, according to Smuts, was largely the same: to grasp or "penetrate" the movement of this physical and spiritual whole toward ever-greater unification of all life, and thus understand it as "no mere aggregation or sum total or compound of part," but as "one and indivisible, a real vital organic unity" which reconciled the "multiplicities of the universes" not as "constituent parts" but as expressions of the whole itself.[48]

Smuts developed these ideas still further in a book he worked on throughout the teens, which was published when he had more time to devote to it after losing his bid for reelection as prime minister in 1924. *Holism and Evolution* was concerned more explicitly than his earlier works with the relationship between the "factor" of holism and the processes of evolution. By Smuts's lights, theologically oriented thinkers like Leibniz had incorrectly conceived of change in purely teleological terms as the "unfolding" of all that was "contained in the past."[49] In contrast, Smuts argued, "Evolution is not merely a process of change, of regrouping of the old into new forms; it is creative, its new forms are not merely fashioned out of the old materials."[50] At times in this text, Smuts presented the process of synthesizing old and new forms as completely self-contained, and the principles of holism and evolution as "self-acting and self-moving." A whole, Smuts argued, "is not actuated or moved by some external principle or force, like a machine or an artificial construction. The source of its activity is internal and of a piece with itself, is indeed itself."[51]

At other times, however, Smuts concluded that some kinds of external stimuli could affect the development of the whole in a way that both changed and improved its fundamental character. "A causal stimulus," he argued, "applied externally to an organism does not merely result in some mechanical movement, but…makes the resulting movement, not the mere mechanical effect of that cause, but the free action of the organism."[52] Smuts seemed particularly concerned with this in his discussion of personality. Expanding upon the theme he first took up at Cambridge, Smuts used the development of the human personality as an example of what he termed "holistic assimilation." "Great minds," he argued, were able to assimilate the stimuli of the world, absorbing new experiences in a manner that "only serves to fructify and enrich them without any detriment to their spiritual wholeness and integrity."[53] And in the process of absorbing these new experiences, great minds were also engaged in a process of ordering the "lower and higher elements" of their personality as they moved closer to wholeness or "purity." Purity, argued Smuts, "means the harmonious co-ordination of the higher and lower elements in human nature," the "sublimation of the lower into the higher, and thus the enrichment of the higher through the lower."[54] Smuts referred to the ordering and coordinating part of the personality as the "central control" which he also argued "emerges in more composite holistic groups in Society."[55] Weaker personalities and weaker social groups have much to learn, he suggested, from the ordering potential of highly organized personalities and peoples. "No organism," he maintained, "has nothing to learn from highly developed Mind in the way of regulation, co-ordination or inner control of structures and functions."[56]

In sum, Smuts's theory of holism evolved between his years at Cambridge and the publication of *Holism and Evolution* from a general attempt to reconcile the whole and its parts (the individual and the social) within a broader notion of evolutionary development, to a worldview that embraced the creative and dynamic power of evolution to change wholes into more complicated and internally diverse forms of themselves, with a clear distinction between higher and lower elements and a clear sense that some personalities and cultures more than others, as Kate Fletcher puts it, "enjoyed a higher level of holistic development."[57] The synthetic, evolving movement of the universe was never toward equality but, rather, toward inner perfection and balance and a proper ordering of parts, toward the creation of "new and higher wholes," arranged "in their various grades."[58]

Contemporary analyses of the relationship between Smuts's holism and his politics are divided as to whether or not this ordered, hierarchical view of the world directly affected his approach to racial politics in South Africa. As Marks has argued, Smuts's "conception of himself as a scholar and a philosopher" never dimmed during those periods when he was most active in politics and, indeed, he wrote "An Inquiry into the Unification of the Whole" while in the midst of multiple administrative duties.[59] Because of this, both Marks and Peder Anker have argued that Smuts the philosopher clearly impacted the thinking of Smuts the politician. By contrast, Noel Garson maintains, "Smuts's philosophical and scientific outlook was neither the determinant of nor the key to his views and policies on racial issues."[60] I argue that a closer look at Smuts's writings on race in South Africa suggests that both views are right. Smuts's early writings and speeches about South African union focus a great deal on the "racial reconciliation" of the Boers and the English in a language redolent with holism. On the one hand, for Smuts, the English and Afrikaners were "already fusing and being fused under the existing form of the Colonial Constitution under which they live."[61] The ongoing process of closer union was, Smuts argued, a goal toward which both communities must continually strive. The "Dutch people in South Africa," he argued, must actively embrace the goal of unification with the British in order to both preserve their culture and create a national body politic capable of becoming a "great people." "We want," he argued in 1917, "to create a blend out of the various nationalities, to achieve a new nationality embracing and harmonizing our various traits and blending them all into a richer national type than could otherwise be achieved."[62] For Smuts, just as the synthetic tendencies of the universe led away from "mere aggregation" toward organic, internally differentiated wholes, so would greater "racial unity" in South Africa create a new "great people" without sacrificing the internal "multiplicities" of British and Afrikaner culture identity.

However, when it came to nonwhite inclusion in this new "racial unity," Smuts's holism—and its commitment to a form of union that both reconciled and preserved difference—seemed to vanish entirely from his political calculus. In his 1917 speech on the future of South and Central Africa, Smuts argued that, "our problem of racial unity is being solved in the midst of the black environment in South Africa," as if the majority of Africans were both there and not there. The sheer fact of their status as the "overwhelming population" ensured their physical presence, but spiritually they stood outside the unifying flow of evolution. "We know that on the African Continent at various times there have been attempts at civilization...Where are those civilizations now?" Smuts asked.[63] For Smuts, the barbarity of the Africans situated them literally before time, in a temporal space apart from that occupied by the white population who were busy consolidating themselves in the present as an organically integrated "great people." Black people, for Smuts, were removed from the great metaphysical push for wholeness; they were not intended to blend in, but simply, it seems, to disappear.

In the context of South Africa, then, Smuts applied his holistic thinking only to the unification of its white populations. He never solved the problem of what to do with black people, whose very existence seemed inexplicable to him, who inhabited the same temporal space as the civilized nations of the world, but who could not be assimilated into the evolutionary progress toward wholeness that he believed both natural and morally necessary. For Smuts, black South Africans stood obdurately in the way of the great march of European civilization in Africa. Black Africans were both his neighbors, his countrymen, and, in Wendy Brown's terms, his "constitutive outside," the men and women against whom he imagined his whole civilizational world.[64] The only way that Smuts could ever manage to respond to this "constitutive outside" was by keeping it outside, by rigorously enforcing laws that physically channeled and corralled black people into separate and unequal social spaces and forms of politics, or, as he explained to his English audience in 1917, rather than "mixing up black and white in the old haphazard way ... we are now trying a policy of keeping them apart as much as possible in our institutions."[65]

Where we do see the interaction between Smut's holism and his racial politics is not in the context of South Africa, but in that sphere to which critical historians interested in his philosophy have paid the least attention: his attempt to reconfigure the British Empire as the basis for a postwar internationalism. Smuts argued, in his tremendously influential *The League of Nations: A Practical Suggestion* that, if properly conceived, it was possible to fashion an approach to internationalism that folded the non-civilized into an organic whole in a manner that not only accounted for the presence of the lower within the whole, but also explained their necessary sublimation to the higher.

Smuts's Liberal, Internationalist Vision: A Practical Suggestion

At the core of Smuts's developing internationalism during the war was his unshakable conviction that the British Empire embodied the "nearest approach to the League of Nations" in the present world.[66] While one can see glimmers of this idea in some of his earlier thinking about South Africa as a dominion, Smuts perfected his story of the Empire as a proto-League of Nations during his time in England in 1917, through a series of lectures he gave for various audiences, collected at the end of that year in a volume entitled *War-Time Speeches*. In his Foreword to this collection, Smuts pointed to the "general unity of ideas" running throughout the speeches, noting that his observations on the British Empire and the "future government of the world" rested "on the same basis of ideas."[67] Smuts stressed two ideas in particular. On the one hand, he insisted that the Empire must always be understood in terms of the unchanging, holistic principles that both described its most essential qualities and enlivened the imperial polity as a whole. These were the "moral principles" of "freedom, equality, and equity."[68] On the other hand, Smuts argued, what made the Empire so rare in the history of the world, and such a model for international governance, was its internal flexibility, its capacity for change, and its ability to accommodate the increased sovereignty of some of its members while still ruling over peoples "speaking different languages, belonging to different races, with entirely different economic circumstances."[69]

The key word that ties Smuts's understanding of holism and evolution to his developing vision of the Empire in these speeches is "actuate." Smuts used the word throughout his writings on holism to refer to the "self acting, self moving" principle present in all biological, social, and political wholes. When speaking of a whole, Smuts argued, it was important to remember that, "It is not actuated or moved by some external principle or force... The source of its activity is internal and of a piece with itself, is indeed itself."[70] In a similar vein, Smuts referred repeatedly, in his wartime speeches, to the principles of "freedom and equality" that have "actuated us so far throughout our history," and that constituted the "spirit which actuates the whole" of the Empire.[71] For Smuts, all other empires since the beginning of time had been "actuated" by "might or force," but in the British Empire "we are actuated by higher motives"—by "liberal principles."[72] These liberal principles both moved and constituted the Empire at its most essential level, they were "internal and of a piece with itself."

At the same time, Smuts combined his understanding of the Empire as holistically "actuated" by liberal principles with a theory of evolution that accounted for its transition over the years from a commercial colonial empire to a complicated, internally variegated, "system" of dominions and dependencies at different stages of self-rule, for which, in Disraeli's words, there was "no example" in "either ancient or modern history."[73] In this sense, Smuts added an evolutionary flair to the kind of history described by the Round Table. By Smuts's lights, the movement of the British Empire through time was "dynamic," "evolving" and "natural."[74] The Empire, he maintained, "has developed along natural lines. The dominions started as Colonies and as settlements of the British Isles. They developed into self-governing Colonies, and now they have become the present dominions. Other parts of the world have been added to the Empire, until today we have really a congeries of nations."[75] But at the same time, Smuts insisted that the object he described was not simply an aggregation but a "whole world by ourselves," an "organism."[76] Thus the process of imperial evolution that Smuts detailed was both synthetic (leading toward greater holism) and evolutionary (leading toward greater internal differentiation.) For this reason, Smuts argued, the word "Empire" was itself misleading "because it makes people think that we are one community to which the word 'Empire' can be appropriately applied."[77] By contrast, he argued that he preferred the word "Commonwealth," and went on to praise this Commonwealth for its internal diversity and flexibility, for the way it folded crown colonies, protectorates, dependencies, and the dominions into a cohesive whole.[78] What differentiated the cohesion of the Commonwealth from other empires was that it did not try to fashion "one nation" out of its constituent parts but, instead, encouraged the development of a "fuller, richer, more various life" in all of its unique communities across the world.

In this respect, and in others, Smuts's vision of the Empire as Commonwealth reflected that of the Round Table although, just as Curtis had eschewed mentioning the Federationists that so clearly influenced his work, so did Smuts avoid crediting the members of the Round Table, many of whom he knew from their days in South Africa.[79] As with, the Round Table, Smuts's vision stressed the British Empire's organic, inner coherence while also celebrating its diversity and insisting upon its liberal, democratic foundations. With the Round Table, Smuts argued that the basic principles of "freedom and equality"—the centrifugal, holistic force that held this political body together while allowing for "the fuller, richer and more various life of all the nations that comprised it"—was grounded in a fraternal bond that sprang from old loyalties and traditions. Like the Round Table, Smuts also stressed that the basis of the Commonwealth lay not in the force it exercised, but the principles that moved it. Thus, the historical narrative that emerged from Smuts's 1917 speeches, like that of the Round Table, is of an Empire "not organized on a military basis" but on a peaceful "commercial basis," that naturally transitioned from its early colonial roots in the eighteenth-century into the wholly unique multinational organ that it was in 1917. "You can see," argued Smuts, "that no political ideas which have been evolved in the past will apply to this world which is comprised in the British Empire."[80]

Because of these basic similarities, Smuts's account of the Commonwealth also allowed him, like the Round Table, to neatly elide the violent and often markedly illiberal history of the Empire by transforming that history into a natural unfolding of the Empire's innermost essence. Smuts's insistence that the Empire "has developed along natural lines" suggested that, like any growing organism, its transitions and expansions were simply part of its movement from one evolutionary development to the next. For Smuts, the "Dominions started as Colonies and as settlements of the British Isles. They developed into self-governing Colonies, and now they have become the present Dominions." Hidden in this slippage from one historical epoch to the next was the actual violence implicit in the eighteenth-century rhetoric of an "empire of liberty," what Karen O'Brien has described as a "cosmopolitan fantasy of the empire as the bringer of a universal British peace and free trade in an era of navigation acts and continuous warfare."[81] Hidden also was the loss of the American colonies and the massive ideological shift in rhetoric required to move from an understanding of the Empire as "bringer of universal British peace and free trade" to an Empire directly and indirectly ruling over populations considered not yet ready for universal British values in the name of other strategic calculations, particularly the need to enhance Britain's reputation as a world imperial power.[82] Smut's smooth contention that "other parts of the world have been added to the Empire" implied that such additions were also natural, and that they followed a similar pattern of development from colonies to free dominions. Smuts's description makes no mention of the historically specific forms of power associated with the Company's expansion in India and establishment of indirect rule, the Opium Wars, or the Scramble for Africa. Along with this language of evolution, Smuts's equally pronounced holism—his relentless insistence that the Empire was a "whole" that was "actualized" by the principles of "freedom and equality"—also erased the current and historical violence of the Empire by constantly reducing the very nature of the Empire to its liberal character. The "spirit of liberty" Smuts claimed, has always been "the guiding principle of British history," the Empire was "built on Freedom," and the City of London "the great bulwark of liberty."[83] With the Round Table, Smuts clearly thought it impossible for the Empire to behave in any other way than its character allowed. Even though, Smuts conceded, the Empire had once veered "off the track" in its dealings with the Boers, he insisted that, once its actuating principles had kicked in, it quickly righted itself and began moving in a liberal direction again.[84]

But Smuts's emphasis on organicism, holism, and evolution allowed him to do something that the Round Table could not: make a case for evolutionary change that moved the Commonwealth idea in a direction other than statehood. Thus, just as Smuts argued in his philosophical texts that evolution amounted to more than "regrouping of the old into new forms; it is creative, its new forms are not merely fashioned out of the old materials," so did he also argue that, with regard to the Empire, "too much, if I may say so, of the old ideas still cling to the new organism which is growing."[85] For Smuts, these old ideas clustered around the fact that the dominions were still "subject provinces" of Great Britain. If he had a suggestion to make for the Commonwealth, it was that the status of the dominions "as equal governments of the King in the British Commonwealth" should be more fully accepted than "is done today."[86] Smuts insisted, however, expanding opportunities for the dominions to exercise autonomy in this way would not be a departure from the moral principles that actualized the Empire as a whole but, rather, would bring the Empire more fully in line with the very traditions upon which it was founded. To Smuts's mind, "our past traditions—the traditions of freedom, self-government, and of the fullest development for all constituent parts of the Empire" provided the obvious solution to the Empire's current problems.[87] Other than its momentary mistreatment of the Boers, the natural evolutionary direction of the Commonwealth and the new organism which was emerging from this process pushed it in the direction of "more freedom and more equality in its constituent parts" and away from a "federal solution."[88]

In contrast to Smuts, and despite their emphasis on the organic, spiritual unity of the Commonwealth and their desire to increase the participation of the dominions in imperial affairs, the Round Table thinkers always understood the Commonwealth as an "international state" whose people were bound together by an allegiance "to the same paramount authority," making them "citizens of one comprehensive state" in which "autocracy has been finally discarded." Smuts, for his part, refused to accept a "federal solution" to the "imperial problem," even one only loosely organized around a "Central Parliament and a Central Executive." Smuts agreed with the Round Table that "the spirit which actuates" the Commonwealth could be found in the "common patriotism and common ideal" expressed by its people, but, he located this spirit in places other than the "instruments of government."[89] In particular, Smuts went out of his way to identify these sites of loyalty with institutions that had only nominal or symbolic power over the dominions, in "hereditary kingship," for instance, and the Imperial Conference system.[90]

Ultimately this vision of a Commonwealth united by sentiment, patriotism, and politically symbolic institutions happened to serve Smuts's political purposes extremely well. It valorized the "common" patriotic ideals of freedom and equality embodied in the whole Commonwealth, while claiming maximal autonomy for increasingly independent white dominions like South Africa. For his part, Smuts envisioned far more autonomy for the dominions than did the Round Tablers, particularly in matters relating to race and immigration. The international ire aimed at Smuts after he arrested Gandhi in 1913 was enough to convince him that South Africa's policies toward Asians and black South Africans could only be maintained in the long run if the country was allowed complete autonomy over its immigration and racial politics.[91] Greater autonomy for the dominions also clearly spoke to Smuts's desire to see white dominions like the increasingly segregationist state of South Africa exercise more control not only over questions of immigration, but also of regional security. Civilizing Africa "from the South" required an expanded mandate for the white dominions to subdue, as they saw fit, their putatively less civilized neighbors in the name of British Commonwealth freedom.

Thus, with respect to the dominions, Smuts's Commonwealth rejected any "federal solution" that gave ultimate authority to London and, instead, grounded his vision almost entirely on a depoliticized, organic conception of the whole in which the relationship between the white dominions and Britain was premised on the "actuating" spirit of "freedom, equality, and equity" that enlivened the Commonwealth at its core rather than on "instruments of government." At the same time, Smuts's evolutionary narrative allowed him to account for this "congeries" of free nations not as a dramatic step away from the "actuating" spirit of the original Empire, but as a "spontaneous" and natural progression from its freedom-loving, commercial and colonial beginnings. There was something amazingly elastic and flexible about the Empire, Smuts argued, that allowed it to evolve toward a more complex and internally differentiated form of itself, and that allowed its dominions greater autonomy, while remaining internally coherent.

Additionally, Smuts claimed that the Empire (or Commonwealth) not only embodied "freedom and equality" at an almost cellular level, he also insisted that the British Empire was not in fact *imperialist* as such. Other peoples and societies were imperialist, but the British Empire understood that its strength lay in its diversity and its principled moral commitments to freedom and equality. By Smuts's lights

> Germany is an Empire. Rome was an Empire. India is an Empire. But we are a system of nations. We are not a State, but a community of States and nations. We are far greater than any Empire which has ever existed, and by using this ancient expression we really disguise the main fact that our whole position is different, and that we are not one State or nation or empire, but a whole world by ourselves, consisting of many nations, of many States, and all sorts of communities, under one flag.[92]

Smuts's aim here was obviously to contrast what he maintained were the homogenizing forces of some forms of imperial domination with the internal diversity between, and the relative autonomy of, the "states" and "nations" that constituted the British Empire. Aside from the fact that the Roman Empire and the Moghul Empire in India were diverse in the ways that Smuts seemed to value, what is most perverse about this claim is Smuts's assertion that while Rome "was" an empire, India "is" an empire, as if India, as a coherent unit, were some how still in the business of imperializing. "The Indian Empire" was a name given to those areas in the Indian subcontinent both directly and indirectly ruled by Britain after the rebellion; the British issued passports after 1876 under that name. Thus, despite the fact that "The Indian Empire" was *imperialized* (not imperializing) in 1917, Smuts took the name and argued that, by its nature, India was imperious, as if there was something about the Indians (and the Germans and the Romans) that made them an imperializing people. In this way, Smuts reduced the very idea of empire to a character trait, something that a society was or was not by its nature, rather than a set of political practices. In holistic terms, Smuts seems to be arguing that what mattered most about a people was not its current political status but its actuating principles, its internal activity that made it "of a piece with itself." Britain's actuating principles were not imperial. India's were.

It is this understanding of empire that made it possible for Smuts to argue that the League of Nations he proposed was a postimperial project even while, at the same time, suggesting that it be modeled upon the British Empire. In another speech entitled "A League of Nations" given in 1917 and also included in *War-Time Speeches*, Smuts maintained, without a hint of irony, that this League be modeled on the British Empire and, at the same time, that the conclusion of the war would establish once and for all that "nations will no longer as in former years be disposed of by alien statesmen and Governments; that they will not be parceled and chopped up so as to be divided among the big Powers of the world."[93] For Smuts, the British Empire was not only grounded on the actuating principles of freedom and equality but was internally flexible, able to meet and absorb the challenges of the world because of its adaptive, evolutionary character. It therefore made a perfect blueprint for a postwar organization that would provide for a sense of international unity and cohesion and simultaneously rest "on the basis of the national."[94]

At the same time, Smuts's philosophical holism was shaped not only by his conviction that wholes, like the Empire, were moved by both internal, actuating principles and the forces of evolution that led toward greater diversity, but that they also were ordered along lines that continually reasserted the superiority of the higher elements over the lower. So while Smuts might have used the word "equality" repeatedly in these speeches to denote the relationship between the metropole and its imperial parts, he certainly did not mean to suggest that each of these parts would be equally autonomous. This is no doubt why Smuts also used the word "equity" when talking about both the Empire's actuating principles ("freedom, equality, and equity") and the relationship between its parts. As political theorists have long observed, the idea of equity assumes a certain level of equality (insofar as all citizens are roughly equal to one another) but, in the name of fairness, argues that neither societal benefits nor advantages need be distributed equally. From Mill to Rawls, liberal political theorists have used the notion of equity to theorize the relationship between liberal equality and fairness in the context of political economy and the unequal accumulation of capital.[95] But Smuts seems to mean something different by the term, something less akin to fairness and more like balance or equilibrium between more or less equal parts.

In this vision, the flexible diversity that Smuts ascribed to the Empire and which he felt differentiated it from all other empires—indeed, made it not imperial—was, above all, an *ordered* diversity in which lower and higher elements were kept in equilibrium. For Smuts, giving the dependencies equal status with the dominions was out of the question and yet, he argued, all were equally members of the Empire. In the Commonwealth, he argued, "you have the United Kingdom with a number of Crown Colonies. Besides that you have a large Protectorate like Egypt, an Empire by itself. Then you have a great Dependency like India, also an Empire by itself, where civilization has existed from time immemorial, where we are trying to see how East and West can work together." In addition, Smuts argued, "we come to the so-called dominions, independent in their government, which have been evolved on the principles of your free constitutional system into almost independent States" that exist alongside the dependencies in "a community of nations."[96] This "community" was holistic, for Smuts, and it was properly ordered, such that the dominions, which had evolved on the principles of freedom, exercised autonomy, while imperious types of people (Egyptians and Indians) who did not understand freedom, remained dependent.

Smuts's holism allowed him to elide any number of what might look like contradictions in the name of liberal equality. The vision of the Empire he developed in these wartime speeches and then championed as a model for the League of Nations was "actuated" by equality but unequally ordered. It was grounded on the freedom of its constituent parts, yet drawn toward the center by its actuating principles. This was a conservative vision of the Empire that constantly referred back to its "traditions" and which suggested very little change to its overall structure, other than greater autonomy for white people in the dominions. At the same time, Smuts claimed that this form of international organization was radically new. When imagining a postwar world, Smuts opined, we "should not follow precedents, but make them" even as he established the precedent of the British Empire as "the only successful experiment in international government that has ever been made."[97]

Smuts also imagined the transition from Empire to League of Nations in similarly holistic and evolutionary terms. "The process of civilization has always been towards the League of Nations," he argued in *A Practical Suggestion*:

> Nations, in their march to power tend to pass the purely national bond; hence arise the Empires which embrace various nations, sometimes related in blood and institutions, sometimes again different in race and hostile in temperament. In a rudimentary way all such composite Empires of the past were leagues of nations, keeping the peace among the constituent nations, but unfortunately doing so not on the basis of freedom but of repression.[98]

Of course what made the British Empire unique was that it was "based on the true principles" of freedom and equality. Therefore, with Zimmern and the Round Table, Smuts argued that the British Empire was both exceptional in the history of the world and a more perfectly true representative of the movement of civilization toward greater perfection more generally and a League of Nations in particular. And yet, it is important to understand that, for Smuts, this movement was not "progressive" in the classically liberal imperial sense, which envisioned historical time marching toward liberal ends. Smuts did not imagine a world where distinct peoples and polities fell somewhere along a temporal axis, closer to or farther away from maturity, either the "caboose of politics" or the engine of civilization. Rather, for Smuts, evolutionary progress implied not forward movement but inner perfection, greater complexity, and more sophisticated, ordered forms of regulation. Polities like the British Empire could serve as models for the world in the same way that all organisms have something "to learn from highly developed Mind in the way of regulation, co-ordination or inner control of structures and functions."

What set Smuts's *A Practical Suggestion* apart from the myriad other suggestions and blueprints for a postwar league circulating in England at the time were his specific suggestions about expanding the Empire's internal hierarchical structure (between dominions and dependencies) to the rest of the world. The end of the German, Ottoman, and Austrian Empires, he believed, meant the liberation of numerous people who were "either incapable of or deficient in the power of self government."[99] A League of Nations, whose "broad features" would closely resemble the British Empire, should be made the "reversionary" of these old empires.[100] "In this debacle of the old Europe," Smuts opined, "the League of Nations is no longer an outsider or stranger, but the natural master of the house."[101] In addition, for those parts of the world not in Europe but left masterless by the end of the German and Ottoman Empires, the League of Nations would actually become, by Smuts's lights, the "real live active heir to the former Empires." For Smuts, there was nothing contradictory about establishing a line of succession between the old empires and the new, while simultaneously insisting that the League itself would be grounded in the triumph of a new world philosophy based on the principles of "self determination and the consent of the governed." But again, in Smuts's mind, "self determination" in this new form of international organization would be modeled on the British Empire—which, he claimed, was not imperial but rather a holistic and evolving composite of peoples and nations at varying degrees of autonomy. And just as the British Empire was actuated by the principles of freedom and equality but internally ordered in such a way that not all of its parts were equal, so was the League of Nations to be actuated by self-determination and the consent of the governed—even when it was internally structured so that only some states and peoples consented to their government.

The extent to which Smuts's understanding of a League of Nations took the entire liberal discourse of civilizational improvement and leading-strings-government out of the grips of time cannot be emphasized enough. In other words, Smuts's approach did not forestall the day when colonized societies would reach the civilizational maturity necessary for self determination; it removed this possibility from consideration by recasting the liberal project in holistic terms, as the increasing diversity and internal perfection of political wholes rather than the linear movement of progress. In this sense, Smuts's language in *A Practical Suggestion* regarding those parts of the world he did not feel were fit for self-governance differed from the language that would eventually be incorporated into the Covenant of the League. Adopted by the Council of Ten on January 30, 1919, Article 22 of the Covenant framed the rationale for what came to be known as the Mandate System in terms of a "sacred trust of civilization":

> To those colonies and territories which as a consequence of the late war
> have ceased to be under the sovereignty of the States which formerly

governed them and which are inhabited by peoples not yet able to stand by themselves under the strenuous conditions of the modern world, there should be applied the principle that the well-being and development of such peoples form a sacred trust of civilization and that securities for the performance of this trust should be embodied in this Covenant... The best method of giving practical effect to this principle is that the tutelage of such peoples should be entrusted to advanced nations.[102]

While Smuts has been credited with both inventing the Mandate System and convincing the leaders at the Paris Conference to adopt it, he rarely used language in *A Practical Suggestion* that linked the League to a project that entailed "tutelage" of those people simply not yet mature enough to stand "by themselves" under the stressful conditions of the modern world. Smuts *did* argue that Great Powers who became administrators of mandated regions should look upon their charge as a "great trust and honour" but he did not imagine these mandated peoples to be equally teachable.

Rather, Smuts spent a considerable amount of time in this text identifying those societies who ought to be mandated and to what extent, using language that attached particular kinds of peoples to particular types of political characters. According to Smut's taxonomy, some societies (primarily in Eastern Europe) were capable of autonomy, and for these groups Smuts preferred to use a language of "development" similar to that which would eventually appear in the Covenant. These new states were not yet "sufficiently capable" of self-governance and required the "guiding hand" of more able League member-states until such time as they could "govern themselves."[103] The wishes of these kinds of people ought to be taken into consideration, Smuts argued, when identifying which state would administrate them in the name of the League. But for the rest of the formerly and still-colonized world, Smuts used words familiar to liberal imperialists like "undeveloped peoples" rather than "developing," or more often, "subject peoples" who were more or less "capable" of autonomy. Most people in those areas of the Middle East soon to fall under League Mandates were "barely capable" of autonomy, while large swaths of Africa and the Pacific were inhabited "by barbarians who cannot possibly govern themselves" for whom "it would be impractable to apply any ideas of political self determination in the European sense."[104] Smuts thus carefully qualified his point by arguing that in a League of Nations system, "the rule of self-determination, or the consent of the governed to their form of government, shall be fairly and reasonably applied."[105] In this way, Smuts could both argue that self-determination was one of the "fundamental principles" upon which the League was grounded while, in the name of applying the principle "fairly and effectively," deny self-determination for most of the world's communities based on their characters as peoples.

There is nothing in *A Practical Suggestion* that would suggest any hope of civilizational development for those who were simply, in Smuts's mind, "incapable" of self-government. Those peoples left ungoverned by the liquidation of former empires would need to be indirectly administered by the League through mandatory states who, not coincidentally, just happened to be great imperial powers. Even less coincidentally, Smuts argued that a few British dominions, like South Africa and Australia, ought to be allowed to administer those areas, formerly occupied by the Germans, in Africa and the South Pacific who "could not possibly govern themselves." Finally, Smuts insisted repeatedly that in all "not completely independent States" (which, in his vision, was much of the world) the policy of "open door, or equal economic opportunity for all, must be laid down."[106] The maintenance of these territories as free trade zones would prevent economic rivalry among the Great Powers, Smuts argued. At the same time, however, ever wary that South Africa might lose control of its racialized immigration policies, Smuts both gestured toward "economic opportunity" and elided the possibility that this could mean the free movement of workers by always immediately following the "open door" suggestion with an equally emphatic claim that military and "police policy" remain in the hands of the mandatory power.[107]

A League of Nations based on the model of the British Empire that Smuts envisioned would provide the "steadying, controlling regulating influence" required to "give stability to progress."[108] In this way, Smuts cannily made the case that the League of Nations would actually *be* progressive, that it would provide the world with a truly new alternative to imperialism while, simultaneously, suggesting that this "progress" was, like the Empire, ordered and regulated, based firmly on an evolving but always hierarchical set of principles, always "of a piece with itself." At the same time, Smuts argued that a new League of Nations could not be simply "superimposed on the pre-existing structure." Like the evolution of all great wholes, it "must be an organic change; it most be woven into the very texture of our political system," it must "flow from the very nature of things political."[109] Again and again in this pamphlet Smuts emphasized the need for a League system that emerged organically out of the Commonwealth, made whole by its "internal" coherence, capable of "inner transformation," organized around a centralized non-center where the Great Powers gathered together to act as a "wise regulator" for the world.[110] In Smuts's rendering of international cooperation and organization, the "vital principles" of freedom, national self determination, and equality gave "development of form and substance to the whole system" but the system itself was geared largely toward internal regulation, toward the maintenance of a harmonious status quo rather than toward a change in the balance of power in the international system or toward the equalization of resources and rights for the worlds' people.

At one point early on in his argument, Smuts gave his readers a glimpse of what such a system might look like:

> The European Empires will all have disappeared; Germany will have become a truly federal democratic State from which the non-German subject peoples will have been disannexed and reunited to their parent peoples. New sovereign States, such as Finland, Poland, Bohemia and Greater Serbia, will have arisen under the aegis of the League. A large number of autonomous States will have arisen, no longer oppressed by their neighbors, but befriended, advised, and assisted in varying degree by individual great States. A smaller number of areas will be directly administered by some or other of the Powers. Over all would be the League as a real live controlling authority.[111]

There is nothing in this picture that necessitates any move toward sovereign equality for those "number of areas" administered by the Great Powers in the name of the League, nor is there any assumption that smaller, emerging nations will ever exercise equal influence over the international system or ever move away from the influence of their "parent" states. We are "called upon," Smuts argued later in the pamphlet, "to decide what we mean by equality in the new system. Will the United States of America count for as much and the same as Guatemala?"[112] Smuts responded with a resounding "no." Perhaps most importantly, in this vision, European empires decidedly would *not* disappear; those "smaller number of areas" directly administered by these Empires, when taken in the context of their total colonial holdings, simply added to the total number of people held in colonial bondage. But for Smuts this did not matter. The whole world would now be imitating the form of the British Empire and the British Empire was not an empire but a "whole world," actuated by freedom and equality, internally variegated, regulated, and above all, well-ordered.

Conclusion

After the War, Smuts was well placed politically to have a significant impact on the actual League of Nations that emerged from the conference in Paris. Lloyd George (who was from the beginning skeptical of any the league of nations idea) had invited Smuts to join his War Cabinet in 1917. Toward the end of 1918, Smuts and Lord Robert Cecil were chosen to represent the British imperial interests in Paris although Smuts, along with Botha, went as an official representative of South Africa.[113] For the British government, the problem with all of the League proposals in circulation at the time was the threat they potentially posed to the sovereignty of the British Empire as a whole, either because they transferred executive power to an external international body or, in the case of Wilson's Fourteen Points, because they suggested that anybody calling themselves a nation—from upstart new states in Eastern Europe to those peoples occupied by the British—ought to be able to participate in a league of nations on the basis of "self determination." Moreover, Point Five of Wilson's missive could potentially call all empires, not just those of the defeated powers, into question by demanding "absolutely impartial adjustment of all colonial claims."[114] At the same time, the government could not ignore the reality that the idea of a league of nations and Wilson's Fourteen Points were wildly popular in Britain, Europe, and America.[115]

Smuts and Cecil were thus sent to Paris with a difficult task: they were meant to appear to be sympathetic to the League idea without sacrificing British imperial interests. Smuts's view, of course, was that an internationalism modeled after the British Empire was not a contradiction because, by his lights, the British Empire was not an empire. Smuts's *Practical Suggestion* (published just before the conference) thus spoke to both British and American interests by combining a practically imperial with a symbolically anti-imperial form of Great Power leadership, tying this understanding of power to a Wilsonian commitment to "national determination," and then reconciling all of this with the Allies' collective desire to both keep and expand their empires by annexing those of the defeated powers in the name of international government. Indeed, Smuts even spoke directly to Wilson's general discomfort with the word "imperialism" by suggesting that the "disposal" of the former German and Turkish colonies ought to be decided "on the principles which President Wilson has laid down in the fifth of his celebrated Fourteen Points."[116] In Mazower's words, *A Practical Suggestion* "squared the circle" between colonial expansion and "Wilsonian idealism" in a manner that allowed imperial states to effectively have their cake and eat it too.[117]

As luck would have it, Wilson read Smuts's suggestion on the way to the Paris Peace Conference. As Smuts described it in a letter he wrote from Paris to his friend Alice Clark, "Wilson has read my pamphlet carefully and the Prime Minister says that he is now beginning to talk enthusiastically of this scheme and will probably end by giving it to the world as his own!"[118] On an institutional level, Smuts's suggestion in his pamphlet for a League framework organized around a conference, a council, and a judicial system was included in every draft brought forward by the British and the Americans at the conference.[119]

The part of the Covenant upon which Smuts clearly had the most impact, however, was the Mandate System.[120] While the system which emerged from the conference excluded Eastern Europe from its purview, as Smuts had originally suggested, and while the final language of Article Twenty-Two put more emphasis on the temporary status of peoples "not yet able to stand by themselves" than did Smuts, Smuts's typology of peoples was incorporated almost word for word into the actual policy language of the Mandate System. According to the description of the system published by the League of Nations Information Section in 1927, "A" Mandates included "certain communities formerly belonging to the Turkish Empire" whose independence could be provisionally recognized. "B" Mandates were described as territories where "self government would be impossible," while "C" Mandates referred largely to indigenous populations in Southwest Africa and the Pacific who "on account of the sparseness of population or their small numbers" and "their remoteness from the centres of civilization" were to be simply absorbed by the Mandatory power as "integral portions of its territory."[121] In addition, the official policy language of the Mandate System committed all Mandatory powers to the "principle of the 'open door'" for all "economic, commercial, and industrial" interests.[122]

Smuts's influence over the final wording of Article Twenty-Two is even more remarkable if we consider that he was able to significantly change and even reverse language that Wilson had added after reading Smuts's original pamphlet. According to Parker Moon, the "wording of the long clauses which were finally inserted into the Versailles treaty as Article 22" were "'due in the main to General Smuts and Mr. Philip Kerr.'"[123] Whereas Wilson had edited Smuts's original language to clarify that those territories intended for mandate were specifically the former colonies of Germany, Austro-Hungary, and Turkey, Smuts responded by artfully changing the language again to those "colonies and territories which as a consequence of the late war have ceased to be under the sovereignty of the States which formerly governed them," thus opening the door for a much more expansive understanding of the Mandate System. Likewise, while Wilson's language had clarified which states would take on responsibility for the mandates under the auspices of the League, Smuts's wording maintained that the "tutelage of such peoples should be entrusted to advanced nations," purposely leaving vague both which nations these would be and how they would be chosen.

Years later, Smuts would become the driving force behind the creation of the United Nations Trusteeship System—which, in almost every meaningful way, resembled the Mandate System. He was also largely responsible for the language of the Preamble to the UN Charter and, just as his holism had allowed Smuts to envision a League of Nations that was both animated by liberal principles and fundamentally unequal, so did he deny any tension between the Charter's commitment to universal human rights and trusteeship.[124] In a very real way, the ability of Smuts's proposal to "square the circle" contributed significantly to the institutional practices and discourses that enabled an ideology of imperialism to exist side by side with emerging norms of internationalism throughout the interwar period and well into the 1960s. Closer to home, South African occupation of the former German colonies in the region would not end until 1988, when Namibia gained its independence.

Even more significantly, traces of Smuts's Mandate System continue to live on in the global institutions that have maintained the international hierarchy between the Global North and the Global South since the inception of the League through the practice of "informal imperialism." According to Antony Anghie, the work of the World Bank and the International Monetary Fund is "continuing the practice of the mandate system, which represented the first occasion on which an international institution, not limited in any way by the sovereignty of a state, could play a direct and unimpeded role in shaping the government, political institutions, and economy of a state."[125] These institutions continue, as per Smuts's insistence, to demand that all "developing" nations maintain an "open door" policy of free trade. Additionally, Smuts's language of international holism continues to thrive in the academic and diplomatic languages of "global governance." While today advocates and scholars of global governance reject words like "barbarian," they are as obsessed with organic notions of "order" between "the governing" and "the governed" as was Smuts.[126] Such thinkers often use words like "holistic" and "spontaneous" to describe what they see as an evolutionary trajectory toward both greater cohesion and greater complexity in the world system.[127] James Rosenau, for instance, argues that all of human development has effectively been leading toward global "government without governance." A "five million year history of human evolution," he argues, "demonstrates a clear pattern of continual growth in 'metabolic memory systems'" which enable "spontaneous" collective action on a global scale.[128]

In sum, Smuts's holism saved the day for liberal imperialism in many ways. At a moment of perceived imperial decline and widespread fears about continued European domination and the decline of the white race, this man from the fringes of the Empire presented liberal pro-League advocates in Britain, Europe, and America with an internationalism that assured European domination in the name of liberal principles like freedom, equality, and self-determination. Unlike other solutions to the "imperial problem" proffered by the likes of the Round Table at the same time, Smuts's proposal removed the language of statehood—and thus, of ruling—from the vocabulary of the British Empire and transformed it into a postimperial, organic, holistic entity actuated by liberal principles and moved by evolution toward greater internal diversity. His vision of the League of Nations thus maintained all of the benefits of ruling without any of the drawbacks (namely, the possibility that the Great Powers would have to surrender their sovereignty over the colonized) and salved the fears of League critics worried about the possibility of a "world state." Smuts's vision also solved liberal imperialism's temporal problem by recasting the linear movement of evolutionary progress as the growth of internally differentiated, overlapping wholes or concentric circles that spontaneously ordered and reordered the world into lower and higher spheres, where the difference between the governed and the governing appeared to be categorical byproducts of nature.

Ironically, what may have appealed most to the legions of adoring liberals drawn to both Smuts and his plan was its barely concealed racism and its conservatism. In this sense, as a political figure, Smuts himself mirrored the racism that English liberals now felt less comfortable expressing, but he did so in a manner that sounded both reasonable and authentic. Smuts's plan seemed to steer a clear-eyed, moderate middle course between the alternatives of white supremacy and total integration, between imperialism and internationalism. The plan was also deeply conservative in its cynically nostalgic conviction that both white, Anglo culture and the entire world could be saved by a return to British traditions, rather than by any uncomfortable accommodation with the increasingly dissatisfied populations in the colonies. At the same time, Smuts's proposal avoided sounding Jeremianic by preserving a language of liberal innovation that imagined both the League of Nations and the British Empire as entirely novel forms of social and political organization. With the Round Table, Smuts's holistic accounting of imperial history allowed both he and his readers to elide the violence of the imperial state and its prolonged dips into illiberality by transforming the Empire's journey through the past into an evolutionary coming to fruition of an anti-imperial character that existed alongside the naturally imperious nature of Indians, Egyptians, and other currently colonized societies.

An analysis of Smuts's vision of the Empire and the League of Nations offers insight into one of the most successful forms of liberal imperial deflection from the early twentieth-century: it also offers us a particularly powerful historical flashpoint for identifying the rhetorical details behind the discursive folding of imperialism into the contemporary language and practice of internationalism, international relations, and global governance. All too frequently these imperialist assumptions remain unstated, emerging in the clusters of imperatives and institutions behind development projects and "good governance" initiatives. However, since the end of the Cold War, and especially since 2001, such assumptions have been breaking through the skin of public international relations discourse, revealing just how close to the surface they really are. In the immediate aftermath of the 2010 earthquake in Haiti, for instance, National Public Radio commentator Daniel Schorr suggested, "What is needed now is some generally accepted authority representing the family of nations. History provides some examples of benign governorship of countries not yet ready for self-government. I am thinking of the Mandate System introduced by the League of Nations after World War I and the Trusteeship System of the United Nations after World War II."[129] Schorr did not feel the need to question the historical circumstances which have rendered Haiti "not yet ready for self-government" (including the French blockade in the nineteenth-century and the years of direct occupation by the United States and its indirect support for puppet governments in the twentieth-century), nor to reflect on the imperialist assumptions that adhere to the phrase "not yet ready for self-government" in the first place. The "family of nations," for Schorr, is a benign household, a place where parent states continue to nurture their children who are always becoming—but not quite yet—ready for self government.

Perhaps more disturbingly, the subject of the final chapter of this book, Michael Ignatieff—an historian who works on international human rights and should have some awareness of League and UN history—ties the notion of trusteeship to benign imperialism without ever acknowledging how the League and the UN used to the term to extend colonialism into the age of internationalism. In the context of "failed states" like Kosovo and Bosnia, he argues in 1995's "The Seductiveness of Moral Disgust" (later reprinted in 2004), that "the next task facing the international community is to devise a form of trusteeship that reproduces the benefits of imperial rule (benefits, that is, for the indigenous population) without reproducing the dynamic of revolt that will destroy what such exercises set out to achieve: a stable and self-determining polity."[130] With this blithe rhetorical gesture, Ignatieff not only strips the League and the UN of their imperial legacies, he empties the word trusteeship of its twentieth-century context and links it with a worldview that imagines international politics and the relationship of Great Powers to the rest of the world in terms of the "benefits of imperial rule." In the same breath, he reduces reactions against imperialism to internecine feuds, a "dynamic of revolt" that appears separable from the overreach of the occupying power. Ignatieff thus evacuates the recent past of its imperial context by returning straight to the source, back to the moment when men like Smuts convinced the white world that their form of empire—always non-imperious, always liberal and democratic, always "internal and of a piece with itself"—was the solution to the violence, instability, and inequality of imperialism.

6

Michael Ignatieff's Tragedy: Just As We Are, Here and Now

In March 2006, the Bush Administration released is updated version of the National Security Strategy for the United States. Perhaps even more notable than the Administration's continued defense of "preemptive" military intervention and the decidedly imperialist implications of the moral, global vision articulated in the report was its fixation with justifying intervention through the language of "character." "In the world today," argued the drafters in terms that would cause realists throughout the world to shudder, "the fundamental character of regimes matters as much as the distribution of power among them."[1] Such thinking—with its emphasis on the fixed, liberal-democratic character of certain peoples and the equally fixed non-liberal-democratic character of others—provided the foundations for the logic of "regime change" that justified the 2003 invasion of Iraq and of the War on Terror more generally. It has also become an accepted part of the post-Bush foreign policy consensus among liberals, conservatives, and neoconservatives in the United States.

This chapter looks at the works of one of the public intellectuals whose work helped shape a post-September 11, 2001 foreign policy climate in America focused on the "fundamental character" of states and peoples: Harvard professor and former leader of the Liberal Party of Canada, Michael Ignatieff. As I have suggested with regard to the work of other contemporary authors explored in this book, the project that Ignatieff confronts in his pro-imperial writings is not uncommon in the history of liberal imperialism and, in particular, it resembles the work of pro-imperial British liberals from a century ago. Like Zimmern, the Round Table authors, and Smuts, Ignatieff must justify empire to an increasingly skeptical liberal audience and make sense out of the niggling disconnect between liberals' historically expressed commitment to human equality, the self-determination of states, and the rule of law, and the actual practices of imperialism which suspend these assumed natural rights for large segments of the world's population, in Ferguson's words, "not just for a few months or years but for decades." What differentiates both Ignatieff and Ferguson from their Edwardian progenitors however, is the extent to which each explicitly acknowledges that liberal imperialism requires the violation of liberal norms for liberal imperial ends, and the way in which both are willing to embrace such violations as an affirmation of the liberal state's identity. But while Ferguson turns to the pained, "self liquidating," conscience of the colonizer as proof positive of the imperial state's liberal character, Ignatieff, a student of Isaiah Berlin, focuses on the moment of tragic choice that the liberal society must confront when facing a barbarous international playing field. As this chapter explores, Ignatieff's sense of tragedy serves a much more complicated purpose than did Berlin's in the sense that tragedy is never, for Ignatieff, merely about loss. Rather, tragedy produces liberal character. In the end, the choice to torture or invade or deprive is important to Ignatieff insofar as it enhances the loss experienced by a ubiquitously liberal, democratic, and eternally innocent "we," while also serving as a painful reminder of just how difficult it is to be liberal in a world of non-believers.

The chapter focuses on the story Ignatieff has told, since September 11, 2001 of the relationship between liberal character, American imperial intervention, and the War on Terror, focusing in particular on the way he constructs this narrative so that the connection between liberalism and American power can only be understood in terms of the tragic choice faced by the liberal society: act illiberally, or allow the world to slip into execrable chaos. At the heart of Ignatieff's vision of the world lies a naturalized image of liberal-democratic, largely Anglophone societies like Canada, Britain, and America forging bravely through time, whose "fundamental characters" justify their actions and whose actions reinforce their "fundamental characters." Ignatieff's narrative here resembles Smuts's story of the British Commonwealth and international politics following World War I, in that both men couch their visions in internationalist and human rights language, but this language is consistently qualified by their rhetorical return to the liberal character of the imperial state. For both men, who "we" are consistently trumps what "we" do by wrapping the imperializing society in the gauzy sheen of a liberal identity that protects it from the barbs of those who are consistently imagined to be illiberal in nature. But, whereas Smuts was able to couch his deeply cynical and segregated vision of the world in a hopeful language that was both internally holistic and externally progressive, Ignatieff's picture of liberal character is premised not on progress but on the loss generated by tragic choice, the blinding pain of which is meant to remind the liberal polity of who it truly is. And at the end of the day, this emphasis on who "we" are not only silences alternative interpretations of the liberal state's own imperial history, it also dampens the radical potential of tragedy itself.

The chapter begins by looking closely at Ignatieff's liberalism, paying particular attention to his pragmatic, Berlin-influenced approach to human rights, deliberation, and empathy. I then move on to look at Ignatieff's post-September 11, 2001 writings, focusing on his emerging conviction that guaranteeing the security of liberal democracies in a world perpetually imperiled by the "chaos" excreted through the porous boundaries of former colonies requires the United States and its liberal Western allies to embrace a policy of military intervention that he calls "empire lite" and a "lesser evil" approach to terrorist suppression. I examine the pastiche of historical vignettes, personal stories, professional policy speak, liberal human rights theory, and ethical torment that Ignatieff constructs to cocoon "the burden," "empire lite," and "the lesser evil" in the anguished glow of what looks like self-reflection and profound moral critique, and which serves to mask the foregone character of his conclusions. The second half of the chapter looks more closely at the role of tragedy in Ignatieff's formulation of liberal character, focusing on the way he transforms the work of Berlin to accommodate an approach that forecloses alternative interpretations of liberal identity in the present and the past. I then briefly examine examples of the kind of approach to tragedy that Ignatieff's work occludes, paying particular attention to the writings of Peter Euben and Richard Ned Lebow. Finally, I conclude by suggesting that Ignatieff's work is *actually* tragic insofar as his hubris blinds him to the possibilities of historicizing and reimagining a more generous, self-critical, democratic "we."

Ignatieff and the Anguish of Liberal "Self-Justification"

Michael Ignatieff holds a joint professional appointment at the Munk School of International Affairs at the University of Toronto and at Harvard University's Kennedy School, where he is a Professor of Practice. Before 2005 he was the Carr Professor of Human Rights Policy at Harvard and previously held academic posts at Cambridge, Oxford, and the London School of Economics. In 2006 he returned to Canada, was elected a member of Parliament, and assumed the leadership of the Liberal Party in 2008, resigning in May 2011 after he lost his Toronto riding. Ignatieff retuned to academia shortly thereafter. An historian by training, Ignatieff is the author of numerous academic and popular books since the late 1970s whose topics range across a number of different disciplines, tackling issues as diverse as human rights, nationalism, political violence, foreign affairs, and minority rights. While his first book, *A Just Measure of Pain: Penitentiaries in the Industrial Revolution, 1580–1850* (1978), was an acclaimed work of history, Ignatieff's publications have, as with Ferguson's, become less scholarly and more popular as his status as a public intellectual has grown. Also like Ferguson, since 2001, Ignatieff has become somewhat of a media darling, serving as a commentator for the BBC and as a regular contributor of op-eds and opinion pieces to *The New York Times, The Globe and Mail, Foreign Affairs,* and other influential publications.

Besides his direct involvement in Canadian politics and his influence as a public intellectual, Ignatieff has garnered a substantial reputation since the 1990s as an expert on questions of international human rights, nationalism, and ethnic violence, particularly after the publication of *Virtual War: Kosovo and Beyond* in 2000 and *Human Rights as Politics and Idolatry* in 2001. He has sat on numerous powerful international commissions, including the Independent International Commission on Kosovo and the United Nations' International Commission on Intervention and State Sovereignty, where he fine-tuned his support for military intervention in states committing human rights abuses. Indeed, Ignatieff's influence on policy makers in these areas during the 2000s has been so great that in 2009 *Foreign Policy* magazine named him sixty-fourth in their list of the "Top 100 Global Thinkers," for "showing that not all academics are irrelevant." "Ignatieff's writing," the editors continued, "on the sometime necessity of 'violence… coercion, secrecy, deception, even violation of rights' to fight terrorism has made him a singular voice among Canadian liberals."[2]

What the editors of *Foreign Affairs* identify as Ignatieff's clear-eyed, realistic take on the need for liberal states to violate liberal norms in the campaign against terrorism reflects what Ignatieff himself describes as his own "pragmatic" approach to liberalism, human rights, and state power. This is an approach that Ignatieff attributes, in large measure, to his former tutor and mentor at Oxford, Isaiah Berlin, the man Ignatieff has described as the person who "next to my father, I love most dearly and (who had) the greatest effect on my thinking."[3] Like Berlin, Ignatieff rejects a comprehensive or foundationalist defense of liberalism, arguing repeatedly, throughout his work, for a more minimalist conception of both liberalism and human rights that does not seek "its ultimate validation in a particular idea of the human good."[4] A firm believer in Berlin's distinction between negative and positive liberty, Ignatieff rejects all "Marxist ideals" as disastrously comprehensive because they are focused almost exclusively, he argues, on "freedom to" rather than "freedom from."[5] Any notion of universal rights ought to privilege the idea of "agency" by which, Ignatieff argues, "I mean more or less what Isaiah Berlin meant by 'negative liberty,' the capacity of each individual to achieve rational intentions without let or hindrance."[6] What makes this approach pragmatic in a Berlinian sense is Ignatieff's awareness that this kind of freedom can only be preserved within a state framework that also restricts freedom. The best kind of state to do this, argues Ignatieff, is a liberal-democratic state animated by a secular civic nationalism, "composed of all those—regardless of race, color, creed, gender, language, or ethnicity—who subscribe to the nation's political creed."[7] Ignatieff's commitment to democracy is thus similarly pragmatic in that he believes it to be the best way to preserve the promise of negative freedom, that is, the promise of enabling individual human agency. In the end, it is his pragmatic faith in liberal, democratic state power to protect human rights that that has fed Ignatieff's growing concern over the last twenty years with the way "failed states" like Kosovo and Afghanistan incubate forms of nationalist, illiberal, and terrorist violence.

However, neither Ignatieff's pragmatic approach to state power nor his refusal to locate the foundations of liberal freedom in a singular vision of the good means that he eschews making moral arguments about the relationship between liberalism, democracy, and civic life. Indeed, for Ignatieff, morality and the political practices of democratic contestation are intimately related, and he insists that a "world of moral equality" is also "a world of conflict, deliberation, argument, and contention."[8] In the same vein, Ignatieff maintains that "moral life" itself is a "process of justification" that requires us to give reasons for opinions and conduct to those who do not share our points of view. Thus the "essence of moral life," according to Ignatieff, "is this process of recurrent, repeated, behavior-changing justification."[9] Additionally, Ignatieff argues that this kind of vibrant and deliberative approach to political life requires no overarching humanist philosophy rooted in a celebratory embracement of human reason or virtue. Nor, he maintains, does this political vision need to be grounded in a spiritual respect for human life more generally. By Ignatieff's lights, the "minimum condition for deliberating with another human being" is not respect for their capacity to reason but "merely negative toleration, a willingness to remain in the same room, listening to claims one doesn't like to hear, for the purpose of finding compromises that will keep conflicting claims from ending in irreparable harm to either side."[10] In other words, endless justification and deliberation are morally good, for Ignatieff, and absolutely necessary for a liberal society to thrive, but such justification and deliberation require no more than the barest, limited, "negative toleration" of others to succeed.

But Ignatieff is not entirely consistent on this issue. While at times he suggests that his approach to liberalism, human rights, and democracy is grounded solely on this thin conception of "negative toleration," at other times he argues for what he terms a "humble humanism" rooted not in the spiritual or critical commonalities between people, but rather on a simple, common "capacity to imagine the pain of others."[11] It is this capacity to imagine the "pain and degradation done to other human beings as if it were our own" that transforms human beings into political agents in the first place insofar as it pushes us to relate, negotiate, and deliberate with people that we might otherwise consider unworthy of our toleration. At other times, Ignatieff takes this "humble humanism" still further by developing it into a political orientation, an empathetic approach to political life that he claims, again, is best illustrated by the political life of Berlin.

One of the things that Ignatieff most admired about Berlin and that he applauds most strenuously in his hagiographic biography of his mentor was Berlin's capacity to think beyond his own limited understanding of negative freedom and "to imagine lives other than his own."[12] What made Berlin such a rare human being, Ignatieff argued in response to an audience question in 1998, was his "tremendous acceptance of otherness, coupled with a capacity to enter into the minds of other people. He was a genius at the business of imagining what it would be to be another person, and that undercut malice, because if you went into another mind and saw the world from the way they saw it, then you wouldn't cut the ground from under their feet."[13]

It is precisely this capacity to "enter into the minds of other people" that Ignatieff, the historian and scholar, has at times striven to bring to his own analysis of politics—an approach most apparent in his early writing and in his work on ethnic nationalism throughout the 1990s. In contrast to most academic writing, Ignatieff's essay-oriented, historically roaming, narrative style often situates the author in relation to his subjects in a manner that clearly indicates the extent to which Ignatieff is himself invested in trying to understand their experiences. *The Needs of Strangers* (1984), for instance, begins with a thick description of the pensioners Ignatieff observers in his neighborhood in London and the ethical complexities that emerge out of the mediated quality of the relationships he can have with them given the structural necessities of the welfare state.[14] In a similar manner, Ignatieff begins his 1994 book *Blood and Belonging: Journeys into the New Nationalism*, by immediately placing himself within the discursive structure of the story he tells. "The itinerary I chose was personal, but, I hoped, not arbitrary," Ignatieff maintains. "I chose places I had lived in, cared about, and knew enough about to believe that they could illustrate certain central themes."[15] Key among those themes to emerge from Ignatieff's travels through Eastern Europe, Kurdistan, Northern Ireland, and Quebec, is his contention that ethnic nationalism is not something Westernized cosmopolitans can dismiss as mere madness. Thus, while Ignatieff ultimately concludes in both *Blood and Belonging* and his next book, *The Warrior's Honor: Ethnic War and the Modern Conscience* (1998), that ethnic nationalism poses the greatest humanitarian threat of the post-Cold War age, the narrative depictions in both books—particularly when read in the context of Ignatieff's own, expressed personal connections to these conflicts—invite the reader to empathize with the emotional and political lure of nationalism.

While Ignatieff has been rightly criticized for both constructing his narratives to illustrate certain foregone conclusions and adopting the voice of authorial innocence to mask his ideological position, the overall picture he paints of ethnic nationalism in these earlier works is both complicated and hopeful.[16] The reader comes away from both *Blood and Belonging* and *The Warrior's Honor* with the sense that not only is nationalism a historical phenomenon with varied, emotionally powerful, and sometimes dangerous manifestations, but that the world can handle it. The existence of humanitarian intervention, the presence of aid organizations, and the uprisings of everyday people against violence all suggest, according to Ignatieff, that nationalism in its most militarized form cannot ultimately dampen the human spirit or (more practically) irrevocably damage fledgling democracies in a manner that threatens to destabilize the global order. "The world is not becoming more chaotic or violent, although our failure to understand and act make it seem so," Ignatieff argues in *The Warrior's Honor.*[17] In other words, for Ignatieff, the rise of ethnically, historically, and politically complicated nationalisms in the wake of the Cold War's well understood patterns of international engagement may seem to imperil the world in heretofore unheard of ways, but that this does not need to be the case. International actors can, Ignatieff maintains, help states torn apart by ethnic nationalism and violence by first understanding nationalism as a complicated historical and emotional phenomenon that speaks to people's needs in diverse ways. "Reconciliation has not a chance against vengeance," he argues, "unless it respects the emotions that sustain vengeance."[18] Again, Ignatieff's decision to structure some of his narratives around his personal family history serves to model, for his readers, what such respectful engagement can look like.

The terrorist attacks on the World Trade Center in September of 2001, however, powerfully impacted Ignatieff's desire to try, in the style of Berlin, to imagine "what it would be to be another person." On a structural level, these post-September 11, 2001, writings on terrorism, imperialism, human rights, and torture resemble his earlier works. Thus, Ignatieff's ode to modern imperialism, *Empire Lite: Nation Building in Bosnia, Kosovo and Afghanistan* (2003) and his tortured grappling with torture, *The Lesser Evil: Political Ethics in an Age of Terror* (2004) are similarly written as collections of essays weaving together several different historical and geographically located narratives that ultimately serve to make Ignatieff's final point, while simultaneously gesturing toward the ethical complexities and contradictions of that point. The tone and assumptions of these writings, however, have shifted significantly away from those earlier empathetic accounts of the possibility of reconciliation. Ignatieff now starts from the premise that the international sphere *is* becoming more "chaotic" and "violent," and that what he had once characterized as a difficult but manageable post-Cold War world peppered by resurgent nationalism is now a "vacuum of chaos and massacre" where transnational terrorists threaten all that liberal society holds dear.[19]

In this environment, Ignatieff maintains, the only way to save liberal society from the chaotic, nihilistic rage of terrorists at loose in a world where insecure states allow transnational violence to fester is not to attempt to understand the motivations and experiences that might drive people to terrorism but rather, to encourage a broad form of liberal retrenchment rooted in a proud acceptance (by American citizens in particular) that the state must reluctantly step in and order the world for the good of all. At times, Ignatieff seems inclined to describe this approach to liberal empire or "empire lite" as something completely novel in American history or the history of the world. Thus,

> The 21st century imperium is a new invention in the annals of political science, an empire lite, a global hegemony whose grace notes are free markets, human rights and democracy, enforced by the most awesome military power the world has ever known. It is the imperialism of a people who remember that their country secured its independence by revolt against an empire, and who like to think of themselves as the friend of freedom everywhere. It is an empire without consciousness of itself as such, constantly shocked that its good intentions arouse resentment abroad.[20]

At other times, Ignatieff frames his desire to see Americans embrace a more self-conscious empire as simply a return to fundamental American values. Since Teddy Roosevelt, he argues, the American state has been attempting to "permanently order the world of states and markets according to its national interest," an interest also tied to the greater good of all.[21] Thus, the Bush Administration's commitment to lead other nations toward a "single sustainable model for national success" is consistent, he argues, with Woodrow Wilson's desire to make the world "safe for democracy." Likewise, Ignatieff asserts, arguments about imperialist intervention in the American press today mirror those from that earlier time.[22] But regardless of whether the argument is new or old, Ignatieff insists, Americans must finally settle in favor of empire and accept that ruling the world—in coalition with other liberal, Western powers—is simply part and parcel of the "burden" they must shoulder in order to save liberal society from the marauding hordes of non-liberal others who he no longer describes in terms that invite empathy but, rather, as "barbarians" who lurk "just beyond the zone of stable democratic states."[23]

However, Ignatieff's enthusiastic support for a self-conscious American imperialism after September 11, 2001 was not an entirely surprising development, given his evolving thoughts on state intervention throughout the 1990s. During this period, while researching *The Warrior's Honor*, Ignatieff traveled extensively through weakened and stateless societies wrecked by ethnic violence and came to the conclusion that, even though military interventions by liberal democracies in the affairs of sovereign but "lawless" states frequently exacerbated many of the problems that led them to become lawless in the first place, such interventions are ultimately worthwhile if, as in Bosnia, Kosovo, and East Timor, they end up saving lives. "For every failed intervention like Somalia," he argued in *The Warrior's Honor*, "there is an Angola, where some hope remains that a durable peace can be brokered."[24] The attacks of 2001 occurred precisely during the period when Ignatieff was most actively involved with the International Commission on Intervention and State Sovereignty, whose final report in December of that year (entitled "The Duty to Protect") concluded that "no one is prepared to defend the claim that states can do what they wish to their own people, and hide behind the principle of sovereignty in so doing."[25] The report continues by arguing that the "international community has a responsibility to act decisively" when states are unwilling or unable to fulfill the basic human rights of their people. In this context, Ignatieff's espousal of "empire lite" after 2001 was simply a more explicit extension of the kind of liberal interventionism he already supported.

But, again, what differentiates his thinking on intervention prior to September 11, 2001 from his thinking on empire in its aftermath is a willingness to empathize with the occupants of failed states. In a 1995 article for *Social Research*, for instance, Ignatieff reflected on humanitarian missions in Somalia, Bosnia, and Kosovo and argued that it was somewhat disingenuous for citizens of liberal Western states to tell themselves that the "interventions of the post-1989 period were humanitarian rather than imperial in their essential motivation."[26] For Ignatieff, such linguistic parsings were merely academic. Humanitarian interventions after 1989 were not without violence, nor were they free of the "ironic interplay between noble intentions and bloody results" that plagued the conscience of liberals like Joseph Conrad one hundred years earlier.[27] And yet, even as he makes the case for a form of humanitarian intervention that more explicitly understands itself as embodying the kinds of tensions produced by the imperialism of Conrad's time, the Ignatieff of 1995 was still clearly moved by a deep empathy for people caught in states that had devolved into paralyzing violence. Ignatieff challenges his readers to call into question their assumption that there is no relationship between the "zones of safety in which 'we' live" and the "zones of danger in which 'they' merely endure."[28] His analysis calls on Americans, Canadians, and Europeans to situate themselves within the context of a world in which their identities and their fates are linked with the occupants of the world's danger zones.

After September 11, 2001, however, Ignatieff's suspicion that it was important to challenge the very distinction between "we" and "they" all but disappears from his writing. One gets the sense from everything Ignatieff writes from his now infamous 2003 article "The Burden" forward that the goals of liberal democracy are now at permanent odds with those actors situated outside the order of liberal states: terrorists, intractable nationalists, warlords, and the hapless occupants of "stateless" societies themselves. Accepting that a self-aware American empire is the only way to bring about world stability also means that the American public must get over its squeamishness about the word "empire" itself and realize that it cannot afford to be orthodox with regard to violating human rights but rather, must accept limited, carefully circumscribed forms of torture and military occupation as necessary byproducts of saving liberalism itself. In 2004's *The Lesser Evil*, Ignatieff attempts to fashion the kind of liberal "political ethics"—a "lesser evil" approach—that could guide a "third way" between a liberal politics that rejects illiberal means altogether and a liberal politics that accepts some violation of its basic principles. He does this by carefully distinguishing between different categories of terrorism, forms of intervention, kinds of human rights, and military and political responses in order to provide his readers with "principles to guide public policy."[29] The hope is, when faced with the "factual uncertainty" that inevitably characterizes terrorist events, policy makers can draw upon these distinctions and learn to uphold state security in a manner that accepts some violations of human rights as inescapable, but strives to keep these violations to a minimum.[30] For the most part, however, there does not seem to be much of a relationship between Ignatieff's distinctions and the "guiding principles" he develops. For instance, despite his careful treatment of the relationship between democracy and torture and his discussion of the difference between torture and "lawful killing" during wartime, it is ultimately unclear why torture limited to "sleep deprivation, permanent light or permanent darkness, disorienting noise, and isolation" is acceptable for Ignatieff and violations of "bodily integrity" are not.[31] What is most startling here, however, is not the fact that Ignatieff is conceptually opaque when it comes to establishing his "guiding principles." Rather, the most chilling aspect of *The Lesser Evil* is the extent to which the book itself is *entirely focused* on the ethical ruminations of those "agents of the liberal democratic state" who should "be able to hold the line that divides intensive interrogation from torture or the line that separates targeted assassinations of enemy combatants from assassinations that entail the death of innocent civilians" with apparently no concern for the perspective of the tortured, the enemy combatants, or the innocent civilians. Rather than challenging the distinction between the "we" and the "they," *The Lesser Evil* radically dehumanizes the "they" in the process of convincing the "we" that "we" are doing the right thing.

Thus, while in his earlier works on nationalism Ignatieff may sometimes have spoken in the affectedly naïve tone of a Westernized "we," he was also willing to press this persona toward developing a real understanding of ethnic nationalism. But "The Burden," *Empire Lite*, and *The Lesser Evil* are all characterized by a notable lack of concern for understanding the emotional or political motivations of those who, by virtue of their actions, place themselves outside of the liberal order. These texts stress not the collective liberal subject's potential affinity with the other, but its absolute difference from those who would seek to destroy its way of life. Thus, in a chapter in *The Lesser Evil* devoted specifically to the dangers posed by terrorism to democratic states, Ignatieff insists that

> Societies under the endless trial of self-justification are apt to feel guilty about their success. But our success is not a fact to feel guilty about, and the failure of other societies is not our fault. It is an illusion, dear to liberal democrats everywhere, especially to Americans, to believe that we are responsible for all the evils of the world and that we are in a position to cure them, if only we possessed the will to do so.[32]

For Ignatieff, the "we" under attack (citizens of liberal states engaged in the "endless trial" of democratic review) are explicitly exempt from any historical responsibility with regards to the "failed states" of the world. Missing entirely from this analysis is the empathy so characteristic of his earlier work. Rather than a world peopled by liberal individuals, states, aid organizations, and humanitarians all struggling together to understand the international situation such that it does not become "more chaotic or violent," the global landscape of Ignatieff's post September 11, 2001 writings looks more like a battlefield, with liberal states and peoples hunkered down in their trenches bent on protecting their way of life from those whose societies are not under the endless trial of justification and for whom they are ultimately not responsible.

    To be fair, in contrast to Ferguson's dismissive assertions about the intransigence of the third world, Ignatieff's often impassioned portrayals of the struggles of Afghan bricklayers or Bosnian villagers suggests that he does feel genuine compassion for the suffering of the occupants of failed states—those past, current, and potential subjects of colonial rule. But like Ferguson's style in *Empire*, his overall argument, particularly in *Empire Lite*, is structured around a storytelling strategy that obscures the humanity and agency of these very same people. Ignatieff strives to put a human face on the contemporary military and humanitarian projects he considers imperial by situating his narratives in Kosovo, Bosnia, Afghanistan, and other embattled locales, and then drawing upon the personal stories and viewpoints of actors involved in each "nation building" endeavor. Thus, the examples in *Empire Lite*, he argues, are intended to "help both sides in the enterprise of nation building, to identify the illusions that make a genuine act of solidarity so difficult."[33] But the only "side" to emerge from these stories as legitimate and as composed of fully formed persons is that of Western nation-builders and diplomats. The primary subject of his discussion of Bosnia, for instance, is the French architect hired to reconstruct a bridge in Mostar, while the story of violence and corruption in Kosovo is told in the context of UN special representative Bernard Kouchner's struggle to fashion a peace between Kosovar Albanians and Serbs. By contrast, imperialized peoples and the hapless subjects of failed states are often described sympathetically but with a wide brush; we see glimpses of "scrofulous" children at school in Afghanistan, and villagers scuttling away from the scene of a bombing in Kosovo, but no one besides the occasional wily warlord appears as a fully formed individual. The overall effect is to repeatedly emphasize for the Western reader that the world is the legitimate purview of the "we," of those able to exercise full humanity: the well-meaning, liberal-minded, Western individuals exerting, in this case, humanitarian order onto a chaotic wash of sympathetic but unfocused masses.

Throughout these pro-imperial texts, Ignatieff often takes what appears to be a pragmatic approach to the interests of the liberal state, often adopting the tone of a detached realist or a hard-nosed observer of imperial politics who recognizes that American and European involvement in Kosovo, Bosnia, Iraq, and Afghanistan involves "just as much callow self-interest as high humanitarian resolve."[34] But, simultaneously, he never once challenges the intentions of the American state and its European allies (however self-interested they may be) precisely because these states are essentially and quintessentially liberal and their commitment to internal forms of legitimate democratic review is beyond question. One sees this uncritical acceptance of the imperial state's moral legitimacy in the extent to which Ignatieff's pro-imperial work dwells on "our" "constitutional identity," as a "free people," as a society "under the endless trial of self-justification."[35] Indeed, whereas Ferguson assumes that that the Anglophone state is liberal in its basic ethos, he does not naturalize this quality to the extent that Ignatieff does. For instance, Ignatieff insists in *The Lesser Evil* that "a liberal democratic society will, by its nature, impose some limitations on what intelligence and counter terror squads can do" and he goes on to argue that democracies "by their very nature, are less capable of vigilance than authoritarian regimes."[36] It is "the very nature of democracy" to limit government, Ignatieff concludes, and it is "also in the nature of democracy that it prevails against its enemies because it does so."[37] In this way, Ignatieff essentializes the liberal-democratic state around a basic set of automatic responses, natural characteristics, and unassailable good intentions that looks strikingly similar to Smuts's notion of the liberal state's "actuating principle": the natural, internal quality that make it both who it is and "of a piece with itself."

In a manner that is also somewhat similar to Ferguson's narrative, Ignatieff uses the pain suffered by the liberal state when it has to act illiberally as a way of reinforcing its liberal credentials. Despite his insistence that liberal societies have nothing to feel guilty about when it comes to their success, Ignatieff simultaneously insists that the collective experience of guilt serves as enduring proof positive of the liberal state's democratic credentials. "Only liberal democracies," he thus maintains, "have a guilty conscience about punishment."[38] Ignatieff's writings differ from Ferguson's, however, in their emphasis. While

Ferguson regards the "liberal critique" of colonial behavior "from within British society" as the "yardstick of liberty" by which history can judge the Empire's fundamental intentions, Ignatieff's collective self-flagellation goes much deeper. Whereas Ferguson demonstrates the Empire's pain through a narrative of history that gestures toward that pain and then moves on, Ignatieff asks his reader to dwell on this pain by keeping questions about the liberal state's imperial mission present in their minds at all times as a precondition of establishing "our" liberal-democratic existence and "our" commitment to democratic practice. In other words, Ignatieff insists that liberal-democratic societies are characterized by a constant process of self-examination and self-justification, both in an institutional and an ideological sense, a quality he literally reenacts through his writing. Thus, "The Burden," *Empire Lite,* and *The Lesser Evil* are studded throughout with contemporary and historical examples of imperialism at work that elicit a stream of difficult questions. What happens, Ignatieff wonders, when the people "we" are occupying do not want "us" there? How does "our" democratic state reconcile its commitment to "self-determination" with empire? What kinds of civil rights can "our" state curtail in the name of freedom? What happens when the goals of nation-building and democracy clash? The overall effect of this barrage of questions is to make it seem as though Ignatieff were, as he wrote the text, boldly seeking to trouble his own reluctant conclusions about imperial necessity by asking seemingly self-undermining questions that cast the whole endeavor in the glow of ethical anguish.

However, there is a deeply performative quality to the restless reiteration of these questions in Ignatieff's work. One is always aware, as one reads him, that Ignatieff has already reached his reluctant conclusions—conclusions apparent from the very titles of the works themselves. A "burden" implies something that must be shouldered. A "lesser evil" suggests that the other option is unacceptable. Thus, the overall effect of his tortured line of questioning is cathartic rather than critical. The liberal subject of the Western democratic state (Ignatieff's intended audience) can feel both as though they've done hard thinking on empire and torture and that, given this hard thinking, can then support the imperial actions of their state. At the same time, we know the state is well meaning in its imperial actions because of the fact that its citizens pose difficult questions. These questions are relentlessly all about "us" (how will imperialism hurt our democracy?) and "our" ethics (should we be involved in this endeavor?), and never about the relationship between "our" liberal state and the history of formal and informal imperialism more generally. After 2001, for Ignatieff, self-justification never goes so far as to question the "self" that is justifying.

The overall effect of this narrative style is that we understand the liberal character of Western states as beyond dispute, as evidenced by the pained, self-justifying practices of liberal-democratic debate in which citizens partake

when faced with difficult issues of national security and intervention. And, given
the fact that the liberal citizenry's "good intentions" are not disputable, terrorism itself can only be understood one-dimensionally as "evil" for Ignatieff, as
an incomprehensible, modern-day "nihilism" with no end. In Ignatieff's words,
"What we are up against is apocalyptic nihilism," and those "honest souls who
believe the terrorists' hatreds must be understood, and that what they hate must
be changed so that they will hate no more, do not understand terrorists."[39] Such
sentiment reflects, again, the fact that after September 11, 2001 the possibility
of empathy all but disappears from Ignatieff's writing, which is why he adopted
the Bush Administration's language of a War on Terror so quickly and with such
obvious enthusiasm, arguing in a lecture delivered in October of that year at
Canada's Royal Military College, that the "ethics of the war on terror involve a
landscape of military action that is completely unfamiliar."[40] As numerous critics have pointed out, what was truly "unfamiliar" in 2001 about using the word
"terror" in relation to military policy was its ineradicable nature, the extent to
which "terror" loomed as a permanent, existential threat in a way never properly
conveyed by the localized implications of "terrorism." A War on Terror is thus
conceivably a war without end.[41]

Ignatieff uses the indeterminateness of "terror" throughout his work, arguing
in his chapter on Kosovo in *Empire Lite*, "terror is terror and its intent is clear; to
force the UN and NATO troops to give up their struggle to keep a Serb minority in Kosovo."[42] In the face of this kind of threat, the only choice liberal societies can make, Ignatieff argues, is to continue to set aside their commitments to
civil liberties, human rights, and sovereign equality and "create order in border
zones essential to the security of the great powers."[43] This necessity will of course
engender all of the uncomfortable questions that a "self-justifying" democracy must confront with regard to its "identity as a free people" (e.g., how will
imperialism hurt our democracy?). But Ignatieff has already made it clear that
self-justifying pain is par for the course, implicit in the "nature" of who "we" are.
Once Americans come to terms with this pain and accept their imperial duty,
the liberal state can face outward into the terror and confront it with a clear conscience, reluctantly resigned to the uncomfortable fact that the "contradictions"
between "empire itself and democracy...are not happy but they are unchangeable."[44] Imperialism may be uncomfortable, Ignatieff argues, but this discomfort
reminds us of our democratic character.

Ignatieff's writings on empire thus perform precisely the kind of reluctant "self reflection" that he deems necessary for the liberal state to be liberal.
However, empire is still a foregone conclusion. Given that the "success" of the
liberal state has nothing to do with structural relations of power, given who
"we" are as a democratic people, and given the "unchangeable" contradictions
between democracy and imperialism, the potential imperializing force has

only two choices: accept the "lesser evil" of empire, or watch the world spiral into a violent chaos that threatens the future of liberal democracy itself. And for Ignatieff, while this choice may be a foregone conclusion, it is also, always already, fundamentally tragic.

Empire's Tragedy

In order to adequately grasp the way that tragic choice works in Ignatieff's writing, it is perhaps useful to begin with a discussion of what he is *not* doing when he frames international relations, imperialism, or politics more generally as a series of tragic choices. There is, of course, a long tradition in the history of political thought of casting the difficult choices that individual political leaders are forced to make as tragic. Berlin, for instance, identified Machiavelli's vision as tragic because Machiavelli understood political life as "a choice between entire worlds"—between a pagan political ethic motivated by courage, fortitude, power, and valor and a Christian political ethic grounded in mercy, charity, and contempt for worldly good.[45] By Machiavelli's lights, Berlin argued, the talented political leader must face the tension between the two with manly *virtù*, ultimately sacrificing one for the other. Weber made a similar argument with his sympathetic description of the politician as tragic hero in "Politics as a Vocation." A true political hero, a "mature man" facing an impossible choice between acting morally and doing what needs to be done for the good of the polity, argued Weber, must act with the "knowledge of tragedy," a tragedy assured by the fact that he is "aware of a responsibility for the consequences of his conduct and really feels such responsibility with heart and soul."[46]

Michael Walzer is similarly concerned with the way individual political leaders must sometimes choose between what is morally right and what is politically necessary (that is, between moral purity and "dirty hands"), and then live with the personal pain and responsibility of having to violate social ethics for the greater good. Walzer begins his 1973 article, "Political Action: The Problem of Dirty Hands," with an examination of Machiavelli and Weber, noting that while we are never entirely sure how Machiavelli's Prince feels about his tragic responsibility, we do know that for Weber it weighed heavily on the mind of the political hero. But Walzer does not agree with Weber that it is enough for the individual political leader to feel personally tormented by his choice. In other words, Weber's political agent is still accountable only to his own pained conscience, whereas Walzer would like to see him punished for his ethical breach, even though this breach might have been politically necessary for the good of the whole. Using the famous example of the "ticking time bomb," Walzer argues that a politician must still be punished for torturing a political prisoner even if torturing that prisoner was essential to obtaining the information necessary to stop a bomb threat.[47] Without such censure, Walzer argues, maintaining society's moral standards becomes impossible.

But while Walzer is somewhat concerned in this article with expanding moral culpability beyond the individual politician—arguing that not only must that political actor pay a price for his or her action but that we, as a political society, must "find some way of paying the price ourselves"—his analysis is still focused almost entirely on the actions of powerful individuals in morally treacherous political situations.[48] Ignatieff, by contrast, is largely concerned not with the discrete acts of individuals making tragic choices but, rather, with the notion of tragic choice *writ large* as a state of being that broadly defines the political. Despite the fact that his writings are filled with stories of individuals grappling with morally ambiguous situations in the context of state intervention and empire (e.g., Kouchner's experiences in Kosovo), Ignatieff usually understands tragic choices as the collective acts of a liberal "we" attached to a liberal state whose moral character is not only beyond reproach, but evident in the collective guilt felt by its people. Nowhere is this approach clearer than in Ignatieff's extended discussion of the War on Terror in *The Lesser Evil*. The lesser evil "approach to a war on terror" that he advocates in this text "acknowledges a tension 'of tragic dimensions,' as Oren Gross puts it, between what is necessary and what is right."[49] The most telling moment in Ignatieff's analysis, however, comes in the next sentence, where he simply refuses to *name* the political agents facing "tragic choices" in a troubled world:

> Saying the choices are tragic is not meant to excuse indecision—decisions will have to be made—but decisions in favor of necessity should be constrained by awareness of the seriousness of the loss in terms of justice.[50]

"Decisions will have to be made," Ignatieff argues in the passive voice, by someone, somewhere, under conditions we cannot know, and yet somehow such choices are to be made with an "awareness" of the loss such decisions engender. But the actors making the decision to imperialize—huddled in the Oval Office, holed up in policy think thanks, scattered throughout Iraq and Afghanistan, typing away in Harvard's hallowed halls—are tightly obscured by layers of security and secrecy, which are then themselves encased in the sheath of democratic accountability and good intentions that Ignatieff feels encase the liberal state.

There is a constant elision, then, in Ignateff's work, between the liberal "we" that is meant to experience the ethical angst of making tragic choices, and those who actually make the choices, between the "fundamental character" of the American, European, and Canadian peoples and the security apparatuses that acts in their name. This slippage is hardly surprising, given the longstand-ing reluctance of political theorists to think critically about sovereignty in an international context, particularly about the relationship between the *demos* and foreign policy, that area of state power in which the people have the least say.[51] Ignatieff's dependence upon the people–state trope, however, exposes a deep flaw in Walzer's argument. Walzer assumes that making the problem of "dirty hands" public and holding political actors to account will help press polities to reflect on their moral codes. By contrast, in Ignatieff's vision, the entity getting its hands dirty is always the collective liberal "we," even though "we" are never privy to the urgent, decision-making moments that constitute life in the world of the ticking time bomb. In Ignatieff's telling words, following the Church hearings of the 1970s that led to a ban on the covert use of assassinations by American intelligence organizations, "We may have betrayed a fatal preference for clean hands in a dark world of terror in which only dirty hands can get the job done."[52] Ignatieff makes no reference to the fact that the Church Hearings were a demo-cratic response to the secret, anti-democratic practices of the CIA. They were, in essence, the "we" speaking back to both the elected and non-elected state actors gathering intelligence and silently killing in "our" name. For Ignatieff, the people ordering drone strikes, targeted killings, invasion, and torture are all bundled into the "us" that has to make tragic choices regarding the use of violence or illiberalism. And after the event, there is no way to reflect because—unlike Walzer's vision where the leader who makes the call to torture is easily visi-ble—the "we" here is diffuse and collectively culpable. Ultimately, the collective wringing of "dirty hands" serves to remind "us" of our liberal identity in the face of tragic inevitability, thus allowing Ignatieff to diffuse tragic choice to the point where everyone, and no one, is responsible.

To a certain extent, Ignatieff's approach to tragic choice as a general condition of political life is, again, not entirely unlike that of his mentor Berlin. In other words, as Ignatieff notes often in his biography of Berlin, Berlin understood that "politics always had a potential for tragedy, because the forces it sought to master were never fully within its grasp."[53] In Berlin's words "If, as I believe, the ends of men are many, and not all of them are in principle compatible with each other, then the possibility of conflict—and of tragedy—can never wholly be elimi-nated from human life, either personal or social."[54] Thus, for Berlin, "tragedy" expressed the permanent presence of incommensurable political visions, and was simply the condition of political life in a world where individuals and states were constantly confronted with the need to make political decisions that would make some people or groups of people unhappy. This ultimately led him to sup-port an indeterminate form of value pluralism embedded in a political process that best enabled the "freedom to choose ends without claiming eternal validity for them." For Berlin, a society guided primarily by a commitment to "negative freedom" was better equipped to foster such an anti-foundationalist approach to political ends, whereas a society oriented toward "positive freedom" will incline toward authoritarianism. Because the liberal state committed to "negative" freedom can provide no totalizing reason for its existence—no claims to sovereign nationhood, people-ness, ideological purity, or self or group actualization—the only permanent fact of its political existence, for Berlin, is the "the necessity and agony of choice" it offers its citizens, choices which are often painful or morally disturbing.[55] However, as committed as he was to negative freedom, Berlin was hardly orthodox about this commitment; he understood that, in the context of making difficult social, political, and economic decisions, negative liberty might not always—and ought not always—to prevail. "Negative liberty must be curtailed if positive liberty is to be sufficiently realized," Berlin argued in 1991, "there must be a balance between the two, about which no clear principles can be enunciated."[56] In other words, when Berlin contemplated the tragedy associated with making difficult choices in a pluralist society, he did not presume the outcome.

However, at the same time, Berlin's approach to international conflict was far more orthodox than his domestic pluralism would suggest, largely because he imagined the world in light of his own experiences with anti-Semitism in Bolshevik Russia and in the bi-polar terms of the Cold War. Berlin understood the conflict between authoritarian states and free societies as a permanent state of affairs, a conflict that mapped perfectly onto his conceptual divide between positive and negative liberty. And it is *this* approach, Ignatieff has argued since September 11, 2001, that it is well worth our while to recapture. Thus, in a 2012 address at an Isaiah Berlin Lecture delivered in Riga, Latvia, Ignatieff took issue with the view, which he identified as prevalent among liberal internationalists today, that seeks to integrate decidedly illiberal states like China and Russian into the new international order. By contrast, in Ignatieff's opinion,

> The generation that came to maturity in 1945—Berlin's generation—thought differently. They thought that the question of how liberal societies should relate to non-liberal powers could not be left to fate and the global division of labour, but was a political, strategic, and moral issue to be decided by democratic peoples... Isaiah Berlin did not live to see these new tyrannies arise in Russia and China and he would have trouble recognizing the world we now inhabit—post 9/11, post-meltdown, post liberal in so many ways—but he did know a lot about living beside barbarians. His Cold War liberalism has much to teach us still.[57]

Ignatieff thus takes Berlin's Cold War understanding of a world permanently structured by the incommensurability between liberal democracies and their

Communist foes and transposes this theory into a post-Cold War key. For Ignatieff, the danger posed by barbarians—those permanent, illiberal threats to liberal order—issue not solely from established states like China and Russia but from everywhere outside the liberal state's purview: in failed states, in sympathetic states, and in the nooks and crannies of an illiberal world, just "beyond the zone" of stability.

And yet, aside from this basic move to recover the certainties of the Cold War for the post-September 11, 2001 world, what makes Ignatieff's evocation of Berlin here most troubling is the extent to which his own attitude toward international politics after the terrorist attacks of that day departs so radically from precisely the attributes that he claims most characterized the sensibilities Berlin brought to international politics: "humility about history, firmness to stand against wrong, and the openness to engage and learn from those we oppose."[58] There is very little humility in Ignatieff's writings on terrorism and the necessities of empire, and no sense that there is anything to be learned from the opposition. Rather, Ignatieff consistently takes Berlin's emphasis on choosing between incommensurable ends and makes *the act of choosing itself*, and not the political conflict that necessitates choosing between ends, the tragedy. In this scenario, there is no moment when it might behoove the liberal state or subject to stop and try to learn from the opposition, because the opposition is only incidental to the larger drama being played out in the War on Terror, a drama focused on the pain of arriving at foregone conclusions about occupation or torture through the vehicle of tragic choice. Ignatieff transforms Berlin's tragic choice by, again, rendering the liberal subject (which Berlin somewhat consistently recognized as both "personal and social") into a constant "we."[59] "We" citizens of liberal democracy must choose between "our" idealistic attachment to liberal human rights and the need to sacrifice human rights to save ourselves. The choice is always "tragic" not because it requires that "we" recognize the permanently unstable nature of politics, but rather, because of the permanent sense of loss it poses to "our" liberal identity. As Ignatieff notes in a 2005 speech,

> Reconciling ultimate ends and responsibility, as Isaiah Berlin emphasized, can be a difficult, sometimes tragic affair. We have to choose, with insufficient evidence, time and insight, just as we are, here and now, and whatever we do, we are bound to lose something. But we must choose.[60]

The entity doing the choosing, for Ignatieff, is the "we" of the liberal society or state facing out into the world. Tragedy lies in this choosing, choosing is inevitable, and choosing involves, for Ignatieff, a letting go of liberal scruples while, at the same time, feeling that loss as an affirmation of "our" liberal identity.

For the post-September 11, 2001 Ignatieff, time is caught in a perpetual loop that replays the urgency of the "dirty hands" scenario over and over again. Living in terrorist time means means liberal societies are forced to make painful choices, again and again, here and now, just as we are, even though the choice to *not* act is never a choice at all. As Ignatieff puts it in *The Lesser Evil*, "In the situation of factual uncertainty, in which most decisions about terrorism have to be taken, error is probably unavoidable." What is notable here is not so much Ignatieff's admission that error is unavoidable, but that decisions "have to be taken" because, as he goes on to insist, "Either we fight evil with evil or we succumb."[61] Ignatieff thus deftly transforms tragic choice into a kind of guilty pleasure, a nasty walk on the wrong side of town that makes "us" feel both sullied and more pure as a collective entity. "As the threat of terrorism targets our political identity," Ignatieff argues, "our essential resource has to be that identity itself."[62] Ignatieff goes on to insist that because the core of that identity is liberal and democratic, we must resist responses to terrorism that eschew open government and public review. But, at the same time, Ignatieff is resolutely unwilling to acknowledge the double bind his own insistence on the pace of terrorist time has enabled. In other words, making tragic choices about whether to torture or invade must happen quickly in Ignatieff's universe, and these decisions must be made in the passive voice by some one or ones, with limited information, who are also "us." Ignatieff goes on to argue that a liberal democracy may not be able to "maintain its own identity in freedom if it rules others without their consent" but, he cautions, actually taking the time to reflect on whether or not invading, occupying, and torturing contradicts our "identity in freedom" is not possible "when a gun is held to your head."[63] In the end, the act of choosing, and the act of accepting the tragic necessity of violating "our" liberal norms, only serves as proof positive of who "we" are because only "liberal democracies have a guilty conscience about punishment." And, Ignatieff argues, "Only in liberal societies have people believed that the pain and suffering involved in depriving people of their liberty must make us think twice about imposing this constraint even on those who justly deserve it. The fact that it is necessary and the fact that it is just do not make it any less painful."[64] For Ignatieff, the "pain and suffering" that liberal societies inflict on others is ultimately only relevant insofar as it causes "us" to feel pain and suffering and, in the process, reminds "us" of who "we" are.

It is in moments like these that Ignatieff's use of Berlin feels particularly crass. Again, while Berlin might have been truly committed to the benefits of negative liberty, he actually believed that the act of making a choice between negative and positive liberty was not a foregone conclusion and that any society worth its salt ought to consider the benefits and problems of valuing one over the other. Weighing these options was an act of genuine social- and self-reflection for Berlin that was tragic insofar as the ends could be incommensurable. But this process

itself was, for Berlin, truly open ended, and politics itself was thus always conditioned by the need to forge an "uneasy equilibrium, which is constantly threatened and in constant need of repair."[65] Negotiation, dialogue, self-reflection, and
political readjustment were all necessary parts of the ongoing process of politics
for Berlin, a process for which there could be no ebb. By contrast, Ignatieff takes
Berlin's understanding of the agonized process of decision-making and makes it
finite by reducing it to momentary disquiet bound to loss, an unease that "we"
must soldier through in order to "choose" empire and torture and know ourselves to be liberal. Even more disturbing, Ignatieff goes so far as to turn liberal
identity into a form of nationalism, and Berlin into a nationalist. "Liberalism,
Berlin taught us," Ignatieff argued in the summer of 2009 before a crowd gathered for the "Isaiah Berlin Lecture" in London, "is not a bloodless breviary for
rootless cosmopolitans. It is a fighting creed for men and women devoted to the
fate of their particular national communities. So it is with me."[66] Berlin understood nationalism as an "inflamed condition of national consciousness which
can be, and has on occasion been, tolerant and peaceful" and he took it seriously
as a world phenomenon that spoke to the desires of newly liberated people for
dignity and equality.[67] At the same time, he was also genuinely worried about
what happens when nations, inflamed by national consciousness, develop "fighting creeds" that are violent and exclusive, when national groups take revenge for
their insulted humanity. The ease with which Ignatieff seems to assume that the
"fighting creed" of liberalism is immune from the siren's song of revenge would
no doubt have confounded Berlin.

To summarize, Ignatieff takes the tragic sensibility that he inherited from
Berlin, collectivizes the subject that must make the tragic choice, and then transforms the moment of choosing into proof of the liberal state's liberal identity.
Beyond the fact that this ends up reinforcing what I consider a very un-Berlinian
commitment to liberalism as a nationalist "fighting creed," Ignatieff's approach
to tragedy and liberal identity also forecloses alternative readings of the relationship between the liberal state (with all of the democratic and self-justifying
practices that Ignatieff values) and the history and contemporary practice of
imperialism.

In order to understand how Ignatieff's work does this, I find it useful to turn
to Romand Coles's analysis of the relationship between tragedy and liberalism more generally in his 2005 book, *Beyond Gated Politics: Reflections for the
Possibility of Democracy*. In this book, Coles examines what he identifies as the
widely held belief that "political liberalism...is oriented by a very deep sense
of tragedy."[68] Coles interrogates this assertion through a close analysis of the
work of John Rawls who, he argues, frames the dialogic space in which liberalism operates by constant reference to the tragic conflict of the European "wars
of religion." For Rawls, political liberalism "starts by taking to heart the absolute

depth of that irreconcilable latent conflict." This depth—that is, its violent and tragic conclusions—thus becomes the reiterated basis of our "self understand-ing" and, according to Coles, the primary logic by which liberals of Rawls's persuasion exclude religion and other forms of "unreasonable" argument from legitimate public discourse. Excluding discussion of "comprehensive doctrines" from the public and political domain may be regrettable, and may constrain the diversity of voices able to engage in democratic practices, but the alternative is a slippery slope into violence and repression. The choice appears tragic because not only must the liberal polity sacrifice engagement with "comprehensive doc-trines" in the name of preventing violence, but this very sacrifice itself requires that "we repeatedly remember" the "mortal and never too distant conflict" that such engagement can produce.

For Coles, tragedy in this Rawlsian context is circumscribed by finitude rather than possibility, critique, and reflection, a characterization that also appropriately describes the kind of "tragic choice" that Ignatieff consistently posits as central to his vision of liberal empire. For Ignatieff, the necessary deci-sions liberal states must make with regard to imperial intervention or torture are quintessentially tragic because they imply collective psychic loss experienced as a challenge to liberal character. Just as Coles characterizes Rawls's re-evocation of the tragic "wars of religion" as a means to exclude particular modes of life from participation in political dialogue, so too does the relentless specter of terror-ism, illiberalism, and barbarism in Ignatieff's analysis force the liberal state (and the liberal "we" that always accompanies it) to make the tragic choice (which is always preordained) to sacrifice its basic generosity and foundational principles regarding civil liberties, human rights, and the self-determination of peoples. In the process, such a choice neatly shuttles alternatives to torture or invasion out of the picture, leaving the stage clear for the next performance of the ticking time bomb scenario and the next agonized choice.

The rapidity of this staging, the extent to which terrorist time piles up one tragic choice after another, forecloses the possibility that there can be any time for reflection on the recent or remote history of the liberal imperial state and the way its actions might have contributed to the political circumstances which now make tragic choice a necessity. Similarly, acting quickly and tragically in a way that affirms the liberal state's character makes it difficult, if not impos-sible, to consider the way this character itself (with its putative commitment to freedom and its endless trial of self-justification) was in some way also shaped by its imperialist practices. Historically speaking, as Tully argues, the modern form of liberal citizenship and understandings of democratic governance in Europe that Ignatieff values, emerged within the context of eighteenth- and nineteenth-century states that were both liberal and imperializing. In this "co-creation" of the West and the non-West we see the discursive and practical fixing over time of global economic practices, governmentalities, and political assumptions about citizenship structured around the relationship between modern and premodern, developed and developing, first and third world, that continues well into the "postcolonial" era through the exercise of American and European economic and military hegemony.[69] Ignatieff's approach to tragic choice also occludes the way these everyday distinctions work to reinforce growing inequality between the Global North and Global South at the level of contemporary practice.[70] In his investigation of global inequality, for instance, Thomas Pogge demonstrates how the desire of Western, liberal, democratic states for cheap natural resources, coupled with an international monetary system that rewards authoritarian and corrupt governments who can deliver these resources, contribute to state failure. There is a *relationship*, Pogge continues, between first-world wants and third-world suffering, between what he terms the "international resource privilege" and the "international borrowing privilege" that encourages the proliferation of illiberal, undemocratic, corrupt regimes in resource-rich but "undeveloped" states.[71]

It is precisely these relationships—between the imperial history of the liberal state and contemporary forms of liberal citizenship, and between thriving liberal economies and global inequality—that Ignatieff's restless reiteration of the tragic choice between liberalism and illiberalism, order and nihilism, good and evil, ignores. To a certain extent, these distinctions were always already baked into Ignatieff's liberalism and were apparent even before he transformed into the tragic imperialist he has become since September 11, 2001. As Bernard Yack observed in his 1996 article "The Myth of Civic Nationalism," the dichotomy between ethnic and civic nationalism that Ignatieff develops in *Blood and Belonging*

> parallels a series of other contrasts that should set off alarm bells: not only Western/Eastern, rational/emotive, voluntary/inherited, good/bad, *ours/theirs*! Designed to protect us from the dangers of ethnocentric politics, the civic/ethnic distinction itself reflects a considerable dose of ethnocentrism, as if the political identities *French* and *American* were not also culturally inherited artifacts, no matter how much they develop and change as they pass from generation to generation.[72]

This ethnocentrism is front and center in all of Ignatieff's work on intervention, empire, and human rights, and, in and of itself, is one of the most obvious and least interesting aspects of his approach. Like liberal imperialists before him, and in the grand tradition of Enlightenment narratives of universal progress, Ignatieff denies the cultural specificity of his universal claims even as he locates their origins in Europe, while simultaneously mocking those phantom critics who see human rights language as "just another cunning exercise in Western moral impe-rialism."[73] The more subtle and insidious underside to Ignatieff's ethnocentrism is, as Yack suggests, the extent to which his dichotomizing naturalizes certain forms of political communities around fixed political identities, and thus shel-ters them from critical inquiry and real self-reflection. In other words, imagining the liberal nation state as timeless and unchanging means that its own origins, its illiberal history, and the complicated genealogy of its current form, are immune from precisely the "process of recurrent, repeated, behavior-changing justifica-tion" that, Ignatieff argues, makes the liberal state liberal in the first place.

When Ignatieff does refer to the history of European or American imperi-alizing, it is usually to make broad, ahistorical claims about intervention as a legitimate political project for the modern world, or to prove a point about the intransigence of terrorists, Islamists, or the illiberal denizens of failed or postco-lonial states. "The history of the British Empire," he thus argues in *Empire Lite*, "is that self-determination and imperial rule are not incompatible." The fault for not being able to make this work in Palestine or India, he argues, lies not with Britain but with the frustrating intransigence of the people who live in those spaces. The British gave themselves "two generations" to school these regions in the ways of imperial self-determination before "throwing up their hands in despair."[74] We get no mention from Ignatieff of Britain's role in systematically under-developing India's economy over two centuries, or its explicit land grab in the Middle East during the Mandate period, much less its role in establishing some of the most troubled regimes in that region.[75] All Ignatieff gives us is a sense of Britain's ulti-mately frustrated commitment to self-government. Likewise, Ignatieff admits that the American state might have aligned itself with some unsavory characters in the Middle East in the past, regimes that have "failed their people," but he is silent with regard to the role of the US in overthrowing democracies, arming friendly dictators, and in general, creating the very "disorder" that now keeps him up at night.[76] The most egregious example of this selective amnesia can be found in *Empire Lite*, the second half of which is devoted to a discussion of NATO troops in Afghanistan. In his exhaustive rumination on the dangers posed by the Taliban to liberal society, Ignatieff fails to mention the origins of the Taliban in the Mujahidin of the 1980s, a group funded and armed by the United States.[77] By Ignatieff's circular logic, the American state's obvious good intentions mean that, while in the past it might have been a bit naïve in its choices of friends, its lib-eral ends insulate it from any responsibility for creating these regimes in the first place, while the pressing need to act and act *now* suggests that it simply does not have the time to dwell on its own past. Simultaneously, making the decision to act illiberally in the face of tragic necessity reaffirms, for Ignatieff, the state's lib-eral identity because only liberal societies "have a guilty conscience about pun-ishment." Hence, even more radically than Ferguson's work, Ignatieff's account of liberal character frees Americans from the weight of historical responsibility—indeed from causation itself—because the urgent burden of dirty hands always outweighs the luxury of reflection. Cause and effect are meaningless in a universe where the decision to act is always already pre-determined by who we are.

Thus, the smooth, ostensibly self-critical, liberal state and its "we" roll through Ignatieff's writing on empire, human rights, and terrorism, like an airtight ball whose internal character insulates it from deeper arguments about its structural relationship to the world in the past, present, and future. Unlike Ferguson, who develops the story of the Anglophone empire from Britain to America in a seamless, linear swoop, Ignatieff lobs the liberal state into recent imperial history with a kind of elliptical abandon, moving back and forth between contemporary narratives, ethical musings on liberal theory, and historical examples. For Ignatieff, the "movements of national liberation that swept through the African and Asian worlds" have "now run their course and in many cases have failed to deliver on their promise to rule more fairly than the colonial oppressors of the past."[78] Ignatieff thus renders the "success" of liberal democracies completely dependent upon their internal qualities, uncoupling that success from the "failure" of postcolonial states. In the spirit of Smuts, whose racial politics he would vocally reject, this approach to liberal imperial identity fixes the liberal character of the imperializing state around an anti-imperial core and frees it from historical reflection altogether, thus rendering it "internal and of a piece with itself."

There is a deep, almost reactionary, nostalgia at work in Ignatieff's desire to freeze the liberal imperial state around a set of eternal liberal practices and expectations that he believes cannot and will not change—a nostalgia which at times resembles an almost blind utopianism in reverse. Ironically, the earlier Ignatieff was intimately familiar with the perils of utopia. Thus, in his thoughtful critique of political community in *The Needs of Strangers*, Ignatieff insisted that most utopias are "a form of nostalgia for an imagined past projected on to the future as a wish...No matter that Greek democracy was built upon the institution of slavery; no matter that the Italian city-states were feuding and unequal oligarchies. Utopias never have to make their excuses to history; like all dreams they have a timeless immunity to disappointment in real life."[79] And yet, there is perhaps no better description of Ignatieff's liberal imperial state than this. Liberal states, under the "endless trial of justification," have nothing to apologize for; they occupy an imagined past projected onto the now and the future as a wish, and they have a similar "timeless immunity" from the illiberalism of the state in history, its forays into slavery and violence, conquest and occupation, torture and evil of the lesser and greater kind.

Additionally, the utopian and nostalgic past also serves a purpose for Ignatieff in the present, insofar as any deviation from its supposed norm becomes an opportunity to experience loss. Thus, Ignatieff often frames the liberal state's choice to act imperially as deeply troubling to its identity, as a wrenching sort of amputation while, at the same time, insisting that the very act of confronting that tragic choice in the name of what is right—of manfully facing up to the fact that "decisions will have to be made" and doing so in the forthright and honest manner of the Victorians alluded to in the very title of "The Burden"—reconfirms the imperial state's liberal character. In the end, it is the sureness of this liberal character that reduces the state's options to empire or death. In Ignatieff's words—which are also, like Ferguson's, eerily similar to Thatcher's—"Nobody likes empires but there are some problems for which there are only imperial solutions."[80] Hence, in the end, by repeatedly gesturing toward the tragic choice of empire, Ignatieff transforms the story of the relationship between political and economic liberalism and European and American imperialism into a timeless clash between these principles and the specter of international chaos, a rhetorical move which effectively erases the deeply complicated and mutually reinforcing history of these endeavors. The story of imperial violence perpetrated by liberals in the name of the liberal state and the global economy is reduced to the same tragic scenario over and over again. And, as with both Smuts and the Round Table, empire becomes the answer to its own question, in Ignatieff's words, the "attempted solution to the crisis of state order that followed two botched decolonizations: the Soviet exit from Europe, and the European exit from Africa and Asia."[81]

And yet, Ignatieff's tragedy not only forecloses historical critique and contemporary reflection, it also shuts out the potentially transformative power of using tragedy itself as a vehicle for facilitating this kind of critique and reflection. Again, by collectivizing tragic choices that are usually made (in an international context in particular) by singular powerful actors, Ignatieff transforms the liberal imperializing state into a single entity confronting incommensurable ends and making painful choices that reconfirm its (and "our") liberal identity. At the same time, Ignatieff uses the confrontation with illiberalism, and the impossibility of this choice, as an opportunity to stage precisely the qualities he believes are so essential to liberal society—in particular, its endless "trial of self justification." Thus, in the early 2000s, Ignatieff argued that, in order to make morally legitimate decisions to invade other sovereign states (e.g., Iraq) and torture terrorists, liberal states must explain and justify these actions "to accountable public bodies, especially the judiciary and elected legislature."[82] But, by setting up the decisions to invade and torture as necessary and already tragic, Ignatieff makes it impossible for the collection of democratic people wrapped inside the liberal whole to actively engage and debate the decisions that must be made "with insufficient evidence, time and insight," transforming the act into a confirmation of "just as we are, here and now." The key to Ignatieff's framing of the moment of choice here is not merely the limited temporal window his emergency necessitates but, again, the fact that the moment of choice is always oriented toward who "we" are, in this moment. This is the performative quality of Ignatieff's liberalism, the way it mimics deliberation without actually deliberating, justifies without justifying, while all the while making its audience feel good about being a liberal, democratic, deliberative people. Ignatieff wants the collective liberal "we" of his audience to embrace the pain of acting against their natures, and then move on to silently sanction more difficult tragic choices made in the passive voice in their name.

But as Peter Euben has deftly illustrated, tragedy as a form of political expression has not always been so preordained. In *The Tragedy of Political Theory: The Road Not Taken* (1990), Euben argues that, in the context of ancient Athens, tragedy (as a literary and performative medium) also served an educative purpose, by setting the context that enabled the *demos* to reflect on the strength or weakness of their society's democratic norms. Dramatists, Euben notes, were political educators, and tragedies were performed in public, during festivals, when the whole of the *demos* would be gathered together. In this public context, actors portrayed scenarios in which characters like Antigone and Creon would take up antithetical positions, forcing the audience to confront the limitations and possibilities of both of these positions, and their own conceptions of justice. As Antigone rages against the law of the state and Creon ignores the law of the gods, the Athenians, as an audience, were invited to reflect upon both as well as to reflect upon the essential democratic quality of *hearing* each other and the dangers of intransigence. For Euben, the most essential transformative quality of the "tragic sensibility" nurtured by these plays is the way it encourages and invites the democratic "we" to approach seemingly incommensurable situations as opportunities to reflect on what kind of democracy "we" want for ourselves and, in the process, expand our political imaginations. In this sense, he argues, the "success" of Aeschylus's trilogy *The Oresteia* lies not in the number of propositions about justice that it "proves" but, rather, "in the number of illuminations it provokes, in the horizons it widens, and in its effectiveness in making us think harder and act differently."[83]

Richard Ned Lebow takes this idea still further, suggesting that international politics are tragic in the Greek sense and that, historically, classical realists like Thucydides and Morgenthau have embraced this sensibility in more revealing and interesting ways than contemporary realists. Approaching international politics as tragedy, for Lebow, means analyzing what look like absolute polarities between states and peoples not in terms that limit such conflicts to opportunities to strategize about the next inevitable clash but, rather, to approach the incommensurables in international life as an invitation to reflect on the complexities of global politics. "Any ontology worthy of attention," argues Lebow, "must start from the premise that these polarities define the extremes of the human condition." Lebow continues by insisting that such a tragic sensibility must seek to "represent, not suppress, the diversity and instability of human identities, interests and motives, and their complex interactions with the discourses, social practices and institutions they generate and sustain."[84] Thucydides, Lebow argues, was a practitioner of this kind of tragic approach to international relations because his description of Athens in *The History of the Peloponnesian War* illuminated the complex "interests and motives" behind the form of overweening pride that compelled it to reject the "constraints, obligations, and other norms traditionally associated with inter-polis relations" in the name of imperial ambition and at the cost of its own democracy.[85]

In essence, Euben's and Lebow's conceptions of tragedy require citizens, scholars, and states to approach seemingly tragic situations as opportunities for reflection on both the political ethics that they hold dear and on the imbricated discourses, social and political practices, and institutions that constitute political life. I would also argue, with Elizabeth Markovits, that tragedies call upon their democratic audiences to think critically about justice in an historical or intergenerational context. Thus, for Markovits, the central characters of *The Oresteia* are not only forced to struggle with justice claims, but also with claims that had their origins in the ethical choices and conflicts of an earlier generation.[86] In Aeschylus's play, Athena and the Athenian community must ultimately judge between these competing claims by creating new institutions and community norms "necessary to deal with Orestes' family history."[87] In staging the play, Markovits argues, Aeschylus provided a civic lesson for his Athenian audience, one that demonstrates the difficulties and sacrifices inherent in establishing a new political vision that can link "the claims of intergenerational justice with those of democracy." A tragic sensibility that takes the past as well as the current moment into consideration would similarly look upon those instances when seemingly intractable worldviews clash as occasions to reflect on the complicated historical circumstances that shaped these conflicting claims in the first place. Tragic choice, from this perspective, invites democratic citizens, scholars, and states to reflect on the past and the present in a way that seems not only perfectly compatible with, but necessary to, Ignatieff's own insistence on debate, trial, and justification.

It is precisely this approach to tragedy that Ignatieff's insistent fixation with immediacy, dirty hands, and collective guilt renders impossible. For Ignatieff, the tragic choice to torture and invade is inevitable: it has already *been made* by someone (us? The state?), brought on by the urgencies of circumstances over which we have no control. In the context of a War on Terror, Ignatieff argues, "further unilateral action is inevitable, given the extent to which the United States remains the first-order target for Al Qaeda and other Islamist groups."[88] Aside from the fact that such an analysis completely sidetracks the extent to which the War on Terror had already become, by 2003, a key ideological tool in America's pursuit of global domination, Ignatieff's fascination with inevitability asphyxiates the possibility that there could be any time—any breathing space—for a democratic people to pause and reflect on the actions of their state in the world and on their complicity in these actions, now and in the past. In the end, Ignatieff's approach to tragedy simply demands that democratic peoples give their imprimatur to empire without critique. At the same time, it encourages them to understand their imperial power as painful but tragic proof of their liberal character as a people. In the process, the past becomes mere prelude, and the future a rote response to the tyranny of events beyond "our" control.

Conclusion: Ignatieff's Liberal Hubris

In a basic sense, Ignatieff's post-September 11, 2001 writings on human rights, empire, and terrorism express a desideratum similar to all of the liberal imperialists discussed in this book: each of these thinkers wants to have it all and pay no political price, to have his imperial cake and eat it too, to theorize a state that is liberal and imperial, free and ordered, well intentioned and powerful, universal and exclusive, subject to the democratic will of the "we" and yet supple enough to respond to the machinations of terrorists with the urgency of a ticking time bomb. And yet anyone familiar with the literary and political tradition of tragedy can discern why approaching the world as a series of tragic choices might not be the best mechanism for juggling and reconciling all of these divergent wants. Tragedians, throughout history, have almost always resisted the path that would allow their heroes an easy reintegration into normal life. Tragic heroes do not learn moral lessons until the damage has been done and, when they come to the realization of what has happened, the pain of the experience destroys them. Thus, when Creon stands over the bodies of Antigone and Haemon, wracked by the knowledge that his actions brought him to this ruin and that it is too late for redemption, he can only weep as the chorus admonishes, "I think you have learned justice—but too late."[89] For Weber and Walzer, the true political hero who makes the decision to torture can never go home again; either he is scarred ethically or the very community he set out to save sanctions him.

Ignatieff's use of tragedy is simply, in the end, too easy to be tragic. For all that he wallows in the pain and guilt that liberal citizens must experience to ultimately grasp the horrible reality of torturing or conquering in order to save the world and themselves from illiberalism, these subjects still get to go home at the end of the day, feeling as though they have truly confronted the ethical complexities of their choices, comfortable in the knowledge of who they/we are, ready to wake up and fight the good fight again. One is reminded here of the scene in "Never on Sunday" where Illia (Melina Mercouri) retells Sophocles' tragedies so that, in the end, "they all go to the seashore."[90]

But it is no coincidence, as Euben and Lebow would no doubt remind us, that the great tragedies of Athens were written in the fifth century B. C. E., at the height of Athenian imperialism, immediately preceding or during the Peloponnesian War. As Thucydides's account of Pericles's Funeral Speech suggests, this was a city that considered itself an "education to Greece," unique from all other people in its ability to deftly balance freedom, democracy, and imperial tutelage. Pericles extolled the miracle of Athens, a city whose greatness sprang entirely from "our constitution and the way of life which has made us great," whose success as a regional power had nothing to do with its status as an imperial power, who never imitated anyone else but, rather, served always as a "model to others."[91] "In this land of our," Pericles insists, "there have always been the same people living from generation to generation up till now, and they by their courage and their virtues, have handed it on as a free country," a country that now wisely ruled much of the known world.[92] The Athenians, in other words, were always, for Pericles, just as they were, here and now. Thucydides, of course, immediately follows the bellicosity of the Funeral Speech with a grossly descriptive account of the radically democratic plague that then befell Athens and "carried away all alike."[93] It is, thus, hardly surprising that tragedies of the period would call on their audiences to cast a wary eye on the kinds of overconfident and insular hubris that leads to historical forgetting and, instead, ask their audiences to wrestle with the debt that "we" owe to others in the past, present, and future.

Ultimately, what makes Ignatieff's hubris particularly doleful is the uncomfortable sense one gets from reading his work that he is vaguely aware of the fact that, by arguing for an explicit increase in American and liberal imperial power, his work falls within the symbolic ambit of a potential historical trap that troubles him deeply; the circular movement of imperial rise and fall. Ignatieff acknowledges somewhat nervously that his theory of "empire lite" could potentially come to resemble the "characteristic delusion of imperial power, " common to the Romans and "repeated by the British imperialists in their turn," a delusion that confuses "global power with global hegemony."[94] But Ignatieff's own delusion lies in his insistence that is possible for liberal states, under the "endless trial of self justification," to stop the tragic repetition of history not by calling the imperial endeavor itself into question, but by halting the cycle through sheer force of liberal will. In essence, Ignatieff wants to claim the insight and the sense of dire urgency that comes with being the subject of a tragic drama, but he is unwilling to admit, despite his own discomfort, that this insight always comes too late. Like Oedipus lying in bed with Jocasta, Ignatieff seems unable to perceive the tragedy that awaits the liberal imperial state he has so insistently bound to a pristine, unchanging character. Thus, he is also unable to admit that "just who we are, here and now" is far more complicated and ethically troubling than it appears.

Conclusion

Is This Who We Want To Be?

On May 23, 2013, President Barack Obama stood before the assembled audience at the National Defense University at Fort McNair and delivered a speech meant to explain the bureaucratic and ethical guidelines of a post-September 11, 2001, defense policy—a policy not conditioned by the threat of a constant, unbounded War on Terror. "America is at a crossroads," the President argued, "we must define the nature and scope of this struggle or else it will define us." From very early on in the speech, however, it became clear that the "us" in danger of being redefined was not open to contestation. Thus, just moments into the speech, before beginning his discussion of the Administration's policies, Obama launched into an extended ode to "who we are":

> For over two centuries, the United States has been bound together by founding documents that defined who we are as Americans, and served as our compass through every type of change. Matters of war and peace are no different. Americans are deeply ambivalent about war, but having fought for our independence, we know a price must be paid for freedom. From the Civil War to our struggle against fascism, on through the long twilight struggle of the Cold War, battlefields have changed and technology has evolved. But our commitment to constitutional principles has weathered every war, and every war has come to an end.[1]

Since its founding, the narrative goes, through wars and domestic conflict and technological change, America's commitment to the liberal principles of its Constitution has remained constant. Obama thus begins his comments with the same deflective gesture we have seen throughout this book by immediately grounding his analysis of "how we act"—that is, how the world's most powerful military hegemon conducts its foreign policy—on the *terra firma* of "who we are."

Throughout the course of the speech, the President utilizes most of the rhetorical strategies at work in the writings of those public intellectuals under consideration here. With Kagan, Obama stresses the somnolent quality of America's imperial past, insisting that it took the events of September 11, 2001 to shake us "out of our complacency." With Ignatieff, Obama couches the Administration's choice to use drones in the context of "heartbreaking tragedies," and argues that the "tragedy" a war with al-Qaeda invites creates situations "where our counterterrorism efforts and our values may come into tension." But, again with Ignatieff, Obama's decision to characterize this tension as tragic is not meant to elicit widespread reflection on America's current security practices or on the history of its foreign policy in the Middle East. Rather, tragic choice in this context serves as a call to arms that abruptly ends discussion. Because the American state has always been true to its constitutional principles and values, and because the danger we face is always immediate and overwhelming, such sustained inquiries appear reckless and self-indulgent. In a world where "who we are" trumps the kinds of critical reflection that tragedy might engender, the only choice available to the hegemon is to do nothing and lose to the terrorists or sacrifice liberal principles in the name of liberalism. But even this suggestion of a "choice" is disingenuous, because the decision to bomb, torture, invade, or surveil has always already been made. "Doing nothing," in Obama's words, "is not an option."[2]

My goal in critiquing this speech is not to lay the blame for the President's deflective approach to foreign policy entirely at the feet of the Administration. Obviously, Obama is a politician working within the tightly circumscribed discursive world of the foreign policy establishment, the semantic limitations of nationalism, and a media culture that often demands almost slavish patriotism from its elected officials. My aim here, rather, is to demonstrate just how thoroughly official policy discourse has been captured by a politics of deflection even at a moment when the President has the opportunity—and the stated desire—to rethink the explicitly imperialist foreign policy of the post-September 11, 2001 era and redefine the "nature and scope" of the War on Terror before it defines us. That such opportunities for reflection snap shut even before they have begun to open reveals just how powerful, and prolix the rhetoric of deflection truly is, and how embedded it remains in the liberal imperialist imaginary.

The real targets of my sustained criticism throughout this book have been those influential public intellectuals who perpetuate deflective and forgetful narratives of the British and American Empires in history—narratives that enable and encourage the kind of foreign policy discourse that reduces politics, again and again, to an agonized need to sacrifice liberal principles or fall victim to the enemy, and in which more and better empire is always the solution to the "imperial problem." And yet, while the kinds of policies and attitudes toward international politics these deflective discourses produce are deeply troubling, their capacity to suck up all the air in the room and obscure alternatives to their narrative logic is equally disturbing. If indeed there is a "lesson" to be learned from an analysis of British liberal imperial discourse in the first decades of the twentieth-century it is not, as Ferguson imagines, that Americans ought to avoid the kinds of critical discourses about the Empire and international politics that he feels crippled Britain at the time. Rather, we ought to be paying closer attention than ever to these voices before they are drowned out by the relentless descant of liberal imperial pundits pushing them aside to put "who we are" back into the center of things.

Paths Not Followed

As I have already alluded to in the individual chapters on Zimmern, the Round Table, and Smuts, each of these authors exercised a considerable amount of influence over the dominant form of liberal internationalism that emerged from the ruins of World War I. During the War, as diplomats and intellectuals were crafting the contours of the League of Nations in American and British think tanks, policy groups, and government circles, Zimmern, some of the key members of the Round Table, and Smuts were all well placed to explain to these architects their visions of an internationalism that expanded, rather than challenged, imperialism. Precisely at the moment when Woodrow Wilson's Fourteen Points were becoming popular in Britain, Round Table stalwart Phillip Kerr became the most influential member regarding foreign affairs in Lloyd George's private secretariat (also known as the "Garden Suburb"), and Zimmern took an important position in the Foreign Office.[3] One of the main objectives of both men seems to have been to challenge Wilson's call for "national self determination" by insisting that the British Empire be recognized as a single state in the new League of Nations Assembly.[4] Zimmern conveyed British opposition to extending statehood to the dependencies in his "Foreign Office Memorandum," which eventually became the backbone of the draft that the British took with them to the Paris Peace Conference.[5] Likewise, Smuts and Kerr were largely responsible for the language of trusteeship that appeared in the Covenant's description of the League's Mandate System.[6] This language, which echoed the Round Table's and Smuts's approach to the perceived "fitness" of colonial populations, provided European imperial powers and a number of newly independent dominions with a powerful rationale for why they needed to govern the mandated regions of the former German and Ottoman Empires and why they needed to maintain their old empires. This same logic also explained why imperial dependencies and

League Mandates should be excluded from the putatively universal "society of nations" gathered in Geneva.

This does not mean, of course, that these thinkers were entirely successful in implementing their particular internationalist visions. Smuts failed to convince the League that newly liberated Eastern European states ought to become League Mandates, and the Round Table was never able to implement its grandiose vision of an imperial parliament. Indeed, with regard to the Round Table, observers as diverse as Hedley Bull and Enoch Powell would for years afterward marvel at the group's willful utopianism and their persistent belief in a "myth" of commonwealth that bore so little relation to reality.[7] However, the transference of these thinkers' worldviews onto the League of Nations, and the extent to which the League then became the model for liberal internationalism in the twentieth-century, tell a different story and speak volumes about the rhetorical power of an ideology that claimed to square the circle between international cooperation and empire. Additionally, not only did this worldview express precisely what discomforted liberal imperialists in Britain and America wanted to hear at that moment, these public intellectuals were often supported by people with real power, kept in business by the financial resources of the Rhodes trust, buoyed by elite connections, and legitimated by the long, intimate relationship between Oxford and imperial administrators. In the end, the combination of their vision's ideological appeal and material resources enabled these thinkers to simply talk over the other voices struggling to make themselves heard at the time—voices urging ordinary people and their leaders to reflect more critically on the very nature of the imperial state and the possibilities of a postwar internationalism not held hostage by the imperial status quo.

Those generating these alternative political visions spoke from positions both at the center and the periphery of the Empire. English pluralist, professor, and journalist G. D. H. Cole, for example, spent the war in Britain as a conscientious objector, writing works of political theory which reimagined the relationship between the state and other political associations in a manner meant to radically decenter the imperializing, war-seeking hegemon.[8] Throughout the war, his political theory evolved into a powerful critique of what he called the "ring fence" approach to sovereignty, or the "introspective method in political theory," that "shuts up the State in the circle of its own ideas."[9] Such an approach to governance, Cole argued, failed to take into account the diverse, rich, and productive forms of politics emerging from associations and locations that refused to conform to the state's legal and geographic parameters. Worse yet, for Cole, an "introspective" approach to the state that accepted the state's *de facto* position as the last and greatest form of political community "leads straight to political Solipsism, which is otherwise known as Imperialism."[10]

Writing from within the belly of the world's greatest imperial state at war, Cole urged his readers in Britain to look out at the global political terrain from a conceptual perspective that regarded the state as "just another association," albeit a powerful one. Cole argued that viewing the development of a League of Nations through lenses that consistently challenged the state's monopoly on sovereignty, exposed the two most widely discussed options for a postwar league—a "world-federation" and a "world state"—for what they were: two sides of the same coin. Both views preserved some notion of ultimate sovereignty that stifled diversity. For Cole, the "abandonment of the view that sovereignty is an absolute possession of the State" led "to the view that the location of sovereignty is a matter of choice."[11] It could then become possible, he maintained, to imagine different forms of political organization and a more democratic world politics.

Cole's main concern in his writing at the time was not to formulate a model for world politics, but rather to demand a shift in perspective that would encourage a reimagining of the global political landscape. The global terrain of Cole's own particular imaginary was a rich tapestry of "mutual relations of individuals and groups extending beyond the boundaries of a single state."[12] These individuals and groups (including local guilds and international workers' organizations) were moved by a wide array of interests and endeavors that focused not only on politics, but also on "art, religion, science, and, we may add, economics."[13] Cole was, I believe, the first observer of international politics to call these groupings "non-governmental organizations," a term that only entered the official vocabulary of international politics through the United Nations Charter.[14] However, Cole's understanding of non-governmental organizations looked distinctly different from today's NGOs, many of which have become the economic and political agents of imperial states and/or transnational financial institutions.[15] Cole, by contrast, envisioned a global landscape in which local and international associations, engaged in acts of communications and solidarity, kept the power of states in check because "a State in which foreign affairs are undemocratically managed has no right to go beyond a voluntary system."[16] In other words, for Cole, associational democracy always trumped state authority and no state had the right to imperialize, invade, surveil, or coerce purely by virtue of its status as a state. Cole's approach thus radically democratized world politics by decentering the state and, in the process, opening up foreign policy decisions to the democratic review of those individuals and associations most affected by them.

From a very different location in 1909—on a boat from England to South Africa—the forty-one-year-old lawyer, activist, and soon to be leading light of the independence movement in India, Mohandas K. Gandhi, penned what would become one of his most important and openly critical texts, *Hind Swaraj* (Indian "self rule" or "home rule"). Writing in Gujarati, Gandhi began and finished the text over the course of the ten-day trip (switching to his left hand when his right hand grew tired), and would translate it himself into English a year later.[17] The main thrust of this text (written as a dialogue between an Editor and a young nationalist Reader) seems, at first glance, to be a typical nineteenth-century, nationalist argument that looks back to what were supposedly the more authentic cultural origins of the national community and then imagines the national movement as a restoration of, or a return to, those origins. Gandhi accompanied this nationalist discourse with a pointed critique of Western civilization that, one hundred years later, Niall Ferguson would dismiss out of hand for the way it "maintained that the European empires had no redeeming future."[18]

In truth, Gandhi's nationalism was never an uncritical rejection of Western civilization, nor was it a slavishly nationalist return to a gloriously "authentic" India. Rather, it was a deeply creative vision of political possibility that relied on the "new spirit born in us" for purging repressive "defects" of the past while fostering a new political theory of practice grounded in economic, social, and political innovations that Leela Gandhi describes as "quite heterodox—even heretical— revisions of religious and social tradition."[19] At the heart of this political vision lay a desire to revive—but not uncritically imitate—an "idea of nationality unknown in other parts of the world," a nationality of diverse local communities knit together in the past through the movement of "leading men" who once traversed India by "foot or in bullock carts."[20] It is this pluralistic understanding of nationhood that Gandhi claims the English had almost destroyed and, as with Cole's political theory, it is a vision that decenters the state even as it calls for the emergence of the Indian nation.[21] Gandhi does this in part by not only critiquing Britain's claim to civilizational superiority, but also by calling into question that nation's "habit of writing history" in a way that privileges "interruptions" (military and otherwise) over the rhythm of lived life.[22] Within this lived life—in the movement of what Gandhi calls "soul force"—a better political community and a better civilization was being forged.

Gandhi's vision for the Indian nation also called upon Indians to conscientiously transform themselves in order to undo the psychological damage of English rule. In perhaps the most famous line of the book, the Editor admonishes the Reader for wanting to imitate the militarist practices of Western states, and then accuses the Reader of desiring "English rule without the Englishman" and "the tiger's nature but not the tiger."[23] That is not, he argued, "the kind of *Swaraj* that I want." In essence, Gandhi's anticolonial project was one of *total* resistance to the colonizer, resistance that transcended mere force or economic and political opposition. He demanded a change of heart, a sustained kind of soul reflection, and a differently oriented worldview that would respond to both the political and psychological repression of the British. For Gandhi, true *Swaraj*, real self-rule, required everyone to think critically and reflectively about their community, their nation, their civilization, and their own souls. As he notes toward the end of the text, "to blame the English is useless... They will either go or change their nature only when we reform ourselves."[24]

How profoundly ironic that a man who had already spent years—some of them in jail—fighting against indentured servitude and for the civic equality of Indians in South Africa (and who had just spent three months in England unsuccessfully petitioning for this cause) would call upon Indians to engage in precisely the kind of critical self-reflection that liberal imperialists like Zimmern, the Round Tablers, and Smuts (the man who imprisoned Gandhi) never once considered for themselves or for their Empire. Rather, as this book has demonstrated, liberal imperialists—increasingly fearful of dissent throughout the Empire—reacted to those who accused the British of hypocrisy, racism, and aggression by consistently holding up British character like it was an airtight, timeless, liberal object, and proclaiming that this character reconciled all of the conflicting tensions inherent in being a liberal empire that behaved illiberally. Despite their calls for reform of the Empire and a thorough investigation of its problems, none of these thinkers ever seemed to ask the question that Gandhi asks of himself and his audience: Is this who we want to be? Is this the *Swaraj* that we want?

I want to be clear that the comparison I am making here between the kind of national reflection demanded by Gandhi, and the adamantine resistance to such reflection apparent in the work of Zimmern, the Round Table members, and Smuts, is not anachronistic. In other words, I am not suggesting these thinkers ought to have read and been familiar with a text of which they could not possibly have been aware. Besides the fact that Smuts corresponded with Gandhi and that he and Curtis both knew Gandhi from South Africa, *Hind Swaraj* was published in English in 1910 and all of them would certainly have known of its existence. Although *Hind Swaraj* did not have a significant impact on the Indian independence movement until it was reissued in 1919, and while reception of it in India and abroad (both by Western-educated nationalist elites and British intellectuals) was sometimes hostile and derisive, it was certainly not being ignored by English liberals.[25] In a 1914 letter to Smuts, for instance, his longtime friend Emily Hobhouse wrote,

> I have been reading Gandhi's book, *Home Rule for India—Hind Swaraj*. Have you read it? I like it *very much*, all about India and the harm English Civilization is doing there. The book has already been prohibited in India—(O foolish authorities, will you never learn wisdom?) but he means to devote his life to it in India... It is a book you would have enjoyed at one period of your life.[26]

The sister of liberal intellectual L.T. Hobhouse and a formidable feminist and peace activist in her own right, Emily Hobhouse was deeply connected to the liberal left in Britain at the time. Her letter both reveals a touching desire to imagine Smuts as more progressive than he actually was (or perhaps a knowing admission that he was not), and suggests that *Hind Swaraj* was making the rounds among English liberals in 1914.

None of these observations are meant to imply, however, that simply because Zimmern, the Round Tablers, and Smuts were aware of Gandhi and *Hind Swaraj* that they naturally *should* have taken his suggestions about critical reflection to heart. Nor do I mean to suggest that, because Cole was a familiar figure to all of these men—he corresponded frequently with Zimmern and his most impassioned critique of the imperial state appeared in a special edition of the *Proceedings of the Aristotelian Society* alongside articles from other major liberal scholars—they obviously should have been more critical of imperial sovereignty.[27] In the spirit of this book, the argument I want to make about the relevance of the past is precisely the opposite. The point of concluding with a brief review of Cole and Gandhi is to argue against the developmental approach to history taken by the liberal imperialists under consideration here—an approach that, despite Ferguson's protestations to the opposite, posits liberal empire as the logical and natural fulfillment of liberal values. Contemporary cosmopolitan authors often do something similar with the League of Nations by reading it as one obvious signpost along the developmental road to Kantian cosmopolitanism.[28] But, as Tully explains in his critical work on global citizenship, history is not "the unfolding of some trans-historical definition that the grand theories claim it to be."[29] Grand Kantian theories of the history of the League of Nations may claim exclusive occupancy of the past, but alternative visions of the possible—of different kinds of local and global politics—circulated right alongside the version of internationalism that Zimmern and Smuts took with them to the Paris Conference. The kind of alternative politics articulated by Cole and Gandhi called for greater reflection on the history of the Empire, the nature of Western civilization, and the status of the dependencies, as well as a differently shaped global politics conceived through the lenses of associational democracy rather than sovereignty or empire. Such visions were ultimately frozen out of the League.

In essence, during that moment toward the end of the war when it seemed that the Empire was at a crossroads, thinkers like Zimmern, the Round Tablers, and Smuts *could have* chosen to "up the ante" (in Mehta's words) for reflection by asking serious questions about the British state's commitment to the liberalism it espoused, or pushed for greater consideration of its role in creating the political instabilities that had led to World War I and to the "imperial problem" in the first place. Instead, they chose to solve the "imperial problem" by closing ranks around narratives of "who we are" in the past, present, and future and, in the process, contributed to the birth of an internationalism that would sustain formal imperialism for decades to come and informal imperialism to this day. Hence, the goal of this comparison has been, in Tully's words, to disclose the "conditions of possibility" that lay behind the "historically singular set of practices of governance" that went into the concretion of the League of Nations and to think more about what these possibilities mean in the context of today's imperial turning point.[30]

Expanding Horizons

Samuel Moyn concludes his important 2010 book, *The Last Utopia: Human Rights in History*, by arguing that the contemporary human rights project "faces a fateful choice: whether to expand its horizons so as to take on the burden of politics more honestly, or to give way to new and other political visions that have yet to be fully outlined."[31] Part of the process of expanding these horizons, Moyn argues, is to turn to history but not, he insists, as a means to "monumentalize human rights by rooting them deep in the past." Rather, historical inquiry broadens our understanding of human rights discourse in its contemporary iteration by exposing it as only the most successful form of utopianism to emerge from the political storm of the 1970s, a storm that left competing visions shipwrecked. Part and parcel of why this contemporary human rights discourse was so successful, Moyn argues, was that it seemed to fulfill the "widespread desire to drop utopia and have one anyway."[32]

The success of liberal imperial narratives of history and visions of the future, from the early twentieth-century until today, can be similarly understood in the context of a widespread desire among liberals in Britain and America to drop empire but have one anyway and, in the process, block out alternative, more expansive horizons for political possibility. As Said might argue, it is not simply easier to *write* political narratives that posit "liberal prescriptions" for the world's problems: such prescriptions are also simply easier to *hear*, particularly for liberals made uncomfortable by the suggestion that our way of life has been made possible, in part, by the military, economic, and political exploitation of others. Neither do these same liberals want to believe that the problems of today's world—problems President Obama associates most closely in his speech with war in the Middle East and domestic terrorism—might have been in some way influenced by the imperial behavior of the American state. In such an environment, the narrative of "who we are" speaks soothingly to our discomfort, assuring us that, in a world of terrible choices, the bravest and most ethical choice is to stay true to "who we are" and ignore "how we act."

The problem, of course, as the example of the British Empire and the League of Nations suggests, is that such "who we are" approaches—as with Zimmern's "Oxford Paradox"—never entirely solve the rhetorical problem of being a liberal state that acts illiberally: they just move it around. In his analysis of Marx's work on crises of capitalism, David Harvey identifies something similar in Marx's contention that capital "cannot abide" a limit. "Every limit appears," Harvey quotes from Marx's *The Grundrisse*, "as a barrier to be overcome."[33] For Harvey, this means that capital solves its problems by shifting them to other financial and geographic locations. When union wages become too costly for capital's liking, industries shift production to countries with fewer labor laws. When wage repression in the 1970s led to a decline in consumer spending, financiers shifted toward a credit economy. One can see a similar impulse at work in the ideology of liberal imperialism over the course of the twentieth-century. When World War I brought imperial foreign policy up hard against the shore of its instability, and when German aggression and dissent in the colonies made British claims to liberal benevolence seem like rank hypocrisy, liberal imperial discourse shifted toward an internationalism that preserved the Empire. When decolonization fully exposed the duplicity of the Trusteeship System in the 1960s, liberal imperialism recast itself as informal international governance under the aegis of the World Bank and the G8. When the events of September 11, 2001 brought home the full horror of American foreign policy in the Middle East during and after the Cold War, liberal imperialism transformed itself into a War on Terror. And as the War on Terror grinds on and President Obama casts about for a new foreign policy language, liberal imperialism waits in the wings—egged on by the prestige of public intellectuals like Kagan, Ferguson, and Ignatieff—ready to become what it needs to be.

What stays constant during these moments of transition, I argue, is the discursive apparatus that responds to every political, historical, and conceptual challenge to liberal consistency by insisting reaffirming the liberal character of the imperial state. As this book has argued, the deflective strategies behind this move become more apparent during moments of intense anxiety about the future of the liberal empire. At the same time, as the examples of Cole and Gandhi remind us, alongside each of these rhetorical shifts in the self-presentation of liberal empire have run what Said calls counter-memories and counter-discourses that articulate different ways of imagining both the trajectory of the past and the current and future political landscape. For example, an incredibly rich pool of scholarship in recent years has sought to decolonize imperial and international history by reexamining those moments when public intellectuals have sought to make the imperials state become "what it has always been."[34] Counter-discourses and democratic practices also thrive during this moment of global economic crisis in ways that unite international citizen groups and associations in a manner reminiscent of Cole's unbounded democratic imaginary.[35]

Ultimately, the goal of this book has been to encourage a widespread wariness toward foreign policy discourses that imagine both international history and contemporary American politics through the lens of "who we are." These discourses can range from Ferguson's bombastic metanarratives, to Ignatieff's tragedies, to the turn of a presidential phrase, but each engages in a politics of deflection that decenters imperial violence while simultaneously positing the necessity of imperial action. The historical comparisons in this book should also encourage us to listen more carefully for counter-memories and counter-discourses too often occluded by liberal imperial claims to be all things to all people—to drop empire and have one anyway. And finally, this book ends with an explicit call for a more courageous politics rooted in sustained *reflection* rather than *deflection*. Such a politics imagines a time when citizens of liberal imperial states move beyond ritualized formulations of "who we are" and ask instead: Is this who we want to be?

NOTES

Introduction

1. Mark Lander, "Obama Promises Thorough Inquiry into Afghan Attack," *New York Times*, March 13, 2012, accessed January 14, 2013, http://www.nytimes.com/2012/03/14/world/asia/obama-promises-thorough-inquiry-into-afghan-attack.html?_r=0.
2. Hillary Clinton: "This is not who we are and the United States is committed to seeing that those responsible are held accountable." "Clinton Expresses Shock, Regret at Afghan Massacre," *Reuters*, March 12, 2012, http://www.reuters.com/article/2012/03/12/us-aghanistan-usa-clinton-idUSBRE82B10I20120312; Leon Panetta: "This is not who we are and it's certainly not what we represent when it comes to the great majority of men and women in uniform." "The American Way of War," *Huffington Post*, May 6, 2012, http://www.huffingtonpost.com/robert-jay-lifton/war-atrocity_b_1490147.htm; General John Allen: "We send our condolences to families who have lost their loved ones and to the people of Afghanistan. This is not who we are." *CNN.com*, March 12, 2012, http://transcripts.cnn.com/TRANSCRIPTS/1203/12/sitroom.01.html. All last accessed January 14, 2013.
3. Michael Ignatieff, "Living Fearlessly in a Fearful World," Whitman College Commencement Address, May 26, 2004. Italics mine. http://www.whitman.edu/newsroom/news/2004/may/whitman-commencement-address-2004-living-fearlessly-in-a-fearful-world, accessed January 14, 2013.
4. One can see this in John Stuart Mill's obsessive concern with national character in *Considerations on Representative Government* (1861) or in Anthony Froude's loving description of the spread of Anglo-Saxon culture in *Oceana: or England and Her Colonies* (London: Longman's, 1886).
5. Milner quoted in J. G. Darwin, "The Fear of Falling: British Politics and Imperial Decline Since 1900," *Transactions of the Royal Historical Society* 36 (1986): 32.
6. See Inderjeet Parmeer's fascinating analysis of this phenomenon in "Foreign Policy Fusion: Liberal Interventionists, Conservative Nationalists and Neoconservatives—the New Alliance Dominating the US foreign Policy Establishment," *International Politics* 46.2-3 (2009): 177–209.
7. George W. Bush, "A Distinctly American Internationalism," Ronald Reagan Presidential Library, Simi Valley, California, November 19, 1999, accessed December 30, 2012. https://www.mtholyoke.edu/acad/intrel/bush/wspeech.htm.
8. Anne-Marie Slaughter, *The Idea that is America: Keeping Faith With Our Values in a Dangerous World* (New York: Basic Books, 2007), 232.
9. For more on this language in the work of the increasingly influential "Princeton Project," see John Ikenberry and Anne-Marie Slaughter's discussion of the long-term American strategy geared toward shaping the world "as we want it to be" in *Forging a World of Liberty Under Law; U.S. National Security in the Twenty First Century, Final Report of the Princeton*

Report on National Security (Princeton University, NJ: The Princeton Project Papers, The Woodrow Wilson School of Public and International Affairs, 2006). See also Obama's speeches and press conferences from April 30, 2013, accessed May 25, 2013. http://www.whitehouse.gov/the-press-office/2013/04/30/news-conference-president and May 23, 2013, accessed May 25, 2013. http://www.whitehouse.gov/the-press-office/2013/05/23/remarks-president-national-defense-university.

10. Slavoj Žižek, *The Sublime Object of Ideology* (London: Verso, 1989), 58.

11. "There is something very characteristic in the indifference which we show towards this mighty phenomenon of the diffusion of our race and the expansion of our state. We seem, as it were, to have conquered and peopled half the world in a fit of absence of mind." Robert Seeley, *The Expansion of England* (Cambridge: Cambridge University Press; 2010), 8.

12. For an insightful analysis of theoretical and scholarly approaches to imperialism and empire see Patrick Wolfe, "History and Imperialism: A Century of Theory, from Marx to Postcolonialism," *American Historical Review* 102.2 (1997): 388–420.

13. See Wolfgang Mommsen, *Theories of Imperialism* (New York: Random House, 1980).

14. Michael Doyle, *Empires* (Ithaca, NY: Cornell University Press, 1986), 45.

15. See Paul A. Kramer's razor-sharp review of some approaches to imperial history in "Power and Connection: Imperial Histories of the United States in the World," *American Historical Review* 116.5 (2011): 1349.

16. See Uday Mehta, *Liberalism and Empire: A Study in Nineteenth-Century British Liberal Thought* (Chicago: University of Chicago Press, 1999), Jennifer Pitts, *A Turn To Empire: The Rise of Imperial Liberalism in Britain and France* (Princeton, NJ :Princeton University Press, 2005); Duncan Bell, *The Idea of Greater Britain: Empire and the Future of World Order, 1860–1900* (Princeton, NJ: Princeton University Press, 2007); and Karuna Mantena, *Alibis of Empire: Henry Maine and the Ends of Liberal Imperialism* (Princeton, NJ: Princeton University Press, 2010).

17. Uday Mehta, "Liberal Strategies of Exclusion," in *Tensions of Empire: Colonial Cultures in a Bourgeois World*, ed. Frederick Cooper and Ann Stoler (Berkeley: University of California Press, 1997), 59.

18. See Ferguson's *Empire: The Rise and Demise of British World Order and the Lessons for Global Power* (New York: Basic Books, 2002) and *Colossus: The Price of America's Empire* (New York: Penguin, 2004) and Zakaria's *The Post American World* (New York: W. W. Norton, 2008).

19. Edward Said, *Culture and Imperialism* (New York: Vintage Books, 1994), 9.

20. Peter Cain, "Empire and the Languages of Character and Virtue in Later Victorian and Edwardian Britain," *Modern Intellectual History* 4.2 (2007): 249–273.

21. Duncan Bell, *The Idea of Greater Britain Empire and the Future of World Order, 1860–1900.* (Princeton, NJ: Princeton University Press, 2009), 10. See also Daniel Deudney's "Greater Britain or Greater Synthesis: Seeley, Mackinder, and Wells on Britain in the Global Industrial Era," *Review of International Studies* 27 (2001): 187–208. Deudney's article concentrates in particular on examples of thinkers who were specifically interested in reimaging the relationship between the Empire and the "inter-state system."

22. Quoted in Darwin, "The Fear of Falling," 32.

23. See Darwin's discussion of tariff reform in "The Fear of Falling," 30. Besides the Round Table, other pro-imperial organizations formed between 1900 and 1914 in Britain included the Royal Colonial Institute, the British Empire League, and the Society of Comparative Legislation.

24. See Samuel Hynes's discussion of this "less confident mood" in *The Edwardian Turn of Mind* (Princeton, NJ: Princeton University Press, 1968), 5–53.

25. Ronald Hyam, "The British Empire in the Edwardian Era," *The Oxford History of the British Empire* (Oxford: Oxford University Press, 1999), 50.

26. See Bernard Porter's *Critics of Empire: British Radicals and the Imperial Challenge* (London: I. B. Taurus, 2008), 60.

27. Gregory Claeys, *Imperial Skeptics: British Critics of Empire, 1850–1920* (Cambridge: Cambridge University Press, 2010). See also Peter Mandler on liberal imperial discussion groups at the

turn of the century in *The English National Character* (New Haven, CT: Yale University Press, 2007), 128–130.

28. Mehta, *Liberalism and Empire*, 107.

29. Dipesh Chakrabarty, *Provincializing Europe: Postcolonial Thought and Historical Difference* (Princeton, NJ: Princeton University Press, 2000). "Mill's historicist argument," argues Chakrabarty, "thus consigned Indians, Africans and other 'rude' nations to an imaginary waiting-room of history" (8).

30. Paul Kennedy, *The Rise of Anglo German Antagonism, 1860–1914* (London: The Ashfield Press, 1989), 393.

31. See Peter Mandler's more extensive discussion of this in *The English National Character*, 131; and Paul Rich, *Race and Empire In British Politics* (Cambridge: Cambridge University Press, 1990), 50.

32. Phillip Kerr, "Anglo-German Rivalry," *The Round Table* 1.1 (1910): 9.

33. Seeley, *The Expansion of England*, 191.

34. For more on this transition see K. N. Panikkar, "From Revolt to Agitation: Beginning of the National Movement," *Social Scientist* 25.9/10 (1997): 28–42. Panikkar argues that the Swadeshi movement, which emerged in reaction to the 1905 partition of Bengal, "shifted the focus of politics from concessions to self reliance." (41). For more on the racialization of the Irish during the nineteenth-century and, in particular, on comparisons between the Indians and the Irish in British visual culture, see Richard Ned Lebow's now-classic *White Britain, Black Ireland: The Influence of Stereotypes on Colonial Policy* (Philadelphia: Institute for the Study of Human Issues, 1976).

35. Phillip Kerr, "India and the English," *The Round Table* 1.1 (1910), 46.

36. Ira Christopher Fletcher, "Double Meanings: Nation and Empire in the Edwardian Era," in *After the Imperial Turn: Thinking With and Through the Nation*, ed. Antoinette Burton (Durham, NC: Duke University Press, 2003), 248.

37. Milner quoted in Bill Schwartz, *The White Man's World* (Oxford: Oxford University Press, 2011), 110.

38. From Richard Jebb's influential *Studies in Colonial Nationalism* (London: Edward Arnold, 1905), 119. In the 1890s, imperialists in Britain were fixated on the possibility of actual separation. Thus, in 1894, Under-Secretary of State for the Colonies Sydney Buxton fretted to the Foreign Office Secretary that surrendering Samoa to the Germans would cause "the devil's own row in Australia and New Zealand" and that the "power and position of the growing party of secessionists would be enormously strengthened." Quoted in Paul Kennedy, *The Rise of Anglo German Antagonism*, 216.

39. Raymond J. Sontag, *Germany and England: Background of Conflict* (London: D. Appleton, 1938), 308.

40. Quoted in James Henry Powers, *Years of Tumult:; The World Since 1918* (New York: W.W. Norton, 1932), 165.

41. See Mommsen's influential *Theories of Imperialism* and Antony Anghie, *Imperialism, Sovereignty and the Making of International Law* (Cambridge: Cambridge University Press, 2007). See also David Harvey's discussion of "informal" imperialism during the postwar years in *The New Imperialism* (Oxford: Oxford University Press, 2003). In particular, Harvey's second chapter, "How America's Power Grew," deals specifically with both "coercive and hegemonic" mechanisms associated with US economic and military power and with the "development of consent" (42) in postcolonial states.

42. Tully refers to this as the "co-creation" of the West and non-West in Chapter Nine, "On Local and Global Citizenship; An Apprenticeship Manual," *Public Philosophy in a New Key. Volume II: Imperialism and Civic Freedom* (Cambridge: Cambridge University Press, 2008). In this chapter, Tully chronicles the historical development of the "rights and duties" associated with informal or "free trade imperialism" and argues that these imperialist ideas are deeply embedded in modern liberal and cosmopolitan notions of global citizenship.

43. John Gallagher and Ronald Robinson, "Free Trade Imperialism," *The Economic History Review* 6.1 (1953): 1–15. For more on "free trade imperialism" see Bernard Semmel's *The Rise of Free Trade Imperialism* (Cambridge: Cambridge University Press, 1970); Wolfgang

Mommsen and Jurgen Osterhammal, *Imperialism and After* (London: Allen and Unwin, 1986); and Harry Magdoff, *Imperialism Without Colonies* (New York: Monthly Review Press, 2003). Magdoff's earlier work makes a similar argument. See *Imperialism from the Colonial Age to the Present* (Monthly Review Press: New York, 1978).

44. See Chakrabarty, *Provincializing Europe*, 43.

45. Said, *Culture and Imperialism*, xii.

46. See Kenneth Morgan's analysis of the impact of slavery on the British Empire up through the twentieth-century in Morgan, *Slavery and the British Empire: From Africa to America* (Oxford: Oxford University Press, 2007). See also Mike Davis's description of the role played by the British in exacerbating the effects of the famine in India from 1876 to 1879 where millions died: "As in Ireland thirty years before, those with the power to relieve famine convinced themselves that overly heroic exertions against implacable natural laws, whether of market prices or population growth, were worse than no effort at all." Mike Davis, *Late Victorian Holocausts* (London: Verso, 2001), 32. Finally, see David Anderson's analysis of the extraordinary violence used by the British to suppress the Mau Mau insurrection in *Histories of the Hanged: The Dirty War in Kenya and the End of Empire* (New York: W. W. Norton, 2005).

47. Richard Immerman, *Empire for Liberty: A History Of American Imperialism from Benjamin Franklin to Paul Wolfowitz* (Princeton: Princeton University Press, 2010), 1. For more on imperial denial in the United States see Andrew Bacevich's introduction to *The Imperial Tense: Prospects and Problems of American Empire* (Chicago: Ivan R. Dee, 2003).

48. Tully, "On Local and Global Citizenship," 261.

49. Philip Golub, *Power, Profit, and Prestige: A History of American Expansion* (London: Pluto Press, 2010), 11.

50. See Michael Cox's discussion of the new attitude toward interventionism and hegemony during the 1990s in "September 11th and US Hegemony—Or Will the 21st Century Be American Too?," *International Studies* 3 (2002): 53–70.

51. Michael Ignatieff, "The Seductiveness of Moral Disgust," *Social Research* 62.1 (1995): 94.

52. Michael Cox, "Empire, Imperialism and the Bush Doctrine," *Review of International Studies* 30 (2004): 588. This article provides an excellent analysis of the transition from a language of "hegemon" to "empire" during this period.

53. Michael Ignatieff, "Barbarians at the Gate?" *New York Review of Books*, February 28, 2002, accessed January 3, 2013. http://www.nybooks.com/articles/archives/2002/feb/28/barbarians-at-the-gate/. Several other authors at this time echo Ignatieff's fixation with barbarians and the fall of Rome, most notably, Harold James, *The Roman Predicament: How the Rules of International Order Create the Politics of Empire* (Princeton, NJ: Princeton University Press, 2006).

54. George W. Bush, "America's Responsibility, America's Mission," in Bacevich, *The Imperial Tense*, 5.

55. George W. Bush, "Transcript of Bush's Remarks on Iraq: 'We Will Finish the Work of the Fallen," *New York Times*, April 13, 2004, accessed December 30, 2012. http://www.nytimes.com/2004/04/14/politics/14BTEX.html.

56. Wendy Brown, *Politics Out of History* (Princeton, NJ: Princeton University Press, 2001), 4.

57. Paul Ricoeur, *Memory, History, Forgetting* (Chicago: University of Chicago Press, 2004), 413.

58. Hayden White, "Guilty of History? The Long Duree of Paul Ricoeur. Review of *Memory, History, Forgetting*, by Paul Ricoeur," *History and Theory* 46.2 (May 2007): 235.

59. Lionel Curtis, *The Commonwealth of Nations: An inquiry into the Nature of Citizenship in the British Empire and the Mutual Relations of the Several Communities Thereof* (London: Macmillan, 1916), 116.

60. Norman Klein, *The History of Forgetting: Los Angeles and the Erasure of Memory* (London: Verso, 2008), 2.

61. Ernst Renan, "What Is A Nation?," in *Nations and Identities: Classic Readings*, ed. Vincent P. Pecora (Oxford: Oxford University Press, 2001), 166.

62. Benedict Anderson, *Imagined Communities* (London: Verso, 1991), 201.

63. See Foucault on repression and the "productive aspect of power" in "Truth and Power," *Power Knowledge: Selected Interviews and Other Writings, 1972–1977* (New York: Pantheon Books, 1980), 119.

64. Judith Shklar, "The Political Theory of Utopia: From Melancholy to Nostalgia," *Daedalus*, 94.2 (1965): 378.

65. Brown, *Politics Out of History*, 7, 8.

66. Brown, *Politics Out of History*, 6.

67. Ian Baucom, *Out of Place: Englishness, Empire, and the Locations of Identity* (Princeton, NJ: Princeton University Press, 1999), 7.

68. Baucom, *Out of Place*, 51.

69. Michael Freeden, *Ideologies and Political Theory: A Conceptual Approach* (Oxford: Clarendon Press, 1996), 1.

70. Freeden, *Ideologies and Political Theory*, 3.

71. See Helen Small's introduction to the edited volume, *The Public Intellectual* (Oxford: Blackwell Publishing, 2002), 1. Also see Stefan Collini, *Absent Minds: Intellectuals in Britain* (Oxford: Oxford University Press, 2006).

72. Jose Harris, "Political Theory and the State," quoted in Bell, *The Idea of Greater Britain*, 6.

73. Bell, *The Idea of Greater Britain*, 6.

74. See Collini's discussion of the idea of "publics" (as opposed to "public" in the singular) in the introduction to *Common Reading: Critics, Historians, Publics* (Oxford: Oxford University Press, 2008).

75. For an analysis of the long-term institutional connections in Britain between Oxford, the colonial service, and the Foreign Office see Richard Symonds, *Oxford and Empire—The Last Lost Cause?* (Oxford: Clarendon Press, 1991).

76. Jan Smuts, *War-Time Speeches: A Compilation of Public Utterances in Great Britain* (New York: George Doran Co., 1917), vii.

77. See Ronald Jacobs's and Eleanor Townsley's lucid analysis of media intellectuals and media space in contemporary America in *The Space of Opinion: Media Intellectuals and the Public Sphere* (New York: Oxford University Press, 2011).

78. Michael Ignatieff, "The Decline and Fall of the Public Intellectual," *Queens Quarterly* 104.3 (1997): 398–399.

79. Donald Kagan, "On Patriotism," *The Yale Review* 99.4 (2011): 25.

80. See Laurence Shoup and William Minter, *Imperial Brain Trust: The Council on Foreign Relations and United States Foreign Policy* (New York: Monthly Review Press, 1977), 11–13.

81. See Inderjeet Parmar's excellent analysis of this foreign policy consensus in "Foreign Policy Fusion: Liberal Interventionists, Conservative Nationalists, And Neoconservatives—The New Alliance Dominating the U.S. Foreign Policy Establishment," *International Politics* 46.2/3 (2009): 177–209.

82. For perhaps the most sustained example of this approach see Quentin Skinner's *Reason and Rhetoric in the Philosophy of Hobbes* (Cambridge: Cambridge University Press, 1996.) Also see Skinner's essay on interpretation in *Meaning and Context: Quentin Skinner and His Critics*, ed. James Tully (Princeton, NJ: Princeton University Press, 1988).

83. Skinner in Tully, *Meaning and Context*, 68–78.

84. Michael Ignatieff, *The Lesser Evil* (Princeton, NJ: Princeton University Press, 2004), 29.

85. Skinner in Tully, *Meaning and Context*, 246–247.

86. Freeden, *Ideology and Political Theory*, 100.

87. Uday Mehta, "Liberal Strategies of Exclusion," 62.

88. Dipesh Chakrabarty, *Provincializing Europe*, 43.

89. James Tully, "Political Philosophy as a Critical Activity," *Political Theory* 30.4 (2002): 534.

90. In his important 2010 book, Moyn argues that the way in which human rights advocates since the 1970s have recast world history as "raw material for the progressive assent of international human rights" makes it difficult for them to admit "that earlier history left open diverse paths into the future, rather than paving a single road toward current ways of thinking and acting." Samuel Moyn, *The Last Utopia: Human Rights in History*, (Cambridge: Harvard University Press, 2010), 5.

91. Edward Said, *Humanism and Democratic Criticism* (New York: Columbia University Press, 2004), 142.

92. Said, *Humanism and Democratic Criticism*, 142.

Chapter 1

1. Alfred Zimmern, "The Greeks and Their Civilization," The Alfred Zimmern Papers (hereafter Bodl. MS. Zimmern) Bodl. MS. Zimmern 135 fols.76,77. Many thanks to the Bodleian Library for allowing me access to the Zimmern papers.

2. Bodl. MS. Zimmern 135 fol. 77.

3. Bodl. MS. Zimmern 135 fol. 99.

4. Alfred Zimmern, "Thucydides The Imperialist" Bodl. MS. Zimmern 136 fol.103.

5. Arnold Toynbee, *Acquaintances* (Oxford: Oxford University Press, 1967), 49. See also Gordon Martel's excellent article on the development of Toynbee's approach to history, "The Origins of World History: Arnold Toynbee Before the First World War," *Australian Journal of Politics and History* 50.3 (2004): 343–356.

6. Graham Wallas Papers, London School of Economics & Political Science, 1/46, fol.8, quoted in Martel, "The Origins of World History," 350.

7. Alfred Zimmern, "United Britain: A Study in 20th Century Imperialism," 1905, Bodl. MS Zimmern 136, fol. 24.

8. H. J. Cunningham, "Review of *The Greek Commonwealth*, by Alfred Zimmern," *The English Historical Review* 27 (1912): 534.

9. For further biographical information on Zimmern see Morefield, *Covenants Without Swords* (Princeton, NJ: Princeton University Press, 2005), and D. J. Markwell, "Sir Alfred Zimmern Revisited: Fifty Years On," *Review of International Studies* 12 (1986): 279–292. Noam Pianko's *Zionism and the Roads Not Taken: Rawidowicz, Kaplan, Kohn* (Indiana: Indiana University Press, 2010) offers an excellent analysis of what until now has been an under-researched component of Zimmern's intellectual life: his exploration of his Jewish identity, his Zionism, and the relationship between these and his analysis of nationhood and internationalism.

10. For more on Zimmern, classics, and Oxford see Paul Millet, "Alfred Zimmern's The Greek Commonwealth Revisited," in *Oxford Classics: Teaching and Learning 1800–2000*, ed. Christopher Stray (London: Duckworth Press, 2007).

11. Toynbee, *Acquaintances*, 53.

12. For more on the history and political theory of New Liberals in Britain see Michael Freeden, *The New Liberalism: An Ideology of Social Reform* (Oxford: Clarendon Press, 1978) and Avital Simhony and David Weinstein, *The New Liberalism: Reconciling Liberty and Community* (Cambridge: Cambridge University Press, 2001).

13. Scholars doing survey work on many of the earliest thinkers involved with the League of Nations have often, incorrectly, stressed what they see as Zimmern's Kantianism. Pagden, for instance, uses Zimmern's "cosmopolitanism" as an example of the way "Kant has left his mark on almost all thinking about the possibility of some future world order, from his own day to this." See Anthony Padgen, *The Enlightenment and Why it Still Matters* (New York: Random House, 2013), 370–371. Zimmern, however, rarely wrote about Kant, and his understanding of a global "*res publica*" looked distinctly different from Kant's *Perpetual Peace*. The one modern political theorist (aside from T. H. Green) who made a regular appearance in Zimmern's writings was Burke.

14. Alfred Zimmern, "The British Workingman," Bodl. MS Zimmern 135 fol. 25.

15. Zimmern, "The British Workingman," Bodl. MS Zimmern 135 fol. 25.

16. Alfred Zimmern, "Preface," in *Nationality and Government* (New York: Robert McBride and Co, 1918), xvii.

17. Zimmern, "Preface," *Nationality and Government*, xvii.

18. Carroll Quigley, *The Anglo-American Establishment: From Rhodes to Cliveden* (New York: Books in Focus, 1981), 5.

19. Markwell, "Sir Alfred Zimmern Revisited," 280.

20. For a fascinating account of Zimmern's important but brief and controversial relationship with UNESCO see John Toye and Richard Toye, "One World, Two Cultures? Alfred

Zimmern, Julian Huxley and the Ideological Origins of UNESCO," *History: The Journal of the History Association* 95.319 (2010): 267–398.

21. Hans Morgenthau and Kenneth Thompson, eds., *Principles and Problems of International Politics* (New York: Knopf, 1952), 18.

22. Julia Stapleton, *Political Intellectuals and Public Identities in Britain Since 1850* (New York: Manchester University Press, 2001), 99. The second chapter looks at Zimmern in the context of other pre-World War I public intellectuals who were similarly committed to reimagining citizenship and democracy through Greece.

23. Zimmern, "Three Doctrines in Conflict," *Nationality and Government*, 334.

24. Alfred Zimmern, *Europe in Convalescence* (London: Mills and Boon Limited, 1922), 50.

25. Alfred Zimmern, *The League of Nations and the Rule of Law* (London: MacMillan, 1936), 177–178.

26. Polly Low, *Interstate Relations in Classical Greece: Morality and Power* (Cambridge: Cambridge University Press, 2007), 17. Paul Rich makes a similar observation in *Race and Empire in British Politics* (Cambridge: Cambridge University Press, 1990).

27. Rich, *Race and Empire in British Politics*, 60.

28. Millet, "Alfred Zimmern's The Greek Commonwealth Revisited."

29. Alfred Zimmern, *The Greek Commonwealth*, 5th ed. (Oxford: Oxford University Press, 1931), 7.

30. Frank Turner, *The Greek Heritage in Victorian Britain* (New Haven, CT: Yale University Press, 1981), 262.

31. G. W. B. "The Greek Commonwealth: Politics and Economics in Fifth-Century Athens," [review of *The Greek Commonwealth* by Alfred Zimmern] *Political Science Quarterly* 27 (1912), 716.

32. Turner, *The Greek Heritage in Victorian Britain*, 1.

33. Turner, *The Greek Heritage in Victorian Britain*, 189.

34. George Grote, *The History of Greece, Volume III* (London: John Murray, 1888), 394.

35. Frank M. Turner, "The Triumph of Idealism in Victorian Classical Studies," in *Contesting Cultural Authority: Essays in Victorian Intellectual Life* (Cambridge: Cambridge University Press, 1993), 325.

36. Turner, *The Greek Heritage in Victorian Britain*, 8.

37. Arlene Saxonhouse, "Athenian Democracy and Modern Mythmakers: A Lesson from Plato about Democracy, Equality, and Gender," *Thamyris* 1.2 (September 1994): 105–122.

38. Robert Knox, *The Races of Men* (Philadelphia: Lea and Blanchard, 1850), 403. As Chapter Three of this book explores in more detail, by 1916, the theory that ancient Greeks had migrated to the Attic Peninsula from Germany, and that the Anglo Saxons came from similar stock and thus were able to form a Greek-like democracy in England as a result of this cultural/racial connection, still played a prominent role in the Round Table's theory of commonwealth. (See Curtis, *The Commonwealth of Nations*, 71–72.)

39. See Duncan Bell's excellent summary of nineteenth-century imperial attitudes toward Greece and Rome in "From Ancient to Modern In Victorian Imperial Thought," *The Historical Journal* 49.3 (2006): 735–759. Also see Adam Rogers and Richard Hingley, "Edward Gibbon and Francis Haverfield; The Traditions of Imperial Decline," in *Classics and Imperialism*, ed. Mark Bradley (Oxford: Oxford University Press, 2010), 189–209.

40. Again, see Bell's argument regarding Seeley and the Imperial Federationists's rejection of Greece in "From Ancient to Modern in Victorian Imperial Thought."

41. Emma Reisz, "Classics, Race, and Edwardian Anxieties," in *Classics and Imperialism*, 210–228.

42. Phiroze Vasunia, "Envoi," *Classics and Imperialism*, 286.

43. Vasunia, "Envoi," 289.

44. Quigley, *The Anglo American Establishment*, 5.

45. Alfred Zimmern, "United Britain," fol. 124.

46. Zimmern, "United Britain," fol. 165.

47. Zimmern, "United Britain," fol. 163.

48. Quigley, *The Anglo America Establishment*, 122.

49. Andrea Bosco and Alex May, *The Round Table: The Empire-Commonwealth and British Foreign Policy* (London: Lothian Foundation Press, 1997), iii. See also Darwin, "The Fear of Falling, British Politics and Imperial Decline Since 1900," *Transactions of the Royal Historical*

Society, Fifth Series 36 (1986): 27–43. Darwin makes a number of connections in this article between the tariff reform movement and a more general Edwardian fear of decline.

50. Alfred Zimmern, "The Seven Deadly Sins of Tariff Reform," Bodl. MS. Zimmern 136 fol. 9.

51. Zimmern, "The Seven Deadly Sins of Tariff Reform," fol. 37.

52. Zimmern, "The Seven Deadly Sins of Tariff Reform," fol. 13.

53. Zimmern, "United Britain," fol. 155.

54. Zimmern, "United Britain," fol. 157.

55. Zimmern, "United Britain," fols. 161, 156,

56. Zimmern, "United Britain," fol. 163.

57. Zimmern, "United Britain," fol. 161.

58. For more on the confusion of race and culture in the writing of early-twentieth-century British authors writing about "imperial citizenship," see Daniel Gorman, *Imperial Citizenship: Empire and the Question of Belonging* (Manchester: Manchester University Press), 50–51.

59. Zimmern, "United Britain," fol. 167.

60. Zimmern, "United Britain," fol. 165.

61. Zimmern, "The Seven Deadly Sins of Tariff Reform," fol. 147.

62. Zimmern, "United Britain," fol. 164.

63. Zimmern, *The Greek Commonwealth*, 7.

64. Letter from Murray to Zimmern, July 6, 1910, Bodl. MS. Zimmern 12 fol. 158.

65. Victor Ehrenberg, "Review of *The Greek Commonwealth,* by Alfred Zimmern," *Gnomon* 1.3 (1925), 146. Many thanks to Karah Kemmerly and David Lupher for their help with the translation of this article.

66. P.A.S "Review of *The Greek Commonwealth,* by Alfred Zimmern," *The Journal of Hellenic Studies* 43 (1923), 68; G. W. B. "The Greek Commonwealth: Politics and Economics in Fifth-Century Athens," [review of *The Greek Commonwealth* by Alfred Zimmern] *Political Science Quarterly* 27 (1912), 716.

67. Ehrenberg, "Review of *"The Greek Commonwealth,"* 142.

68. Zimmern, *The Greek Commonwealth*, 446.

69. Zimmern, *The Greek Commonwealth*, 378.

70. Zimmern, *The Greek Commonwealth*, 156.

71. Zimmern, *The Greek Commonwealth*, 139.

72. Zimmern, *The Greek Commonwealth*, 381. For more on evolving attitudes toward Athens in the nineteenth-century and Zimmern's relationship to this trend, see Turner, *The Greek Heritage in Victorian Britain*, 259–263.

73. Zimmern, *The Greek Commonwealth*, 386.

74. Zimmern, *The Greek Commonwealth*, 386. By the time *The Greek Commonwealth* was published in 1911, Zimmern had already made a name for himself as a defender of Greek slavery. According to Zimmern, slavery in fifth-century-B. C. E Athens was actually a widely misinterpreted form of apprenticeship. See his 1909 article "Was Greek Civilization Based on Slave Labour?" from the *Sociological Review* reprinted in Zimmern, *Solon and Croesus and Other Greek Essays* (Freeport, NY: Books for Libraries Press, 1968). Also see Zimmern's thoughts on "manumission" in his review article, "Calderini's Manomissione," *The Classical Review* 24:1 (1910): 21–22.

75. Ehrenberg, "Review of *The Greek Commonwealth,*" 142. Again, many thanks to David Lupher for his translation help and suggestions here. The translations in brackets are mine.

76. Zimmern, *The Greek Commonwealth*, 59.

77. Ehrenberg, "Review of *The Greek Commonwealth,*" 141.

78. Zimmern, *The Greek Commonwealth*, 207 (Thucydides, *The History,* 2.43.2).

79. See Richard Crawley's 1874 translation, *The History of the Peloponnesian War* (London: J.M. Dent & Sons, 1914); Rex Warner's 1954 translation, *The History of the Peloponnesian War* (Harmondsworth, Eng., Baltimore: Penguin Books, 1972); Benjamin Jowett's 1881 translation, *The History of the Peloponnesian War* (New York: Washington Square Press, 1963). For examples of scholars who translate *koine* as a noun, see Blanco, *The Peloponnesian War* (New York: W.W. Norton and Company, 1998), and C. F. Smith's 1915 translation, *Thucydides: History of the Peloponnesian War* (New York: Loeb Classical Library, 1965). Thanks to Professor Joseph Lane for his guidance with the translation.

80. Richard Schlatter, ed. *Hobbes's Thucydides* (New Brunswick, NJ: Rutgers, 1975), 135.

81. Zimmern, *The Greek Commonwealth*, 58.

82. For more on Burke's odd appropriation of Cicero through Bolingbrook in this quotation see Paddy Bullard, *Edmund Burke and the Art of Rhetoric* (Cambridge: Cambridge University Press, 2011), 14.

83. Zimmern, *The Greek Commonwealth*, 106.

84. Zimmern, *The Greek Commonwealth*, 368.

85. Zimmern, *The Greek Commonwealth*, 367.

86. Zimmern, *The Greek Commonwealth*, 345.

87. H.J. Cunningham, review of, *The Greek Commonwealth*," by Alfred Zimmern, *The English Historical Review*, 27 (1912), 534.

88. Zimmern, *The Greek Commonwealth*, 63.

89. Zimmern, *The Greek Commonwealth*, 343, 93.

90. Zimmern, *The Greek Commonwealth*, 217, 247, 293.

91. See Kendle's discussion of the Round Table and India, in John Kendle, *The Round Table Movement and Imperial Union* (Toronto: University of Toronto Press, 1975), 227.

92. Zimmern, *The Greek Commonwealth*, 186.

93. Zimmern, *The Greek Commonwealth*, 181.

94. Zimmern, *The Greek Commonwealth*, 74. Zimmern's treatment of this "Indian influence" in the Appendix is extremely vague.

95. Zimmern, *The Greek Commonwealth*, 21.

96. Zimmern, *The Greek Commonwealth*, 193.

97. Zimmern, *The Greek Commonwealth*, 292

98. Zimmern, *The Greek Commonwealth*, 227.

99. Zimmern, *The Greek Commonwealth*, 373.

100. Zimmern, *The Greek Commonwealth*, 183. In this moment, Zimmern argued, Greece came into "self-consciousness."

101. Zimmern, *The Greek Commonwealth*, 193. By the time the fifth edition of *The Greek Commonwealth* was published in 1931, Zimmern most certainly would have been aware of the recently discovered "Coinage Decree" that demonstrated the extent of the coercion involved in Athens's standardization of currency. But he never corrected his interpretation. For more on the "Coinage Decree" see C. W. Fornara, *Archaic Times to the End of the Peloponnesian War* (Cambridge: Cambridge University Press, 1991), 105. See also Meiggs on the significance of the "Coinage Decree" in Russell Meiggs, *The Athenian Empire* (Oxford: Clarendon Press, 1992), 167–173. Thanks to Professor Kyra Nourse for her help finding information on the Coinage Decree. At the same time, Zimmern was also wrong about the way Britain handled currency issues in India. For more on this see Sunanda Sen, "Tributes and Transfers from Colonial India," in *India in the World Economy, 1850–1950*, ed. G. Balachandran (Oxford: Oxford University Press, 2003), 104–106.

102. Zimmern, *The Greek Commonwealth*, 189.

103. Zimmern, *The Greek Commonwealth*, 191.

104. Zimmern, *The Greek Commonwealth*, 184.

105. Zimmern, *The Greek Commonwealth*, 195.

106. Zimmern, *The Greek Commonwealth*, 194.

107. Zimmern, *The Greek Commonwealth*, 369, 372.

108. Thucydides, *The History of the Peloponnesian War*, trans. Rex Warner (Penguin: Harmondsworth, UK, 1972), I.1.23. Other scholars translate this similarly as "real cause" (Crawley in *The Landmark Thucydides: A Comprehensive Guide to the Peloponnesian War* [New York: Free Press, 1998]), "real or unavowed cause" (Benjamin Jowett, *The History of the Peloponnesian War* [New York: Washington Square Press, 1963] and Richard, Livingston, *The History of the Peloponnesian War* [Oxford: Oxford World Classics, 1972]), "truest cause" (Steven Lattimore, *The Peloponnesian War* [New York: Hacket, 1998]), "truest explanation" (G. E. M. de Ste. Croix, *The Origins of the Peloponnesian War* [Ithaca, NY: Cornell University Press, 1972]).

109. Zimmern, *The Greek Commonwealth*, 374.

110. Diodorus is also widely believed to have significantly miscalculated dates. In his 1948 article, "The Foundation of Thurii," for example, Ehrenberg noted Wade-Gery's reliance on

Diodorus and then groused, "everybody knows what this fact involves." *The American Journal of Philology* 69.2 (1948): 149.

111. Zimmern, *The Greek Commonwealth*, 374.

112. Zimmern, *The Greek Commonwealth*, 369.

113. The nineteenth-century Oxford classicist Evelyn Abbot praised the Panhellenism of Thurii in *Pericles and the Golden Age of Athens* (New York: Putnam and Sons, 1891), 148. Zimmern does not cite Abbott in *The Greek Commonwealth*.

114. Mason Hammond, "Ancient Imperialism: Contemporary Justifications," *Harvard Studies in Classical Philology* 58 (1948): 130.

115. See Zimmern's footnote on Wilamowitz and the timing of the Funeral Speech in the first footnote on p. 199 of *The Greek Commonwealth*.

116. Zimmern, "Thucydides the Imperialist," Bodl. MS. Zimmern 136 fol. 98.

117. Zimmern, "Thucydides the Imperialist," fol. 98.

118. Zimmern, *The Greek Commonwealth*, 199.

119. Zimmern, *The Greek Commonwealth*, 199.

120. Thucydides's text, argued Hobbes, proved that "democracy was wrong and one man was far wiser than a throng." From Hobbes's biography quoted in Maurice Pope, "Thucydides and Democracy," *Historia: Zeitschrift für alte Geschichte* 37.3 (1988): 276. See Saxonhouse for a discussion of *phusis* (human nature) in Thucydides's discussion of democracy and external politics. Arlene W. Saxonhouse, "Nature & Convention in Thucydides' History," *Polity* 10.4 (1978): 480. On Thucydides as a critic of empire and hubris, see Jacqueline de Romilly, *Thucydides and Athenian Imperialism* (New York: Barnes and Noble, 1963) and Francis MacDonald Cornford, *Thucydides Mythistoricus* (London: Edward Arnold, 1907). Finally, for an account of Thucydides as an "amoral" chronicler of empire, see the Introduction to de Ste. Croix's *Origins of the Peloponnesian War*, 5–34.

121. Zimmern, *The Greek Commonwealth*, 196.

122. Zimmern, *The Greek Commonwealth*, 196.

123. Zimmern, "Thucydides the Imperialist," Bodl. MS. Zimmern 136 fol. 98.

124. Zimmern, *The Greek Commonwealth*, 196.

125. Thucydides asserted that he wrote his *History* "not as an essay which is to win the applause of the moment, but as a possession for all time," in (Warner I.1.22).

126. Zimmern, "Thucydides the Imperialist," in *Solon and Croesus* (New York: Books for Libraries Press, New York, 1928), 104. I have used the published version of the essay here because the 1905 draft is missing its final page.

127. Zimmern believed that Thucydides was "under the influence" of the Sophists. See "Thucydides the Imperialist," fol. 110.

128. Zimmern, "Thucydides the Imperialist," fol. 104.

129. Zimmern, "Thucydides the Imperialist," fol. 105.

130. Bonnie Honig, *Political Theory and the Displacement of Politics* (Ithaca, NY: Cornell University Press, 1993), 2.

131. Zimmern, *The Greek Commonwealth*, 430.

132. Michael Lang also assumes that Zimmern wrote "The Ethics of Empire." See "Globalization and Global History in Toynbee," *Journal of World History* 22.4 (2011): 747–783.

133. Alfred Zimmern, "The Ethics of Empire," *The Round Table* 311 (1913): 495.

134. Zimmern, "German Culture and the British Commonwealth," *Nationality and Government*, 31.

135. Carroll Quigley Papers, Georgetown University Library Special Collections Research Center, Washington, D.C., Box 37 of 63, letter from Zimmern to Quigley, July 2, 1948. Thanks to the Georgetown Library for allowing me access to these papers.

136. Carroll Quigley Papers, Box 37 of 63, from Quigley's notes on his discussions with Zimmern.

137. Carroll Quigley Papers, Box 37 of 63, letter from Quigley to Zimmern, Nov. 16, 1949.

138. Zimmern, "Ethics of Empire," 488.

139. Zimmern, "Ethics of Empire," 488–489.

140. Zimmern, "German Culture and the British Commonwealth," 10.

141. Zimmern, "Ethics of Empire," 498.

142. Zimmern, "Ethics of Empire," 499.

143. Zimmern, "The Ethics of Empire," 497.

144. Zimmern, "The Ethics of Empire," 500.

145. Zimmern, "The Ethics of Empire," 494.

146. Zimmern, "The Ethics of Empire," 501.

147. See both David Armitage and Herman Lebovics on the imperial threads in Locke's political philosophy. David Armitage, "John Locke, Carolina, and the 'Two Treatises of Government,'" *Political Theory* 32.5 (2004): 602–627; Herman Lebovics, "John Locke, Imperialism, and the First Stage of Capitalism," in *Imperialism and the Corruption of Democracies* (Durham, NC: Duke University Press, 2006). See Anthony Pagden for a broader discussion of early modern rights theory and empire in Europe. Anthony Pagden, "Human Rights, Natural Rights, and the Europe's Imperial Legacy," *Political Theory* 31.2 (2003): 171–199.

148. Round Table Papers, MS.Engl.hist.c817, fols. 153–154. Letter from Zimmern to John Hobson, September 13, 1916. Thanks again to the Bodleian for allowing me access to these papers.

Chapter 2

1. Irvin Kristol, "The Neoconservative Persuasion: What It Was and What It Is," in *The Neoconservative Reader*, ed. Irwin Stelzer (New York: Grove Press, 2004), 35–36.

2. Douglas Murray, *Neoconservatism: Why We Need It* (New York: Encounter Books, 2006), 45.

3. Donald Kagan, "World War I, World War II, World War III," *Commentary* 83.3 (1987): 31.

4. Donald Kagan and Frederick Kagan, *While America Sleeps: Self-Delusion, Military Weakness, and the Threat to Peace Today* (New York: St. Martin's Press, 2000), 5.

5. Kagan, "World War I, World War II, World War III," 21.

6. Warner translates Thucydides's famous claim in I.23 as "the real reason for the war." See Rex Warner's translation, *The History of the Peloponnesian War* (New York: Penguin, 1972). Jowett refers to "real or unavowed cause." See Jowett's translation, *The History of the Peloponnesian War* (Oxford: Clarendon Press, 1900), 17. See also Richard Crawley's 1874 translation in Robert Strassler, *The Landmark Thucydides* (New York: The Free Press, 1998), 16.

7. As David Marshall explains, political theorists like Sheldon Wolin and Jean Elshtain have used this term in reference to Hannah Arendt. See Marshall, "The *Polis* and its Analogues in the Thought of Hannah Arendt," *Modern Intellectual History* 7.1 (2010): 125, footnote 6.

8. Donald Kagan, *The Peloponnesian War* (New York: Viking, 2003), xxvi.

9. Donald Kagan, "Athenian Strategy in the Peloponnesian War," in *The Making of Strategy: Rulers, States, and War*, ed. Williamson Murray (Cambridge: Cambridge University Press, 1994); Donald Kagan, *On the Origins of War and the Preservation of the Peace* (New York: Doubleday, 1995).

10. Barry Strauss, "Donald Kagan: The Scholar and Teacher," *Historically Speaking* 7.1 (2005): 44.

11. Strauss, "Donald Kagan," 43.

12. Jacob Heilbrunn, *They Knew They Were Right: The Rise of the Neocons* (New York: Doubleday, 2008), 215.

13. Bruce Fellman, "Lion in Winter," *Yale Alumni Magazine*, April 2002, accessed December 11, 2012, http://www.yalealumnimagazine.com/issues/02_04/kagan.html.

14. William A. Percy and Pedro J. Suarez, "Today's Western and World Civilization College Texts: A Review," *The History Teacher* 17. 4 (1984): 580.

15. Elliott Abrams, Gary Baur, Donald Kagan, et al., "Statement of Principles," The Project for a New American Century, accessed December 11, 2012, http://www.newamericancentury.org/statementofprinciples.htm.

16. Donald Kagan, Gary Schmitt, and Thomas Donnelly, "Rebuilding America's Defenses: Strategy, Forces, and Resources for a New Strategy," *A Report of the Project for a New American Century* (Washington, D.C.: Project for a New American Century, 2000), iv.

17. Brady Johnson Program in Grand Strategy, Yale University, accessed December 11, 2012 http://iss.yale.edu/grand-strategy-program.

18. Amy Dockser Marcus, "Where Policy Makers Are Born," *The Wall Street Journal*, December 20, 2008, accessed December 13, 2012. http://online.wsj.com/article/SB122973925559323583.html.

19. John Lewis Gaddis, Charles Hill, Paul Kennedy, Walter Russell Mead, John Negroponte, and Paul Solman, "Studies in Grand Strategy," 2010 syllabus, accessed December 12, 2012 http://iss.yale.edu/node/41/attachment.

20. Donald Kagan, *Pericles of Athens and the Birth of Democracy* (New York: The Free Press, 1991), 10.

21. Donald Kagan, *The Outbreak of the Peloponnesian War* (Ithaca, NY: Cornell University Press, 1969), x.

22. Ronald S. Stroud, "Review of *The Outbreak of the Peloponnesian War*," *Classical Journal* 67.1 (1971), 88.

23. Arnold Toynbee, *Acquaintances* (Oxford: Oxford University Press, 1967), 49.

24. Murray, *Neoconservatism*, 44–45.

25. See, for example, Barry Hughes, *Continuity and Change in World Politics* (New York: Prentiss Hall, 1991), or David Boucher, *Political Theories and International Relations* (Oxford: Oxford University Press, 1998.)

26. See Morgenthau's discussion of Thucydides in *Politics Among Nations* (Boston: McGraw-Hill, 1993).

10; Kenneth Waltz, *Theory of International Politics* (Reading, MA: Addison-Wesley, 1979), 127 and 186–187; and Robert G. Gilpin, "The Richness of the Tradition of Political Realism," *International Organization* 38 (1984), 287–304.

27. Robert Connor, *Thucydides* (Princeton, NJ: Princeton University Press, 1984), 3.

28. Louis J. Halle, "A Message From Thucydides," *Foreign Service Journal* (1952) [quoted from an article reprinted in Halle, *Civilization and Foreign Policy: An Inquiry For Americans* (New York: Harper, 1955), 262].

29. Alfred Zimmern, "Our Greek Augustan Age," *The Classics Journal* 46.7 (1951): 327–328.

30. Hans Morgenthau, "We Are Deluding Ourselves in Vietnam," *New York Times Magazine*, April 18, 1965. Many neorealists had similar reactions to the Bush administration's invasion of Iraq. See most importantly Mearsheimer's 2005 op-ed, in which he framed his critique as an ode to Morenthau. "Hans Morgenthau and the Iraq War: Realism versus Neo-Conservatism," excerpted as "Realism is Right," in *The National Interest* 81 (Fall 2005), 10.

31. Thucydides, *History* (Warner, 1.23.6).

32. Robert Keohane and Joseph Nye, *Power and Interdependence* (New York: Little, Brown, 1977), 42.

33. A sampling of IR reconsiderations of the realist Thucydides include several excellent articles by Richard Ned Lebow, including "Thucydides as a Constructivist," *American Political Science Review* 95.3 (2001); "Thucydides and Hegemony: Athens and the United States," *Review of International Studies* 27.4 (2001). See also Laurie M. Johnson Bagby, "The Use and Abuse of Thucydides," *International Organization* 48.1 (1994); and John Zumbrunnen's *Silence and Democracy: Athenian Politics in Thucydides' History* (University Park, PA: Pennsylvania State University Press, 2008).

34. Kagan, *Pericles of Athens*, 273.

35. See in particular Gordon M. Kirkwood, "Thucydides' Words for 'Cause,'" *The American Journal of Philology* 73.1 (1952): 37–61; Lionel Pearson, "Prophasis and Aitia," *Transactions and Proceedings of the American Philological Association* 83 (1952): 205–223.

36. Donald Kagan, "The First Revisionist Historian," *Commentary* 85.5 (1988): 43.

37. Kagan, "The First Revisionist Historian," 45. Donald Kagan, *Thucydides: The Reinvention of History* (New York: Penguin, 2009), 225.

38. Kagan, "The First Revisionist Historian," 45.

39. Hobbes, for instance, read Thucydides's *History* as a warning about the dangers of democratic governance. See Hobbes's autobiography, quoted from Maurice Pope, "Thucydides and Democracy," *Historia: Zeitschrift für alte Geschichte* 37.3 (1988): 276.

40. Thucydides, *History* (Warner, 2.65.10).

41. See Zumbrunnen's *Silence and Democracy* for a counterintuitive reading of the *demos* in *The History*.

42. See, for example, Arlene W. Saxonhouse, "Nature & Convention in Thucydides' History," *Polity* 10.4 (1978): 480.

43. "Personally," began Cleon, "I have had occasion often enough already to observe that a democracy is incapable of governing others and I am all the more convinced of this when I see how you are now changing your minds about the Mytilenians." Thucydides, *The History*

(Warner, 3.37.1). Scholars are just as likely to translate the word *archē* (rule, governance, or dominion) in this sentence as "empire." See, for instance, Jowett.

44. See Jacqueline de Romilly, *Thucydides and Athenian Imperialism* (New York: Barnes and Noble, 1963, English translation).

45. Kagan, *Thucydides*, 113.

46. Kagan, *Thucydides*, 113.

47. Victor Ehrenberg, "The Foundation of Thurii," *The American Journal of Philology* 69.2 (1948): 170. In *The Outbreak*, Kagan also thoroughly unpacks Theodore Wade-Gery's challenge to Plutarch's claim that Pericles was not the elected general when Thurii was founded. See Wade-Gery, *Essays in Greek History* (Oxford: Oxford University Press, 1959.) Wade-Gery's argument remains a contentious one that ancient historians interested in Thurii continue to accept or put aside. See, for instance Neil O'Sullivan's 1995 article in which he argues that, regarding Plutarch's claim, "what follows will only have relevance to this paper's title if that is accepted as accurate." O'Sullivan, "Pericles and Protagorus," *Greece & Rome*, Second Series 42.1 (1995): 16.

48. Kagan, *The Outbreak of the Peloponnesian War*, 161, 165.

49. Kagan, *The Outbreak of the Peloponnesian War*, 169.

50. See, for instance, M. E. White's "Review of *The Outbreak of the Peloponnesian War*, by Donald Kagan," *Phoenix* 25.4 (1971): 380–383.

51. Samuel K. Eddy, "Review of *The Outbreak of the Peloponnesian War*, by Donald Kagan," *Classical Philology* 68.4 (1973): 309.

52. See Thucydides's account of the debate at Sparta, Thucydides, *The History* (Warner, I.75.4).

53. Kagan, *Pericles of Athens*, 111.

54. Kagan, *The Outbreak of the Peloponnesian War*, 122.

55. Thucydides, *The History* (Warner, 1.22.1).

56. Romilly, *Thucydides and Athenian Imperialism*, 111.

57. Saxonhouse, "Nature & Convention in Thucydides' History," 465. While some authors have argued that the speeches in *The History* were pure literary inventions, most see them as, if not invented, at least deeply constructed. Even the more literally minded Orwin notes that, "Like the poets…Thucydides embellishes the truth; he 'orders things for the better.'" See Clifford Orwin, "Thucydides' Contest: Thucydidean 'Methodology' in Context," *The Review of Politics* 51.3 (1989): 350.

58. Zimmern, "Thucydides the Imperialist," Bodl. Ms. Zimmern 136, fol. 104.

59. Donald Kagan, "The Speeches in Thucydides," *Studies in the Greek Historians*, Yale Classical Studies, 24,, ed. Donald Kagan (Cambridge: Cambridge University Press, 1975), 78.

60. Kagan, *Thucydides*, 56.

61. Jack Cargill, "Review of *The Peace of Nicias and the Sicilian Expedition*, by Donald Kagan," *The American Historical Review* 88.1 (1983): 87.

62. Kagan, *Thucydides*, 50.

63. Kagan, *The Outbreak of the Peloponnesian War*, 129.

64. Kagan, *On The Origins of War*, 74.

65. Donald Kagan, *The Fall of the Athenian Empire* (Ithaca, NY: Cornell University Press, 1987), x.

66. Kagan, *The Fall of the Athenian Empire*, x.

67. Kagan, *The Peloponnesian War*, xxvi.

68. Anne Norton, *Leo Strauss and the Politics of American Empire* (New Haven, CT: Yale University Press, 2004), 200. While I believe Norton's observations on Kagan's political agenda are correct, Norton's assumption that Kagan is a Straussian seems based entirely on his associations with neoconservative thinkers (and perhaps on his decision to leave Cornell in 1969.) There is an argument to be made that Kagan's approach to theorizing out of historical gaps bears certain similarities to Strauss's "esoteric" reading between the lines of political philosophy, but Norton does not make it. In addition, Kagan has made it perfectly clear over the years that he disagrees with Strauss's ahistorical reading of texts. As Justin Vaisse puts it, Kagan "argued endlessly with his Cornell colleague Allan Bloom on Strauss' interpretation of Plato's *Republic*. Kagan father and son deem Straussians to be fundamentally wrong…" See Justin

Vaisse, *Neoconservatism: The Biography of a Movement* (Cambridge, MA: Harvard University Press, 2010), 273.

69. Daniel Mendelsohn, "Theaters of War," *The New Yorker*, January 2004, accessed December 15, 2012, http://www.newyorker.com/archive/2004/01/12/040112crat_atlarge?currentPage=all. Mendelsohn himself is a classically trained scholar whose first book was an important study of Euripides, *Gender and the City in Euripides' Political Plays* (Oxford: Oxford University Press, 2002).

70. Since Cornford's *Thucydides Mythohistoricus*, many scholars have read the Melian Dialogues as an example of Thucydides's use of the literary style of tragedy. As Cornford notes, this event sets the tone for what happened in Sicily. "Hubris and cruel madness which fell upon the Athenian people just before the Sicilian expedition—her entrance we have marked in the Melian Dialogue." Cornford, *Thucydides Mythisticus* (London: Edward Arnold, 1907), 194.

71. Kagan, *The Peloponnesian War*, 247.

72. Kagan, *The Peloponnesian War*, 487.

73. Kagan, *The Outbreak of the Peloponnesian War*, 355.

74. Argues Kagan, "it is evident to everyone who has studied the matter that during the recent war against Iraq the generals did a terrible job. They screwed up in every conceivable way, and the president didn't even fire them." Randall J. Stephens, "Thucydides and the Lessons of Ancient History: An Interview With Donald Kagan," *Historically Speaking* 11.5 (2010): 29.

75. Donald Kagan, *Pericles of Athens*, 258.

76. Kagan, *Pericles of Athens*, 273.

77. Thucydides, *History* (Warner, 2.43.1).

78. Saxonhouse makes this critique of a number of different "modern mythmakers" about Athens. See Saxonhouse, "Athenian Democracy: Modern Mythmakers and Ancient Theorists," *PS: Political Science and Politics* 26.3 (1993): 489.

79. See, for instance, Clifford Orwin, "Periclean Democracy: Merit and Relevance? Review of *Pericles of Athens*, by Donald Kagan," *The Review of Politics* 55.1 (1993): 159–162.

80. Kagan, *The Outbreak of the Peloponnesian War*, 355.

81. Kagan, *The Outbreak of the Peloponnesian War*, xi.

82. Kagan, *The Outbreak of the Peloponnesian War*, 236–237.

83. Murray, *Neoconservatism*, 46. The term "moral clarity" comes up often in neoconservative descants against "political correctness" and was particularly present in the discourse about foreign policy following the attacks of September 11, 2001. See, for example, William Bennett, *Why We Fight: Moral Clarity and the War on Terror* (New York: Doubleday, 2002), 84.

84. See Kagan's comparison of Athenian "defeatists" and critics of the war in Iraq in Donald Kagan, "On Patriotism," *The Yale Review* 99.4 (2011): 29.

85. Kagan, *On The Origins of War and the Preservation of the Peace*, 74.

86. Donald Kagan, "Lessons of the Great War," *Commentary* 108.3 (1999): 52.

87. Donald Kagan, Steven Ozment, and Frank Turner, *The Western Heritage: Teaching and Learning Classroom Edition* (Upper Saddle River, NJ: Prentice Hall, 2007), xxviii.

88. Kagan and Kagan, *While America Sleeps*, 435.

89. Maurice Halbwachs, *On Collective Memory* (Chicago: University of Chicago Press, 1992), 39.

90. Donald Kagan, "From Ancient Greece to Modern America: Why Western History Matters," *Current* 371 (March/April 1995): 37.

91. Plato, "The Apology," *The Trial and Death of Socrates*, trans. G. M. A. Grube (Indianapolis: Hackett, 2000), 33 (31.a).

92. For more on Strauss's attitude toward democracy, Socrates, and Athens see Thomas Pangle's "Introduction" in *The Rebirth of Classical Political Rationalism: An Introduction to the Thought of Leo Strauss* (Chicago: University of Chicago Press, 1989).

93. Kagan, *Pericles of Athens*, 24–25.

94. Donald Kagan, "Response Letter, *Commentary*," 86 (July, 1988), accessed January 4, 2013, http://www.commentarymagazine.com/article/socrates/.

95. Kagan, "From Ancient Greece to Modern America," 37.

96. Donald Kagan, "Terrorism and the Intellectuals," *The Intercollegiate Review* 37.2 (2002): 7.

97. Interview with Jim Puplava, "Financial Sense Newshour," transcription of audio interview, June 27, 2001, accessed January 4, 2013, http://www.financialsensearchive.com/transcriptions/2001/Kagan1.html.
98. Zimmern, *The Greek Commonwealth*, quoted in Kagan, *Pericles of Athens*, 271.

Chapter 3

1. Hobson to Zimmern, September, 16, 1916, Round Table Papers, Bodl. MS. Engl.hist.fol. 142. Curtis dismissed Hobson's incredulity with regard to British imperial motivations by declaring him a misanthrope. "One's heart bleeds for Hobson," he declared in a 1916 letter to Zimmern (written from India.) "It must hurt I should imagine to think so ill of men in general." [Bodl. MS. Curtis 817, fol. 170.]
2. Lionel Curtis, "The Green Memorandum," Bodl. MS. Curtis. 156/4–6, p. 6.
3. Andrea Bosco and Alex May, *The Round Table: The Empire/Commonwealth, and British Foreign Policy* (London: Lothian Foundation Press, 1997), i.
4. The Round Table also published a shorter book for popular consumption titled *The Problem of the Commonwealth* (London: Macmillan and Co., 1916).
5. For a discussion of the Round Table in the context of other pro-imperial groups of the Edwardian era see Bruce Ziff, *Unforeseen Legacies* (Toronto: University of Toronto Press, 2000), 22. See Peter Mandler's discussion of the Round Table's relationship to other liberal imperial discussion groups at the turn of the century in *The English National Character: The History of an Idea from Edmund Burke to Tony Blair* (New Haven, CT: Yale University Press, 2006), 128–130.
6. Mandler, *The English National Character*, 147.
7. Mandler, *The English National Character*, 147.
8. W. K. Hancock, *Survey of British Commonwealth Affairs*, vol.1 (Oxford: Oxford University Press, 1937), 53.
9. Inderjeet Parmar, "Anglo-American Elites in the Interwar Years: Idealism and Power in the Intellectual Roots of Chatham House and the Council on Foreign Relations," *International Relations* 16.1 (2002): 53.
10. See Andrea Bosco, "Lothian, Curtis, Kimber, and the Federal Union Movement," *Journal of Contemporary History* 23 (1988): 465–502; Deborah Lavin, *From Empire to International Commonwealth: A Biography of Lionel Curtis* (Oxford: Clarendon Press, 1995); John Kendle, *The Round Table Movement and Imperial Union* (Toronto: University of Toronto Press, 1975); and D. C. Ellingwood, Jr., "Lord Milner's 'Kindergarten': The British Round Table Group and the Movement for Imperial Reform, 1910–1916," (unpublished Ph.D. thesis, Washington University, 1962). Articles and collections that look at the impact of the Round Table on British foreign and imperial policy include: Andrea Bosco and Alex May, *The Round Table, The Empire/Commonwealth, and British Foreign Policy*; Roberta M. Warman, "The Erosion of Foreign Office Influence in the Making of Foreign Policy, 1916–1918," *The Historical Journal* 15 (1972): 133–159; Peter Yearwood, "'On the Safe and Right Lines': The Lloyd George Government and the Origins of the League of Nations, 1916–1918," *The Historical Journal* 32 (1989): 131–155.
11. See Antony Anghie, "The Evolution of International Law: Colonial and Postcolonial Realities," *Third World Quarterly* 27.5 (2006): 739–753.
12. Archibald Rosebery, *Questions of Empire* (New York: T. Y. Crowell, 1901), 6 [quoted in S. R. Mehrotra, "On the Use of the Term Commonwealth," *The Journal of Commonwealth Political Studies* 2 (1963–64): 10.]
13. Richard Higgott and Diane Stone, "The Limits of Influence: Foreign Policy Think Tanks in Britain and the USA," *Review of International Studies* 20.1 (1994): 17. See also Bosco and May, *The Round Table: The Empire/Commonwealth, and British Foreign Policy*, iii.
14. See Bosco and May's discussion of the group's funding, *The Round Table: The Empire/Commonwealth, and British Foreign Policy*, xi.
15. Lionel Curtis, "Draft Preface for the Published Edition of 'The Problem of the Commonwealth,'" Bodl. MS. Curtis 838, fol. 6.

16. Letter from Curtis to Zimmern, July 1914, MS. Eng.hist 786, fol. 98.

17. Quoted in Kendle, *The Round Table Movement and Imperial Union*, 181.

18. Kendle, *The Round Table Movement and Imperial Union*, 171.

19. For Curtis's description of the group's method see the "Introduction" to *The Commonwealth of Nations*. See also "Introduction" to the "Green Memorandum," Mss. Curtis. 156, 4–6, p. 6.

20. The London group included most of the original members of the "kindergarten" plus Milner himself, Muir, Grigg, Kerr, Zimmern, Reginald Coupland, Graeme Peterson, Lord Selborne, Starr Jameson, Abe Bailey, and Lord Robert Cecil [Kendle, *The Round Table Movement and Imperial Union*, 159.] According to M. S. Donelly, while "several hundred pages of comment" came in from Round Table groups in the dominions, these comments "produced only tactical changes in the plan Curtis had proposed to the Central London group in 1911, before comment had been invited." M. S. Donelly, "J.W. Dafoe and Lionel Curtis—Two Concepts of the Commonwealth," *Political Studies* 8 (1960): 175.

21. Letter from Curtis to Charles Edward Wood ("Lord Irwin"), Bodl. MS. Curtis 5, fol. 1.

22. Kendle, *The Round Table and Imperial Union*, 185–187.

23. Kendle, *The Round Table and Imperial Union*, 10.

24. Schwartz describes Milner's approach to Empire as "mystical," Kendle prefers "religious," and Bosco and May use "spiritual," but whatever we call it, this vision was bound to a basic faith in a natural and patriotic connection between the populations of the colonies and the mother country. See Bill Schwartz, *The White Man's World* (Oxford: Oxford University Press, 2012), 92; Bosco and May, *The Round Table, The Empire/Commonwealth, and British Foreign Policy*, 38; Kendle, *The Round Table and Imperial Union*, 96.

25. Richard Symonds, *Oxford and Empire—The Last Lost Cause?* (Oxford: Clarendon, 1993), 45.

26. J. R. Seeley, *The Expansion of England* (Cambridge: Cambridge University Press, 2010), 221.

27. This omission, as David Armitage has argued, "masked the fact that the British Empire in South Asia was precisely the kind of 'inorganic quasi state' that Seeley deplored in his *Introduction to Political Science*." David Armitage, *The Ideological Origins of the British Empire* (Cambridge: Cambridge University Press, 2000), 20.

28. Paul Rich, *Race and Empire in British Politics* (Cambridge: Cambridge University Press, 1990), 50, 58. See Peter Mandler's more extensive discussion of this in *The English National Character: The History of an Idea from Edmund Burke to Tony Blair*, 131.

29. Phillip Kerr, "Anglo-German Rivalry," *The Round Table* 1.1 (1910): 9.

30. Rich, *Race and Empire In British Politics*, 55. Round Table members who dissented from this view, such as Robert Henry Brand, argued that the primary reason the Empire was worth preserving was to ensure that the "white European races, and particularly the Anglo-Saxon branches of it, will be fortified and their ideals, religion, method of government, and civilisation preserved wherever they are now quartered on the globe, in fact that the white races will by that means be better able to 'live well.' " [Comments from Brand on a draft of *The Project of a Commonwealth*, May 1914. In Bodl.MS.Eng.hist.836, fol. 106.]

31. Phillip Kerr, "India and the English," *The Round Table* 1.1 (1910): 46.

32. Marcello de Cecco, *Money and Empire: The International Gold Standard, 1890–1914* (Oxford: B. Blackwell, 1974), 62 [quoted in Harry Magdoff, *Imperialism: From the Colonial Age to the Present* (New York: Monthly Review Press, 1978), 8–9.]

33. Round Table thinkers like Kerr and Curtis were also equally worried that losing India would prompt the "intervention of some other civilized Power" in the region that would, they maintained, seriously disrupt the global balance of power. Curtis, "The Original Egg," Bodl. Mss. Curtis. 156, fols. 156/4-6, 1910, 26.

34. Enoch Powell, "The Myth of Empire," in *Empire to Commonwealth, 1910–1970 / The Round Table, Diamond Jubilee Number*, ed. W. H. Morris-Jones (Oxford: Oxford University Press, 1970), 441.

35. S. R. Mehrotra, "Imperial Federation and India, 1868–1917," *The Journal of Commonwealth Political Studies* 1.1 (1961): 36.

36. Curtis, *The Problem of the Commonwealth*. See graphic on page 69 entitled, "Population of the World Divided According to States."

37. Zimmern to Hobson, Bodl. MS. Curtis 817, fol. 147.

38. Curtis and Kerr, "Green Memorandum," 1910, Bodl. MS Curtis 156, 17.

39. See the "Populations of the World Divided According to States," that appeared in the Round Table Studies, Second Series, Installment A, in 1912. Bodl. MS. Curtis 156.5.

40. Curtis, quoted in Gorman, *Imperial Citizenship*, 51.

41. Curtis, *The Commonwealth of Nations*, 699.

42. Duncan Bell, "Beyond the Sovereign State: Isopolitan Citizenship, Race, and Anglo-American Union," *Political Studies*, 2 (2013-01-01).

43. Curtis refers to the "actuating principle" or "actuating force" of the Commonwealth throughout *The Commonwealth of Nations*.

44. Curtis, Memo to London Group, 1914, Bodl. MS. Curtis 836, fol. 19.

45. For more on what happened to many British Idealists and those thinkers associated with the revival of Hegelian state theory in Britain during the war see D. C. Band, "The Critical Reception of English Neo-Hegelianism in Britain and America, 1914–1960," *The Australian Journal of Politics and History* 23 (1980): 228.

46. Hobson to Zimmern, Bodl. MS. Curtis 817, fol. 142. One reviewer went even farther, noting that "in the background" of the ideas that informed the group's approach "is Treitschke rather than T.H. Green." [D. A. MacGibbon, "Review article; *The Commonwealth of Nations* by L. Curtis," *The Journal of Political Economy* 25 (1917): 514.]

47. Bodl. MS. Curtis 836, fol. 116. Italics mine.

48. Lionel Curtis, "The Green Memorandum," Bodl. MS. Curtis. 156 /4–6, 6.

49. Curtis, *The Problem of Commonwealth*, 231.

50. Kerr, "The Anglo-German Rivalry," 7.

51. See Armitage, *The Ideological Origins of the British Empire*, on the commercial character of the early Empire.

52. Alfred Zimmern, "United Britain," Bodl. MS Zimmern, 136, fol. 157.

53. Dougal Malcolm, "Notes on Printed Draft of Part III of the Report, April 27, 1914," Bodl. MS. Curtis 836, fol. 108. Italics mine.

54. The draft "eggs" were differentiated by the color of their covers (e.g. the "Strawberry egg," the "Green egg.") References to "eggs" appear throughout Round Table correspondences during this period. See in particular Bodl. MS. Curtis 836.

55. Grigg, Bodl MS. Curtis 836, fol. 112.

56. Both Kendle, and Bosco and May, argue that Curtis and the Round Table "introduced" the term "commonwealth" into the political debate in their article, "The Spirit of the Coronation," *Round Table* 1.4 (1911). However, while the article definitely suggests the need for a spiritual and political community that looked like what the Round Table would eventually call the commonwealth, the word itself does not yet appear.

57. See memo circulated by Curtis to the Round Table, which he described as "an attempt to analyze the argument of the first 24 pages of the Strawberry Memorandum." [Bodl. MS. Curtis 836, fol. 91.]

58. A circulated memo from Curtis, May 22, 1914, MS. Eng.hist.c.836, fol. 91.

59. See Kerr's reflections on commonwealth in his 1922 article, "From Empire to Commonwealth," *Foreign Affairs* 1.2 (1922): 94.

60. Curtis, *The Commonwealth of Nations*, 8.

61. Curtis, *The Commonwealth of Nations*, 11.

62. Lionel Curtis, *The Project of a Commonwealth* (London: Macmillan and Co., 1915), 691.

63. Nicholas Mansergh, *The Commonwealth Experience* (Toronto: University of Toronto Press, 1969), 22. See also Bernard Shaw, *Fabianism and the Empire* (London: BibiloLife, 2009); Goldwin Smith, *Commonwealth or Empire* (Toronto: W. Tyrrell, 1900). Rosebery, who would later write a book on Oliver Cromwell, was undoubtedly aware of the historical parallel he was drawing between English Commonwealth history and the international body politic he described in 1884, but he never elaborated on this inference. A. Rosebery, *Oliver Cromwell: A Eulogy and an Appreciation* (London: A. Melrose, 1899).

64. W. K. Hancock, *Survey of British Commonwealth Affairs*, vol. I (Oxford: Oxford University Press, 1937), 53.

65. I am indebted to Duncan Bell's work on Victorian debates over international federation. Duncan Bell, "The Victorian Idea of the Global State," in *Victorian Visions of*

Global Order: Empire and International Relations in Nineteenth-Century Political Thought (Cambridge: Cambridge University Press, 2007), 159–185.

66. Daniel Gordon, "Lionel Curtis, Imperial Citizenship, and the Quest for Unity," *Historian* 66 (2004): 81. Gorman no doubt assumes this to be the case because of the Round Table's connections to Milner and because the policy suggestions implicit in their later thinking about commonwealth assumed a similar federalism.

67. Lionel Curtis, "World Order," *International Affairs* 18 (1939): 304. In addition, because their theory was based on a number of patently "idealist"-sounding concepts (such as "organic union"), Curtis and the Round Table would have had a strong incentive to put as much distance as they could between themselves and the legacy of the Federationists, and insist instead that what they were concerned with were "stern realities." [Curtis, *The Problem of the Commonwealth*, 137]

68. See Anthony Froude, *Oceana: Or, England and Her Colonies* (New York: Longmans, Green, and Co., 1898), 10.

69. Curtis and Kerr, "The Spirit of the Coronation," 427.

70. Curtis, *The Commonwealth of Nations*, 1.

71. Zimmern to Hobson, 13th of Sept. 1916, MS.Engl.hist.c817, fol. 139.

72. Bodl. MS. Curtis 836, fol. 122. This is from a memorandum commenting on the draft of Section Three of the Commonwealth project, probably written by Grigg.

73. Michael Doyle, *Empires* (Ithaca, NY: Cornell University Press, 1986), 45.

74. Dipesh Chakrabarty, *Provincializing Europe: Postcolonial Thought and Historical Difference* (Princeton, NJ: Princeton University Press, 2007), 8.

75. Uday Singh Mehta, *Liberalism and Empire: A Study in Nineteenth-Century British Liberal Thought* (Chicago: University of Chicago Press, 1999), 97.

76. Mehta, *Liberalism and Empire*, 94.

77. Kerr, "Anglo German Rivalry," *The Round Table* 1.1 (1910): 12.

78. Kerr, "Anglo German Rivalry," 12.

79. Curtis, *The Commonwealth of Nations*, 320. See the description of how Curtis imagined this process in Lavin, *From Empire to International Commonwealth*, 106–132. See also Curtis, *Report on the Green Memorandum Prepared by the Oxford University Segment of the Round Table Society* (Toronto: Toronto University Press, 1910), 10. ("It was provided that a Dependency might become a Dominion if a Bill to that effect obtained a three-fifths majority in both Houses of the Imperial Parliament sitting together.")

80. Ian Baucum, *Out of Place: Englishness, Empire and the Locations of Identity* (Princeton, NJ: Princeton University Press, 1999), 14. See also Mandler, *The English National Character: The History of an Idea from Edmund Burke to Tony Blair,* and Linda Colley, *Britons: Forging the Nation, 1707–1837* (Yale, CT: Yale University Press, 1992).

81. Colley, *Britons: Forging the Nation*, 6. Edmund Burke developed his understanding of the English constitution as a scheme of government that "has existed since time out of mind" at the same time he was giving speeches condemning the rapine of the East India Company and its violation of all that was good about Englishness. [Edmund Burke, *Selected Writings and Speeches*, ed. Peter James Stanlis (New York: Transaction Publishers, 2006), 397.] In the mid- to late nineteenth-century, Freeman wrote extended accounts of English history that exalted the nascent democracy of the Teutonic Saxons. See for instance, E. A. Freeman, *The Growth of the English Constitution from the Earliest Times* (New York: Frederick and Stokes Co., 1890), and *The History and Conquest of the Saracens* (London: Macmillan and Co., 1877).

82. Parker, for instance, refers to Freeman as an "ardent opponent of imperial federation." See Parker, "The Failure of Liberal Racialism: The Racial ideas of E. A. Freeman," *The Historical Journal* 24.4 (1981): 827. Edmund Burke's particular brand of anti-imperialism has been extensively studied by many, including Uday Mehta in *Liberalism and Empire* and Jennifer Pitts in *A Turn To Empire* (Princeton, NJ: Princeton University Press, 2005).

83. See J. R. Seeley, *The Expansion of England* (Cambridge: Cambridge University Press, 2010). For more on race in the political theory of the "Federationists," see Duncan Bell, *The Idea of Greater Britain* (Princeton, NJ: Princeton University Press, 2008).

84. Phillip Ker, "Foreign Affairs, The Anglo German Rivalry," *The Round Table* 1.1 (1910): 8.

85. Curtis, *The Problem of Commonwealth*, 11.

86. Curtis and Kerr, "The Spirit of the Coronation," 433.

87. For more on the lasting impact of Hegelian idealism on early-twentieth-century Oxford internationalists see Jeanne Morefield, *Covenants Without Swords: Idealist Liberalism and the Spirit of Empire* (Princeton, NJ: Princeton University Press, 2005).

88. Hayden White, *Metahistory: The Historical Imagination in Nineteenth-Century Europe* (Baltimore, MD: Johns Hopkins University Press, 1973), 7.

89. John M. Hobson, *The Eurocentric Conception of World Politics* (Cambridge: Cambridge University Press, 2012), 170.

90. Curtis, *The Commonwealth of Nations*, 19, 23–24.

91. Kendle refers to Zimmern's book as a very "useful" study of the "ideas of citizenship in the Athenian city." See, *The Round Table Movement*, 171. Close examination of the early chapters of *The Commonwealth of Nations* suggest that Curtis framed his interpretation of Athens almost entirely in terms culled from *The Greek Commonwealth* and that the definition of commonwealth that he would eventually place at the axis of the group's argument mirrors Zimmern's interpretation of the Athenian polity almost in its entirety. Other sources on Athens used less extensively by Curtis included Grote's *History of Greece* and Freeman's *Greater Greece and Greater Britain*.

92. Curtis, *The Commonwealth of Nations*, 43.

93. Alfred Zimmern, "German Culture and the British Commonwealth," *The War and Democracy*, ed. Seton Watson (London: St. Martin's Press, 1915), 380.

94. Curtis, *The Commonwealth of Nations*, 11.

95. Curtis, *The Commonwealth of Nations*, 11.

96. Curtis, *The Commonwealth of Nations*, 29.

97. Curtis, *The Commonwealth of Nations*, 49.

98. Curtis, *The Commonwealth of Nations*, 54.

99. Carlyle wrote in a letter to Emerson, "what is to hinder huge London from being to universal Saxondom what small Mycale was to the Tribes of Greece…a meeting of all the English ought to be as good as one of all the Ionians…" Letter, August 18, 1841, in Nell Irvin Painter, *The History of White People* (New York: W. W. Norton, 2012), 161. See E. A. Freeman, *Greater Greece and Greater Britain* (London: Macmillan, 1886), 60.

100. Curtis, *The Commonwealth of Nations*, 71.

101. W. Ridgeway, *The Early Age of Greece* (Cambridge: Cambridge University Press, 1931), 683. While Curtis never mentions these scholars by name, Zimmern spent a considerable amount of time on their work, identifying Myres's scholarship on the southward movement of Greek migration in particular as being "especially helpful," noting that it established "the beginning of a new era for English classical teaching in this respect." [Zimmern, *The Greek Commonwealth*, 459.] In addition, Zimmern began his own book with a rhapsodic description of the unique call of the Mediterranean to ancient Northern ears. From their "cold Northern homes," Zimmern argued, the "prehistoric Achaeans and Dorians... the Galatians and Goths and Longbeards and Vandals and Avars" all "heard the call of the South and thousands of them obeyed it." [17–18.] For more on the relationship between Victorian theories of race and ancient Greece see Debbie Challis, "The Ablest Race: The Ancient Greeks in Victorian Racial Theory," *Classics and Imperialism in the British Empire*, ed. Mark Bradley (Oxford: Oxford University Press, 2010), 94–122.

102. W. Stubbs, *The Constitutional History of England* (Chicago: University of Chicago Press, 1979), 2. Stubbs and Freeman's preference for "Teutons" also expressed itself in their emphatic hostility toward the East. (See, for instance, Freeman's *The Turks in Europe*, (New York: Harper & Brothers, 1877). Curtis's sympathy for Freeman's ideas might also help explain his equally vehement antipathy toward "Oriental despots." For more on the relationship between nineteenth-century racial science and "Saxon" histories, see Parker, "The Failure of Liberal Racialism: The Racial Ideas of E. A. Freeman"; R. Horsman, "Origins of Racial Anglo-Saxonism in Great Britain before 1850," *Journal of the History of Ideas* 37.3 (1976): 387–410. For more on Whig historians and "Teutonic" myths of origin, see R. Janns, "Democratic Myth in Victorian Medievalism," *Browning Institute Studies* 8 (1973): 129–149.

103. E. A. Freeman, *The History of the Norman Conquest*, vol. 5 (Oxford: Clarendon, 1875), 387. Freeman also noted that because of this continuity, "the holders of Liberal principles

in modern politics need never shrink from tracing up our political history to its earliest beginning." [E.A. Freeman, *The Growth of the English Constitution from the Earliest Times* (New York: Frederick and Stokes Co., 1890), 8.]

104. E. A. Freeman, *Comparative Politics* (London: Macmillan and Co., 1896), 24. Freeman maintained in this text that Greek, Roman, and "Teuton" civilizations represented distinct nations within the Aryan linguistic "family." Other authors later complained that Freeman's "theory of Teutonic origins" kept him from appreciating the existence "of representative assemblies in antiquity." [see J. A. O Larsen, "Representation and Democracy in Hellenistic Federalism," *Classical Philology* XL (1945)]. For more on the eighteenth- and nineteenth-century traditions in both Germany and Britain that link Indo-European/Aryan language groups with Greece often in contrast to, or distinction from, "Semitic" languages, see Martin Bernal, *Black Athena: The Fabrication of Ancient Greece* (Rutgers, NJ: Rutgers University Press, 1987).

105. J. Myres, *Geographical History in Greek Lands* (Oxford: Clarendon, 1953), Preface.

106. Zimmern, *The Greek Commonwealth*, 7.

107. Curtis, *The Commonwealth of Nations*, 72.

108. Curtis, *The Commonwealth of Nations*, 90. Curtis relied, in particular, on Freeman's "History of England," *Encyclopedia Britannica*, 10th ed., vol. 8.).

109. Curtis, *The Commonwealth of Nations*, 79.

110. Indeed, this move to link England to Greece had even deeper historical precedents, such as Geoffrey of Monmouth's location of the origins of British history in ancient Troy. See Hugh MacDougal, *Racial Myth in English History* (Montreal: Harvest House Limited, 1982).

111. Curtis, *The Commonwealth of Nations*, 49.

112. In linking the Greek commonwealth to the English Commonwealth to the British Empire, the Round Tablers departed politically from Freeman himself, who opposed British imperial expansion. Curtis was thus forced to spend a considerable amount of time refuting Freeman's stance in a lengthy endnote entitled "Professor Freeman's Expression of the Feeling That the Government of Dependencies is Not in Harmony with the Development of the Principles of the Commonwealth" (*The Commonwealth of Nations*, 227–230). In addition, Curtis's take on the relationship between the Athenian *polis* and the Empire also put the Round Table at odds with the way most nineteenth-century Federationists focused their inquiries on Athenian colonization rather than on the *polis* itself. For more on the federalists' uses of classical history see Duncan Bell, "From Ancient to Modern in Victorian Imperial Thought," *The Historical Journal* 49.3 (2006): 735–759.

113. Curtis, *The Commonwealth of Nations*, 97.

114. Curtis, *The Commonwealth of Nations*, 89.

115. Curtis, *The Commonwealth of Nations*, 147.

116. Curtis, *The Commonwealth of Nations*, 141.

117. Curtis, *The Commonwealth of Nations*, 181.

118. Curtis, *The Commonwealth of Nations*, 146.

119. James Tully, *Public Philosophy in a New Key*, vol. 2 (Cambridge: Cambridge University Press, 2008), 259. In his lucid conclusion to this book, Tully also makes an argument for the presence of a "correlative duty of hospitality" on the part of the host country or the colonized (p. 258). See also Antony Anghie's discussion of the "right" to free trade both in the context of early modern trading companies, late-nineteenth-century international law, and contemporary human rights discourse in *Imperialism, Sovereignty, and the Making of International Law* (Cambridge: Cambridge University Press, 2004).

120. Curtis, *The Commonwealth of Nations*, 62.

121. Kenneth Morgan, *Slavery, Atlantic Trade, and the British Economy, 1660–1800* (Cambridge: Cambridge University Press, 2000), 97.

122. Curtis, *The Commonwealth of Nations*, 166.

123. Curtis, *The Commonwealth of Nations*, 172.

124. See Morgan's discussion of twentieth-century slavery in parts of the British Empire in the Epilogue to *Slavery and the British Empire: From Africa to America* (Oxford: Oxford University Press, 2007), 203.

125. Curtis, *The Commonwealth of Nations*, 173.

126. Curtis, *The Commonwealth of Nations*, 13, 14.

127. Curtis, *The Commonwealth of Nations*, 80.

128. Curtis, *The Commonwealth of Nations*, 148, 150.

129. See for instance John Stuart Mill's "East India Company Petition to Parliament" (1858).

130. Curtis, *The Commonwealth of Nations*, 153.

131. Curtis, *The Commonwealth of Nations*, 14.

132. Curtis, *The Commonwealth of Nations*, 156.

133. Curtis, *The Commonwealth of Nations*, 156.

134. Curtis, *The Commonwealth of Nations*, 14.

135. "The project of a commonwealth is the noblest enterprise yet conceived in the cause of liberty, for it has played a part greater than any before in joining together without binding in chains the diverse families of mankind" (Curtis, *The Commonwealth of Nations*, 177).

136. Curtis, *The Commonwealth of Nations*, 173.

137. Curtis, *The Commonwealth of Nations*, 173.

138. Curtis, *The Commonwealth of Nations*, 175.

139. Curtis, *The Commonwealth of Nations*, 175. Italics mine.

140. Curtis, *The Commonwealth of Nations*, 11.

141. T.H. Marshall, *Citizenship and Social Class* (Cambridge: Cambridge University Press, 1950), 28–29.

142. The Levellers, for instance, argued that all men were "capable of being elected to that supreme trust" of citizenship except for anyone who was a servant, received alms, or "served the late king in arms." [John Lilburne, et al., "An Agreement of the Free People of England," in *The English Levellers* (Cambridge: Cambridge University Press, 1998), 170.] The American Founders obviously excluded slaves from their citizenship calculations, and nearly all the world's democratic states excluded women from suffrage until the early to mid-twentieth-century.

143. See Derek Heater's analysis of Jim Crow laws and "second class citizens" in *A Brief History of Citizenship* (New York: New York University Press, 2004), 92–93.

144. A memo summarizing the argument Curtis was developing in *The Commonwealth of Nations* circulated among the group on May 22, 1914. Mss.Eng.hist.c.836, fol. 91.

145. Curtis, *The Commonwealth of Nations*, 176.

146. Curtis, *The Commonwealth of Nations*, 155.

147. Thomas Babington Macaulay, "Minute of 2 February 1835 on Indian Education," in *Prose and Poetry*, selected by G. M. Young (Cambridge, MA: Harvard University Press, 1957), 721–724.

148. Curtis, *The Commonwealth of Nations*, 176.

149. Curtis, *The Commonwealth of Nations*, 702.

150. Mss.Eng.hist.c.836fol. 117. An internal draft, possibly by Griggs.

151. Bodl. MS. Curtis 836, fol. 91.

152. Curtis, *Commonwealth of Nations*, 176.

153. Mill argued, "a people must be considered unfit for more than a limited and qualified freedom who will not cooperate actively with the law and public authorities in the repression of evil doers...Hindoos will perjure themselves to screen the man who has robbed them rather than take trouble to expose themselves." John Stuart Mill, "On Representative Government," in *On Liberty and Other Essays* (Oxford: Oxford World Classics, 1998), 209.

154. Curtis, *The Problem of the Commonwealth*, 228.

155. For more on the relationship between the Round Table, Curtis, and Kerr in creation of the "trusteeship" component of the Mandate System see William Bain, "The Idea Of Trusteeship in International Society," *The Round Table* 368 (2003): 69. See also Rayford W. Logan, "The Operation of the Mandate System in Africa," *Journal of Negro History* 13.4 (1928): 426.

156. See Parmar's analysis of Curtis's 1936 letter to Kerr where he discusses the origins of Chatham House, in "Anglo-American Elites in the Interwar Years," 56. In this letter, Curtis admitted that "Chatham House was the outcome of Round Table Work" and thus represented merely a "tactical change" in the organization's overall goal which was to continue advocating for a vision of Anglo imperial hegemony—couched as a universal project.

Chapter 4

1. Niall Ferguson, "Is the U.S. an Empire in Denial? A Lecture by Niall Ferguson," Foreign Policy Association Event, September 17, 2003, accessed November 3, 2013, http://www. fpa.org/topics_info2414/topics_info_show.htm?doc_id=193437.

2. Niall Ferguson, *Civilization: The West and the Rest* (New York: Penguin, 2011), 299–300.

3. Niall Ferguson, "An Empire in Denial," *Harvard International Review* 25.3 (2003): 64.

4. Niall Ferguson, *Colossus: The Price of America's Empire* (New York: Penguin, 2004), x. In Bush's words, "These values of freedom are right and true for every person, in every society—and the duty of protecting these values against their enemies is the common calling of freedom-loving people across the globe and across the ages."

5. Niall Ferguson, "Recovering our Nerve," *The National Interest* 76 (2004): 51.

6. Niall Ferguson, "The Problem of Conjecture," in *To Lead The World,* eds. Melvyn P. Leffler and Jeffrey E. Legro (New York: Oxford University Press, 2008), 234.

7. Niall Ferguson, "The Problem of Conjecture," 234, 235.

8. Ferguson, *Civilization,* 299.

9. Niall Ferguson, "Complexity and Collapse," *Foreign Affairs* 89.2 (2010): 22, 30.

10. Ferguson, *Civilization,* 300.

11. Ferguson, *Colossus,* 170.

12. Pankaj Mishra, "Watch This Man," *London Review of Books* 33.21 (November 3, 2011), 8.

13. Examples of this kind of critique were particularly apparent in August and September of 2012 after the publication of Ferguson's article for *Newsweek,* "Hit the Road Barack." I discuss these critiques in more detail below.

14. Pankaj Mishra, "Watch This Man," 10.

15. Ferguson, *Civilization,* 323.

16. Niall Ferguson, "America's 'Oh Sh*t!' Moment," Newsweek, Oct 30, 2011, http://mag.news-week.com/2011/10/30/niall-ferguson-how-american-civilization-can-avoid-collapse.html.

17. Niall Ferguson, "Sinking Globalization," *Foreign Affairs* 84.2 (2005): 68.

18. For more on Ferguson's role in revamping history in British schools see Charlotte Higgins, "Rightwing Historian Given School Curriculum Role," *The Guardian,* Sunday May 30, 2010, accessed October 3, 2013, http://www.guardian.co.uk/politics/2010/may/30/niall-ferguson-school-curriculum-role.

19. For more on McCain's "kitchen cabinet" see John Broder, "McCain Mines Elite of G.O.P. for 2008 Team," *The New York Times,* August 21, 2006, accessed October 3, 2013, http://www.nytimes.com/2006/08/21/washington/21mccain.html?_r=2&oref=slogin&.

20. Michael Lind, "Niall Ferguson and the Brain-Dead American Right," *Salon,* May 24, 2011, accessed October 3, 2013, http://www.salon.com/2011/05/24/lind_niall_fergsuon/.

21. For more on T. H. Green's influence on the Round Table see Kendle, *The Round Table and Imperial Union,* 17–18. Zimmern himself has been credited with coining the term "welfare state" during the 1930s to contrast those European states committed to the social good of all with "warfare states" like that of Nazi Germany. See Kathleen Woodroofe, "The Making of the Welfare State in England: A Summary of its Origin and Development," *The Journal of Social History* 1.2 (1968): 303.

22. See my discussion in Chapter One of Milner, Zimmern, and tariff control.

23. As Ferguson told the *Harvard Magazine* in a 2007 interview, he had become attracted to Thatcherites while an undergraduate at Oxford because they were "clearly the most interesting people there." See Jane Tassel, "The Global Empire of Niall Ferguson," Harvard Magazine, May–June 2007, accessed October 3, 2013, http://harvardmagazine.com/2007/05/the-global-empire-of-nia.html.

24. David Harvey, *A Brief History of Neocolonialism* (New York: Oxford University Press, 2005), 65. For more on the relationship between informal neoliberal imperialism and neoconservative globalism see Martin Orr, "The Failure of Neoliberal Globalization and the End of Empire: Neoliberalism, Imperialism, and the Rise of the Anti-globalization Movement," *International Review of Modern Sociology* 33 (2007): 105–122.

25. Since 2001 there has been a steady stream of publications dealing with the connections between the Bush Administration and the neoconservatives associated with the Project for a

New American Century. Political theorists have been particularly drawn to the connections between the Project and former students of Leo Strauss. See, for instance, Anne Norton, *Leo Strauss and the Politics of American Empire* (New Haven, CT: Yale University Press, 2005) and Nicholas Xenos, "Leo Strauss and the Rhetoric of the War on Terror," *The Logos Reader*, eds. Stephen Bronner, Michael Thompson, (Lexington, KY: University of Kentucky Press, 2006), 59–73. For more on neoliberal economics and the politics of American Empire after 2001, see Susan Roberts, Anna Secor, and Matthew Sparke, "Neoliberal Geopolitics," *Antipode* 35.5 (2003): 886–897.

26. National Bureau of Economic Research, *Globalization in Interdisciplinary Perspective: A Panel* (Chicago: University of Chicago Press, 2003), 556.

27. Mishra, "Watch This Man," 3.

28. Niall Ferguson, *Empire: The Rise and Demise of the British World Order and the Lessons for Global Power* (New York: Basic Books, 2002), xxiii.

29. For one of the first uses of the term by an international economist see Theodore Levitt, "The Globalization of Markets," *Harvard Business Review* 61 (1983): 92-102.

30. Niall Ferguson, "Globalization Without Gunboats?" *Historically Speaking* 4.4 (2003): 34.

31. Ferguson, "Globalization Without Gunboats?" 34.

32. Frederich Hayek, "Notes on the Evolution of Systems of Rules of Conduct," in *Studies in Philosophy, Politics, and Economics* (Chicago: University of Chicago Press, 1967), 77.

33. Niall Ferguson, *Civilization*, 301. For an interesting look at the early work of the Santa Fe Institute see Robert Pool's "Strange Bedfellows," *Science* 245.4919 (1989): 700–703.

34. See, for example, Samir Rihani, *Complex Systems Theory and Development Practice* (London: Zed Books, 2002) and Neil Harrison, *Complexity in World Politics: Concepts and Methods of a New Paradigm* (Albany, NY: SUNY Press, 2007).

35. Ferguson, "Complexity and Collapse," 2.

36. Ferguson, "Complexity and Collapse," 3.

37. Niall Ferguson, "Fiscal Crisis and Imperial Collapses: Historical Perspective on Current Predicaments," Ninth Annual Niarchos Lecture, Even Transcript, Peterson Institute for International Economics, Washington, DC, May 13, 2010, 17, accessed October 3, 2013, http://www.petersoninstitute.org/publications/papers/niarchos-ferguson-2010.pdf.

38. Ferguson, "Complexity and Collapse," 2.

39. Ferguson, "Complexity and Collapse," 3.

40. Ferguson, *Civilization*, 298, 299. Ferguson's examples of historians who imagine time in terms of cycles or patterns include not only historical figures like Toynbee, Spengler, Marx, and Hegel, but also contemporary scholars like Paul Kennedy and Jared Diamond.

41. Andrew Haldane, "Rethinking the Financial Network," speech delivered at the Financial Student Association, Amsterdam, Bank of England, accessed November 3, 2013 http://www.bis.org/review/r090505e.pdf.

42. Ferguson, "Complexity and Collapse," 2.

43. Ferguson, "Complexity and Collapse," 3.

44. Niall Ferguson, "Our Currency, Your Problem," New York Times, March 13, 2005, accessed October 3, 2013, http://www.wright.edu/~tdung/AsianBanks_NiallFerguson.pdf.

45. David Harvey, *The Enigma of Capital and the Crisis of Capitalism* (New York: Profile Books, 2011), 107–108.

46. Ferguson, "Complexity and Collapse," 4.

47. Ferguson, *Civilization*, xx.

48. Michel Foucault, *The Order of Things: An Archaeology of the Human Sciences* (New York: Vintage Books, 1994), 109. [Originally published 1970.]

49. Hayden White, *The Content of the Form: Narrative Discourse and Historical Representation* (Baltimore, MD: The John Hopkins University Press, 1990), ix.

50. Niall Ferguson, *Virtual History: Alternatives and Counterfactuals* (New York: Basic Books, 1999), 63.

51. Ferguson, "Complexity and Collapse," 3.

52. Niall Ferguson, "A Powerful Leap From Chaos," *Nature* 408.2 (2000): 21.

53. Niall Ferguson, *The Cash Nexus: Money and Power in the Modern World, 1700–2000* (New York: Basic Books, 2001), 6.

54. Ferguson, *Virtual History,* 89.

55. Ferguson, *Virtual History,* 89.

56. Ferguson, *Virtual History,* 88..

57. Ferguson, *Colossus,* xii.

58. Ferguson, *Civilization,* xx.

59. See Niall Ferguson, *The Pity of War* (New York: Basic Books, 1999), 51–52 and Ferguson, *Virtual History,* 237–238. Not only is Ferguson's point the same in these two books, his prose is also identical.

60. See Bernard Porter's excellent analysis of the impact of the South African War on anti-imperial thought in Britain in *Critics of Empire* (London: IB Taurus, 2008). For a closer treatment of Fabian pro-imperialism during this period, see Gregory Claeys, *Imperial Skeptics* (Cambridge: Cambridge University Press, 2010), 180–198.

61. Ferguson, *Empire,* 267.

62. Ferguson, *Empire,* 267–270.

63. Ferguson, *Colossus,* xxviii, 287.

64. Ferguson, "Recovering our Nerve," 54.

65. Ferguson, "Ninth Annual Niarchos Lecture, Fiscal Crises and Imperial Collapses: Historical Perspectives on Current Predicaments," 3.

66. Ferguson, "America's 'Oh Sh*t!' Moment," 1.

67. Ferguson, "America's 'Oh Sh*t!' Moment," 3.

68. Ferguson, "Complexity and Collapse," 5.

69. Ferguson, *Civilization,* 311.

70. Ferguson, *Civilization,* 324.

71. Ferguson, *Civilization,* 325.

72. Priyamvada Gopal, "The Story Peddled by Imperial Apologists is a Poisonous Fairytale," *The Guardian,* Wednesday June 28, 2006, accessed October 3, 2013, http://www.guardian. co.uk/britain/article/0,,1807642,00.html.

73. Matthew O'Brien, "A Full Fact-Check of Niall Ferguson's Very Bad Argument Against Obama," *The Atlantic,* Aug. 20, 2012, accessed October 3, 2013, http://www.theatlantic. com/business/archive/2012/08/afull-fact-check-of-niall-fergusons-very-bad-argument-a gainst-obama/261306/.

74. Matthew O'Brien, "The Age of Niallism: Ferguson and the Post-Fact World," *The Atlantic,* August 24, 2012, accessed October 3, 2013, http://www.theatlantic.com/business/ archive/2012/08/the-age-of-niallismferguson-and-the-post-fact-world/261395/.

75. Eric Zuesse, "The Shamefulness of Niall Ferguson," *The Huffington Post,* August 23, 2012, accessed October 3, 2013, http://www.huffingtonpost.com/eric-zuesse/ the-shamefulness-of-niall_b_1824651.html75.

76. Ferguson, *Civilization,* 76.

77. See, for example, Bruce Masters, *Christians and Jews in the Ottoman Arab World: The Roots of Secularism* (Cambridge: Cambridge University Press, 2001). According to Masters, the autonomy granted by Ottoman sultans to "various social groupings" afforded "the Christians and Jews in the Ottoman world fairly wide ranging freedom to order their communal affairs as they saw fit" (42). The religious communities, he argued, "were psychologically separated from each other if not separated by law" (17).

78. Ferguson, *Civilization,* 210.

79. Karl Marx and Friedrich Engels, "The Manifesto of The Communist Party," in *The Marx-Engels Reader,* ed. Robert C. Tucker (New York: W. W. Norton, 1978), 488.

80. Michel Foucault, "On The Ways of Writing History," *Aesthetics, Method, and Epistemology: Essential Works of Foucault, 1954–1984* (New York: The New Press, 1999), 280.

81. Niall Ferguson, "Hegemony or Empire," *Foreign Affairs* 82.5 (2003): 1.

82. Ferguson, *Colossus,* 2.

83. Ferguson discusses his fears about the decline of Europe's white population in "Eurabia?," *The New York Times Magazine,* April 4, 2004, accessed October 3, 2013, http://www.nytimes. com/2004/04/04/magazine/04WWLN.html. For Ferguson's recent thoughts on China

see his 2012 series for Channel 4, "China, Triumph and Turmoil." Phillip Sherwell sums up both the series and Ferguson's understanding of the potentially dangerous impact of a new Chinese Empire in an article for *The Telegraph*, "Niall Ferguson: China's Got the Whole World in its Hands," March 11, 2012, accessed October 3, 2013, http://www.telegraph.co.uk/news/worldnews/asia/china/9135590/Niall-Ferguson-Chinas-got-thewhole-wo rld-in-its-hands.html.

84. Again, see John M. Hobson's account of the "Aryan/Teutonic relay race" at the heart of some of last century's imperial histories, including those of Woodrow Wilson. Hobson, *The Eurocentric Conception of World Politics*, 170.

85. For Ferguson, it is precisely when freedom (in this case, freedom of trade) is stymied and when we see a rise of "protectionism in less developed countries" that "global prosperity declines." *Colossus*, 177.

86. Ferguson's thoughts on the third world and tariffs in *Colossus*, 166.

87. For Ferguson's full thoughts on the relationship between anti-capitalism and "radical Islam" see his 2006 interview with the *Boston Globe*. "The great category error of our time," he argues, "is to equate radical Islamism with fascism. If you actually read what Osama bin Laden says, it's clearly Lenin plus the Koran. It's internationalist, revolutionary, and anti-capitalist rhetoric far more of the left than of the right. And radical Islamism is good at recruiting within our society, within western society generally. In western Europe, to an extent people underestimate here, the appeal of radical Islamism extends beyond Muslim communities." Harvey Blume, "Q and A with Niall Ferguson," *Boston Globe*, September 24, 2006.

88. "Civil government," Smith thus observed, "so far as it is instituted for the security of property is in reality instituted for the defense of the rich against the poor, or of those who have some property against those who have none at all." Adam Smith, *An Inquiry Into The Nature and Causes of The Wealth of Nations: Selected Passages* (Oxford: Oxford University Press, 1998), Book V, Part II.

89. Ferguson, *Empire*, 310.

90. G. A. Cohen, "Capitalism, Freedom, and the Proletariat," in *The Idea of Freedom: Essays In Honour of Isaiah Berlin*, ed. Alan Ryan (Oxford: Oxford University Press, 1979), 11.

91. Ferguson, "Globalization in Interdisciplinary Perspective: A Panel," 566.

92. James Tully, "Lineages of Contemporary Imperialism," in *Lineages of Empire: The Historical Roots of British Imperial Thought*, ed. Duncan Kelly (Oxford: Oxford University Press, 2009), 11.

93. Ferguson, *Empire*, 308.

94. Ferguson, *Empire*, 304.

95. Niall Ferguson, "China Marches Again, Tyrannous and Toxic," *The Telegraph*, September 9, 2007, accessed October 3, 2013, http://www.telegraph.co.uk/comment/personal-view/3642553/China-marches-again-tyrannousand-toxic.html.

96. See James Tully's excellent summation of informal imperialism in "Lineages of Contemporary Imperialism." Anghie's genealogy of contemporary international law in *Imperialism, Sovereignty, and the Making of the Modern State* (Cambridge: Cambridge University Press, 2007) also traces the vestiges of imperial forms of economic and political domination in contemporary international institutions.

97. For more on Ferguson's lawsuit see Peter Beaumont, "Niall Ferguson Threatens to Sue Over Accusation of Racism," *The Guardian*, November 26, 2011, accessed October 3, 2013, http://www.guardian.co.uk/books/2011/nov/26/niall-ferguson-pankaj-mishra-review.

98. Ferguson, *Empire*, 24.

99. Ferguson, *Civilization*, 71, xxvii.

100. A notable absence in most of Ferguson's work is any mention of Gandhi's reading of Western civilization in 1909's *Hind Swaraj*. Ferguson quotes *Hind Swaraj* briefly in *Civilization*, but only to misinterpret Gandhi's meaning. For an excellent and detailed overview of some of the nineteenth-century Asian intellectuals whose ideas have been largely ignored by imperial historians see Pankaj Mishra, *From the Ruins of Empire* (New York: Farrar, Straus and Giroux, 2012).

101. Said, *Culture and Imperialism*, 22.

102. Ferguson, *Civilization*, xxvii.

103. Ferguson, *Empire*, xv, 155, 59.

104. Ferguson, *Civilization*, 11–113.

105. Bill Ashcroft, *Post-Colonial Transformation* (New York: Routledge, 2001), 101.

106. Ferguson, *Civilization*, 8.

107. Ferguson, *Empire*, xxv.

108. Ferguson, *Civilization*, 8.

109. Ferguson, *Empire*, xxi.

110. Ferguson, *Civilization*, 49

111. Ferguson, *Colossus*, 174.

112. Ferguson, *Empire*, xxvi.

113. Thanks to Onur Ulas Ince both for directing me toward the Fischer book and for his own work on disavowal in his dissertation, "Colonial Capitalism and the Dilemmas of Liberalism."

114. Sibylle Fischer, *Modernity Disavowed: Haiti and the Cultures of Slavery in the Age of Revolution* (Durham, NC: Duke University Press, 2004), 38.

115. Fischer, *Modernity Disavowed*, 38.

116. Fischer, *Modernity Disavowed*, 38.

117. Ferguson, *Empire*, xxii.

118. Ferguson, *Empire*, 90.

119. Ferguson, *Empire*, 163.

120. Ferguson, *Colossus*, 184.

121. Ferguson, *Colossus*, 26.

122. In 1947 Harold Laski would use precisely this language to declare that now "America bestrides the world like a colossus; neither Rome at the height of its powers nor Great Britain in the period of its economic supremacy enjoyed an influence so direct, so profound, pervasive." Harold Laski, "America—1947," *The Nation* 165 (1947), 641.

123. Ferguson, *Colossus*, 26.

124. Ferguson, *Civilization*, 311.

125. Ferguson, *Empire*, 185.

126. Ferguson, *Empire*, 268.

127. Ferguson, *Empire*, 269

128. Ferguson, *Empire*, 275.

129. Ferguson, *Empire*, 279–278.

130. Ferguson, *Empire*, 284.

131. Ferguson, *Empire*, 288.

132. Ferguson, *Empire*, 316.

133. For an example of Ferguson's occasional tendency to put his foot in his mouth in a spectacular way, look to the 2013 John Maynard Keyenes episode. See Paul Harris, "Niall Ferguson apologises for remarks about 'gay and childless' Keynes," *The Gaurdian*, May 4, 2013, accessed October 3, 2013, http://www.guardian.co.uk/books/2013/may/04/niall-ferguson-apologises-gay-keynes.

134. The article's author, David Austin Walsh, felt that interviewing two members of the department was sufficient enough evidence to conclude that all of his colleagues, except his LGBT colleagues, supported him. See article, May 13, 2013, accessed October 3, 2013, http://hnn.us/articles/niall-fergusons-harvard-colleagues-support-him-not-lgbt-historians.

Chapter 5

1. Jan Smuts, *The League of Nations: A Practical Suggestion* (London: Hodder and Stoughton, 1918), 10.

2. Smuts, *The League of Nations*, 32.

3. Smuts, *The League of Nations*, 10, 26, 8.

4. Smuts, *The League of Nations*, 11, 9.

5. Smuts, *The League of Nations*, 30, 32, 29. Smuts's text vacillates between capitalizing and not capitalizing "league" and "nations" seemingly without attention to context.

6. Mark Mazower, *No Enchanted Palace: The End of Empire and the Ideological Origins of the United Nations* (Princeton, NJ: Princeton University Press, 2009), 30. Mazower's chapter on Smuts provides an excellent analysis of Smuts's long-term influence on both interwar internationalism and the Charter of the United Nations.

7. Jan Smuts, "The Future Constitutional Relations in the Empire," in *War-Time Speeches: A Compilation of Public Utterances in Great Britain* (New York: George Doran Co., 1917), 16.

8. Bill Schwarz, *The White Man's World* (Oxford: Oxford University Press), 280.

9. See F. S. Crafford's discussion of Smuts the imperial "Handyman" in *Jan Smuts: A Biography* (New York: Doubleday, 1943), 106, 132.

10. Mazower is one of the few contemporary critics of Smuts who reads his international thought as a "political expression of his own philosophy of holism." See *No Enchanted Palace*, 58.

11. Robert Lansing, "A Memorandum by Robert Lansing on Wilson's First 'Paris Draft' of the Covenant of the League of Nations," quoted in William Bain, *Between Anarchy and Society: Trusteeship and the Obligations of Power* (Oxford: Oxford University Press, 2003), 93.

12. Letter from Maitland to Smuts, June 15, 1894, in W. K. Hancock, *Selections from the Smuts Papers: Volume 1, June 1886–May 1902* (Cambridge: Cambridge University Press, 1966), 33.

13. Jan Smuts, *A Century of Wrong* (London: Review of Reviews Office, 1900), ix.

14. Jan Smuts, "The British Commonwealth of Nations," in *War-Time Speeches*, 5.

15. See Shula Marks's fascinating exploration of Smuts's relationship to liberals and English feminists in "White Masculinity: Jan Smuts, Race, and the South African War," *Proceedings of the British Academy* 11 (2001): 199–203, 206.

16. Interview with Edward Marshall, "Democracy and the War," in *War-Time Speeches*, 99.

17. *Daily Telegraph*, October 5, 1917, from "Preface," in *The Coming Victory, A Speech Made By General Jan Smuts, Oct. 4, 1917* (London: Hodder and Stoughton, 1917).

18. Carroll Quigley, *The Anglo-American Establishment: From Rhodes to Cliveden* (New York: Books in Focus, 1981), 77.

19. Letter from Smuts to J. X. Merriman, March 13, 1906, in *Selections from the Smuts Papers*, vol. II, 288.

20. Letter from Smuts to Isie Smuts, June, 2 1901, in *Selections from the Smuts Papers*, vol. II, 394.

21. Smuts, "Memorandum to Labour Commission, 1903," in *Selections from the Smuts Papers,*, vol. II, 130.

22. W. K. Hancock, *Smuts, The Sanguine Years, 1870–1919*, (Cambridge: Cambridge University Press, 1962), 346. Smuts's conflict with Gandhi during this era is well known. His highly sympathetic biographer, Crafford, mirrored Smuts's own population paranoia when he noted that, in facing down Gandhi, Smuts took on "Mother India with her teeming millions." See F.S. Crafford, *Jan Smuts: A Biography*, 63.

23. In a 1914 speech before the Union Parliament entitled "The Syndicalist Conspiracy in South Africa; A Scathing Indictment," Smuts used the miners' attempted strike as "an example to the people of South Africa of what might happen if there was a general strike, if the white people of the country started fighting and anarchy was afoot. A body of about 9,000 natives broke out of the compound at the Jagersfontein mine and invaded the town and had it not been for the extremely gallant behavior of the inhabitants of Jagersfontein very much more terrible might have occurred." Jan Smuts, "The Syndicalist Conspiracy in South Africa; A Scathing Indictment. Revised, Published by the Authority of the Minister of Defense, General J.C. Smuts" (Printed and Published by the Cape Times Limited, 1914), 21.

24. Jan Smuts, 1909 speech to the Legislative Council of the Transvaal Colony, in *Selections from the Smuts Papers*, vol. II, 556.

25. Smuts, 1909 speech to the Legislative Council, 554.

26. Smuts, "South and Central Africa," *War-Time Speeches*, 81.

27. Jan Smuts, Letter to D. Moore, March 2, 1947, *Selections From the Smuts Papers*, vol. VII, 136.

28. Hancock recounts the general tenor of Smuts's correspondences with "friends in Britain," who were, according to Hancock, "prone to put the blame [for the war] upon the British Government," or, in Emily Hobhouse's words, "our wretched Imperialists." See Hancock, *Smuts, The Sanguine Years*, 377

29. Letter from Merriman to Smuts, March 18, 1906, in *Selections from the Smuts Papers*, vol. II, 245.

30. Saul Dubow, "Smuts, the United Nations, and the Rhetoric of Race and Rights," *Journal of Contemporary History* 43 (2008): 51.
31. See Schwarz's analysis of this in *The White Man's World*, 305–308.
32. Schwarz, *The White Man's World*, 305–308.
33. Dubow, "Smuts, the United Nations, and the Rhetoric of Race and Rights," 57.
34. Marks, "White Masculinity: Jan Smuts, Race, and the South African War," 213.
35. See "Jan Christiaan Smuts, The Round Table's Oldest Friend," *The Round Table* 41 (1950): 3–21.
36. Crafford, *Jan Smuts: A Biography*, 140.
37. A letter from Hancock to Canon C. E. Raven, January 8, 1952, quoted from Kosmas Tsokhas, "A Search for Transcendence: Philosophical and Religious Dialogues in W. K. Hancock's Biography of J. C. Smuts," *The Round Table* 358 (2001): 72. Also see Hancock's *Smuts: The Sanguine Years*, 310–311.
38. For an examination of Smuts's influence on systems theory see J. C. Poynton, "Smuts's Holism and Evolution Sixty Years On," *The Royal Society of South Africa* 46 (1987). Peder Anker also has an extensive discussion of Smuts's relationship with philosophers of holism, including Quine, in *Imperial Ecology: Environmental Order in the British Empire, 1895–1945* (Cambridge, MA: Harvard University Press, 2001). For a discussion of Smuts's reception by holistic psychology, see Camilo E. Khatchikian, "A Holistic Perspective on Natural Sciences," in *Striving for Wholeness: Creating Theoretical Synthesis*, ed. Rainer Diriwachter (London: Transaction Publishers, 2008). Christina Steyn identifies Smuts as a "prophet" of New Age philosophy in "South African New Age Prophets: Past and Present," *Religion and Theology* 9 (2002): 282–296. Andrew Dobson includes an excerpt from Smuts's *Holism and Evolution* in *The Green Reader* (along with Vandana Shiva, Rachel Carson, and Aldous Huxley.) According to Dobson's introduction, Smuts's philosophical holism ought to be read as an "attempt to heal the wounds between human beings and the natural world." *The Green Reader* (San Francisco, CA: Mercury House, 1991), 255.
39. Notably, Anker's 2001 book *Imperial Ecology* takes a close look at the relationship between Smuts's holism, his writings as an amateur botanist, and his understanding of race in South Africa. See also Marks's "White Masculinity: Jan Smuts, Race, and the South African War," and Noel Garson, "Smuts and the Idea of Race," *South African Historical Journal* 57 (2007): 153–178. Finally, Schwarz's excellent chapter on Smuts in *The White Man's World* explores the memorializing of Smuts in the context of his racism, his holism, and his long-term interest in imperial politics.
40. Hancock returns repeatedly to Smuts's love for nature, synthesis, and holism in *The Sanguine Years*. See also Kate Fletcher's interesting analysis of his relationship to Oxford liberal Hegelians in "Smuts, Philosophy, and Education," *South African Historical Journal* 34 (1996): 106–126.
41. Jan Smuts, "Law, A Liberal Study," quoted from Naphtali Levy, *Jan Smuts, Being a Character Sketch of Gen. the Hon. J.C. Smuts, K.C., M.L.A., Minister of Defense, Union of South Africa* (London: Longman's, 1917), 13.
42. See excerpt from this manuscript in *Selections from the Smuts Papers*, vol. I, 59.
43. Smuts, *Selections from the Smuts Papers*, vol. I, 59.
44. Again, Smuts's efforts in this regard also recall the work of British idealists, particularly those like Hobhouse who were, at the time, reformulating Spencer's approach to evolution along more liberal lines that reflected their concern both for human agency and social cooperation. See Fletcher, "Smuts, Philosophy, and Education."
45. Marks, "White Masculinity: Jan Smuts, Race, and the South African War," 204.
46. Smuts, "An Inquiry Into the Unification of the Whole," *Selections from the Smuts Papers*, vol. III, 69.
47. Smuts, "An Inquiry Into the Unification of the Whole," 83.
48. Smuts, "An Inquiry Into the Unification of the Whole," 70.
49. Jan Smuts, *Holism and Evolution* (New York: Macmillan, 1926), 91.
50. Smuts, *Holism and Evolution*, 91.
51. Smuts, *Holism and Evolution*, 103.
52. Smuts, *Holism and Evolution* 316.

53. Smuts, *Holism and Evolution*, 312.

54. Smuts, *Holism and Evolution*, 291.

55. Smuts, *Holism and Evolution*, 109.

56. Smuts, *Holism and Evolution*, 240.

57. Fletcher, "Smuts, Philosophy, and Education," 117.

58. Smuts, *Holism and Evolution*, 344–345.

59. Marks, "White Masculinity: Jan Smuts, Race, and the South African War," 204.

60. Gerson, "Smuts and the Idea of Race," 159.

61. Smuts, Speech on the Draft Constitution made to the Legislative Council of the Transvaal Colony, April 3, 1909, *Selections from the Smuts Papers*, vol. II, June 1902–May 1910, 556.

62. Smuts, "The Future of South and Central Africa," in *War-Time Speeches*, 75.

63. Smuts, "The Future of South and Central Africa," in *War-Time Speeches*, 77

64. Wendy Brown develops this notion of "constitutive outside" briefly in her discussion of Marcuse in *Edgework: Critical Essays on Knowledge and Politics* (Princeton, NJ: Princeton University Press, 2005), but gives a fuller account in *Politics Out of History* (Princeton, NJ: Princeton University Press, 2001), particularly in Chapter One.

65. Smuts, "The Future of South and Central Africa," in *War-Time Speeches*, 80.

66. Smuts, *The League of Nations*, 29.

67. Smuts, "Foreword," in *War-Time Speeches*, v.

68. Smuts, "The War and Some Empire Problems," in *War-Time Speeches*, 7.

69. Smuts, "Constitutional Relations," in *War-Time Speeches*, 14.

70. Smuts, *Holism and Evolution*, 103.

71. Smuts, "The War and Empire Problems," in *War-Time Speeches*, 6; Smuts, "The Commonwealth of Nations," in *War-Time Speeches*, 32.

72. Smuts, "Constitutional Relations," in *War-Time Speeches*, 11.

73. Quoted in Anthony Pagden, "Fellow Citizens and Imperial Subjects: Conquest and Sovereignty in Europe's Overseas Empires," *History and Theory* 44.4 (2005): 42.

74. Smuts, "The Commonwealth of Nations," in *War-Time Speeches*, 26.

75. Smuts, "Constitutional Relations," in *War-Time Speeches*, 12.

76. Smuts, "The British Commonwealth of Nations," in *War-Time Speeches*, 27; Smuts, "Constitutional Relations," in *War-Time Speeches*, 12.

77. Smuts, "The British Commonwealth of Nations," in *War-Time Speeches*, 26.

78. Smuts, "The Future Constitutional Relations of the Empire," in *War-Time Speeches*, 16.

79. According to Quigley, Smuts knew Curtis and Kerr, and was friends with Rhodes and Milner, and worked with them closely both after the Boer War and again in 1917 at the Imperial War Conference (*The Anglo American Establishment*, 77–79). When Smuts died he was memorialized in the *Round Table* journal in an article titled "Jan Christiaan Smuts, The Round Table's Oldest Friend."

80. Smuts "Commonwealth of Nations," in *War-Time Speeches*, 27.

81. From Karen O'Brien's "Protestantism and the Poetry of Empire," quoted in P. J. Marshall, "Britain and the World in the Eighteenth Century: Reshaping the Empire," *Transactions of the Royal Historical Society* 8 (1998): 5.

82. P. J. Marshall deals with the period between Britain's loss of much of the empire in North America and solidification of empire in India in *The Making and Unmaking of Empires: Britain, India, and America, c. 1750–1783* (Oxford: Oxford University Press, 2007). His 1998 article, "Britain and the World in the Eighteenth Century," speaks specifically to the shift in rhetorical explanations of the Empire's purpose that accompanied this change.

83. Smuts, "The War and the Empire," in *War-Time Speeches*, 36; Smuts, "The War and Empire Problems," in *War-Time Speeches*, 6; Smuts, "Freedom," in *War-Time Speeches*, 64.

84. Smuts, "The War and the Empire," in *War-Time Speeches*, 34.

85. Smuts, "Constitutional Relations," in *War-Time Speeches*, 12.

86. Smuts "Constitutional Relations," in *War-Time Speeches*, 13.

87. Smuts, "Commonwealth of Nations," in *War-Time Speeches*, 29.

88. Smuts, "Constitutional Relations," in *War-Time Speeches*, 13, 14.

89. Smuts, "The British Commonwealth of Nations," in *War-Time Speeches*, 32.

90. The King, Smuts thus argued, "is not your King, but the King of all of us, ruling over every part of the whole Commonwealth of nations." "The British Commonwealth of Nations," in *War-Time Speeches*, 29.

91. In Crafford's words, Smuts's conflict with Gandhi "resolved itself into a duel" that was "watched with interest by almost the whole of the English-Speaking world outside America" (Crafford, *Jan Smuts: A Biography*, 69). Smuts was forced to deal with Gandhi first as Transvaal Colonial Secretary and then as Minister of the Interior. Their negotiations and conflicts were so prolonged that Huttenback subtitled a chapter of his 1971 book "Gandhi versus Smuts." See Robert Huttenback, *Gandhi in South Africa: British Imperialism and the Indian Question, 1860–1914* (Ithaca, NY: Cornell University Press, 1971).

92. Smuts, "The Commonwealth of Nations," in *War-Time Speeches*, 26.

93. Smuts, "A League of Nations," in *War-Time Speeches*, 55.

94. Smuts, "A League of Nations, in *War-Time Speeches*, 55.

95. See, for example, Mill's discussion of equity and "reasonable wages" for workers and "reasonable profits" for capitalists in *Principles of Political Economy*, vol. I (New York: D. Appleton and Co., 1896), 442. More recently, Rawls explored the relationship between equity and equality in his much lauded and criticized notion of "the difference principle." See Chapter 13 of *A Theory of Justice* (Cambridge, MA: Harvard University Press, 2003).

96. Smuts, "The Commonwealth of Nations," in *War-Time Speeches*, 27.

97. Smuts, "The War and Empire Problems," in *War-Time Speeches*, 6; Smuts, "The Future Constitutional Relations of the Empire," in *War-Time Speeches*, 11.

98. Smuts, *The League of Nations: A Practical Suggestion*, 9.

99. Smuts, *The League of Nations*, 11.

100. Smuts, *The League of Nations*, 12.

101. Smuts, *The League of Nations*, 12.

102. "The Covenant of the League of Nations," The Avalon Project: Documents in Law, History, and Diplomacy, accessed January 12, 2012, http://avalon.law.yale.edu/20th_century/leag-cov.asp#art22.

103. Smuts, *The League of Nations*, 6.

104. Smuts, *The League of Nations*, 15.

105. Smuts, *The League of Nations*, 16.

106. Smuts, *The League of Nations*, 22.

107. Smuts, *The League of Nations*, 22.

108. Smuts, *The League of Nations*, 71.

109. Smuts, *The League of Nations*, 47.

110. Smuts, *The League of Nations*, 71.

111. Smuts, *The League of Nations*, 29.

112. Smuts, *The League of Nations*, 33.

113. Alice Clark reminded Smuts of this in a letter she wrote to him later that spring, after Smuts broke with Lloyd George over the terms of the Armistice. "You are not appointed by Lloyd George," she wrote, "and you are only responsible for South Africa." Letter from Alice Clark, May, 19, 1919, *Selections from the Smuts Papers*, vol. IV, 171.

114. Woodrow Wilson's Fourteen Points, The Avalon Project: Documents in Law, History, and Diplomacy, January, 8, 1918, accessed January 12, 2013, http://avalon.law.yale.edu/20th_century/wilson14.asp.

115. In Britain and America, this popularity was due in large part to lobbying by pro-League groups during the war such as the League of Nations Society. See Henry Winkler, *The League of Nations Movement in Great Britain* (New Brunswick, NJ: Rutgers University Press, 1952).

116. Smuts, *The League of Nations*, 15.

117. Mazower, *No Enchanted Palace*, 45.

118. Smuts, letter to Alice Clark, January 15, 1919, *Selections from the Smuts Papers*, vol. IV, 42.

119. See Christian Reus-Smit, "The Constitutional Structure of International Society and the Nature of Fundamental Institutions," *International Organization* 51.4 (1997): 580.

120. For more on Smuts's influence on the Mandate System and the changes to Smuts's original plan see Antony Anghie, "Colonialism and the Birth of International Institutions: Sovereignty, Economy, and the Mandate System of the League of Nations," *New York University Journal*

of International Law and Politics 35 (2002): 513–633. See also, George Curry, "Woodrow Wilson, Jan Smuts, and the Versailles Settlement," *American Historical Review* 66.4 (1961): 968–986.

121. League of Nations, Secretariat, Information Section, *The League of Nations: The Mandate System* (Geneva: Information Section, League of Nations Secretariat, 1927), 7–8.

122. *The League of Nations: The Mandate System*, 17.

123. Parker Moon, *Imperialism and World Politics* (New York: MacMillan, 1930), 480.

124. See Peter Marshall, "Smuts and the Preamble to the UN Charter," *Round Table* 358 (2001): 55–65. See also, Otto Spijker, "Global Values in the United Nations Charter," *Netherlands International Law Review* 59.3 (2012): 361-397.

125. Antony Anghie, "Decolonizing the Concept of 'Good Governance,'" in *Decolonizing International Relations*, ed. Branwen Gruffydd Jones (New York: Rowman and Littlefield, 2006), 124.

126. See, for example, "Our Global Neighborhood," Report of the UN Commission on Global Governance, 1995.

127. James Rosenau, "Governance in the Twenty First Century," in *The Global Governance Reader*, ed. Rorden Wilkinson (New York: Routledge, 2005), 46.

128. James Rosenau, "Citizenship in a Changing Global Order," in *Governance Without Government: Order and Change in World Politics*, ed. James Rosenau (Cambridge: Cambridge University Press, 1992), 278.

129. Daniel Schorr, "Haiti Quake Highlights Need for Trusteeship," National Public Radio, January 20, 2010, accessed October 4, 2013, http://www.npr.org/templates/story/story.php?storyId=122777067.

130. Michael Ignatieff, "The Seductiveness of Moral Disgust," *Social Research* 71.3 (2004): 566.

Chapter 6

1. "Overview of America's National Security Strategy," *The National Security Strategy of the United States of America*, March 2006, accessed November 5, 2013, http://georgewbush-whitehouse. archives.gov/nsc/nss/2006/sectionI.html.

2. "The Foreign Policy Top 100 Global Thinkers," *Foreign Policy*, December 2009, accessed October 7, 2013, http://www.foreignpolicy.com/articles/2009/11/30/the_fp_top_100_global_thinkers?print=yes& hidecomments=yes&page=full.

3. Linda Diebel, "Ignatieff Apologizes for Isreali War Crime Comment," *Toronto Star*, April 14, 2008, A3.

4. Michael Ignatieff, *Human Rights as Politics and Idolatry* (Princeton, NJ: Princeton University Press, 2001), 55.

5. Michael Ignateiff, "The Myth of Citizenship," in *Theorizing Citizenship*, ed. Ronald Beiner (Albany, NY: SUNY Press, 1995), 65.

6. Ignatieff, *Human Rights as Politics and Idolatry*, 57.

7. Michael Ignatieff, *Blood and Belonging: Journeys into the New Nationalism* (New York: Farrar, Strauss, and Giroux, 1994), 6.

8. Michael Ignatieff, "The Attack on Human Rights," *Foreign Affairs* 80.6 (2001): 116.

9. Michael Ignatieff, "Reimagining a Global Ethic," *Ethics and International Affairs* 26.1 (2012): 18.

10. Ignatieff, *Human Rights as Politics and Idolatry*, 84.

11. Ignatieff, *Human Rights as Politics and Idolatry*, 88.

12. Michael Ignatieff, *Isaiah Berlin: A Life* (New York: Metropolitan Books, 1998), 291.

13. Michael Ignatieff, "Berlin in Autumn: The Philosopher in Old Age," Doreen B. Townsend Center Occasional Papers, 16, Berkeley, CA, 50.

14. Michael Ignatieff, *The Needs of Strangers* (New York: Viking, 1985).

15. Ignatieff, *Blood and Belonging, Journeys into the New Nationalism* (New York: Farrar, Strauss, and Giroux, 1993), 14.

16. See, for instance, Smaro Kamboureli's critique of Ignatieff in "Staging Cultural Criticism: Michael Ignatieff's *Blood and Belonging* and Myrna Kostash's *Bloodlines*," *Journal of Canadian Studie,* 31 (1996): 166–187.

17. Michael Ignatieff, *The Warrior's Honor: Ethnic War and the Modern Conscience* (New York: Metropolitan Books, 1998), 8.

18. Ignatieff, *The Warrior's Honor*, 190.

19. Michael Ignatieff, "The Burden," *The New York Times Magazine*, January 5, 2003, 25.

20. Ignatieff, "The Burden," 24.

21. Michael Ignatieff, *Empire Lite: Nation Building in Bosnia, Kosovo and Afghanistan* (London: Vintage, 2003), 2.

22. Ignatieff, "The Burden," 24.

23. Michael Ignatieff, "Barbarians at the Gate?" *New York Review of Books*, February 28, 2002, accessed October 7, 2013, http://www.nybooks.com/articles/archives/2002/feb/28/barbarians-at-the-gate/.

24. Ignatieff, *The Warrior's Honor*, 7–8.

25. "The Responsibility to Protect," *Report of the International Commission on State Sovereignty*, co-chairs, Gareth Evans, Mohamed Sahnoun (Ottawa: International Development Research Centre, 2001), 75.

26. Michael Ignatieff, "The Seductiveness of Moral Disgust," *Social Research* 71.3 (2004, originally published Spring 1995): 549.

27. Ignatieff, "The Seductiveness of Moral Disgust," 550.

28. Ignatieff, "The Seductiveness of Moral Disgust," 566.

29. Michael Ignatieff, *The Lesser Evil: Political Ethics in an Age of Terror* (Princeton, NJ: Princeton University Press, 2004), 146.

30. Ignatieff, *The Lesser Evil*, 19.

31. Ignatieff, *The Lesser Evil*, 137, 138, 47.

32. Ignatieff, *The Lesser Evil*, 168.

33. Ignatieff, *Empire Lite*, 25.

34. Ignatieff, *Empire Lite*, 23.

35. Ignatieff, *The Lesser Evil*, 142, 168.

36. Ignatieff, *The Lesser Evil*, 135, 153.

37. Ignatieff, *The Lesser Evil*, 23.

38. Ignatieff, *The Lesser Evil*, 17.

39. Michael Ignatieff, "It's War—But It Doesn't Have to Be Dirty," *The Guardian*, September 30, 2001, accessed October 7, 2013, http://www.guardian.co.uk/world/2001/oct/01/afghanistan.terrorism9.

40. Michael Ignatieff, "Ethics and the New War," *Canadian Military Journal* (Winter 2001–2002): 5.

41. For a concise analysis of some key work on the "War on Terror" written during the 2000s, see Yves Winter's review essay "Critical Theory, The War on Terror, and the Limits of Civilization," *Political Theory* 35.2 (2007): 207–214. See also my review of Ignatieff's *Lesser Evil* in *Perspectives on Politics*, 3.3, (September 2005): 688–689.

42. Ignatieff, *Empire Lite*, 63.

43. Ignatieff, *Empire Lite*, 109.

44. Ignatieff, *Empire Lite*, 17.

45. Isaiah Berlin, "The Originality of Machiavelli," in *Against the Current: Essays in the History of Ideas* (New York: Viking Press, 1980), 63.

46. Max Weber, "Politics as Vocation," in *Essays in Sociology* (New York: Oxford University Press, 1946), 27.

47. Michael Walzer, "Political Action: The Problem of Dirty Hands," *Philosophy and Public Affairs* 2 (1973): 167.

48. Walzer, "Political Action: The Problem of Dirty Hands," 180.

49. Ignatieff, *Lesser Evil*, 29.

50. Ignatieff, *Lesser Evil*, 29.

51. This has not always been the case, however. Early-twentieth-century pluralist thinkers such as Harold Laski and G. D. H. Cole were extremely interested in the relationship between the "external relations" of the state and democracy. See G. D. H. Cole, "The Nature of the State and Its External Relations," *Proceedings of the Aristotelian Society* 16 (1915–1916): 290–325, and Harold Laski, "The Apotheosis of the State," *The New Republic* 7 (1916): 302–304. The

end of the Cold War has also brought about a resurgence of interest among political theorists in questions of sovereignty although, again, these theorists are not particularly concerned with foreign policy and democracy. See in particular William Connolly, *Pluralism* (Durham, NC: Duke University Press, 2005), and Wendy Brown, *Walled States, Waning Sovereignty* (New York: Zone Books, 2010).

52. Michael Ignatieff, "Lesser Evils," *The New York Times*, May 2, 2004, 49–50.

53. Ignatieff, *Isaiah Berlin*, 124.

54. Isaiah Berlin, "Two Concepts of Liberty," in *Four Essays on Liberty* (Oxford: Oxford University Press, 1969), 169.

55. Berlin, "Two Concepts of Liberty," 168.

56. See Berlin's comments on "Two Concepts" thirty years later in Ramin Jahanbegloo, *Conversations with Isaiah Berlin* (New York: Charles Scribner's Sons, 1991), 40–43.

57. Michael Ignatieff, "Isaiah Berlin, The Soviet Union and the Captive Nations," Isaiah Berlin Lecture delivered in Riga, Latvia, June 6, 2012, accessed October 7, 2013, http://ibriga.files. wordpress.com/2012/06/milecture2012.pdf.

58. Ignatieff, "Isaiah Berlin, The Soviet Union and the Captive Nations," 12.

59. For more on Berlin's somewhat complicated rendering of the liberal subject as both "personal and social" see Connie Aarsbergen-Ligtvoet's *Isaiah Berlin: A Value Pluralist and Humanist View of Human Nature and the Meaning of Life* (Amsterdam: Rodopi, 2006).

60. Michael Ignatieff, "The Foreign and Domestic: Getting the Balance Right," Address to Apex Symposium, National Arts Center, Ottawa, June 1, 2005, 5. http://www.apex.gc.ca/ uploads/symposia/2005/michael%20ignatieff-bil.pdf. See also a speech Ignatieff gave at Wolfson College, Oxford, May 24, 2007, "Isaiah Berlin On Political Judgment," for similar thoughts on Berlin and choice. Note that this speech was formerly available at http://www. michaelignatieff.ca/about/speech/2007_Berlin_On_Political_Judgement.aspx but has since been removed along with Ignatieff's web page. Last accessed May, 2011.

61. Ignatieff, *The Lesser Evil*, 19.

62. Ignatieff, *The Lesser Evil*, 154.

63. Ignatieff, *The Lesser Evil*, 132.

64. Ignatieff, *The Lesser Evil*, 17.

65. Isaiah Berlin, *The Crooked Timber of Humanity* (Princeton, NJ: Princeton University Press, 1998), 19.

66. Michael Ignatieff, "Isaiah Berlin Lecture: Liberal Values in Tough Times," The Isaiah Berlin Lecture, National Liberal Club, Whitehall Place, London, July 8, 2009, 5, last accessed November 5, 2013. http://www.liberal.ca/newsroom/speeches/ isaiah-berlin-lecture-liberal-values-in-tough-times/. Note that this speech was originally posted on Ignatieff's web page. It now appears at http://www.liberal-international.org/edi- torial.asp?ia_id=1849.

67. Isaiah Berlin, "The Bent Twig: A Note on Nationalism," *Foreign Affairs* 51.1 (October 1972): 17.

68. Romand Coles, *Beyond Gated Politics: Reflections for the Possibility of Democracy* (Minneapolis, MN: University of Minnesota Press, 2005), 6.

69. James Tully, "On Global and Local Citizenship," in *Public Philosophy in a New Key, Volume II, Imperialism and Civic Freedom* (Cambridge: Cambridge University Press, 2008).

70. For an in-depth look at the crisis in global inequality and why it matters see Branko Milanovic, *Worlds Apart: Measuring International and Global Inequality* (Princeton, NJ: Princeton University Press, 2005).

71. Thomas Pogge, "Economic Justice and National Borders," *Revision* 22.2 (1999): 29.

72. Bernard Yack, "The Myth of the Civic Nation," *Critical Review* 10.2 (Spring 1996): 196.

73. Ignatieff, *Human Rights*, 58. Ignatieff has not altered this insouciant tone in any way in his recent work. In "Reimagining a Global Ethic," for instance, Ignatieff engages in very little "reimagining." Universal human rights institutions still, in this narrative, are supposed to look for "buy in" from the particular, local, non-Western other. "The universal takes the form, often enough, of a humanitarian aid worker or public health nurse. The local takes the form of a village political system in which power is held by elders and where women may not have voice or influence." Ignatieff, "Reimagining a Global Ethic," 15.

74. Ignatieff, *Empire Lite*, 114–115.

75. For a thorough examination of Britain's economic underdevelopment of India in the twentieth-century, see Hugh Tinker, *Separate and Unequal: India and the Indians in the British Commonwealth, 1920–1959* (Vancouver: University of British Columbia Press, 1976). Keith Wattenpaugh gives a concise analysis of the lingering effects of the colonial mandate in Iraq after World War I and its current impact on US policy in "The Guiding Principles and the U.S. 'Mandate' for Iraq: 20th Century Colonialism and America's New Empire," *Logos*, 3.1 (Winter 2003): 26–37.

76. Ignatieff, *Lesser Evil*, 100.

77. See David Harvey's discussion of this irony in *The New Imperialism* (Oxford: Oxford University Press, 2005), 52–53.

78. Ignatieff, *Empire Lite*, 9.

79. Ignatieff, *The Needs of Strangers*, 107.

80. Ignatieff, *Empire Lite*, 11.

81. Ignatieff, *Empire Lite*, 123.

82. Michael Ignatieff, "Human Rights, the Laws of War, and Terrorism," *Social Research* 69.4 (2002): 1139.

83. Peter Euben, *The Tragedy of Political Theory: The Road Not Taken* (Princeton, NJ: Princeton University Press, 1990), 94.

84. Richard Ned Lebow, *The Tragic Vision of Politics: Ethics, Interests, and Orders* (New York: Cambridge University Press, 2003), 374.

85. Lebow, *The Tragic Vision of Politics*, 390. Lebow argues that Morgenthau and Clausewitz shared Thudycides's sensibilities regarding tragic hubris.

86. Elizabeth Markovits, "Birthright, Freedom, and Democratic Comportment in Aeschylus' *Oresteia*," *American Political Science Review* 103.3 (2009): 427–441.

87. Markovits, "Birthright, Freedom, and Democratic Comportment in Aeschylus' *Oresteia*," 457.

88. Ignatieff, *Lesser Evil*, 166.

89. Sophocles, "Antigone," in *Sophocles I*, ed. David Grene and Richmond Lattimore, trans. Elizabeth Wyckoff (Chicago: University of Chicago Press, 1991), 209.

90. Thanks to David Lupher for reminding me of this scene and of the fact that journalists were making a similar analogy as early as 2006. See Spengler, "Victor Davis Hanson Goes to the Seashore," *Asia Times*, January 4, 2006, accessed October 7, 2013, http://www.atimes.com/atimes/Middle_East/HA04Ak02.html.

91. Thucydides, *History of the Peloponnesian War*, trans. Rex Warner (New York: Penguin Classics, 1972), 2.37.1.

92. Thucydides, *History*, 2.36.1. "This land of ours" is Warner's translation of "the land." (τὴν χώραν).

93. Thucydides, *History*, 2.51.3.

94. Ignatieff, *Empire Lite*, 4.

Conclusion

1. Remarks by President Obama at the National Defense University, May 23, 2013, Accessed October 8, 2013, http://www.whitehouse.gov/the-press-office/2013/05/23/remarks-president-national-defense-university.

2. One particularly stark example of this duplicity is the revelation in *The Guardian*, a scant two weeks after Obama gave these remarks, that the Administration had widened the scope of the Bush Administration's domestic surveillance program by using a provision in the Patriot Act to compel the communications company Verizon to give the National Security Administration information on all telephone calls in its system on "an ongoing, daily basis." (See Glenn Greenwald, "NSA Collecting Phone Records of Millions of Verizon Customers Daily," *The Guardian*, June 5, 2013, accessed October 8, 2013, http://www.guardian.co.uk/world/2013/jun/06/nsa-phone-records-verizon-court-order.) In the May 23 speech, Obama had explicitly distanced himself from the Patriot Act by suggesting that, "in some cases, I believe we compromised our basic values—by using torture to interrogate our enemies, and detaining individuals in a way that ran counter to the rule of law."

3. For more on Kerr and Lloyd George see Warman, "The Erosion of Foreign Office Influence in the Making of Foreign Policy, 1916–1918," *The Historical Journal* 15 (1972): 133–159; Peter Yearwood, "'On the Safe and Right Lines': The Lloyd George Government and the Origins of the League of Nations, 1916–1918." *The Historical Journal* 32 (1989): 131–155. For information on Zimmern's relation to the Foreign Office, see Paul Rich, "Reinventing Peace: David Davies, Alfred Zimmern and Liberal Internationalism in Interwar Britain," *International Relations* 16 (2002): 117–133.

4. Thus, in a 1916 letter attached to a copy of the Fourteen Points, Zimmern told Kerr, "Wilson asks me to send enclosed on to you. I should be very grateful of candid criticism. I have not been through it carefully yet, but I'd be glad if you'd back me up in getting him to modify his view about the necessary sovereign independence of nationalities." (Bodl. MS. Curtis 817, fol. 44.)

5. According to Paul Rich, the proposals embodied in this draft "did much to weaken some of the idealism of Woodrow Wilson's plan and to limit the League's role to one where it was an expansion of the concert of Europe." ("Reinventing Peace," 120.) League historian J. D. B. Miller would later refer to this more limited approach to the League as "the Zimmern Vision." (Miller, "The Commonwealth and World Order: The Zimmern Vision and After," *The Journal of Imperial and Commonwealth History* 8 (1979): 159–174.)

6. See John Kendle, *The Round Table Movement and Imperial Union* (Toronto: University of Toronto Press, 1975), 253–256.

7. Hedley Bull, "What is the Commonwealth?", *World Politics* 11 (1959): 577–587. Enoch Powell, "The Myth of Empire," in *Empire to Commonwealth, 1910–1970*, ed. W. H. Morris-Jones (London: Oxford University Press, 1970).

8. Throughout the 1910s Cole was, in David Runciman's words, "the most significant champion of polyarchic, or federalist political theory" in Britain, influenced by both the intellectual lights of the English pluralist tradition (namely Maitland and Figgis) and the "functionalist," decentralizing impulses of guild socialism. See David Runciman, *Pluralism and the Personality of the State* (Cambridge: Cambridge University Press, 1997), 164–165.

9. G. D. H. Cole, "The Nature of the State and Its External Relations," *Proceedings of the Aristotelian Society, New Series* 16 (1915–1916): 311.

10. Cole, "The Nature of the State and Its External Relations," 325.

11. Cole, "The Nature of the State and Its External Relations," 325.

12. Cole, "The Nature of the State and Its External Relations," 313.

13. Cole, "The Nature of the State and Its External Relations," 324.

14. The drafters of the United Nations Charter would popularize the term when they argued that the Economic and Social Council might, if it so chose, "make suitable arrangements for consultation with non-governmental organizations." The use of the term was institutionalized in Article 71, Chapter 10, of the United Nations Charter. ""The Economic and Social Council may make suitable arrangements for consultation with non-governmental organizations which are concerned with matters within its competence. Such arrangements may be made with international organizations and, where appropriate, with national organizations after consultation with the Member of the United Nations concerned." [See "Charter of the United Nations," The Avalon Project, accessed October 8, 2013, http://www.yale.edu/law-web/avalon/un/unchart.htm#art71. Steve Charnovitz argues that the "first use of the term 'non-governmental organization' in international law scholarship may have been an article by Lasswell and McDougal in 1943." See Steve Charnovitz, "How Non-governmental Actors Vitalize International Law," in *Looking to the Future: Essays on International Law in Honor of W. Michael Reisman*, ed. Mahnoush H. Arsanjan (Leiden, The Netherlands: Koninklijke Brill, 2010), 137.

15. See T. Wallace, "NGO Dilemmas: Trojan Horses for Global Neoliberalism?" *Socialist Register* (2003): 202–219.

16. Cole, "The State and its External Relations," 322.

17. See Anthony Parel's fascinating "Introduction" in Mohandas K. Gandhi, *Hind Swaraj and Other Writings* (Cambridge: Cambridge University Press, 2009), xiv. *Hind Swaraj* is the only one of his writings that Gandhi translated himself.

18. Niall Ferguson, *Civilization: The West and the Rest* (New York: Penguin, 2011), 171.

19. Gandhi, *Hind Swaraj*, 69. Leela Gandhi, *Postcolonial Theory: A Critical Introduction* (New York: Columbia University Press, 1998), 20.

20. Gandhi, *Hind Swaraj*, 48.

21. For an interesting account of Gandhi's pluralism, see Karuna Mantena's excellent article, "Gandhi's Critique of the State: Sources, Contexts, Conjunctures," *Modern Intellectual History* 9.3 (2012): 535–563.

22. Gandhi, *Hind Swaraj*, 86.

23. Gandhi, *Hind Swaraj*, 27.

24. Gandhi, *Hind Swaraj*, 115.

25. For more on this reception, see Anshuman Mondal, "Gandhi, Utopianism, and the Construction of Colonial Difference," *Interventions: International Journal of Postcolonial Studies* 3:3 (2001): 419–438.

26. "Letter from Emily Hobhouse to Jan Smuts, April 23, 1914," in *Selections from the Smuts Papers, vol. 3, June 10–November 1918*, ed. Keith Hancock (Cambridge: Cambridge University Press, 2007), 174.

27. Other thinkers with interesting articles on the state in this issue include fellow conscientious objectors Bertrand Russell and C. Delisle Burns.

28. The most recent author to take this approach is Anthony Pagden, who claims that the idea of Enlightenment cosmopolitanism has been "the inspiration behind the League of Nations and the United Nations, behind the International Court of Justice and the beleaguered, but still enduring, belief in the possibility for a truly international law." Pagden, *The Enlightenment: And Why it Still Matters* (New York: Random House, 2013), 8.

29. James Tully, "On Local and Global Citizenship," *Public Philosophy in a New Key* (Cambridge: Cambridge University Press, 2008), 245.

30. James Tully, "Political Philosophy as a Critical Activity," *Political Theory*, 30.4 (2002): 534.

31. Samuel Moyn, *The Last Utopia: Human Rights in History* (Cambridge, MA: Belknap Press, 2010), 225.

32. Moyn, *The Last Utopia*, 175.

33. David Harvey, *The Enigma of Capital: And the Crises of Capitalism* (Oxford: Oxford University Press, 2010), 47.

34. See for instance, Pankaj Mishra's close reading of Indian and Chinese intellectuals' responses to the hypocrisy of the West which completely recasts the story of the Paris Peace Conference of 1919. Pankaj Mishra, *From the Ruins of Empire: The Intellectuals Who Remade Asia* (New York: Farrar, Strauss, and Giroux, 2012), particularly Chapter Four, "1919, 'Changing the History of the World.'" Likewise, Antony Anghie's very different, but equally careful, tracing of imperial themes in international law—from de Vitoria to the Mandate System to the World Bank—shines a bright light on the disciplinary structures at work in international law and the discourse of global governance. Antony Anghie, *Imperialism, Sovereignty, and the Making of International Law* (Cambridge: Cambridge University Press, 2005). See also John M. Hobson, *The Eurocentric Conception of World Politics* (Cambridge: Cambridge University Press, 2012).

35. See, for example, Boaventura de Sousa Santos, *The Rise of the Global Left: The World Social Forum and Beyond* (London: Zed Books, 2006). See also Tully, "On the Global Multiplicity of Public Sphere: The Democratic Transformation of the Public Sphere?" in *Beyond Habermas: Democracy, Knowledge, and the Public Sphere*, eds. Christian J. Emden and David Midgley (New York: Berghahn Books, 2013). See also the special online edition of *Tikkun* (Spring 2012) on the tactics, political theory, and spirituality of the Occupy movement, http://www.tikkun.org/nextgen/online-exclusives-on-the-occupy-movement.

INDEX